Implicit Cognition

Implicit Cognition

Edited by
GEOFFREY UNDERWOOD
Professor of Cognitive Psychology,
University of Nottingham

Oxford New York Tokyo
Oxford University Press
1996

This book has been printed digitally in order to ensure its continuing availability

OXFORD
UNIVERSITY PRESS

Great Clarendon Street, Oxford OX2 6DP

Oxford University Press is a department of the University of Oxford.
It furthers the University's objective of excellence in research, scholarship,
and education by publishing worldwide in

Oxford New York

Auckland Bangkok Buenos Aires Cape Town Chennai
Dar es Salaam Delhi Hong Kong Istanbul Karachi Kolkata
Kuala Lumpur Madrid Melbourne Mexico City Mumbai Nairobi
São Paulo Shanghai Singapore Taipei Tokyo Toronto

with an associated company in Berlin

Published in the United States
by Oxford University Press Inc., New York

Reprinted 2002

A catalogue record for this book is available from the British Library

Library of Congress Cataloging in Publication Data
Implicit cognition / edited by Geoffrey Underwood. – 1st ed.
Includes bibliographical references and index.
1. Subconsciousness. 2. Cognition. 3. Implicit learning. 4. Human information
processing. I. Underwood, Geoffrey (Geoffrey D. M.)
BF315.146 1996 153—dc20 95-18291

ISBN 0-19-852311-4 (Hbk)
ISBN 0-19-852310-6 (Pbk)

Preface

The discussions presented here explore the range of behaviour that can be influenced by information that is not available to consciousness, and in so doing they help to describe the relationship between consciousness and cognition. What do we gain by being aware of our cognitions, and what kind of behaviour is under the influence of unconscious knowledge? Can we perceive and record events without being aware of their presence, and later behave differently as a result of those still unconscious events? The essays here evaluate the evidence for these implicit effects upon behaviour in the domains of perception, memory, learning, and thinking.

The possibility of a dissociation between consciousness and behaviour has a long history. Psychologists have long been intrigued by demonstrations of perception without awareness, or subliminal perception. These demonstrations have had a very mixed reception, and our essays here contain echoes of ancestral debates about methodological problems in attempts to separate those effects that are controlled by conscious cognitions from those effects in which awareness has played no part. The long history of subliminal perception has allowed the opportunity for some wild claims to be made about the efficacy of subliminal techniques in clinical therapy, in the marketing of self-help audio tapes ('stop smoking', 'play better golf', 'improve your sexual confidence', 'lose weight' ...), and as a theft deterrent in shops, among the popular applications. Legislation in some countries specifically prohibits the use of subliminal messages for marketing purposes. The existence of commercial applications, and legislation to restrict their use, does not mean that subliminal messages are effective, of course, merely that some people believe them to be effective. The evidence has not been overwhelming. Laboratory effects tend to be small even when they are reliable. This problem leads to questions about the generality of subliminal effects, and questions about methodology. If effects are small and inconsistent, then what can their influence be upon everyday behaviour? Size and inconsistency may be simply a product of laboratory methods failing to capture the critical conditions in which unnoticed events result in cognitive records. Just as proponents of the generality of subliminal perception have appealed to the evolutionary advantages of monitoring environmental events while dedicating mental resources to the main task in hand, proponents of implicit learning have suggested that it must be pervasive because consciousness is an evolutionary recent phenomenon. Animals without consciousness can learn, and so they are learning, by definition, implicitly. This begs the question of how we can know that an animal, or indeed another person is conscious, and while avoiding a path reserved for philosophers we can record progress in our investigative methods. A major part of the discussion in the following essays is taken by a concern for methodology. The concern is to know when an implicit effect has been demonstrated, whether this is perception without awareness, remembering with having an explicit memory available, learning without knowing what we have learned, or solving problems with knowledge that is implicit.

How do we know when someone has become aware of a stimulus event, and when they have been infuenced by information but remain unaware of the information or its influence? This is more tricky with animals, but in the case of humans we could just ask them. If a subject in an experiment is aware of a presentation on a screen, for example, they could be asked to give a verbal report as a measure of stimulus identification. This sets the threshold for awareness at the threshold for verbal report. While it may be appropriate for some stimuli and some tasks, and can lead to difficulties with a stimulus that a viewer is unable to describe even though perception is clear. A complex stimulus that did not lend itself readily to verbal classification, for example, might then be considered to be a subliminal percept because a verbal report was not forthcoming. More stringently, we could set the threshold at the point at which the viewer reports that the stimulus is undetectable—the subjective threshold—or even more stringently, at the point at which the viewer is unable to respond better than chance on a forced-choice detection task—the objective threshold. A related problem awaits those seeking to determine whether well-perceived events can influence subsequent behaviour. The experimenter's task is to demonstrate that what someone is remembering or has learned is not influenced by their awareness of what they are remembering or of the rules underlying the learned relationships. Their retrieval of information may change depending upon the presence of unconscious cognitions, but how can we be certain that there is no awareness of these influences? Or are these unconscious cognitions in some way contaminated by memories that our subject has in his or her consciousness? Separating the effects of conscious and unconscious cognitions is a problem that continues to receive attention.

The contributors to this volume deserve my thanks for the enthusiasm and intellectual vigour with which they have addressed the problem of accounting for the implicit and explicit cognitions that influence behaviour, and for making the task of editor an explicitly pleasurable experience. I must also take this opportunity of thanking Dianne Berry, Vanessa Whitting, and Sue Jeffery who were, in various ways, instrumental in bringing it all together.

Nottingham G.U.
July 1995

Contents

Contributors

Dianne C. Berry Department of Psychology, University of Reading, Earley Gate, Whiteknights, Reading RG6 6AL

James E. H. Bright School of Psychology, University of New South Wales, Sydney, NSW 2052, Australia

Zoltan Dienes Laboratory of Experimental Psychology, University of Sussex, Brighton, Sussex BN1 9QG

Jennifer Dorfman Department of Psychology, University of Memphis, Memphis, Tennessee 38152, USA

John M. Gardiner Department of Psychology, City University, Northampton Square, London EC1V 0HB

Rosalind I. Java Laboratory of Experimental Psychology, University of Sussex, Brighton, Sussex BN1 9QG

John F. Kihlstrom Department of Psychology, Yale University, P. O. Box 208205, New Haven, Connecticut 06520–8205, USA

Josef Perner Laboratory of Experimental Psychology, University of Sussex, Brighton, Sussex BN1 9QG

Eyal M. Reingold University of Toronto, Department of Psychology, 100 St. George Street, Toronto, Ontario M5S 1A1, Canada

Alan Richardson-Klavehn School of Psychology, Middlesex University, Queensway, Enfield, Middlesex, EN3 4SF

Victor A. Shames Department of Psychology, University of Arizona, Tucson, Arizona 85721, USA

Jeffrey P. Toth Rotman Institute of Baycrest Centre, 3560 Bathurst Street, Toronto, Ontario M6A 2E1, Canada

Geoffrey Underwood Department of Psychology, University of Nottingham, University Park, Nottingham, NG7 2RD

1

Cognition with and without awareness

Geoffrey Underwood and James E. H. Bright

What does awareness do for cognition? By attending to part of the environment we can gain awareness, but apart from this change in the quality of conscious experience is awareness associated with a cognitive change? Is it necessary to be conscious of an event in order to perceive it, to remember it, or to incorporate it into our abstracted representations? These questions about the relationship between performance and our mental states during performance have been part of psychology for many generations, and have undergone as many formulations. The contemporary debate about the distinction between implicit and explicit processes again foregrounds the question of whether we can process information without explicit knowledge of the cognitive processes that are involved. The purpose of this chapter is to introduce some of the issues involved in establishing the implicit/explicit distinction, and to set the current debate in the context of a longer running argument about the necessity of awareness for information processing.

Much of the evidence to be reviewed here suggests that the recognition of simple stimuli can be achieved without attention, and even without awareness. This does not imply that attention serves no purpose or that awareness adds nothing to cognition, however. When we focus our attention not only do we become selectively aware of some parts of the environment to the exclusion of others, but these changes in our personal perceptions can be observed in our behaviour. Johnston and Wilson (1980) compared the effects of focused attention against the effects of asking subjects to listen to two messages at once, using a dichotic listening task. The direction of attention was manipulated by either informing the listener as to which message would contain the target word (pre-cueing), or providing no information upon which selection of messages could be made. Johnston and Wilson first established that with attention divided between the two messages, performance is influenced by the word presented at the same time as the target. This effect disappeared when the subjects were pre-cued as to which message would contain the target, and could therefore focus upon an attended message. The comparison between the conditions which induced divided and focused attention provides us with a demonstration of the effects of inattention. Non-targets in an unattended message were unable to influence the detectability of simultaneous targets: the influence of their meaning might be said to have been 'attenuated' by the listeners focusing upon the attended message. A similar effect can be observed in the case of visual attention. When attempting to name simple line-drawings of common objects viewers are influenced by the presence of printed words. If attention can be focused upon a single target location the effect is relatively small, and is only seen with words that are associates of the drawings. When attention is divided, however, the effect is larger, and is also greater for unassociated words (Underwood 1976). Attention may not be necessary for the processing of simple stimuli, such as single words, but the pattern of processing changes when attention can be focused.

Investigations of the effects of attention upon detection provide a straightforward conclusion: when a message is unattended there is poor detection of the targets contained in it. Failing to attend to a message results in a failure to respond to single words within that message, and the Johnston and Wilson (1980) experiment provides evidence to suggest that effects of non-target words can be eliminated by directing attention away from them. These effects of attention are not confounded by attended and unattended messages competing for limited response systems, and are most easily interpreted as being due to unattended messages failing to gain the perceptual analysis required for target detection. Although unattended words are not readily detected (that is, they are not available for verbal report, nor available to awareness), they can continue to influence ongoing behaviour, as has been demonstrated in the dichotic shadowing experiments reported by Lewis (1970) and Underwood (1977). This indicates that they have not been recognized at the level where a conscious representation has been formed, but that recognition can be independent of availability for report.

The distinction between *implicit* and *explicit* memories has been used to describe performance in amnesic, hypnotic, and anaesthetized subjects and in normal subjects who show evidence of remembering without awareness of their memories. Whereas we can reflect on some past events in personal experience and provide a verbal report on the context in which an event occurred, there are other forms of knowledge which may not be available for verbal report but which are available only in the sense that our behaviour is changed. These are explicit and implicit forms of knowledge respectively, and there are now a number of demonstrations of implicit memory in the absence of explicit memory. A subject in a memory experiment may be unable to provide an item as a response in a recall task, but may offer the item in a word association task, or show an effect of priming from this 'unavailable' item, or may know some obscure fact without knowing from where the knowledge originated. Memories that do not have a conscious representation are not necessarily dormant, and this can be demonstrated to exist by their indirect effects upon other activities. Eich (1984) used the distinction between implicit and explicit memories to demonstrate the semantic processing of unattended messages with a dichotic listing task. Recognition of unattended spoken words remained at chance level (i.e. no explicit influence), even when the words had influenced the interpretation of homophones (i.e. an implicit influence). Awareness of an event is neither a necessary consequence of cognition nor a necessary condition for cognition.

1.0 SEMANTIC ACTIVATION WITHOUT CONSCIOUS IDENTIFICATION

Can messages be recognized even when we have no conscious representation of them? The debate over the effectiveness of subliminal messages (messages presented at a stimulus intensity insufficient for the perceiver to gain awareness of them) has been extended to cover unattended messages and to cover demonstrations of implicit memory and implicit learning. A critical methodological problem is the consideration of the means used to prevent awareness and the method of inquiring of the perceiver's state of awareness. There are a number of means by which a stimulus can be presented so as to be out of conscious access: a spoken message may be presented too quietly and a visual message too briefly or too dimly for the perceiver to be able to give a report, or masking techniques can be employed. For example, in the case of visually presented words, the message may be followed immediately by a backwards mask in the form of a second stimulus. This masking stimulus is most effective when it is a random display of letter-like features (i.e. it is a 'pattern mask'), and other techniques involve the use of masking displays of randomly placed dots and other non-linguistic features, and the use of dichoptic masking, in which the message is presented to one eye while relatively bright light is presented to the other.

Reviews of studies using these techniques have been provided by Dixon (1981) and Holender (1986), with opposing conclusions. The question of whether there are any convincing demonstrations of the semantic processing of subliminal messages hinges on the issue of whether the perceiver has been aware of the effective message. A priming word presented under subliminal conditions may have an effect upon a subsequent target word, for example, as in the experiments of Fowler *et al.* (1981), Balota (1983), and Marcel (1983), but the critics of these experiments query the measures taken to ensure that the 'subliminal' prime was not available for conscious scrutiny. Part of the problem here is that the experimenter is obliged to rely upon verbal report as the only index of the level of conscious representation. If the subject can say what the word is, then it is a supraliminal presentation, otherwise it is subliminal, but this objective measure does not necessarily match with subjective impressions. The perceiver may be unable to identify a word well enough for verbal report while still knowing something of the presentation. While verbal reports are all-or-none, the process of becoming aware of a stimulus may be more gradual. The moment immediately before we are able to give a verbal report extensive processing will have been completed, and it is this processing which may be responsible for the positive results obtained in studies of subliminal words.

With subliminal demonstrations, the dissociation between objective and subjective discrimination thresholds has the perceiver declaring that nothing can be seen, while being affected by the stimulus, or while otherwise being able to make forced-choice guesses better than chance. Part of the controversy over demonstrations of processing without awareness involves the choice of the awareness threshold. Subjective thresholds rely upon the perceiver's verbal reports of their awareness of a stimulus, whereas objective thresholds are determined by the perceiver's ability to make a discriminative response regardless of their verbal reports of discriminability (Cheesman and Merikle 1984). The problem with the use of subjective thresholds is that the perceiver is left with the decision as to what counts as awareness. Some perceivers may adopt more stringent criteria than others, and the criterion may be biased by the instructions given during the experiment. The problem with the use of objective thresholds alone is that it may be so strict as to make it impossible to demonstrate unconscious processing that was in reality taking place.

Given that there are separate objective and subjective thresholds, and given that perceivers are not often asked after each presentation whether they were able to report the subliminal word, the critics of the notion of 'semantic activation without conscious identification' have good reason to be doubtful. We cannot be certain that the perceivers were unaware of the messages at the time of presentation. What is needed is a converging operation, whereby a secondary index of processing would give support to the claim that the effective message has not been available as a conscious representation. A dissociation between the two measures would allow us to conclude that unconscious processing was in evidence (Reingold and Merikle 1988). One measure would take into account the perceiver's verbal reports (explicit performance) and the other measure would take account of changes in discrimination performance that are unavailable for report (implicit performance). A demonstration of processing without conscious identification would require that the implicit measure should show sensitivity to the stimulus in the absence of sensitivity in the explicit measure.

Dixon (1981) has suggested that the use of converging measures ideally should provide a qualitative change in the effect of the stimulus under subliminal and supraliminal conditions. When the perceiver can report the message its effect should be not only different in magnitude from when it cannot be reported, but the effect should also vary in type or direction. This would provide an independent assessment of whether the perceiver was aware of the message. Of course, if processing with awareness involved not a change in the nature of processing but a change in the extent of processing, then the adoption of this criterion would define subliminal processing as impossible to demonstrate. We would never be able to demonstrate subliminal processing because our criterion requires a qualitative change that would not exist. Processing with awareness does, at least in some circumstances, involve a qualitative change, however.

One example of a qualitative change is provided by Marcel (1980), in which the effect of an ambiguous word was observed under masking conditions. A set of three words terminated with a target, and it was the response to the target that was measured. The first word and the target were not related in meaning, but both were related to the second word, through its two meanings. For example, in the triplet *save—bank—river* the first word might prime the second, but once the second word is interpreted it should not prime the terminal word. This, in fact, was the pattern of results obtained when all three words were presented supraliminally, but when the second word was pattern-masked, and unavailable for verbal report, then a qualitative change was observed in the results. With a subliminal second word a priming effect was found. Other demonstrations of this qualitative change have been reported for auditory and visual investigations of subliminal presentations by, for example, Groeger (1984, 1986). The distinction between implicit and explicit memories may again be an appropriate framework for regarding these demonstrations, in that events which are prevented from achieving a conscious level of representation are recorded as having influences upon the processing of other events. Implicit representations are inferred by their effects which can be observed even when the representations themselves are not available for verbal report.

A recent investigation of the effects of subliminal messages also demonstrates the necessity of a check on the reportability of the stimulus. This demonstration comes from one of the few attempts to observe the effects of subliminal messages in a national television broadcast (Underwood 1994). The demonstration was part of a popular science programme (the BBC TV series 'Tomorrow's World') that was concerned with the psychology of perception. We asked viewers to make a judgement about the emotion expressed in a still photograph of a woman's face. More than 35 000 viewers telephoned one of two numbers to indicate that they had seen the face as being happy or sad. What they had not been told was that half of the BBC TV regions had been presented with a smiling version of the same face subliminally just before the neutral face. Viewers in the other regions received no subliminal stimuli. The subliminal smiling face was presented for just 20 ms, and was superimposed over one frame of a film about two infants playing with an adult. The brevity of the display combined with its low contrast was, we hoped, sufficient to ensure that the frame was unreportable. There was no way of estimating the reportability of the stimulus during the broadcast without alerting the participants to the existence of the very stimuli that we wanted to remain subliminal. The explicit measure had to remain undetermined at this stage.

The frame was shown seven times during this 25 s film, and it had an effect upon judgements about the neutral face. Hence, we had sensitivity on the implicit measure. Viewers exposed to the smiling face tended to make more 'sad' judgements than those seeing no frames prior to the judgement. The presence of a subliminal stimulus had a contrast effect upon the perception of the neutral face—having been exposed to a subliminal version of a smiling face the viewers tended now to see her as being sad. The indication of sensitivity on the implicit measure of processing is a negative contrast effect. The explicit measure was observed in a separate experiment prior to the TV broadcast. In a laboratory study with the same film, subjects who were informed that subliminal frames were present and who were instructed to look for them and to describe them, no-one reported seeing a smiling face. The explicit measure confirmed that the frames were unavailable for conscious report. These subjects also tended to see the neutral face as being sad, just as the TV viewers had reported.

We have no information about the perceptions of the TV viewers in this study, other than their single judgement about the neutral face. There was no opportunity to determine whether the superimposed frames were subliminal or not during the actual broadcast. We had to rely upon a separate study to complete the dissociation between the implicit and explicit measures. It may have been, of course, that for some viewers the 20 ms exposure was above the threshold for report, even with the low contrast achieved by displaying the smiling face at the same time as the film. A study from Paula Niedenthal's Ph.D. thesis (1987) supports the conclusion that the frames were subliminal, however. A negative contrast effect observed in her subliminal condition changed to a positive priming effect when the stimuli were presented supraliminally. There was a qualitative change in the effect as perceiver's became aware of the effective stimulus. In her experiments subjects saw faces in combination with pictures of objects. Either a subliminal face was presented together with a supraliminal object, or the other way round for other subjects. With supraliminal objects the task was to name them, and with supraliminal faces subjects named the emotional expression. After this slide-naming task the subjects read short descriptions of personal behaviours and wrote down a personality label to best describe the person characterized by the behaviour. The descriptions called for positive labels (e.g. 'adventurous') or for negative labels (e.g. 'reckless'). The slides of the faces either depicted positive or negative emotions—the face was either smiling or scowling.

Niedenthal found that subliminal faces produced a negative contrast effect, as they did in Underwood's (1994) TV experiment. Subjects seeing a smiling face were more likely to make a negative judgement about the behavioural description than were subjects seeing a subliminal scowling face. On the other hand, supraliminal faces had a positive priming effect upon these judgements. Having seen a smiling face, subjects were more likely to consider the descriptions to represent someone who was thrifty, adventurous, persistent, or self-reliant. Subliminal slides produced an effect of opposite direction to that found when they were presented supraliminally, suggesting qualitatively different processes. In the 'Tomorrow's World' study the effect was similar in direction to that in Niedenthal's subliminal condition, supporting the suggestion that our smiling faces were indeed presented subliminally.

The problem of deciding whether a stimulus has been processed without awareness that has long been of concern to investigations of attention and investigations of subliminal processing is now a central issue in investigations of implicit and learning and implicit memory. It is a problem that emerges in a number of the discussions in this volume.

1.1 IMPLICIT LEARNING AND IMPLICIT MEMORY

Although much of the work on implicit cognition has been concerned with information processing without attention or without awarness, the notion of implicit cognition more traditionally embraces implicit learning and implicit memory. So far we have introduced some of the evidence purporting to show the degree to which semantic representations can be accessed in the absence of normal conscious attentional mechanisms. Typically subjects are unaware that any relevant stimulus has been presented to them. This can be contrasted with implicit learning and implicit memory where the materials from which learning proceeds or memorization takes place are (generally) explicitly presented. In the following sections, the major studies in the tradition of implicit learning are described and from these the key issues motivating current thinking in this area are highlighted and evaluated. Points of contact with implicit memory are discussed in terms of possible common underlying cognitive structures.

There is now a large literature claiming to have demonstrated 'implicit learning' (e.g. Reber 1967, 1969, 1976; Berry and Broadbent 1984, 1988;

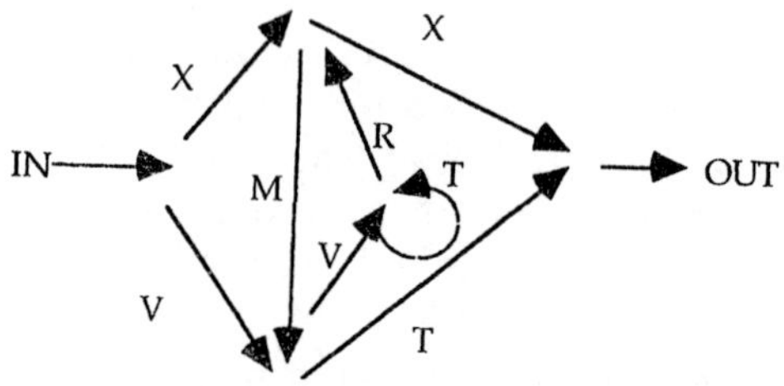

Fig. 1.1 A typical Reber grammar.

Lewicki 1985, 1986; Lewicki *et al.* 1987; Lewicki *et al.* 1988). At its most general, implicit learning is said to occur when there is an increase in task performance without an accompanying increase in verbal knowledge about how to carry out the task. That is, there is evidence of procedural knowledge in the absence of declarative knowledge. Furthermore the learning tends to be associated with incidental conditions (Berry 1993). The earliest experimental demonstrations of learning that were dubbed 'implicit' were carried out by Reber (e.g. 1967). In his studies, subjects successfully learned to classify novel letter strings as being grammatical or ungrammatical, having previously memorized valid exemplars that were generated by an artifical grammar. Learners did not appear to appreciate the basis on which they made their judgements in that they were unable to report on the rules of the grammar that guided their behaviour.

The rules that governed the generation of letter strings were based upon Markov grammars such as that depicted in Fig. 1.1. Grammatical strings are generated using this type of grammar by following the arrows and loops. Using the grammatical string generator in Fig. 1.1, the first letter must always be either V or X. Following a V, the only legal continuations are V and T. The third letter may (following VV) be either R or T, and so on. For instance, the following letter strings are grammatical:

VVTRX, VVTTRX, XMVTTRX, VT

whereas the following would be ungrammatical:

VVXMR, MRTV, XVVMRXX, etc.

In a typical Reber task, subjects were instructed to memorize short lists of grammatical strings produced from one grammar (see, for example, Reber 1967). A control group of subjects were given random strings to memorize. Subjects were not told at this stage about the existence of an underlying grammar. Memory for these strings was then tested in free recall to determine criterial levels of learning. Once subjects could recall accurately the criterial proportion of the strings, they were assumed to have learnt them. At this stage subjects were informed of the existence of a grammar, and were then given a surprise grammar discrimination test. This comprised a list of mixed grammatical and ungrammatical strings which subjects had to sort into grammatical and ungrammatical sets. Subjects claimed that they had no basis upon which to make these discriminations and reported guessing; however, they performed above chance on this task. Typically, subjects correctly classified about 65 per cent of grammatical strings indicating they had learnt a considerable amount about the grammar (Dienes *et al.* 1991). Subjects were unable to offer any accurate insights into the structure of the grammar. Reber argued that subjects were implicitly learning abstract rules in this and subsequent studies. Furthermore, Reber (1969) demonstrated that subjects' grammatical learning remained intact to the same degree when the symbols making up the grammar were changed between learning and test whilst preserving the sequential structure of the underlying grammar. In this experiment, subjects learnt the rules of combination with strings such as XMT, VVRMT, etc., and were then tested on 'CHFF, CHF', etc. Figures 1.1 and 1.2 provide examples of changed letter sets that preserve the same grammatical structure.

The observed dissociation between task performance and verbal knowledge of the principles that guided performance was found to be even more impressive when subjects were encouraged to think about the underlying grammar during learning. Reber (1976) compared groups memorizing letter strings naïve with respect to the grammar and those who were informed that the letter strings all obeyed a grammar. Furthermore, these groups were told that attempts to ascertain the nature of the grammar would help in memorizing the strings. Such explicit search instructions actually lead to a *decrease* in subsequent classification performance.

A second approach to investigating implicit learning came from Broadbent's group who, whilst maintaining a stimulus set that was complex in nature, presented subjects with a more realistic task to perform (see, for example, Broadbent and Aston 1978; Berry and Broadbent 1984, 1988). This involved subjects interacting with a computer program which would take inputs from the subjects and use these to alter some 'real life' scenario

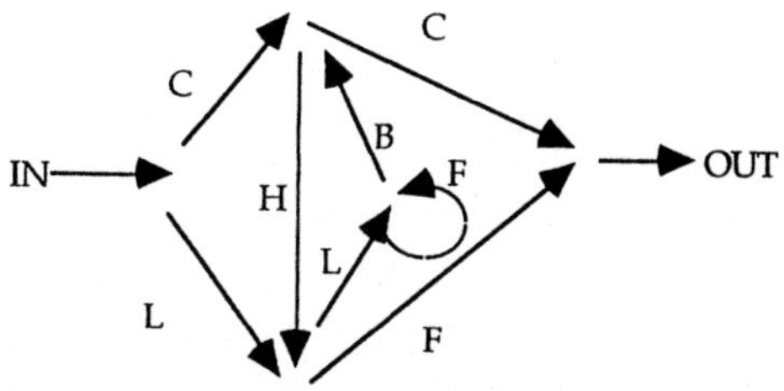

Fig. 1.2 A new letter set with the same underlying grammar.

according to the underlying rules of the program. In one such task, subjects were in control of an imaginary city transport system in which they had to control two variables, the number of passengers using buses and the number of empty car parking spaces. They were able to exert control over these variables by varying the cost of car parking and the intervals of departure of the buses. The bus load and parking fee variables were related by underlying equations which the subjects were not informed about. Subjects were given initial values for each of the variables and a target figure of car spaces and bus intervals to reach for each trial. Subjects' performance in quickly attaining the targets was observed to improve over trials although this was not accompanied by an associated increase in verbal knowledge. When they were asked to complete questionnaires on the relationships within the system, they were unable to provide accurate insights into the system's workings.

Implicit memory is distinct from implicit learning in that it is characterized as the influence of a previously memorized piece of information on a task without the explicit or deliberate attempt to recall the memory. Researchers have tended to treat the two phenomena separately. Berry and Dienes (1991) point out that implicit memory and implicit learning are logically independent. They give the example of a person who might be able to remember an episode in which they learnt to make a right decision without being able to justify the decision.

Savings during relearning is the phenomenon where a previously learnt task is learnt *faster* on a subsequent occasion due to the influence of the previously learnt material. These savings can be used as an indication of the implicit availability of information that may not necessarily be available for explicit recall. Nelson (1978) presented subjects with a series of material which was later re-presented, and found that they were quicker to respond to the items during test, despite being unable to recall or recognize the items. The implicit effects of subliminally presented material has been demonstrated by Kunst-Wilson and Zajonc (1980). Subsequently, subjects were unable to remember the items when tested on a forced-choice test, but showed a tendency to 'prefer' the previously seen shapes over unseen shapes on a preference rating task. In both of these tasks material that is explicitly unavailable was observed to influence performance. Repetition priming effects have also been used to demonstrate savings in subsequent tasks. This facilitation of the processing of a stimulus due to the previous presentation of the same stimulus has been demonstrated with a variety of tasks, including lexical decision tasks (Scarborough *et al.* 1979), word identification (Jacoby and Dallas 1981), and word-stem completion (Tulving *et al.* 1982; Warrington and Weiskrantz 1974). Preserved learning in amnesics has been repeatedly demonstrated by Warrington and Weiskrantz (e.g. Warrington and Weiskrantz 1974). Amnesic patients were found to be able to show normal retention of a list of familiar words when tested by word-stem or word completion, but showed impaired performance on free-recall and recognition tests.

Evidence that implicit memory (as opposed to explicit memory) is tied to surface characteristics rests upon the failure for an effect to transfer across presentation formats. This has generally taken the form of a modality shift (e.g. from visually to auditorally presented). For instance, Jacoby and Dallas (1981) found that perceptual identification priming was reduced when a prime was presented auditorally and tested visually. Changing the presentation of items within a mode, such as the shape or font in which a letter string is presented, also reduces the priming effect. Berry and Dienes (citing Berry and Broadbent 1988) argue that this trait is shared with implicit learning where transfer of learning from one complex control system to another only occurred when the two systems were perceptually similar. Several other studies, however, have shown transfer between representations. For instance, Reber (1969) has shown that subjects learning on one set of letters from an artificial grammar can discriminate novel strings made up of a new letter set from the same underlying grammar. One problem with this line of comparison is to obtain a measure of similarity. In these implicit learning studies it is not clear what similarity means. For instance, there is no metric of similarity between one complex system and another or between one letter set and another generated from the same grammar.

The durability of implicit learning has not been extensively researched. One paper that reports on this issue is Allen and Reber (1980) who retested subjects who had participated in the Reber and Allen (1978) artificial grammar learning study. They demonstrated that subjects could still discriminate between grammatical and ungrammatical strings without any further training two years after first learning the grammar. With an implicit memory task Jacoby and Dallas (1981) found that priming effects of perceptual identification lasted over months.

Very few implicit learning studies have systematically compared the effects of different study processing tasks upon what is learnt. Implicit learning has been characterized as automatic and effortless (e.g. Hasher and Zacks 1984), so maybe one would not expect to find any effect of study processing. The impact of study *instructions* has been manipulated, with Reber (1976) and Berry and Broadbent (1988) reporting that learning is either unaffected or impaired when subjects are encouraged to use a deliberate hypothesis testing strategy. Implicit memory appears to be unaffected by study processing, Jacoby and Dallas (1981) reported no effect of study processing on a word meaning/identification task on indirect measures of memory, but a marked effect upon direct measures.

The stochastic independence of implicit learning from explicit learning has largely been based upon zero or negative correlations between performance on an implicit task and performance on an explicit task. For instance, Berry and Broadbent (1984) found a negative correlation between task performance and verbalizable knowledge. Those who were better at controlling the dynamic system were worse at answering questionnaires about the system. Tulving *et al.* (1982) have also demonstrated that primed word fragment completion was independent of yes/no decisions for recognizing study words.

Although both Berry and Dienes (1991) and Schacter (1987) see great similarities between implicit learning and implicit memory, the theoretical basis for this position is not exactly clear. In particular, in the implicit learning field, as Berry and Dienes point out, there are many gaps, so that comparisons between characteristics of the two phenomena are based on comparatively few studies. For instance, the role of transfer between learning and test has not yet been adequately explored for a definite conclusion to be reached. As Berry and Dienes (1991) highlight, the role of study processing has almost been ignored in studies of implicit learning. The notions of automaticity, and intentional versus unintentional learning, need to be addressed in greater depth to provide a description of the role of study processing.

1.2 ISSUES IN IMPLICIT LEARNING

Many of the claims made by researchers in implicit learning are still controversial. In particular, it is possible to highlight three key issues that have yet to be resolved. These concern: the degree to which the acquired knowledge is really implicit, the nature of the underlying representations, and the degree to which the learning is unintentional. Each of these issues will now be examined in turn.

1.2.1 Verbal reports and conscious knowledge

One of the strongest claims made about the character of implicit learning is that it leads to verbally inaccessible knowledge, indeed to knowledge of which the subject is unaware. This state of knowing has been described with a variety of labels, including 'noetic consciousness' (Tulving 1984*b*); 'independent of consciousness' (Reber 1989); 'inaccessible to free recall' (Berry 1994); 'unavailable for conscious evaluation and verbal communication' (Hayes and Broadbent 1988); and 'not consciously recognized or controlled' (Lewicki *et al.* 1987), and these give an indication of the characteristics of knowing without awareness of the knowledge. Arguments opposing this position can be characterized by those who argue that the knowledge acquired is explicit (e.g. Dulaney *et al.* 1984, 1985; Perruchet and Pacteau 1990; Perruchet and Amorim 1992; Shanks and St.

John 1994), and those that argue that the knowledge becomes available to consciousness at a different rate or in incomplete form (e.g. Sanderson 1989; Dienes *et al.* 1991). The first group tend to argue for 'the primacy of the declarative' (Perruchet and Pacteau 1990)—that knowledge initially has a declarative form. Those who argue that explicit knowledge sometimes lags behind implicit knowledge retain the view that the acquisition of knowledge may proceed in the opposite direction—from procedural to declarative.

The denial of implicit processes in learning

Dulaney *et al.* (1984) argue that Reber's various demonstrations of implicit learning do not show unconscious processing of the materials. Instead, they suggest that it is at least as plausible that explicit learning strategies could account for Reber's observed results. They modified Reber's basic grammar learning test procedure, so that when subjects classified strings as grammatical or ungrammatical they were instructed to underline the critical portions of grammatical strings and cross out critical portions of strings that violated the grammar. Underlining was used as a test of awareness of the grammar. Different groups of subjects in the Dulaney *et al.* experiment were either shown all the learning exemplars on one slide or shown them sequentially. Within each of these groups subjects either learnt with prior knowledge of the existence of an underlying grammar or with no such knowledge. A fifth 'control' group were just given the test items and told that other groups had been prior-exposed to a series of letter strings. Dulaney *et al.* broadly replicated Reber's earlier findings that subjects exposed to grammatical items can classify novel grammatical and ungrammatical exemplars. However, they also found that the rules extracted from subjects' underlinings and crossing out were sufficient to account for their observed performance on the classification task. This result suggests that the learning of grammatical rules is accompanied by awareness of the rules.

Carlson and Dulaney (1985) also found no evidence of unconscious processes in a task similar to the artificial grammar task. Subjects were presented with a series of letters that were members of ill-defined categories based on letter features. Letters from a limited set appeared with varying probabilities in categories defined by the presence of either an 'R' or an 'S'. As in the Dulaney *et al.* (1984) task, in which subjects classified strings as belonging to one category or the other, they were asked to underline the constellation of letters that aided their decisions. The underlining gave an indication of the explicit information that was guiding their classifications. Across a variety of strategy conditions (e.g. neutral, hypothesis testing, and focused) conscious rules predicted classification performance well, again suggesting that performance is associated with awareness.

Reber *et al.* (1985) rebut Dulaney *et al.*'s (1984) assertions that the acquired rules are explicit, arguing that changing the procedure in the learning situation—as they did by introducing the 'underlining' task—might alter the nature of the learning. This argument has been used by Reber and his associates on previous occasions to defend the nature of implicit learning. For instance, Brooks' (1978) criticisms about the nature of the underlying mechanisms in grammar learning were also countered by pointing out the subtle changes in procedure. This will discussed further in the following section.

Reber *et al.* (1985) argue that the 'underlining' task did not elicit explicit knowledge, suggesting that, although a small proportion of explicit rules are typically reported by subjects in free recall, these cannot account for performance. They point out that Dulaney *et al.* (1984) used a technique more akin to a recognition test than recall, and propose that this represents a test of implicit knowledge. Essentially, Reber *et al.* argue, subjects are merely reassessing and recognizing the grammatical validity of the strings rather than expressing any explicit knowledge about the underlying rules of the grammar. It is even possible that subjects were guessing at possible rules. They argue that Dulaney *et al.* (1984) blurred the distinction between implicit and explicit processing by blurring the distinction between recognition and recall.

These criticisms were rejected by Dulaney *et al.* (1985) on the basis that the chances of subjects guessing at the underlying rules given their efficacy would be 'about once in 10 billion occasions'. Furthermore, they rejected the idea that the rule extraction procedure was a recognition task, suggesting instead that the task was 'assessment at the moment of judgement'. They argued that it is odd to reserve the term 'explicit' for only those rules that can be recalled excluding 'rules in consciousness when there is something at hand to be categorized'.

Perruchet and Pacteau (1990) extended the findings of Dulaney *et al.* (1984) by considering the nature of the possibly explicit knowledge found in artificial grammar learning experiments. Their approach centred around the acquisition of bigram and trigram knowledge—the knowledge of short sequences of letters within categorization strings. Reber and Lewis (1977) noted that such substrings were particularly salient to subjects. Perruchet and Pacteau (1990) argued that fragmentary knowledge is sufficient to account for grammar classification performance and that this knowledge is consciously held. They found that performance was not impaired if the learning materials consisted of legal bigrams rather than the more usual longer strings. The ordering of the bigrams was found to be the major basis of classification decisions, although knowledge of the position of bigrams was also acquired. Finally, they demonstrated that this knowledge of the bigrams was consciously held. After a normal learning phase, subjects were asked to rate bigrams on a six-point scale from 'sure this wasn't present in strings studied' through to 'sure that this was present'. Classification performance was found to be good and they argued that performance on this response scale equated to explicit knowledge of the bigrams.

Reber (1990) made methodological arguments in defence of his position against Perruchet and Pacteau (1990) similar to those made against earlier attacks upon the notion of unconscious knowledge (cf. Dulaney *et al.* 1984; Reber *et al.* 1985). He argued that the conditions of learning in the Perruchet and Pacteau study were likely to give rise to explicit learning and he disputed their use of data produced under such 'free' conditions in subsequent simulations that purport to demonstrate explicit strategies. This position was also supported by Mathews (1990), who defended the unconscious nature of grammar knowledge by comparing the Mathews *et al.* (1989) study with that of Perruchet and Pacteau (1990). He concluded that the Perruchet and Pacteau study is limited in a variety of ways. In particular, he argued that the relative lack of positional knowledge demonstrated by Perruchet and Pacteau's subjects was due to the use of a grammar and a procedure that made spatial information less important (e.g. through the use shorter string lengths). Secondly, he argued that subjects were not given enough exposure to the grammar in order to develop rich representations. Finally, as demonstrated in the general abstraction processing system (GAPS) model (Tulving 1983), recall can be a more sensitive measure than recognition as it allows for unanticipated forms of knowledge to be elicited. Mathews argued that more sensitive recall techniques fail to find explicit knowledge.

Evidence for explicit processing in another task previously deemed to be implicit—the Nissen and Bullemer (1987) serial reaction time task—has been reported by Perruchet and Amorim (1992). In this task subjects were reported to show an improvement in reaction time to visually presented targets on a computer screen. As the same pattern of presentation of targets was repeated successively (unbeknown to subjects), the response time to locate the target falls. Subjects showed no knowledge of the pattern sequencing. This conclusion is based on a 'generation task'. As a test of explicit knowledge, subjects were presented with a target and asked to press a button indicating where the next target would appear. When the correct response was made, the next item was presented. Reaction times were significantly better, compared to controls, but there was no difference in the proportion of correct responses.

Perruchet and Amorim (1992) claimed that the generation task is akin to a test of implicit memory as subjects were not informed they were being tested on previously presented sequences (although they might guess this). Furthermore, the process of feedback on the test trials provided extra learning opportunities, making much of the later response data for each subject dubious. They repeated the task with explicit instructions relating the study and test phases and without the feedback at the test stage. They also looked at the hypothesized relation between portions of the sequences where reaction times improve and conscious knowledge of the structure of these portions. They found that subjects were able to recognize consciously sequenced components and it was these components that were associated with improved reaction times (learning).

However, this position has been challenged by the recent findings of Curran and Keele (1993), who found that sequential knowledge was preserved across distraction and distraction-free conditions during learning, but that awareness of the sequences was not. They argued that this is due to the existence of two parallel forms of learning—attentional and non-attentional learning.

Finally, in a recent review of implicit learning, Shanks and St. John (1994) have argued that no sound evidence exists to support the hypothesis that the learning can be unconscious. They invoke the notions of an Information Criterion and a Sensitivity Criterion to support their argument. The match between the information responsible for performance and the information revealed by tests of awareness is the Information Criterion, whereas the Sensitivity Criterion is the degree of sensitivity of the conscious knowledge test. The force of their criticism is that many researchers have disregarded information proffered by subjects about their performance, which is inconsistent with the researcher's own model of the information requirements for task performance. Furthermore, many tests of conscious knowledge do not capture all the relevant knowledge. This argument is discussed in more detail in Dianne Berry's chapter (Chapter 5).

Differential rates of attaining explicit knowledge

Even many of those firmly committed to the orthodox implicit learning explanations (e.g. Reber 1989; Berry and Broadbent 1988) do not deny that some explicit encoding also occurs. For instance Reber (1989, p. 229) points out that:

> . . . knowledge acquired from implicit learning procedures is knowledge that, in some raw fashion, is always ahead of the capability of it's possessor to explicate it . . . it is misleading to argue that implicitly acquired knowledge is completely unconscious . . .

Reber and Lewis (1977) make this point in observing that subjects highly practised in artificial grammar learning over a period of four days produced far more 'complete and accurate' verbal reports than had been found in previous studies. They argue that as performance improves, it is no coincidence that verbal report should improve, but they note that even with improved performance there is still a considerable lag between performance and verbal report.

This position has been borne out in a study of the control of complex systems by Stanley *et al.* (1989). They found that on both the personal interaction task and the sugar production task subjects could pass on useful advice to novices, but that this was only after extended practice of 570 trials, and even then this advice only became reportable after first seeing personal improvements in performance of the subjects.

A similar finding has been reported by McGeorge and Burton (1989). They used the sugar production task presented to subjects for 90 trials with the helpful feedback of a graph of the system's input—output characteristics for the previous 10 exchanges. After this learning period subjects were able to report heuristics under free recall conditions. These heuristics were then entered into a computer simulation of the system. They reported that for 5 out of 14 cases, simulated performance based on a particular subject's reported heuristics was superior to their actual performance.

Mathews *et al.* (1989) provided evidence of the role of limited explicit processes in artificial grammar learning. They adopted a 'teach-aloud' procedure during the acquisition of the grammar in which subjects were periodically stopped on the discrimination task and asked to give verbal instructions as though to help somebody else complete the task. These heuristics were later given to yoked subjects who had to perform the discrimination task without the help of prior exposure to the learning exemplars. The experiment included an extended learning period over four weeks. It was found that yoked subjects outperformed control subjects over the duration of the experiment and closely shadowed the subjects in the experimental group. This demonstrated the transmission of explicit and accurate knowledge to yoked subjects. However, the yoked subjects' performance was always inferior to those exposed to the learning exemplars. Thus, although some explicit knowledge was transferred in the artificial grammar learning experiment, it was over an extended practice period and was attenuated compared with the abilities of those who possess it.

Although Lewicki (1986) stated that implicit learning is totally separate to explicit learning and that implicit knowledge is totally inaccessible to explicit report, this position can be seen at an extreme in the implicit learning literature. Most authors who maintain that there is such a process argue that although some of what is learnt is available to explicit retrieval not everything that is learnt implicitly is available.

The debate between Dulaney *et al.* (1984, 1985), Perruchet and Pacteau (1990), and Reber *et al.* (1985) serves to sharpen the focus on some of the less than satisfactory terminology that has been used in the implicit learning debate. As Berry (1994) has pointed out, many authors have failed to define what they mean by conscious and unconscious. It is clear that Reber feels a process is unconscious if it cannot be reported through the process of recall, whereas a recognition test can tap implicit knowledge. However, Dulaney *et al.* (1984, 1985) have argued that recognition tests elicit explicit knowledge. The following section reviews the debate over these different tests of knowledge.

Tests of knowledge

The previous section highlighted some of the methodological problems associated with testing for implicit and explicit knowledge. A variety of different tests have been used in implicit learning studies (recognition, recall, verbal report, generation, forced-choice recognition, false recognition, anagram solutions, etc.) which can make it difficult to compare directly experimental results. However, this becomes doubly difficult when tests such as forced-choiced tests are simultaneously interpreted as a test of implicit knowledge by some and a test of explicit knowledge by others (cf. Reber *et al.* 1985; Dulaney *et al.* 1984).

Recall has variously been characterized as more sensitive than recognition tests in some circumstances (e.g. Mathews 1990) and as less so in others (e.g. Dienes *et al.* 1991). Intriguingly, both sides cite Tulving (1983) in support of their respective cases. Recourse to Tulving does not provide a simple determination of this argument. As Tulving (1983) argues, in support of his general abstraction processing system (GAPS) model, recall can be superior to recognition under certain circumstances (e.g. Tulving and Thompson 1973). The encoding specificity principle predicts improved retrieval performance when there is a match between the encoded information and the information available at the time of retrieval. However, as recognition provides a 'copy cue', providing the environment in which the encoding and testing remain consistent, recognition should be more sensitive than recall. Free recall is also criticized by some for being insensitive and incomplete (e.g. Dienes *et al.* 1991; Brody 1989), but Mathews (1990) argues that free recall can often pick up classification information missed by forced-choice approaches.

It has been argued that recall and recognition differ in that recall depends upon declarative memory, whereas recognition is dually based upon declarative memory and upon implicit processes. Jacoby and his colleagues have argued that recognition benefits from a measure of the facility with which the recognition cue is processed (Jacoby and Dallas 1981; Jacoby 1983; Johnston *et al.* 1985). This so-called 'perceptual fluency' helps determine recognition performance and is based upon the notion of perceptual priming. Perceptual priming is seen as a non-conscious process that increases the facility of recognition of a perceptual pattern due to its prior exposure (e.g. Shimamura 1986; Tulving and Schacter 1990).

The relatedness of recall and recognition measures is demonstrated by

Haist *et al.* (1992) in a series of experiments on implicit memory that demonstrated that perceptual fluency judgements do not seem to influence recognition performance. They argued that if recognition depends upon perceptual fluency, then recognition and recall behaviour would be different in amnesics compared to controls. Recognition should be relatively much better than recall in amnesic patients as the implicit perceptual fluency process remains intact whereas the declarative store is inaccessible. Using amnesic patients and controls, they reported that both recall and recognition judgements were proportionally impaired in amnesic patients along with confidence ratings of their judgements. This suggests that both processes interrogate the same (declarative) store.

The testing debate seems a futile approach to implicit learning as there is no authoritative theory to help us decide upon one approach of testing over another. What is clear is that, under some encoding conditions, knowledge of a particular character seems to be acquired, which yields itself to particular testing methods and not to others. It is not the tests that are important but the fact that these variations occur. Defining the unconscious in such a way as to suggest that there is absolutely no way of observing its contents is such a restrictive definition as to be almost entirely unhelpful. Such a definition misses the crucial point that some methods of acquiring knowledge occur without the typical insight associated with learning. The mechanisms that give rise to this type of behaviour should be the focus of future research. The next section addresses the problem of the representation of the knowledge in implicit learning.

1.2.2 The underlying representations—rules vs. analogies?

Reber (1989), quoting Rosch and Lloyd (1978), suggests that every discourse on mental processes must address the nature of the representation of the knowledge held. Within the implicit learning literature this has largely centred on the claim that the knowledge acquired is abstract (e.g. Reber 1969, 1989). Others have demonstrated that performance in 'Reber tasks' can be explained in terms of similarity to specific stored exemplars by analogical processing (e.g. Brooks 1978). Shanks and St. John (1994) have also argued that learning taxonomies would be more usefully based upon rule versus instace-based learning than upon implicit versus explicit learning. The argument over representation carries with it a series of assumptions about the processes of the learning mechanism based upon the retrieval mechanisms posited for each representational approach. In this way arguments for the discrete storage of individual learnt exemplars can be accommodated in MINERVA 2 (Hintzman 1986) and also within Medin and Schaffer's (1978) categorization model. Whereas such a hypothesized mechanism is incompatible with agglomerative memory models such as the connectionist models of Dienes (1992; Dienes and Perner, Chapter 6, or Cleeremans and McClelland 1991).

The abstractionist (rule-based) position

Reber (1967) started out by characterizing the grammar learning performance he reports as being similar in nature to the perceptual learning processes described by E. Gibson and J. J. Gibson (1955). In their paper, they argue for two learning mechanisms based on enrichment and differentiation. Enrichment, as the word suggests, is a process of adding extra information to a stimulus to improve the perception of it, whereas differentiation involves an increasing sensitivity to the existing information held within the stimulus. Perceptual learning was then seen to be a process of differentiation. However, Reber (1969) had further developed these views about the nature of the process. By showing that subjects could transfer their newly acquired knowledge to strings composed of new letter sets (but based on the same grammar), Reber argued that the knowledge stored must be abstract in nature.

Reber and Lewis (1977) demonstrated that the knowledge held is not confined to surface features. They found that subjects could accurately solve anagrams based upon grammatical strings after a prior learning phase. In solving these anagrams, subjects demonstrated sensitivity to letter pairs and triplets (bigrams and trigrams). Subjects tended to learn about bigrams with high relational invariances more so than low invariant pairs. Furthermore, positional factors, such as first letters and initial letter sequences, tended to be apprehended better than end ones, which in turn are better than middle letters and sequences. This knowledge of bigram structure did not correlate with the actual frequency of occurrence of the bigrams in the study phase and so cannot be ascribed to superficial surface encoding. Thus, they argue that the knowledge acquired is representative of the deep structure of the grammar. Reber and Lewis argued that performance deficits were due to 'gaps' in the acquired knowledge rather than the acquisition of inappropriate rules.

The abstractionist position, based on a series of demonstrations in the artificial grammar learning paradigm, argues that deep, abstract, rule-governed knowledge is acquired in a passive, unconscious manner. Knowledge about the deep structure of the grammar and the interrelations between elements of that grammar are acquired in an effortless, although verbally inaccessible fashion.

The analogy-based position

The abstractionist view of implicit learning is controversial, and has been challenged regularly (e.g. Brooks 1978; 1987; Brooks and Vokey 1991;

Vokey and Brooks 1992; Nosofsky 1988; Nosofsky *et al.* 1989; Jacoby 1983). Brooks (1978, p. 208) challenges the view that human behaviour can be described by a series of centralized abstract rules and suggests that much of our knowledge is:

> . . . a looser confederation of special cases in which our knowledge of the general is often overridden by our knowledge of the particular.

Brooks (1978) makes a distinction between analytic and non-analytic modes of concept formation. Analytic processes are the typical processes of the scientific method in that they involve rule induction and logic used to provide abstract generalizations about a body of knowledge that will hold for all cases. He contrasts this with non-analytic processing which deals with special instances and circumstances personal to the individual. Reber's (1967, 1969, 1976) results are open to alternative interpretation due to the methodology they employ. By not showing grammar-violating strings during acquisition, Reber's subjects could have been basing their classification decisions upon 'sort-of-like-old' decisions based upon specific previously seen learning items. Secondly, Reber's subjects may have been misled by the memorization process during learning which was followed by a concept formation test. Finally, the classification test of knowledge might induce a different strategy to other forms of response. Brooks was essentially highlighting issues relating to the mechanism of learning, the encoding process, and the testing process. These, he argued, are biased to the extent that the results will appear to be due to abstraction, whereas similarity to previously seen instances will account for performance.

Brooks (1978) tested these claims in a series of three experiments. He adopted a paired associate learning method in the artificial grammar learning paradigm. Subjects had to learn strings based upon two underlying grammars. These items were then associated with either cities or animals which came from either the 'old-world' or the 'new-world'. Items from grammar A were associated with 'old-world' items such as 'Paris', 'Zebra', etc., whereas grammar B items were associated with 'new-world' items such as 'beaver', 'Montreal', etc. Under these conditions, the animal versus city dimension was salient whereas the new-world versus old-world dimension was not. Having reached criterial performance, subjects were shown a novel series of strings from both grammars. They were informed of the existence of the new-and old-world categories and were told that half the strings belonged to one and half belonged to the other. Subjects were able to discriminate successfully between the novel strings based upon these categories. In this way, Brooks demonstrated that the learning effect can occur with the presence of non-grammatical learning exemplars, in the sense that grammar B strings were ungrammatical with respect to grammar A and vice versa.

Brooks argued that this performance cannot be based upon deep knowledge of the two grammars as subjects were unaware of the presence of the two. Consequently, it is more likely that subjects were drawing specific analogy to individual learning exemplars when making the classification decisions. He illustrated this point with an example of how such a 'sort-of-like-old' process may work. For instance, if a subject saw the letter string MRMRV and decided it was similar to MRRMRV which was known to be associated with Vancouver, then MRMRV could be classified as a 'new-world' item on the basis of this similarity. Note that subjects do not need to know about the categories 'new-world' and 'old-world' during learning for this mechanism to work. Reber and Allen (1978, p. 192) characterize this as follows:

> . . . a novel four legged beast is perceived as a dog, not because it fits with the viewer's abstract feature system for dog but rather because it reminds him of specific critter he has met before which was identified as a dog.

This mechanism has received support from studies demonstrating the role of similarity mechanisms in concept formation (e.g. Nosofsky 1988; Nosofsky *et al.* 1989) and in complex control systems research (e.g. Stanley *et al.* 1989). Berry and Broadbent (1988) proposed a similar mechanism for the dynamic systems task when they postulated the notion of a look-up table for the contingencies between variables in these tasks.

It should be noted, however, that the encoding procedures adopted by Brooks (1978) were at variance with the approach of Reber (1967, 1969, 1976). Particularly, the change from memorization to paired associate learning may have served to change the nature of the observed learning. Reber and Allen (1978) argued that this paired associate learning (PAL) technique serves to make it 'highly unlikely' that subjects could abstract deep structures. The PAL technique serves to amplify the importance of individual exemplars and this is reflected in each of them being stored in memory separately. By comparing the PAL technique and an observation technique that involved looking at each string for 10 seconds, they reported that the PAL technique led to the storage of individual exemplars. This result replicates the report by Brooks (1978), but the observation technique led to the general abstraction of the underlying properties of the grammar. Furthermore, this technique was associated with superior learning.

McAndrews and Moscovitch (1985) failed to find support for the strong version of the instance-based account of categorization. In a grammar learning experiment they reported that subjects were able to determine the grammaticality of non-grammatical strings that were closely similar to previously presented grammatical strings and vice versa. Strong instance-based accounts would predict misclassification of these types of strings. The result is important, as in previous grammar learning experiments it could be argued that grammaticality and similarity were confounded, thereby making a determination between the two accounts impossible. Studies of the relationship between encoding processes and retrieval processes in problem solving have come to the similar conclusion that performance is maximized when the encoding and retrieval processes are either both rule- or analogy-based (e.g. Caplan and Schooler 1990).

Brooks *et al.* (1991) contended that similarity is not restricted to special cases outside general knowledge, as has been suggested by Reber (1989). They demonstrated that in the case of medical diagnosis, performance was facilitated by similar cases previously seen in the same context more so than by dissimilar cases from the same diagnostic category. They argued that the facilitation must be due to similarity mechanisms and not the activation of the diagnostic category as a whole.

Abstract analogies—general vs. particular

Reber's argument that the knowledge acquired is abstract in nature rests upon two main strands of evidence: that subjects show good transfer from one letter set to another with the same underlying grammar (e.g. Reber 1969; Mathews *et al.* 1989), and that the knowledge of bigrams and trigrams is deeper than frequency of occurrence detection (e.g. Reber and Lewis 1977). Recent research by Brooks and Vokey (1991) and Perruchet *et al.* (1992) has disputed both of these claims.

Brooks and his colleagues have argued that categorization can be executed through reference to particular previously stored instances in memory using similarity mechanisms (e.g. Brooks 1978, 1987; Vokey and Brooks 1992). This account has been extended to allow for the same types of mechanisms to explain the transfer effects demonstrated by Reber (1969) and Mathews *et al.* (1989). They have suggested that letter strings, such as MXVVVM, could be seen as similar to BDCCCB in that they both contain a letter triplet and both start and end with the same letters. They refer to this as *abstract* or *relational analogy* which can be contrasted to *literal analogy*. The strings BHCCCB and BDCCCB would be literally similar. Abstract analogies capture the within-item correspondences of features across two (or presumably more) types of presentation of a given underlying structure. They demonstrated how abstract analogies can account for grammar learning in an experiment where similarity to learning items was unconfounded with the grammaticality of the strings. Items were classified as 'similar' if they differed from a learning item by one letter or 'far' if they differed from a learning item by more letters. They found that the similarity variable accounted for more of the variance than grammaticality even in transfer conditions.

This theory seems underspecified in several respects. It can be seen how the notion of similarity may be applied in a very restricted sense to strings generated by artificial grammars, but it is not clear whether this view has a wider application. For instance, the question of 'abstraction' is somewhat obscure. What is clear is that abstractive processes operate upon particular instances rather than across the general deep structure of the grammar. However, this is based upon a particular sort of instance-based account of memory than defines any performance not based on this tight measure of similarity to be due to knowledge beyond the exemplars (e.g. knowledge of the grammar). This nearest-neighbour model of instance memory is not relevant to most instance theories (e.g. Whittlesea and Dorken 1993; Hintzman 1986; Estes 1986; Nosofsky 1988).

The work of Brooks and Vokey (1991) highlights more specifically the essence of the abstraction debate, namely whether categorization occurs with reference to specific whole instances (Brooks) or whether it occurs across a range of materials (Reber). They argued that the similarity to specific episodes accounts for the grammar learning studies. While abstraction is agreed to occur, the focus of this debate essentially is whether it occurs to form an abstraction over many instances or whether it occurs at the level of each episode.

This complex issue is further confused by evidence from Perruchet and Pacteau (1990, 1991) who demonstrated that classification performance can be achieved through knowledge of the incomplete fragments of the letter strings (bigrams). Whittlesea and Dorken (1993) argued that this may come about due to the 'degenerate' encoding of the learning strings. For instance, subjects may only encode pairs of letters from the strings (bigrams), which Perruchet *et al.* (1992) have shown to be sufficient to account for classification performance. Thus, the representation stored is abstract with respect to the instances but is not the product of an abstraction mechanism. Brooks and Vokey (1991) argued that in usual grammar learning studies the memorization process will result in more than just bigrams being stored (Whittlesea and Dorken 1993) or being available to report (Perruchet and Pacteau 1990).

The second case made for abstraction by Reber (1989) is that knowledge of bigrams goes beyond surface knowledge such as frequency of occurrence (Reber and Lewis 1977). Perruchet and Pacteau (1992) have reinterpreted this result attributing the original conclusions to a series of experimental biases found in the Reber and Lewis procedure. They reported that subjects learning on just bigrams—which they argue precludes any high level learning of rules—produce the same pattern of results as those learning on strings and thus the knowledge acquired is not deep as Reber maintains.

Do we use abstracted representations?

Historically, the ground has shifted in the debate over the nature of the representation of knowledge from an argument over whether abstraction occurs or not (Brooks 1978; Reber and Allen 1978), to a position where abstraction is a phenomenon accepted by many (e.g. Reber 1989; Brooks and Vokey 1991). Differences now focus on whether the abstraction is across many exemplars (Reber) or local to each specific instance (Brooks and Vokey). The simple position is complicated by Perruchet and Pacteau (1992) who argue that the knowledge is neither abstract nor based upon entire exemplars. Furthermore, the terminology is confused with Brooks and Vokey's position being described as 'global' by Perruchet and Pacteau as each whole exemplar is studied and 'particular' (as opposed to 'general') by Whittlesea and Dorken (1993) because particular exemplars are studied and not the exemplars in general.

Therefore, there appear to be three levels at which similarity is being invoked in this debate. Reber (1989) seems to be arguing for similarity measured across the range of learning exemplars, Brooks and Vokey (1991) argue for similarity at the level of the exemplar, and Perruchet and Pacteau (1992) argue for similarity at the level of the bigram within the exemplar. Reber argues that similarity at the exemplar level only occurs under specific encoding conditions that do not normally obtain (e.g. Reber and Allen 1978; Reber 1989), Brooks argues that similarity at the bigram level may be a phenomenon of the encoding and testing regimes (Brooks and Vokey 1991), and Perruchet and Pacteau (1992) deny that the knowledge is abstract.

It is clear that in addition to untangling the semantic confusion between these studies, there remains empirical work that needs to be done in order to resolve the issue of abstraction. However, two recurring themes in the debate revolve around testing (discussed earlier) and the encoding process. We now turn to the issue of the nature of encoding, and in particular, the claim that it may occur automatically.

1.3 WHAT DO WE HAVE TO DO TO LEARN? THE ROLE OF ORIENTING TASKS, FREQUENCY DETECTION, AND AUTOMATICITY

A central claim made by several researchers is that implicit learning is an automatic, passive process (e.g. Reber 1989; Berry and Dienes 1991; Berry and Broadbent 1988; Hasher and Zacks 1984). Indeed, Shanks and St. John (1994) argue that instance-based learning should be characterized in this way. These claims will now be discussed in the light of evidence from automaticity studies, implicit learning, and implicit memory.

1.3.1 Automatic and effortful processes

Implicit learning has often been described as an automatic process in the sense that it occurs without the intention to learn (e.g. Berry, Chapter 5; Reber 1976; Kemler-Nelson 1984, etc.). This closely resembles the definition of automaticity provided by Logan (1990) who views an automatic process as one which requires minimal attentional resources, is effortless, and is obligatory in that it does not require attention to instigate or to end the process. Logan's (1988, 1990) model of attentional processes has a lot in common with the instance-based models of categorization such as those advocated by Hintzman (1986) and Jacoby (1983). Before evaluating the idea that implicit learning is an automatic process, we shall consider the implications that are associated with this designation.

The defining characteristics of automatic activities are that they: develop with extensive practice; are performed smoothly and efficiently; are resistant to modification; are unaffected by other activities; do not interfere with other activities; are initiated without intention; are not under conscious control; and do not require mental effort. Some of these characteristics can be observed in the laboratory while those that involve intention, conscious control, and mental effort are either inferred or they come from subjective reports. The list is descriptive rather than definitive and is taken from a variety of sources. There is, however, no agreed criterion for categorizing an activity as being automatic rather than volitional.

1.3.2 Proponents of the two-process view

It is possible to argue that processes can be split up into those which are automatic and those which are attentional and that automaticity can be considered as all-or-none (Posner and Synder 1975; Shiffrin and Schneider 1977). More recent views have emphasized the notion of a continuum of automaticity, with new, unskilled activities at the conscious control end, and familiar, highly practised activities at the automatic end (Kahneman and Chajzyck 1983; Cohen *et al.* 1990). As more experience of an activity within a constant environment is encountered, then so the activity moves from the controlled end towards the automatic end. The arguments put forward by proponents of the continuum view is that automatic processes acquire the characteristics of automaticity with practice and still show effects of attentional factors even when they are considered to be automatic.

If, as seems likely, activities are neither completely automatically or completely consciously controlled, then in analysing the automatized components of an activity we have three options available. The first two options continue to use the assumption that behaviour can be under automatic or conscious control, but the third option simply says that the distinction has no value in that activities do not fall into one or other of these categories.

The first option is to propose that there exists a continuum of automaticity, with new, unskilled activities at one end and with familiar, highly practised activities at the other end. This description gives a one-dimensional impression of the nature of skill, however, and it also assumes that skills are static rather than vulnerable to changes with practice. This effect of practice can be described in terms of the acquisition of automatization.

The second option to handle these problems is to propose that skills are organized hierarchically, and that the automatization of the low-level sub-skills progresses through practice. Skill acquisition is then seen as the increasing automatization of the component subskills. Attention may be directed initially at the control of the low-level components, but as practice is increased these components are automatized and attention can be released for higher-level activities. The LaBerge and Samuels (1974) model of automatic processes in reading provides a good example of hierarchical processes. A low-level component would be recognizing a letter or a familiar word, and a higher-level component would be transforming an idea into the surface form of a sentence. The skilled reader will have the impression that details concerning the identity of the visual pattern can take care of themselves, and that thought should be given to decisions about the inferences that should be drawn about the meaning of the text. This model requires us to describe the mechanism whereby practice allows attention to move up the skill hierarchy, releasing attention from visual analysis so that the skilled reader can focus upon meanings.

The overt indices of performance change with practice, but can we give any weight to the verbal reports of reflections upon our own skilled activities? If these reflections do not correlate with any externally observable change in performance, then they have little credibility. On the other hand, if the subjective reports of attention-free behaviour coincide with changes in performance, such as speed and accuracy improvements, then we are entitled to look at the reports in more detail. They may emerge after the event, in which case they are not very interesting. For instance, it may simply be that the performer noticed an improvement in performance, and now attributes that change to a particular state of awareness. If this has happened, then we cannot know whether a change in performance has been accompanied by a change in attentional control. Did the change in attention accompany the change in performance or did it follow this change? These are not mutually exclusive possibilities, of course. The subjective reports of automatized behaviour are obtained after the behaviour has been produced, and so perhaps we simply have unreliable memories of skilled performances. Perhaps we think that the performance was attention-free for the reason that we did not record a memory during performance. In this case, attention may have been allocated, but when no memory is recorded we subsequently have the impression that we were behaving without attention. We must be very cautious of subjective reports from skilled performers, as it is not clear whether their impressions of changes in attention come as an accompaniment to changes in performance or as a result of changes in performance.

Practice allows a physical action to be performed faster, more accurately, and more smoothly and the change can also be described in terms of a change in the cognitive structure which mediates performance. Motor performance can be categorized according the feedback necessary for successful execution. Adams (1976), Reason (1979), Underwood (1982), and others have described novel activities as requiring closed-loop control, in that performance of the individual components of the activity requires individual checking. The 'closed-loop' here refers to feedback from execution of an individual action being used to check the match between intention and action. If there is a match, then the next individual action can be executed. Behaviour under closed-loop control is halting, slow, and variable, and practice has the effect of eliminating the need to use feedback. The skilled performer issues a command for action and does not check that the individual action matches the individual intention. The elimination of feedback from the sequences of actions is described as the change to open-loop control, and is equivalent to a change to automatized performance.

Feedback in the open-loop control mode is not used to check the intention—action match and performance becomes smoother because there are no longer any interruptions to the flow of action. Performance becomes faster because the time taken to check the feedback is eliminated, and accuracy is improved because the performer is now able to issue instructions for action based upon overlearnt associations. The evidence in favour of this view of a change from closed-loop to open-loop control is reviewed by Underwood (1982), where the use of feedback is identified with attention. The subjective impressions that accompany a highly skilled action under open-loop control result from the removal of attention from the production of the action sequence. The model applies equally well to motor skills and to cognitive skills such as recalling familiar facts (e.g. simple multiplication calculations, the names of certain capital cities, and world politicians). Provided that the performer does not need to check the intention—action match, then attention will be unnecessary for behaviour.

An alternative view of the effects of practice is proved in Logan's (1988) instance-based theory of automatization in which practice has the effect of taking the performer from a reliance upon algorithm-based actions to a reliance upon memories. The algorithms must be calculated each time an unskilled action is performed, while the practised action can rely upon a memory of the stimulus and its accompanying action. Calculation and operation of the algorithm requires mental resources, while memory-based performance is free of attention. The two models are compatible, of course, if Logan's algorithm requires the use of feedback and can be described as running under closed-loop control, and if the reliance upon memories is free of feedback and runs under open-loop control.

Hasher and Zacks (1979) contrasted automatic and effortful processes by assuming that there is a continuum of attentional requirements among encoding processes and that attentional capacity varies with the encoding task. Automatic and effortful processes are at opposite ends of this continuum. Automatic processes operate continually, encoding attributes of the stimuli being attended to. The process is independent of awareness or intention and is robust in the face of even high attentional demands. However, they say that the knowledge gained by automatic processes is available to consciousness. It is arguable that the contents of automatic processes are not *necessarily* available to consciousness, of course, as an automatic process can be initiated, performed, and completed without awareness. The skilled car driver may change gear, in response to a change in engine speed, many times on a journey without being aware of the conditions that prompted the response or of the act of changing gear itself. The driver may know that several gear changes must have occurred, without awareness of any specific action. This would be knowledge through reasoning, however, rather than knowledge through phenomenal experience. There are a number of ways by which we can come to know that something has happened, and awareness at the time of occurrence is not necessarily implied.

Effortful processes are characterized as being intentional, conscious, planned, and controlled. Shiffrin and Schneider (1977) suggested there are two types of conscious process, the accessible and the veiled. Accessible processes are slow and are capable of being monitored 'on-line' and altered during execution whereas the veiled processes are quicker and afford less opportunity to alter them. The use and ability to introspect about effortful processes develops at the same rate. This can be compared with Berry and Broadbent's (1984, 1988) findings that their subjects' abilities to introspect about the processes they engage in does not improve at the same rate as the process. In time, these processes could become automatic.

1.3.3 Frequency detection in implicit learning

For implicit learning to be described as effortless it seems likely that it must be composed, at least in part, of automatic processes. One process that has been suggested to underlie implicit learning is frequency detection (e.g. Hasher and Zacks 1984; Kellogg and Dowdy 1986; Hayes and Broadbent 1988; Hintzman, *et al.* 1992; Wattenmaker, 1993; Perruchet and Pacteau, 1990). For instance, Hayes and Broadbent (1988), in delineating two separate learning mechanisms, argue that frequency information is unselectively 'aggregated' in U-mode learning (implicit learning).

Hasher and Zacks (1979) proposed that frequency encoding in memory for instances is an automatic process. They defined an automatic process as one that does not interfere with other ongoing cognitive activity. In a series of studies they showed that kindergarten children, college students, the elderly, and the depressed can equally accurately estimate the frequency of occurrence of the presentation of pictorial information. Furthermore, college students performed equally well in incidental and intentional learning modes. Supporting evidence comes from Hintzman (1969) who reported that subjects can accurately estimate the frequency of occurrence of words in a list. Furthermore, Zacks *et al.* (1982) reported that event frequency encoding was not influenced by practice, appropriateness of practice, accuracy of test predictions, or by competing demands. Our knowledge of the frequencies of events appears to be gained without effort.

Hasher and Zacks (1984) reviewed the evidence that suggests that incidental frequency judgements are indeed made in a variety of natural situations. For instance, the occurrences of letters, syllables, surnames, professions, and sources of morbidity and mortality are events to which people show frequency sensitivity. Hasher and Zacks argue that these sorts of events are unlikely to have been intentionally encoded. A fascinating example of this sensitivity to natural events comes from Coren and Porac (1977) who surveyed a large number of works of art portraying figures engaged in 'handed' activity. From prehistoric times to 1977, the number of left-and right-handed people portrayed in the pictures matched actual frequencies of differing handedness. It is not clear why left-handed people are so accurately portrayed, as it was the practice of many cultures to dissuade actively left-handedness, associating it with a variety of negative attributes such as evil, sloth, and ignorance.

Further support for the role of feature frequency counting in concept learning comes from Kellogg (1982), who suggested that people learn about the relative frequency of features in a set of exemplars through automatic processes. This knowledge is necessary and sufficient to account for concept acquisition. Wattenmaker (1993) examined feature frequency sensitivity across incidental and intentional learning conditions, finding that feature frequencies were encoded equally well across a range of learning conditions.

Not all the evidence is in favour of automatic feature frequency detection. Greene (1984) reported two experiments investigating the effect of learning intentions upon memories for frequencies of words in a list. Subjects were either not informed that there would be a specific frequency estimation test after learning or were told that there would be a memory test for the words presented on a list. Subjects in the intentional group outperformed those in the unintentional group. Thus, frequency judgements were better for those that were specifically informed of a memory test.

Kellogg and Dowdy (1986) also concluded that sensitivity to frequency knowledge is acquired through an effortful process, on the basis of a series of experiments where subjects attending to instances of a concept were later asked to estimate feature frequency. Concepts were defined by a conjunction of stimulus features that were systematically varied in frequency of presentation during learning. Learning was either incidental or intentional and the rate of presentation of the items was also varied. The stimulus features consisted of letters and subjects in the intentional learning group had to try to work out which features defined the concept that they were told linked the exemplars. The subjects in the incidental learning group had to decide if the letters were an anagram of a word or not. The defining features of the concept appeared 100 per cent of the time and other varyingly similar features appeared 80 per cent, 60 per cent, 40 per cent 20, per cent and 0 per cent of the time.

Concept learning was tested by asking the subjects to distinguish as 'familiar' old instances, new instances, and new non-instances in a recognition test. All conditions showed a frequency sensitivity up to 60 per cent, but only the intentional learners produced accurate frequency estimates above this level, suggesting that feature frequency detection is not an automatic process. Furthermore, longer presentation rates (4 s vs. 8 s) led to increased accuracy of estimates. Subjects in both groups were able to distinguish instances from non-instances yet those in the incidental group were unable to verbalize the defining features of the concept. On the basis of these results Kellogg and Dowdy (1986) argued that feature frequency detection is not automatic. They suggest that it is more accurately described as being a veiled process (Shiffrin and Schneider 1977) that is difficult to modify and is not easily open to introspection.

The possibility therefore arises that if frequency detection is not strictly automatic and effortless, then this may also be the case in implicit learning tasks. Kellogg and Dowdy (1986) criticized Hasher and Zacks (1979) for using a weak measure of intentional versus incidental learning, and this may account for differences in their conclusions. In other studies where markedly different orienting tasks lead to markedly different processing (e.g. Fisk and Schneider 1984)—between semantic and graphical orienting tasks—different estimates of frequency have been found. Thus, it may be that a closer control of the conditions of study processing may be required to determine the case for automaticity of implicit learning.

1.3.4 Effects of instructions on learning

The issue of instruction during learning is discussed in this section. Implicit learning has been characterized as operating maximally when 'subjects are not trying to break the code' (Reber 1976) or tends to be associated with incidental learning conditions (Berry, Chapter 5). Studies that have addressed this claim often have used the approach adopted in Greene's (1984) study of frequency detection. Typically, subjects are given hints or instructions about the nature of a subsequent test or about the existence of some underlying structure they must hypothesize about. The assumption made in these studies is that the experimental instructions will affect the manner in which subjects attempt to tackle the problem. As has been noted previously, both Reber and Berry have argued that implicit learning occurs when the stimulus materials to be learnt represent a complex pattern or structure, so consequently we can conclude that certain approaches to the material will result in more or less implicit learning than others.

One reason that implicit learning studies have tended to ignore the role of study processing, as Berry and Dienes (1991) point out, could be because it has been used to explain results contrary to the implicit learning hypothesis (e.g. Brooks 1978; Reber and Allen 1978). Some studies have attempted to alter the nature of instructions given to subjects, and the results from these are illuminating.

Reber (1976) reported an artificial grammar learning study where subjects were either instructed to memorize strings (neutral condition) or were told that the strings obeyed a complex set of rules that governed which letters could follow others and that discovering these rules would facilitate memorizing the items. He found that subjects in the intentional group were worse at memorizing the strings and also in their subsequent classification performance. Kemler-Nelson (1984) provided some support for this view in reporting that subjects learn about categories that have a strong family-resemblance structure more easily under incidental conditions than in intentional conditions. The finding that instructions impair performance is controversial. Reber *et al.* (1980) failed to replicate the Reber (1976) effect, as did Dienes *et al.* (1991).

Recently, a study by Bright and Burton (1994) indicated that study instructions had a significant effect upon learning. Subjects were exposed to a series of 30 analogue clock faces all bearing a different time falling in the range 6–12 o'clock. Subjects in one group were instructed to write out the time shown on each clock and subjects in the other group were instructed to rate the clocks for aesthetic appeal. Neither group of subjects was informed about the invariant rule defining the times. After this encoding phase subjects were given a surprise forced-choice pseudo-recognition test comprising 10 pairs of times (in digital format). One member of each pair was a time that was novel yet consistent with the invariant rule and the other time fell outside this range. Subjects were asked to circle the time they thought they had seen before, or failing that to guess. Whilst both groups selected these times better than chance performance, the group that were asked to rate the clock-face appearances were significantly worse at test than the group that wrote the times out. Neither group were able to offer any accurate information about their performance and many expressed surprise when debriefed. Thus, this study seems to indicate a learning mechanism impaired by study instructions but not inhibited by them.

The disconfirmation of a negative effect of intention upon learning by Bright and Burton (1994) does not rule out a second weaker claim that intention has no effect upon learning. Evidence for this position comes from complex systems studies such as Berry and Broadbent (1988). They found that search instructions did not have an effect on performance on the person-interaction task. Both Berry and Broadbent (1988) and Reber *et al.* (1980) reported that search instruction has a differential effect in relation to the complexity of the study materials. Both report that the search instruction facilitates learning when the underlying structure of the stimuli are relatively salient. In the Berry and Broadbent (1988) study, when the relationship was salient, performance was positively correlated to question answering which was good. However, when the relationship was less salient, performance was poorer and was not correlated with question answering which was also poor.

1.3.5 Automatic and implicit processes

This evidence, taken with the evidence on frequency detection, again produces a complicated story. It has been variously suggested that implicit learning is an automatic process that may depend upon frequency detection as one of its basic subprocesses. The evidence from frequency detection studies casts doubts on the extreme view that the process is totally automatic as defined by Hasher and Zacks (1979). Implicit learning may not be automatic if it depends upon this process. It has also been suggested that implicit learning proceeds optimally under passive learning conditions. However, it can be seen that manipulations of the conditions of learning can lead to the criticism that these manipulations inhibit implicit learning processes from operating at all. Thus, when impaired performance is observed with such manipulations one cannot rule out the alternative possibility that the performance is due to fragmentary explicit learning instead. Therefore, it is important to attempt to address these issues without confounding inhibitory effects within the learning mechanism with inhibiting the mechanism itself.

The issues of consciousness, representation, and encoding conditions represent the focus of research in the field at present. The Shanks and St. John (1994) review, denying unconscious learning processes, has sharpened the debate about the use of such terms as *consciousness, implicit,* and *explicit*. Recent work by McGeorge and Burton (1990), Wright and Burton (in press), Bright and Burton (1994), Cock *et al.* (1994) has started to address issues of representation and encoding using paradigms that avoid some of the procedural problems that have beset artificial grammar learning. The following chapters provide a detailed view of the variety of different approaches currently being used to tackle the problems of justifying the implicit—explicit distinction and in determining the extent of its usefulness.

REFERENCES

Adams, J. A. (1976). Issues for a closed-loop theory of motor learning. In *Motor control: issues and trends,* (ed. G. E. Stelmach). Academic Press, London.

Allen, R. and Reber, A. S. (1980). Very long-term memory for tacit knowledge. *Cognition,* **8** 175–85.

Balota, D. A. (1983). Automatic semantic activation and episodic memory encoding. *Journal of Verbal Learning and Verbal Behavior,* **22** 88–104.

Berry, D. C. (1993). Implicit learning: reflections and prospects. In (ed. A. Baddeley and L. Weiskrantz). *Attention: Selection, awareness, and control,* Oxford University Press.

Berry, D. C. and Broadbent, D. E. (1984). On the relationship between task performance and associated verbalisable knowledge. *Quarterly Journal of Experimental Psychology,* **36A**, 209–31.

Berry, D. C. and Broadbent, D. E. (1987). The combination of implicit and explicit learning processes. *Psychological Research,* **49**, 7–15.

Berry, D. C. and Broadbent, D. E. (1988). Interactive tasks and the implicit-explicit distinction. *British Journal of Psychology,* **79**, 251–72.

Berry, D. C. and Dienes, Z. (1991). The relationship between implicit memory and implicit learning. *British Journal of Psychology,* **82**, 359–73.

Bright, J. E. H. and Burton, A. M. (1994). Past midnight: Semantic processing in an implicit learning task. *Quarterly Journal of Experimental Psychology,* **47A**, 71–89.

Broadbent, D. E. and Aston, B. (1978). Human control of a simulated economic system. *Ergonomics,* **21**, 1035–43.

Brody, N. (1989). Unconscious learning of rules: Comment on Reber's analysis of implicit learning. *Journal of Experimental Psychology: General,* **118**, 236–8.

Brooks, L. R. (1978). Non-analytic concept formation and memory for instances. In *Cognition and categorisation,* (ed. E. Rosch and B. Lloyd). Erlbaum, Hillsdale, NJ.

Brooks, L. R. (1987). Decentralized control of categorisation: The role prior processing episodes. In *Concepts and conceptual development: Ecological and intellectual factors in categorization*, (ed. U. Neisser). Cambridge University Press.
Brooks, L. R. and Vokey, J. R. (1991). Abstract analogies and abstracted grammars: Comments on Reber (1989) and Mathews *et al.* (1989). *Journal of Experimental Psychology: General*, **120**, 316–23.
Brooks, L. R., Norman, G. R., and Allen, S. W. (1991). Role of specific similarity in a medical diagnostic task. *Journal of Experimental Psychology: General*, **120**, 278–87.
Caplan, L. J. and Schooler, C. (1990). Problem solving by reference to rules or previous episodes: The effects of organized training, analogical models, and subsequent complexity of experience. *Memory and Cognition*, **18**, 215–27.
Carlson, R. A. and Dulaney, D. E. (1985). Conscious attention and abstraction in concept learning. *Journal of Experimental Psychology: Learning, Memory, and Cognition*, **11(1)**, 45–58.
Cheesman, J. and Merikle, P. M. (1984). Priming with and without awareness. *Perception and Psychophysics*, **36**, 387–95.
Cleeremans, A. and McClelland, J. (1991). Learning the structure of event sequences. *Journal of Experimental Psychology: General*, **120**, 235–53.
Cock, J., Berry, D. C., and Gaffan, E. A. (1994). New strings for old: the role of similarity processing in an incidental learning task. *Quarterly Journal of Experimental Psychology*, **47A**, 1015–34.
Cohen, J. D., Dunbar, K., and McClelland, J. L. (1990). On the control of automatic processes: a parallel distributed processing account of the Stroop effect. *Psychological Review*, **97**, 332–61.
Coren, S. and Porac, C. (1977). Fifty centuries of right-handedness: The historical record. *Science*, **198**, 631–2.
Curran, T. and Keele, S. (1993). Attentional and nonattentional forms of sequence learning. *Journal of Experimental Psychology: Learning, Memory, and Cognition*, **19**, 189–202.
Dienes, Z., Broadbent, D. E., and Berry, D. C. (1991). Implicit and explicit knowledge bases in artificial grammar learning. *Journal of Experimental Psychology: Learning, Memory, and Cognition*, **17**, 875–87.
Dixon, N. F. (1981). *Preconscious processing*. Wiley, Chichester.
Dulaney, D. E., Carlson, R. A., and Dewey, G. I. (1984). A case of syntactical learning and judgement: How conscious and how abstract. *Journal of Experimental Psychology: General*, **113**, 541–55.
Dulaney, D. E., Carlson, R. A., and Dewey, G. I. (1985). On consciousness in syntactic learning and judgement: A reply to Reber, Allen and Regan. *Journal of Experimental Psychology: General*, **114**, 25–32.
Eich, E. (1984). Memory for unattended events: Remembering with and without awareness. *Memory and Cognition*, **12**, 105–11.
Estes, W. K. (1986). Memory storage and retrieval processes in category learning. *Journal of Experimental Psychology: General*, **115**, 155–74.
Fisk, A. D. and Schneider, W. (1984). Memory as a function of attention, level of processing, and automatisation. *Journal of Experimental Psychology: Learning, Memory, and Cognition*, **10**, 181–97.

Fowler, C. A., Wolford, G., Slade, R., and Tassinary, L. (1981). Lexical access with and without awareness. *Journal of Experimental Psychology: General*, **110**, 341–62.

Gibson, E. and Gibson, J. J. (1955). Perceptual learning: differentiation or enrichment? *Psychological Review*, **62**, 32–41.

Greene, R. L. (1984) Incidental learning of event frequency. *Memory and Cognition*, **12**, 90–5.

Groeger, J. A. (1984). Evidence of unconscious semantic processing from a forced error situation. *British Journal of Psychology*, **75**, 304–14.

Groeger, J. A. (1986). Predominant and non-dominant analysis: Effects of level of presentation. *British Journal of Psychology*, **77**, 109–16.

Haist, F., Shimamura, A. P., and Squire, L. R. (1992). On the relationship between recall and recognition memory. *Journal of Experimental Psychology: Learning, Memory, and Cognition*, **18**, 691–702.

Hasher, L. and Zacks, R. T. (1979). Automatic and effortful processes in memory. *Journal of Experimental Psychology: General*, **108**, 356–88.

Hasher, L. and Zacks, R. T. (1984). Automatic processing of fundamental information. *American Psychologist*, **39**, 1372–88.

Hayes, N. A. and Broadbent, D. E. (1988). Two modes of learning for interactive tasks. *Cognition*, **28**, 249–76.

Hintzman, D. A. (1969). Recognition time: effects of recency, frequency, and the spacing of repetitions. *Journal of Experimental Psychology*, **79**, 192–4.

Hintzman, D. L. (1986). Schema abstraction in a multiple trace memory model. *Psychological Review*, **93**, 411–28.

Hintzman, D. L., Curran, T., and Oppy, B. (1992). Effects of similarity and repetition on memory: registration without learning? *Journal of Experimental Psychology: Learning, Memory, and Cognition*, **18**, 667–80.

Holender, D. (1986). Semantic activation without conscious identification in dichotic listening, parafoveal vision and visual masking: A survey and appraisal. *Behavioral and Brain Sciences*, **9**, 1–66.

Jacoby, L. L. (1983). Remembering the data: Analyzing interactive processes in reading. *Journal of Verbal Learning and Verbal Behavior*, **22**, 485–508.

Jacoby, L. L. and Dallas, M. (1981). On the relationship between autobiographical memory and perceptual learning. *Journal of Experimental Psychology: General*, **110**, 306–40.

Johnston, W. A. and Wilson, J. (1980). Perceptual processing of non-targets in an attention task. *Memory and Cognition*, **8**, 372–7.

Johnston, W. A., Dark, V. J., and Jacoby, L. L. (1985). Perceptual fluency and recognition judgements. *Journal of Experimental Psychology: Learning, Memory, and Cognition*, **11**, 3–11.

Kahneman, D. and Chajzyck, D. (1983). Tests of the automaticity of reading: dilution of Stroop effects by colour-irrelevant stimuli. *Journal of Experimental Psychology: Human Perception and Performance*, **9**, 497–509.

Kellogg, R. T. (1982). When can we introspect accurately about mental processes. *Memory and Cognition*, **10**, 141–4.

Kellogg, R. T. and Dowdy, J. C. (1986). Automatic learning of the frequencies of occurrence of stimulus features. *American Journal of Psychology*, **99**, 111–26.

Kemler-Nelson, D. G. (1984). The effects of intention on what concepts are acquired. *Journal of Verbal Learning and Verbal Behavior*, **23**, 734–59.

Kunst-Wilson, W. R. and Zajonc, R. B. (1980). Affective discrimination of stimuli that cannot be recognized. *Science*, **207**, 557–8.
LaBerge, D. and Samuels, S. J. (1974). Toward a theory of automatic information processing in reading. *Cognitive Psychology*, **6**, 293–323.
Lewicki, P. (1985). Nonconscious biasing effects of single instances on subsequent judgements. *Journal of Personality and Social Psychology*, **48**, 563–74.
Lewicki, P. (1986). Processing information about covariations that cannot be articulated. *Journal of Experimental Psychology: Learning, Memory, and Cognition*, **12**, 135–46.
Lewicki, P., Hoffman, H., and Czyzewska, M. (1987). Unconscious acquisition of complex procedural knowledge. *Journal of Experimental Psychology: Learning, Memory, and Cognition*, **13**, 523–30.
Lewicki, P., Hill, T., and Bizot, E. (1988). Acquisition of procedural knowledge about a pattern of stimuli that can not be articulated. *Cognitive Psychology*, **20**, 24–37.
Lewis, J. L. (1970). Semantic processing of unattended messages using dichotic listening. *Journal of Experimental Psychology*, **85**, 225–8.
Logan, G. D. (1988). Towards an instance theory of automatisation. *Psychological Review*, **95**, 492–527.
Logan, G. D. (1990). Repetition priming and automaticity: Common underlying mechanisms? *Cognitive Psychology*, **22**, 1–35.
McAndrews, M. and Moscovitch, M. (1985). Rule-based and exemplar-based classification in artificial grammar learning. *Memory and Cognition*, **13**, 469–75.
McGeorge, P. and Burton, A. M. (1989). The effects of concurrent verbalization on performance in a dynamic systems task. *British Journal of Psychology*, **80**, 455–65.
McGeorge, P. and Burton, A. M. (1990). Semantic processing in an incidental learning task. *Quarterly Journal of Experimental Psychology*, **42**, 597–610.
Marcel, A. J. (1980). Conscious and preconscious recognition of polysemous words: Locating the selective effect of prior verbal context. In *Attention and performance, VIII*, (ed. J. Long and A. Baddeley). Erlbaum, Hillsdale, NJ.
Marcel, A. J. (1983). Conscious and unconscious perception: experiments on visual masking and word recognition. *Cognitive Psychology*, **15**, 197–237.
Mathews, R. C. (1990). Abstractness of implicit grammar knowledge: Comments on Perruchet and Pacteau's analysis of synthetic grammar learning. *Journal of Experimental Psychology: General*, **119**, 412–16.
Mathews, R. C., Buss, R. R., Stanley, W. B., Blanchard-Fields, F., Cho, J., and Druham, B. (1989). Role of implicit and explicit processing in learning from examples: a synergistic effect. *Journal of Experimental Psychology: Learning, Memory, and Cognition*, **15**, 1083–100.
Medin, D. L. and Schaffer, M. M. (1978) Context theory of classification learning. *Psychological Review*, **85**, 207–38.
Nelson, T. O. (1978). Detecting small amounts of information in memory: Savings for nonrecognized items. *Journal of Experimental Psychology: Human Learning, Memory, and Cognition*, **4** 453–68.
Niedenthal, P. (1987). *Unconscious affect in social cognition*. Unpublished D. Phil. thesis. University of Michigan.
Nissen, M. J. and Bullemer, P. (1987). Attentional requirements for learning: Evidence from performance measures. *Cognitive Psychology*, **19**, 1–32.

Nosofsky, R. M. (1988). Exemplar-based accounts of relations between classification, recognition and typicality. *Journal of Experimental Psychology: Learning, Memory, and Cognition*, **14**, 700–8.

Nosofsky, R. M., Clark, S. E., and Shin, H. J. (1989). Rules and exemplars in categorization, identification and recognition. *Journal of Experimental Psychology: Learning, Memory, and Cognition*, **15**, 282–304.

Perruchet, P. and Amorim, M. A. (1992). Conscious knowledge and changes in performance in sequence learning: Evidence against dissociation. *Journal of Experimental Psychology: Learning, Memory, and Cognition*, **18**, 785–800.

Perruchet, P. and Pacteau, C. (1990). Synthetic grammar learning: Implicit rule abstraction or explicit fragmentary knowledge? *Journal of Experimental Psychology: General*, **119**, 264–75.

Perruchet, P. and Pacteau, C. (1991). Implicit acquisition of abstract knowledge about artificial grammar: some methodological and conceptual issues. *Journal of Experimental Psychology: General*, **120(1)**, 112–16.

Perruchet, P., Gallego, J., and Pacteau, C. (1992). A reinterpretation of some earlier evidence for abstractiveness of implicitly acquired knowledge. *Quarterly Journal of Experimental Psychology*, **44A**, 193–210.

Posner, M. I. and Snyder, C. R. R. (1975). Facilitation and inhibition in the processing of signals. In *Attention and perfomance V* (ed. P. M. A. Rabbit and S. Dornic). Academic Press, London.

Reason, J. (1979) Actions not as planned: The price of automatisation. In *Aspects of consciousness*, Vol. 1, (ed. G. Underwood and R. Stevens). Academic Press, London.

Reber, A. S. (1967). Implicit learning of artificial grammars. *Journal of Verbal Learning and Verbal Behavior*, **6**, 855–63.

Reber, A. S. (1969). Transfer of syntactic structure in synthetic languages. *Journal of Experimental Psychology*, **81**, 115–19.

Reber, A. S. (1976). Implicit learning of synthetic languages: The role of instructional set. *Journal of Experimental Psychology: Human Learning and Memory*, **2**, 88–94.

Reber, A. S. (1989). Implicit learning and tacit knowledge. *Journal of Experimental Psychology: General*, **118**, 219–35.

Reber, A. S. (1990). On the primacy of the implicit: Comment on Perruchet and Pacteau. *Journal of Experimental Psychology: General*, **119**, 340–2.

Reber, A. S. and Allen, R. (1978). Analogic and abstraction strategies in synthetic grammar learning. *Cognition*, **6**, 189–221.

Reber, A. S. and Lewis, S. (1977). Implicit learning: An analysis of the form and structure of a body of tacit knowledge. *Cognition*, **5**, 333–61.

Reber, A. S., Kassim, S. M., Lewis, S., and Cantor, S. (1980). On the relationship between implicit and explicit modes of learning a complex rule structure. *Journal of Experimental Psychology: Human Learning and Performance*, **6**, 492–502.

Reber, A. S., Allen, R., and Regan, S. (1985). Syntactical learning and judgement, still unconscious and still abstract: Comment on Dulany, Carlson and Dewey. *Journal of Experimental Psychology: General*, **114**, 17–24.

Reingold, E. M. and Merikle, P. M. (1988). Using direct and indirect measures to study perception without awareness. *Perception and Psychophysics*, **44**, 563–75.

Rosch, E. and Lloyd, B. B. (1978). Representations. In *Cognition and categorization* (ed. E. Rosch and B. B. Lloyg). Erlbaum, Hillsdale, NJ.

Sanderson, P. M. (1989). Verbalizable knowledge and skilled task performance: Association, dissociation and mental models. *Journal of Experimental Psychology: Learning, Memory, and Cognition*, **15**, 729–47.

Scarborough, D. L., Gerard, L., and Cortese, C. (1979). Accessing lexical memory: The transfer of word repitition effects across task and modality. *Memory and Cognition*, **7**, 3–12.

Schacter, D. L. (1987). Implicit memory: History and current status. *Journal of Experimental Psychology: Learning, Memory, and Cognition*, **13**, 501–18.

Shanks, D. and St. John, M. (1994). Characteristics of dissociable learning systems. *Behavioral and Brain Sciences*, **17**, 367–447.

Shiffrin, R. M. and Schneider, W. (1977). Controlled and automatic human information processing. II: Perceptual learning, automatic attending and a general theory. *Psychological Review*, **84**, 127–90.

Shimamura, A. P. (1986). Priming effects in amnesia: Evidence for dissociable memory function. *Quarterly Journal of Experimental Psychology*, **38**, 619–44.

Stanley, W. B., Mathews, R. C., Buss, R. R., and Kotler-Cope, S. (1989). Insight without awareness: On the interaction of verbalisation, instruction and practice in a simulated process control task. *Quarterly Journal of Experimental Psychology*, **41**, 553–77.

Tulving, E. (1983). *Elements of episodic memory*. Oxford University Press.

Tulving, E. (1984*a*). Multiple learning and memory systems. In *Psychology in the 1990's*, (ed. K. M. J. Lagerspetz and P. Niemi). Elsevier, Amsterdam.

Tulving, E. (1984*b*). Precis of elements of episodic memory. *Brain and Behavioral Sciences*, **7**, 223–68.

Tulving, E. and Schacter, D. L. (1990). Priming and human memory. *Science*, **247**, 301–6.

Tulving, E. and Thompson, D. M. (1973). Encoding specificity and retrieval processes in episodic memory. *Psychological Review*, **22**, 142–7.

Tulving, E., Schacter, D. L., and Stark, H. A. (1982). Priming effects in word-fragment completion are independent of recognition memory. *Journal of Experimental Psychology: Learning, Memory, and Cognition*, **8**, 336–42.

Underwood, G. (1976). Semantic interference from unattended printed words. *British Journal of Psychology*, **67**, 327–38.

Underwood, G. (1977). Contextual facilitation from attended and unattended messages. *Journal of Verbal Learning and Verbal Behavior*, **16**, 99–106.

Underwood, G. (1982). Attention and awareness in cognitive and motor skills. In *Aspects of consciousness*, Vol. 3, (ed. G. Underwood). Academic Press, London.

Underwood, G. (1994). Subliminal perception on TV. *Nature*, **370**, 103.

Vokey, J. R. and Brooks, L. R. (1992). The salience of item knowledge in learning artifical grammars. *Journal of Experimental Psychology: Learning, Memory, and Cognition*, **18**, 328–44.

Warrington, E. K. and Weiskrantz, L. (1974). The effect of prior learning on subsequent retention in amnesic patients. *Neuropsychologia*, **12**, 419–28.

Wattenmaker, W. D. (1993). Incidental concept learning, feature frequency and correlated properties. *Journal of Experimental Psychology: Learning, Memory, and Cognition*, **19**, 203–22.

Whittlesea, B. W. A. and Dorken, M. D. (1993). Incidentally, things in general are particularly determined: An Episodic-processing account of implicit learning. *Journal of Experimental Psychology: General*, **122**, 227–48.

Wright, R. L. and Burton, A. M. (In press). Implicit learning of an invariant: Just say no. *Quarterly Journal of Experimental Psychology*,

Zacks, R. T., Hasher, L., and Sanft, H. (1982). Automatic encoding of event frequency: further findings. *Journal of Experimental Psychology: Learning, Memory, and Cognition*, **8**, 106–16.

2

Beyond perception: conceptual contributions to unconscious influences of memory

Jeffrey P. Toth and Eyal M. Reingold

Whenever knowledge of the possible interpretation or *conceptualization* of something helps in perceiving that thing, we say the processing is conceptually driven. That is, the process starts with conceptualization of what might be present and then looks for confirming evidence, biasing the processing mechanisms to give the expected result . . . Conceptually driven processing and data-driven processing almost always occur together, with each direction of processing contributing something to the total analysis. (Lindsay and Norman 1977, p. 13)

2.0 OVERVIEW

In what ways can a person be unconsciously influenced by the past? In the last quarter century, there has been a great deal of research directed at answering that question. However, the majority of that research has focused on the transfer of prior perceptual or data-driven processing. Much less emphasis has been placed on conceptual factors in the production of unconscious influences even though events are never processed in conceptual isolation—without a meaningful or interpretive context. The purpose of this chapter is to address the question of whether memory for prior meaning-based processing can unconsciously influence subsequent thought and behaviour—that is, the question of 'conceptual priming'. More generally, we describe how conceptually driven or 'top-down' processes may play a role in all forms of priming, both perceptual and conceptual.

We had three specific goals in writing this chapter. First, we wanted to point out the inadequacies of indirect tests as measures of unconscious influences, especially as they relate to the question of conceptual priming. This goal seems important because, if we are to truly understand the way prior conceptual processing affects subsequent thought and behaviour, we need to begin with unequivocal demonstrations of such effects. Our second goal was to identify some of the conditions necessary for the transfer of prior meaning-based processing. To anticipate, we argue that conceptual transfer depends on reinstating the context surrounding the prior event in which conceptual processing took place. Our third goal was to point out what we see as an important but missing factor in contemporary theories of unconscious influences—the subject's *set* or 'level of attunement' (Bransford *et al.* 1977) for task processing. We relate cognitive set to current notions of 'executive' processing (e.g. Norman and Shallice 1986), but argue that, rather then being absolute, unconscious (automatic) influences are relative to the context set by intentions (Jacoby *et al.* 1993*a*; Neumann 1984).

The chapter is organized as follows. We begin by giving a brief overview of research on unconscious influences of memory ('implicit memory'). We then take a selective look at early research on unconscious influences. Aside from general historical interest, the purpose of this section is to provide a background for evaluating contemporary research on unconscious influences of memory. Early investigations provide an elegant contrast for contemporary studies because, whereas the issues of set and context were viewed as critical by early investigators, these issues have been largely ignored in modern studies. The largest portion of the chapter is devoted to reviewing contemporary evidence for unconscious conceptual influences of memory. Here, we focus mainly on indirect tests of memory and on evidence from the process dissociation procedure. We conclude by assessing how our review informs theorizing about the nature of memory; and, what it implies for the nature of conceptual unconscious influences.

2.1 PERCEPTIONS OF CURRENT RESEARCH ON UNCONSCIOUS INFLUENCES OF MEMORY

An influential study in the modern characterization of unconscious influences was published by Winnick and Daniel in 1970. In the first phase of their experiment 2, subjects were shown words, pictures of objects, and definitions, and were required to pronounce the words depicted by the different stimuli. Subjects were then asked to recall the words, and, as expected, words generated from pictures and definitions were better recalled than those evoked from the printed words themselves. However, a very different pattern emerged in the following test of tachistoscopic identification. For this test, words that had been pronounced at study were flashed very briefly for identification although 'no indication was given that the same words would be used'. Results showed that performance in tachistoscopic identification was almost the opposite of that in free recall: words originally presented in printed form showed the greatest facilitation (i.e., the lowest identification thresholds), whereas words previously elicited by definitions or pictures had thresholds nearly indistinguishable from non-presented control words. Winnick and Daniel (1970, p. 80) described their findings as indicative of 'a kind of perceptual sensitization'.

Winnick and Daniel's (1970) results were replicated in a number of later studies using word identification as well as other indirect tests such as stem and fragment completion (e.g. Jacoby 1983*b*; Jacoby and Dallas 1981; Graf and Mandler 1984; Weldon and Roediger 1987; for a review see Roediger and McDermott 1993). In addition to words generated from pictures or definitions, these experiments showed that other conceptual manipulations, such as levels of processing (Craik and Lockhart 1972), which are known to have large effects on recognition and recall, had little or no effect on indirect tests using physically degraded ('data-limited') retrieval cues. Similar to the account given by Winnick and Daniel (1970), one of the most straightforward explanations of these effects appealed to 'transfer-appropriate processing' the notion that memory reflects the overlap in processing requirements at encoding and retrieval (Jacoby 1983*b*; Kolers and Roediger 1984; Morris *et al.* 1977; Roediger and Blaxton 1987). Unlike generating, reading isolated words requires that specific visual patterns—the printed words—be perceptually analysed. Similarly, tests, such as word indentification and stem completion, require the subject to perform a visual or 'data-driven' analysis of the degraded test cues in order to garner evidence as to their identity. Thus, because of their prior visual processing, read words show a larger benefit than generated words in subsequent identification or completion tests. Also, because semantic elaboration occurs subsequent to identification, levels of processing has little effect on these tests.

At around the same time the above findings were being reported in normals, curious findings were emerging in research with memory-impaired populations such as those with Korsakoff amnesia (for a review see Moscovitch *et al.* 1993). In a classic series of studies, Warrington and Weiskrantz (1968, 1970, 1974) found that amnesics, who showed little recollection of prior experience on traditional tests such as recognition and recall, showed nearly normal retention when provided with fragments of the target items (e.g. word-stems). Warrington and Weiskrantz (1974) used these results to argue that amnesia reflected a deficit in retrieval marked by an extreme susceptibility to interference, and that this deficit could be ameliorated by providing sufficient environmental support at retrieval. Further evidence, however, suggested a more complex account of the memory impairment in amnesia. Most important, amnesics given fragmented retrieval cues did not report that they were remembering previous events but rather claimed to simply be guessing. Additional research validated the amnesic's subjective reports by showing that their memory performance was sensitive to the instructions given at test. When provided with word-stems, for example, and told to complete them only with items they remembered being presented earlier, they performed very poorly. However, performance with these same cues improved dramatically when the patients were told to complete the stems with 'the first word that came to mind' (e.g. Graf *et al.* 1984).

Taken together, the experiments with normals and amnesics provide two critical findings that will have to be accounted for by any general theory of memory. First, contrary to the notion that elaborating the meaning of an event always leads to better memory (e.g. Craik and Lockhart 1972), performance on certain tests can be relatively immune to the effects of prior meaningful elaboration. More generally, this finding suggests that there is no complete or absolute memory for prior events. As captured by the notions of encoding specificity (Tulving 1983) and transfer appropriate processing (Morris *et al.* 1977), memory performance always reflects the interaction between encoded information and information available in the retrieval environment. The second finding, perhaps related to the first, is that an intentional orientation to remember is not a prerequisite for demonstrating the effects of prior experience. Memory can be expressed incidentally or unconsciously as a facilitation in the identification (Winnick and Daniel 1970), production (Gardiner *et al.* 1973), or reprocessing of stimuli (Cohen and Squire 1980), or as a bias in the interpretation of ambiguous stimuli (Jacoby and Witherspoon 1982). It is important to emphasize the impact these results have had on our conceptualization of memory. Prior to these findings, memory was a conscious activity and meaningful elaboration was the best way to enhance it. After these findings, memory could occur unconsciously and when it did, prior perceptual operations seemed to best mediate the effects of the past.

Could it be that conscious uses of memory are inherently conceptual and unconscious influences inherently perceptual? At least in broad strokes, this is the impression one gets from surveying both 'structural' and 'processing' theories of memory. For example, Tulving and colleagues (Tulving 1983, 1985; Tulving and Schacter 1990) have argued that explicit memory is subserved by an episodic memory system which records the context and meaning of prior events, whereas implicit memory or 'priming' is based on the operation of a 'presemantic, perceptual representational system'. Similarly, Squire (1992, p. 212) states that repetition priming 'occurs as changes in early-stage perceptual processing systems in posterior cortex, before conceptual or semantic analysis is carried out and before the involvement of the hippocampal formation and the development of declarative memory'. Finally, Roediger (1990, p. 1049) states that 'most explicit tests draw on the encoded meaning of concepts, or on semantic processing, elaborative encoding, and the like . . . [M]ost implicit tests (and all those tests in which impoverished perceptual information is presented) rely heavily on the match between perceptual operations between study and test'.

It seems likely that at least part of the current emphasis on perception stems from the fact that, as was the case in Winnick and Daniel's (1970) experiment 2, many of the studies investigating dissociations between memory and awareness confound task demands with test instructions. That is, tests using indirect memory instructions have also tended to have perceptual (or lexical) task demands, whereas tests using direct memory instructions have tended to ask for information about the meaningful aspects of prior experience, although such conceptual demands are often tacit.[1] Recently, investigators have begun to correct this confound and are beginning to investigate the possibility that memory for prior conceptual processing may produce unconscious influences (e.g. Blaxton 1989). Surprisingly, one of the earliest modern demonstrations of conceptual priming can be found in the same paper that had such a large role in launching the current focus on perceptual unconscious influences. Even more interesting, that demonstration was obtained using what today is considered by many to be the definitive data-driven test: word ('perceptual') identification.

Although Winnick and Daniel's (1970) second experiment had a large impact on theoretical approaches to memory, their first experiment produced a finding that is not as easily incorporated. In their experiment 1, two groups of subjects generated a limited number of the US states (e.g. Arizona, Kentucky, etc.). One group performed this task visually by writing the states on a sheet of paper while another group performed an auditory version of the task by naming the states aloud. Following the generation task, the subjects were given an indirect test of tachistoscopic identification for five of the states they had named (or written), five unnamed states, and five control words. Results showed that previously generated states were identified at a threshold significantly lower than that for unnamed states and matched control words. Interestingly, the reduction in threshold was the same whether the subjects had originally written the states or simply named them aloud. Even more important,

1. That direct tests generally ask for conceptual information can be appreciated by considering a visual recognition test for words presented aurally. When presented with a visual test word (e.g. 'boat'), subjects will often say that they recognize it as having been previously presented even though, technically, a visual word form was not presented. It follows that what a subject recognizes (or recalls) in this situation is not the repetition of a specific perceptual pattern but rather the repetition of a concept (i.e. the referent of a perceptual pattern; in this case, a craft that floats on the water). Thus, although there are important exceptions (e.g. Blaxton 1989; Fisher and Craik 1977; Morris *et al.* 1977), in general the question asked by a direct test of recall or recognition is a conceptual question (for further discussion see Roediger and Blaxton 1987; Roediger *et al.* 1989).

the unnamed states, although not physically presented at encoding, were identified more readily than control words. Winnick and Daniel (1970, p. 76) cast their results in terms of a subject's 'response set' and concluded that 'in order for prior experience with words to facilitate their subsequent [identification], it is not necessary that the words be seen in the first stage'.

What can we make of these results? By not informing their subjects that test items included previously encountered words, Winnick and Daniel's experimental methodology conforms to current standards for assessing implicit memory. Moreover, they used a test that is generally considered to be perceptual and data-driven, yet showed priming for words that had not been presented in the experimental context. The finding of enhanced identification of non-presented words strongly conflicts with current theoretical approaches which uniformly identify priming effects in word identification with perceptual processes or presemantic memory systems (Roediger 1990; Tulving and Schacter 1990). Of course, a proponent of those theories might argue that Winnick and Daniel's results offer only weak support for unconscious conceptual effects because conscious response strategies would have produced effects in the same direction. Subjects were surely aware that the majority of test words were from the same conceptual category and this knowledge, this awareness, may have altered the nature of the test. We agree that the pattern of data obtained by Winnick and Daniel may have been influenced by consciously controlled processes but question whether more recent demonstrations of priming—both conceptual and perceptual—do not reflect similar influences. But conscious contamination notwithstanding, we believe that what distinguishes Winnick and Daniel's experiment 1 from more recent investigations of conceptual priming is their use of a retrieval environment that contained a coherent set of related words. By having the majority of their test words be US states, Winnick and Daniel may have created a retrieval context—a 'response set'—specific enough to recruit the conceptual operations used in the original generation task.

Why are we framing contemporary memory research with a study conducted over twenty years ago? We believe the Winnick and Daniel (1970) paper encapsulates an important change in the way memory is studied. Indeed, their paper can be viewed as signifying a 'paradigm shift' in memory research—not in the Kuhnian sense, but rather methodologically—from an emphasis on processing meaningful, interrelated material (experiment 1) to processing unrelated items presented 'out of context' (experiment 2). Modern studies of unconscious influences are more similar to Winnick and Daniel's experiment 2 than their experiment 1. However, if we are correct that the retrieval context and the subject's set play a critical role in priming, then there may be something to learn from looking more closely at the theoretical precursors of Winnick and Daniel's first experiment.

2.2 A SELECTIVE REVIEW OF EARLY RESEARCH ON UNCONSCIOUS INFLUENCES

Research and theorizing on unconscious influences has a long history in psychology, perhaps beginning with Helmholtz's unconscious inference. However, it is probably in Freud's psychoanalytic approach that non-perceptual unconscious influences were given their strongest statement (see Erdelyi 1985). Freud was interested in how hidden anxieties, impulses, and expectancies drive thought and behaviour. In this sense, much of psychoanalysis can be viewed as an attempt to understand unconscious influences mediated by the meaning of prior events. Indeed, phenomena such as action slips and slips of the tongue, as well as repression phenomena such as memory distortions, all suggest unconscious conceptual influences. As noted by others (e.g. Khilstrom 1987), contemporary views of unconscious influences bear more relation to automaticity as described in the attention literature (e.g. Shiffrin and Schneider 1977) and to habit as described by James (1890) than to the psychoanalytic unconscious. Nevertheless, there are interesting similarities between the psychoanalytic approach to unconscious influences and the current cognitive approach. For example, the study of action slips continues to inform theories of attention, memory, and 'executive processes' (Norman 1981; Norman and Shallice 1986; Reason 1984, 1990) and unconscious influences from emotional (Isen and Diamond 1989; Niedenthal 1992) and motivational sources (Bargh 1990; Jacoby and Kelley 1990)—all of which are related to a subject's conceptualization of prior events—are central topics in social cognition.

Another similarity concerns the methodological strategies used to infer unconscious influences. For both the cognitive and psychoanalytic approaches, unconscious influences are often inferred from the structure that subjects impose on ambiguous stimuli under non-directed ('implicit') test conditions. In this sense, an indirect test is similar to a Rorschach and can be as potentially difficult to interpret (see Jacoby *et al.* 1992*b*). There are, however, important differences in the way psychoanalytic and cognitive approaches treat performance on tests such as the Rorschach. One that is particularly interesting is that, like many indirect test cues, a Rorschach ink blot is more of a perceptual, than a conceptual, stimulus; yet, responses to a Rorschach have rarely been used to infer the nature of perceptual processing or the status of a subject's perceptual memory systems. Rather, they are used to interpret a subject's needs, fears, and motivations; in short, their conceptual state. What this difference in emphasis suggests is that it is not the nature of the stimulus (perceptual or conceptual) that determines the subject's response to it, but rather the question being asked about that stimulus. We return to this issue below. For present purposes, we simply want to note that the first systematic experiments using what are now called perceptual indirect tests were not directed at perception *per se*, but rather in how perception is influenced by non-perceptual factors, such as drives, emotions, expectancies, and a somewhat vague entity known as 'set'. A nice example is provided by the work of Sanford.

Sanford (1936) was interested in the effects of motivational factors on 'imaginal' processes. To investigate the issue, he gave children word-association and ambiguous-pictures tests immediately before or after a regular meal and found significantly more food-related responses (e.g. 'meat') on both tests from the hungry group. A follow-up study using a more rigorous design (Sanford 1937) compared the performance of fasting and non-fasting college students on five tests: word association, interpretation of ambiguous pictures, chained associations, completion of fragmented pictures, and stem completion. Interestingly, Sanford (p. 147) went to great lengths to disguise the nature of his tests: '[T]o be sure that the giving of food responses was not influenced by some conscious and deliberate determination . . . [a]ll subjects were told that the experiments had to do with speed of response under different conditions.' Thus, in the word association tests, subjects were told to respond 'as quickly as possible with the first word which came to mind' and for the chained associations tests they were told to 'write as rapidly as they could' (p. 146). In addition, the critical tests followed a number of 'irrelevant "speed tests"' (p. 148).

As in his previous study with children, Sanford found that the fasting college students gave the highest number of food-related responses and, for the non-fasting students, food-related responses increased as a function of time since their previous meal. How would we explain Sanford's findings in current parlance? Can hunger be viewed as a priming manipulation? If so, one might expect priming on conceptual tests (e.g word association), but Sanford also found facilitation on data-driven tests (e.g. stem completion) suggesting some perceptual mediation. Are motivations and expectancies perceptual or conceptual? Perhaps Gibson (1941, p. 783), in his extensive, critical review of the concept of set, summed it up best:

> At about the turn of the century it began to be realized that the events in a psychological experiment—reactions, associations, judgments, or thoughts—were determined by something other than the reportable events themselves and that this was itself a psychological problem . . . [T]his phenomenon of set established by the Wurzburg psychologists was conceived as something quite distinct from association, from reaction, and from ordinary conscious content. It was not any of these things, but was a determiner of them all.

Sanford's work represents one of many experiments directed at the issue of set and it is in this context that a variety of indirect tests were invented. For example, Rees and Israel (1935) used anagrams and Siipola (1935) used 'skeleton words' (word fragments) to study the effects of set on the organizational nature of perception. In one study, Rees and Israel (1935) gave subjects a series of 40 anagrams, the first 20 of which could be completed only with words from a specific category ('eating solutions' or 'nature solutions'). By use of this 'training series' they hoped to influence the solutions given to the 20 anagrams in the second half of the test; these anagrams could also be completed with categorically related words but allowed for unrelated completions as well. Not surprisingly, they found that the categorical set established by the first 20 anagrams had a large influence on subsequent performance; in comparison with control subjects, those given the training series were more likely to solve ambiguous (multiple completion) anagrams using words congruent with the categorical set established in the first half of the test. Interestingly, Rees and Israel (1935, p. 11) used subjective reports to determine 'the degree to which the sets involved a conscious attitude of search for the related words. Of the 34 subjects, only 11 reported awareness of such an attitude accompanying realization of the relatedness of the words. For the others, the reports indicated that the sets had operated automatically'. Of course, methodological issues limit the conclusions that one can draw from this research. Nevertheless, it is of interest in showing apparent automatic influences of conceptual information on an ostensibly data-driven test, in its use of self-report techniques to assess awareness, and in the questions it raises for current methodological approaches to unconscious influences.

The investigation of set reached its zenith in the research movement known as the 'newlook' in perception. The central idea in the newlook movement was that perception was an act of *categorization*. As stated by Erdelyi (1992): 'Perception, according to the New Look, was an interaction phenomenon: Organismic factors such as needs, expectancies, and defenses interact with the input, and perception is the end result'. Newlook researchers pushed set to its logical extension by investigating the effects of a variety of non-perceptual factors, such as emotional state and economic value, on perception. One classic example was the finding that coins were judged to be larger than metal or cardboard discs that were objectively equivalent in size; also, identical coins were judged as larger by children from families with low, as compared to high, socioeconomic status (Bruner and Goodman 1947).

Although it has been claimed that the newlook movement died for lack of empirical support (Greenwald 1993; but see Erdelyi 1992), its influence nevertheless spilled over into more cognitive research. For example, in a study conceptually similar to Winnick and Daniel's 'response-set' experiment, Corteen and Wood (1972; Corteen and Dunn 1974) presented subjects with a list of words, some of which were city names that were paired with a mild electric shock thereby causing a increase in autonomic nervous activity as measured by galvanic skin response. In a subsequent dichotic listening task, shock-associated city names, city names that had not been previously presented, and control words were presented on the non-attended channel. Despite the fact that both shadowing performance and direct memory testing revealed no awareness of their presentation, shock-associated words produced an increase in autonomic activity in comparison to control words. More importantly, words (i.e. city names) neither previously presented nor associated with shock, but semantically related to shock-associated words, also increased autonomic activity over baseline. Corteen and Wood's (1972) findings, like those of Winnick and Daniel (1970) and the early newlook researchers, suggest that unconscious retrieval processes can be affected by the conceptual information available in the retrieval environment as well as by the motivational concerns subjects bring to the experimental setting.

What does this brief historical survey tell us about the nature of unconscious influences? We see four facets that are worth emphasizing. First, in addition to prior perceptual and conceptual processing, unconscious influences may originate from a variety of sources including long-standing motivational and emotional concerns. Although this point is recognized today—most clearly by social psychologists—it has yet to be incorporated into contemporary theories of memory. We believe that these various sources of influences are contextually embedded in the events that later serve as the basis for unconscious influences of memory. The second point is that unconscious influences are most likely to occur in retrieval environments that reinstate the prior context in which that earlier processing took place. This is especially true for unconscious influences of prior conceptual information. Again, although this point may seen obvious, one would not get that impression by looking at the retrieval environments used in modern investigations of priming. Thirdly, tests and test stimuli by themselves do not determine the nature of the psychological processes that are used in response to those tests and stimuli. Thus, not only is it questionable whether indirect tests provide process-pure measures of unconscious influences (Toth *et al.* 1994), it also seems unlikely that 'perceptual' or 'conceptual' indirect tests uniformly provide process-pure measures of perception or conception (Hunt and Toth 1990).

The final, most important, point is that a subject's cognitive set is an integral constituent of all psychological acts including those that reveal unconscious influences of memory. Although set has been interpreted in a variety of ways (see Gibson 1941), its most basic meaning is a state of anticipation or a readiness to respond to stimuli in a particular way (e.g. Woodworth and Schlosberg 1954). As a form of expectancy, set is similar to descriptions of conceptually driven processing (see quote by Lindsay and Norman on p. 41 of this book). Also, by incorporating the notions of task-orientation and goal-state, cognitive set is akin to modern characterizations of executive processes. Models of executive processes attempt to characterize how a large number of distinct neurocognitive processes are organized and co-ordinated so as to produce coherent, goal-oriented behaviour (e.g. Moscovitch 1992; Norman and Shallice 1986; Stuss 1991). However, most contemporary models draw a sharp distinction between executive control processes and the more automatic processes (or 'special purpose processing systems') through which the 'mechanics' of perception, thought, and behaviour are actually carried out. That is, they assume that automatic processes are highly modular and thus independent of the context in which processing occurs. In contrast, we assume that automatic (and unconscious) processes are sensitive both to the processing context and to the intentional state of the system as a whole. In our view, memory for prior processing (perceptual, conceptual, emotional, or motivational) can influence thought and behaviour, but only in the context of an overriding intention, goal, or set.

An elegant example of the context specificity of automatic influences is provided in a personal anecdote related by Shallice (1982). He describes walking into a very familiar room and finding himself making an unusual 'pulling movement' with his arm. At first this movement was unintelligible to him, but he soon realized that the light in that room was controlled by a cord which had become hooked up in a cupboard door. Shallice (1988, p. 328) looks upon this incident as showing how the 'initiation and execution of this action [is] not normally controlled by a conscious intention to execute it'. True enough, but this analysis fails to acknowledge the context in which the action occurred. It seems likely that Professor Shallice does not make this unusual pulling movement at random, or even upon walking into most rooms. Rather, we expect that this movement would occur only in the context of that, or a highly similar, room. We would further argue that the movement was triggered not only by the specific room, but also by a specific goal: to turn on the light.

We propose that cognitive set—the executive, 'top-down' processes involved in maintaining a goal or task orientation—forms an integral aspect of the operations involved in most, if not all, memory experiments. Some of the implications of this perspective are explored near the end of the chapter. First, we examine contemporary evidence for unconscious conceptual influences of memory. Few modern studies have investigated the relationship between set and memory (but see Bransford *et al.* 1977), and so we say little about that relationship for much of our review of contemporary empirical findings. However, it is possible to cast current results in terms of *context*, which can be viewed as one of the major cognates of set. As our review progresses, we increasingly find contextual factors to be critical for the production of unconscious influences of memory.

2.3 CONTEMPORARY EVIDENCE FOR CONCEPTUAL UNCONSCIOUS INFLUENCES OF MEMORY

Studies of unconscious influences of memory are often separated into two classes based on the type of cue provided at retrieval. The first, most popular, class of tests are those that measure responses to single, often physically degraded, stimuli presented in isolation; examples of such *perceptual indirect tests* include word identification and fragment completion. The second major class of tests are those that measure responses to semantic cues in the absence of perceptual information that could directly elicit the target response; tests of this type are referred to as *conceptual indirect tests* and include word association and category-examplar generation. A final set, often treated as a variety of conceptual indirect tests, are those that measure responses to a mixture of perceptual and conceptual cues, such as the time to read connected discourse (i.e. text), or responses to degraded cues (e.g. word-fragments) presented in the context of intact words that are associatively related to the correct response.

Although apparently straightforward and certainly useful for descriptive purposes (e.g. the organization of chapters), classifying tests as perceptual or conceptual has a number of drawbacks that often go unacknowledged. One of the main problems with this classification scheme is that it leads to terminological confusions in the description of results, and to circularity in their interpretation. For example, if a conceptual study manipulation such as self-generation affects performance on a perceptual indirect test, is that conceptual priming? Or should 'conceptual priming' be reserved for performance on conceptual indirect tests? More importantly, how should such an effect be interpreted? A rapid survey of the literature reveals little consensus on the matter with some researchers interpreting such effects as perceptual (e.g. Gardiner 1988*a*; Roediger and McDermott 1993), and others as conceptual (Hirshman *et al.* 1990). Echoing our review of early research on unconscious influences, we question whether it is theoretically sound to define underlying processes in terms of the cues provided at retrieval.

A second problem with the distinction between perceptual and conceptual indirect tests is the notion that the former measure processing 'out of context' while the latter measure processing 'in context'. We take issue with this characterization and assume that there is always a context for processing; the important questions concern the way in which one context (e.g. the isolated-word-paradigm context) differs from others, and the implications of those differences for the operation of memory. A related issue concerns the role of context at encoding. Many researchers tacitly assume a form of exclusivity between perception and conception such that the two trade-off in processing. For example, it has been argued that isolated stimuli engage relatively more perceptual than conceptual processing, and vice versa for items presented in larger groups such as word pairs, connected text, etc. (Jacoby 1983*b*; MacLeod 1989; Roediger and Blaxton 1987). The notion of a processing trade-off is perhaps best formalized in Roediger *et al.*'s (1989) claim that data-driven and conceptually driven processing represent 'endpoints on a continuum'. However, a single continuum is inconsistent with much of the theorizing surrounding the perceptual/conceptual distinction (e.g. Craik 1991; Jacoby in press; Weldon 1991) and cannot explain a number of experimental findings reviewed below.

Despite these problems, we follow the current zeitgeist and organize our review in terms of the perceptual/conceptual indirect test distinction. Indeed, explicitly using this structure helps us to reveal its inadequacies. We should warn readers that, although we are interested in the unconscious effects of prior conceptual processing, much of our review is dedicated to showing that there are few unquestionable examples of such effects. The major issue is whether indirect tests can be treated as process-pure measures of unconscious influences (Dunn and Kirsner 1989; Jacoby 1991; Reingold and Merikle 1990). If they can (e.g. Rajaram and Roediger 1993), then examples of conceptual unconscious influences abound. If they cannot (e.g. Toth *et al.* 1994), then it becomes more difficult to unequivocally identify such examples (see Reingold and Toth, Chapter 4). In our review of the literature, we rely on the results from the process dissociation procedure (Jacoby 1991; Jacoby *et al.* 1993*b*), as well as from other methods (e.g. post-test interviews) to evaluate results gained from indirect tests of memory.

2.3.1 Conceptual influences on 'perceptual' indirect tests

Levels of processing and self-generation.

One basis for the claim that conceptual processing can unconsciously influence subsequent performance comes from findings of levels of processing (LoP) and generation effects on perceptual indirect tests. In the LoP paradigm, subjects are presented with single words at encoding and asked to focus their attention on either semantic (meaningful) or non-semantic (physical or lexical) aspects of the word (Craik and Lockhart 1972). LoP effects in memory performance (i.e. semantic > non-semantic) are thought to provide some of the most straightforward evidence of conceptual influences because, it is assumed, perceptual encoding is equated in the semantic and non-semantic encoding conditions and only the degree of meaningful elaboration is varied (see Challis and Brodbeck 1992, for alternative characterizations). The generation paradigm also involves a manipulation of conceptual processing, but that manipulation is usually confounded with differences in perceptual processing. The general encoding procedure is for subjects to read some words in isolation, and generate others on the basis of semantic cues. There is usually some limited amount of perceptual information provided in the generate condition, but not enough to completely specify the target. Priming from self-generated items (i.e. generated > new) has been taken to indicate conceptual transfer. Even stronger evidence for conceptual transfer is provided by a 'generation effect' (Slamecka and Graf 1978) in which generated items (which lack complete perceptual specification) facilitate performance significantly more than items that are read (and thus are fully specified perceptually).

Despite initial evidence that LoP and self-generation do not effect performance on tests of word identification and stem completion (e.g. Jacoby 1983*b*; Jacoby and Dallas 1981; Graf *et al.* 1982), such effects have now been produced in a number of independent laboratories and on a wide range of 'perceptual indirect tests'. For example, significant LoP effects in word-fragment completion were observed by Challis and Brodbeck (1992), who also reviewed previous investigations of this variable. They found that in 33 of 35 cases (experiments or experimental conditions) priming was greater in the semantic, as opposed to non-semantic, condition. In a more extensive review, Brown and Mitchell (1994) surveyed 166 cases from 38 studies and found that 79 per cent yielded positive LoP effects, over half of which were statistically significant. Interestingly, there was no statistical difference between the percentage of LoP effects found on perceptual versus conceptual indirect tests. Also worth nothing is that both the elderly (Chiarello and Hoyer 1988) and memory-impaired patients with various aetiologies (Graf *et al.* 1984) have shown reliable LoP effects on ostensibly perceptual indirect tests.

Similar to results using the LoP paradigm, words generated on the basis of semantic cues and incomplete perceptual specification have also been found to produce significant priming (generated > new) on perceptual indirect tests. Tests showing such effects include auditory and visual word-stem completion (Bassili *et al.* 1989), word-fragment completion (Blaxton 1989; Weldon 1991), anagram solution (Srinivas and Roediger 1990), picture-fragment completion (Hirshman *et al.* 1990), and word identification (Masson and MacLeod 1992). Even more remarkable, significant generation effects (generate > read) have been found on word-fragment completion (Gardiner 1988*a*, 1989), anagram solution (Gardiner *et al.* 1989), and word identification (Toth and Hunt 1990). The generation effects appear to depend on the complete reinstatement of the physical cues used to constrain generation at encoding. Gardiner (1988*a*) had subjects generate or read intact words in the context of short definitions (e.g. *It swings in a clock*: -E-D-L-M). In a subsequent indirect fragment completion test, subjects showed significantly greater priming for previously generated, as compared to read, words but only when the test fragment was identical to that presented at encoding. Changing the test fragment by only one letter elimnated the generation effect (Gardiner *et al.* 1989).

Analogous results in a word identification test were found by Toth and Hunt (1990, experiment 1) who had subjects generate words in absence of semantic guidance in order to equate better the nature of encoding in the generate and read conditions. Subjects read single words and generated others from isolated word-fragments that were missing one interior letter. This study manipulation was crossed with the type of test cue given in word identification; subjects were given masked presentations either of complete words or of word-fragments that were missing the same letter as that at encoding. When complete words were flashed, generated and read word showed an equivalent amount of priming (0.21 vs. 0.19). In contrast, when a fragment was flashed, previously generated words were identified significantly more often than words that had been read (0.33 vs. 0.20). Interestingly, this effect occurred even though subjects could not reliably discriminate between the type of stimulus presented at test (whole words vs. fragments).

The Toth and Hunt (1990) results, as well as those by Gardiner and colleagues (1988*a*, 1989; Gardiner *et al.* 1989), suggest that generation effects on perceptual indirect tests only occur when retrieval cues are perceptually similar to the generation cues used at encoding; the effects do not appear to generalize to non-specific test stimuli such as different fragments, different anagrams, or complete words in word identification. Do these effects reflect the recruitment of prior conceptual processing? Gardiner (1988*a*; see also Roediger and McDermott 1993) has argued that these effects reflect perceptual priming but this interpretation seems circular in that the nature of processing proposed to underlie the effect is defined by the assumed perceptual nature of the test. However, as demonstrated in the studies reviewed above, it is not at all clear that so-called perceptual indirect tests can be viewed as reflecting only prior perceptual processing. Moreover, it seems unusual to label a *generation* effect 'perceptual' when the facilitation in performance is actually greater for stimuli having fewer perceptual characteristics at encoding. Our view is that the generation effects obtained by Toth and Hunt (1990) and Gardiner (1988*a*) reflect context-specific recruitment of prior encoding operations, both perceptual and conceptual (see also Masson and Freedman 1990; Masson and MacLeod 1992). Although the particular conceptual operations involved in this task may be relatively low-level (e.g. lexical), they still reflect inferential processes that go beyond the perceptual information given. We thus view these experiments as indicative of a more general principle: reinstating contextual features of a prior event—including specific *perceptual* features—can be sufficient to recruit prior conceptual (or inferential) processes which occurred in the same episode.

Results from LoP and generation studies show that, contrary to initial reports, perceptual indirect *tests* can be affected by prior conceptual processing. The important question is whether these effects truly reflect conceptual unconscious influences or are the result of other factors such as undetected conscious uses of memory. Toth *et al.* (1994) addressed this issue by manipulating LoP and comparing performance on an indirect stem completion test with estimates of conscious and unconscious influences derived from the process-dissociation procedure. Replicating previous studies, performance following indirect test instructions showed a small but highly significant LoP effect (semantic = 0.51, non-semantic = 0.45). In contrast, estimates of unconscious influences showed no effect of LoP (0.45 vs. 0.44). Importantly, the estimate of unconscious influences following non-semantic study was nearly identical to performance on the indirect test for that condition. This convergence is to be expected if the two paradigms are measuring the same construct and the implicit test is uncontaminated by conscious uses of memory. Evidence for the lack of contamination was provided by estimates of conscious uses of memory which were quite high following semantic study (0.27) but near zero following non-semantic study (0.03). Bowers and Schacter (1990), using post-test interviews, also found evidence for conscious contamination: 'test-aware' subject showed large LoP effects (0.20) but 'test-unaware' subjects had a small non-significant effect (0.03). Both studies, then, suggest that previous findings of LoP effects on indirect tests are the by-product of conscious uses of memory.

Toth *et al.* (1994) also examined whether generation from semantic cues produces subsequent unconscious influences. Subjects read isolated words or generated words from sentences and the first letter of the target word (e.g. *The witch gave Snow White a poisoned a*______). In the test phase, subjects given indirect test instructions showed a typical pattern of results: read words were given as completions more often than generated words (0.54 vs. 0.44) but both conditions were well above baseline (0.30). It is the difference between baseline and the generation condition that some researchers have claimed shows conceptual priming (e.g. Hirshman *et al.* 1990; Masson and MacLeod 1992). Application of the process-dissociation procedure, however, suggested a very different conclusion. Whereas generated words afforded significantly more conscious control than read words (0.34 vs. 0.21), they were at a large disadvantage in producing unconscious transfer (0.32 vs. 0.51). Indeed, comparing the unconscious estimate for generated items to baseline (0.32) indicated that generated items produced no unconscious influence. Jacoby *et al.* (1993*b*) found a similar cross-over interaction of processes using anagrams as the cues for generation. In contrast to indirect test performance which showed significant priming for words derived from previously presented anagrams, estimates of unconscious influences did not differ from baseline. Taken together, results from Toth *et al.* (1994) and Jacoby *et al.* (1993*b*) suggest that generation effects on indirect tests may often reflect conscious uses of memory.[2]

In summary, a large number of studies have shown that conceptual processing manipulations, such as LoP and self-generation, can significantly influence performance on ostensibly perceptual indirect tasks. On closer examination, however, many of these effects appear not to reflect conceptual priming but rather are mediated by more conscious uses of memory. With the possible exception of studies using perceptually specific cues (Gardiner 1988*a*; Toth and Hunt 1990), it would appear that unconscious influences obtained with isolated stimuli are mediated completely by prior perceptual processing. Such a conclusion would be consistent with Winnick and Daniel's (1970) claim that priming of unrelated words in tests such as word identification reflects 'perceptual sensitization'; and with more recent claims that priming on perceptual implicit tests is due to modification of presemantic representation systems (Moscovitch 1992; Schacter 1992; Tulving and Schacter 1990), or the selective transfer of perceptual or data-driven processing (Roediger 1990).

There is, however, at least one curious anomaly in these theoretical accounts. If item-specific priming is due only to changes in the nature of perception, then it would seem to follow that such changes could be detected as an enhancement of perceptual sensitivity. But experiments explicitly designed to test that idea using signal detection methods have shown that performance in many of the so-called perceptual indirect tests are driven, not by enhancement of perceptual sensitivity, but rather by changes in *response bias* (Masson and Freedman 1990; Ratcliff and McKoon 1993; Ratcliff *et al.* 1989). Response bias is generally thought to reflect a post-perceptual stage of processing although Ratcliff *et al.* (1989) argued for the notion of a 'perceptual bias' to characterize priming in perceptual indirect tests. Nevertheless, the signal detection studies point to the presence of some form of decision processes in these tests. Thus, while we find little evidence for the influence of prior conceptual processing in the experiments reviewed above, there *is* data suggesting that the priming effects observed involve processing that goes beyond perception *per se*.

2. As pointed out by Masson (personal communication), the process dissociation procedure has not been applied to the word identification task, leaving open the possibility that conceptual effects in this task (Masson and MacLeod 1992; Toth and Hunt 1990) reflect unconscious uses of memory.

Cross-form priming

Another set of empirical findings that have been linked to conceptual factors is that of cross-form priming. Cross-form priming refers to enhanced performance on a test stimulus that is perceptually dissimilar from the nominal stimulus originally presented at encoding—as, for example, when auditory presentation of a word increases its subsequent production on a visual word-stem completion test. A number of different types of cross-form priming have been investigated, including changes in typography (e.g. Kolers and Roediger 1984; Jacoby and Hayman 1987), the size and orientation of objects (e.g. Biederman and Cooper 1991, 1992; Jolicoeur 1985), voice characteristics in auditory priming (e.g. Jackson and Morton 1984; Schacter and Church 1992), and stimulus clarity (e.g. Jacoby *et al.* 1989; Snodgrass and Feenan 1990). Here, however, we focus on studies in which the encoded stimuli have no physical overlap with their respective retrieval cues (i.e. cross-modality and picture/word priming) because these cases bear most directly on the question of conceptual priming (for more general reviews of the cross-form priming literature see Kirsner *et al.* 1989; Roediger and McDermott 1993).

Changing presentation modality from study to test was one of the first manipulations compared on direct and indirect tests of memory. Although early experiments suggested that priming effects were completely modality-specific (e.g. Ellis 1982; Jacoby and Dallas 1981; Kirsner and Smith, 1974) it now seems clear that modality-specificity is the exception, not the rule. Cross-modality priming has been found on word identification (Clarke and Morton 1983; Kelley *et al.* 1989; Weldon 1991), fragment completion (Blaxton 1989; Hunt and Toth 1990), auditory and visual stem completion (Bassili *et al.* 1989; Rajaram and Roediger 1993), anagram solution (Srivinas and Roediger 1990), and lexical decision (Kirsner *et al.* 1983). Although within-modality priming is generally about twice that observed across modalities, significant cross-modality priming is a common finding on indirect tests. Weldon and Roediger (1987; Roediger *et al.* 1989; Weldon 1993) suggested that cross-modality priming may reflect the contribution of conceptual processes to indirect test performance. A related hypothesis is that cross-modality priming reflects the operation of a modality-independent representation or process (Kirsner *et al.* 1983, 1989; see also Weldon 1991, 1993). Note that both hypotheses would be unnecessary if cross-modality 'priming' was due to conscious uses of memory.

In addition to cross-modality effects, picture-to-word priming has also been reported by a number of researchers (e.g. Brown *et al.* 1991; Durso and Johnson 1979; Kirsner *et al.* 1986; Roediger *et al.* 1992; Weldon and Roediger 1987). Weldon (1991, 1993) has argued that picture-to-word priming reflects lexical activation due to spontaneous covert naming of the picture at study. However, manipulations designed to influence the probability of covert naming of pictures have little or no effect on word-fragment completion (Weldon and Roediger 1987; but see Weldon and Jackson-Barrett 1993) or word identification performance (Kirsner *et al.* 1986). Also, the covert naming hypothesis does not explain why covert picture naming either fails to occur or fails to produce priming in some situations (Rajaram and Roediger 1993; Weldon 1991), but produces complete picture-to-word transfer in others (Alejeno and Carr 1991; Brown *et al.* 1991).

Along with enhanced word processing from prior presentation of pictures, word-to-picture priming has also been demonstrated both in the identification of fragmented pictures (Hirshman *et al.* 1990) and in picture naming (Durso and Johnson 1979). Using the latter test, Brown *et al.* (1991) found cross-form (word-to-picture) priming to be as great as within-form (picture-to-picture) priming when the type of prime was manipulated between subjects. In within-subject designs, cross-form priming was reduced but still significant when picture and word primes were presented in separate blocks at study; when primes were presented in a completely mixed fashion, cross-form priming was eliminated (cf. Challis and Brodbeck 1992). On the surface, Brown *et al.*'s results would appear to represent an extreme violation of transfer appropriate processing. Mediation from prior lexical activation (Weldon 1991) may provide some reconciliation but, in addition to the inconsistencies noted above, there is no obvious reason why the lexical contribution from word primes should change as a function of list composition (mixed vs. blocked). These same criticisms apply to explanations based on unconscious conceptual mediation.

Importantly, lexical or conceptual explanations of cross-form priming would only be required if such priming represented true unconscious influences of memory. Recent results question that assessment. Jacoby *et al.* (1993*b*) had subjects read and hear different lists of words and then used a process-dissociation procedure to estimate conscious and unconscious influences in a visual stem-completion task. In two experiments, prior visual exposure produced significant unconscious influences as estimated by the process-dissociation procedure but prior auditory experience produced little (experiment 1a) or no (experiment 1b) effect. The small effect found in experiment 1a was attributed to subjects pronouncing the stems at test, thus producing an auditory retrieval cue, rather than to automatic cross-modal transfer. In two other experiments, Jacoby *et al.* (1993*b*) found that anagrams presented visually and solved aloud did not drive estimates of unconscious influences above baseline. These results cast doubt on a general lexical activation hypothesis (Weldon 1991) and instead suggest that cross-form priming is a by-product of controlled strategies, such as pronouncing the stem or consciously retrieving list items.

Using a fragment-completion tests, Jacoby *et al.* (in press) also examined cross-modality priming as assessed by the process-dissociation procedure, indirect test instructions, and a subjective-report ('remember/know') technique (Tulving 1985; Gardiner 1988*b*). Under the assumption that conscious and unconscious influences make independent contributions to performance, estimates of unconscious influences from both the process-dissociation procedure and the remember/know technique showed *no* cross-modality transfer. In contrast, indirect tests showed significant cross-modality priming. However, when attention was divided at study, thereby reducing conscious recollection and the possibility of conscious contamination, the cross-modality effect on the indirect test was totally eliminated. For the other two measures, estimates of conscious influences were significantly reduced by the divided-attention manipulation, but estimates of unconscious influences did not change. These results strongly suggest that cross-modality priming arises from conscious uses of memory. Similar arguments can be made for picture/word priming (see Toth *et al.* 1994, for further discussion). At the very least, these results recommend divided attention or speeded retrieval (Weldon and Jackson-Barrett 1993) as a converging operation for establishing the validity of an indirect test as a measure of unconscious influences.

In summary, as was the case for LoP and self-generation, cross-form priming effects appear to be the by-product of conscious uses of memory. What do these findings imply? One specific implication is that there may be no need to postulate modality-independent representations of the form advocated by Kirsner and others (Kirsner *et al.* 1983, 1989; Rajaram and Roediger 1993). More generally, because conscious processes enable a person to translate symbolic stimuli into a variety of perceptual forms, contaminated indirect tests may often underestimate the specificity of the effects of prior experience. Cross-form 'priming' is a ubiquitous phenomenon in the memory literature and stands as one of the primary sources of support for theories postulating abstract, context-independent mental representations. In contrast to these views, the present analysis suggests that the unconscious influences may be more episodically based than has been appreciated (Jacoby and Brooks 1984; Logan 1988; Jacoby and Kelley 1987, 1990).

2.3.2 Conceptual influences on 'conceptual' indirect tests

In all of the studies described above, effects of prior experience were assessed by presenting subjects with isolated stimuli under degraded (data-limited) conditions. The subject's goal in these tasks is to identify or generate members of a particular class (e.g. English words) on the basis of the surface information presented. It is also possible to present subjects with retrieval cues containing no perceptual information that could directly elicit the target response; rather, the test cue consists of semantic or associative information and the subjects' task is to generate a response that is meaningfully related to the cue. One of the earliest modern uses of such a conceptual indirect test is attributable to Storms (1958) who found that presenting words for a subsequent memory test increased the frequency with which these words were produced on an intervening, indirect word-association task. Storms had originally described the phenomenon as a 'recency' effect but Segal and Cofer (1960), who replicated Storms' findings, renamed it 'priming' to avoid confusion with the recency effect found in list learning experiments. Thus, in what is an interesting historical twist, the term priming, which has been treated as an exclusively perceptual phenomenon (Tulving and Schacter 1990), was originally used to describe unconscious influences in a *conceptual* task.

Semantic cues

Perhaps the first systematic review of performance on what are now called conceptual indirect tests was done by Cofer in 1967. Coming from the verbal learning tradition, Cofer was interested in the effects of context on production of responses in a variety of verbal-association tasks. Although this work contains no explicit discussion of unconscious influences, many of the experiments described made use of free-association tests, interpolated between a mnemonic study and test phase, and thus anticipated more recent experiments using conceptual indirect tests. Experiments on 'direct priming' showed that previously studied words were often given as responses to associatively related cues (Clifton 1966; Storms 1958; Grand and Segal 1966; Segal and Cofer 1960). Also, experiments on indirect or 'mediated priming', in which presentation of an item or set of items increases subsequent responses with related stimuli, are suggestive of unconscious influences of associative information. For example, Cramer (1964, 1966) presented sets of four words (e.g. *dark, black, moon, dream*) and had subjects free-associate to the last one. Results showed that the first three words—which are known to elicit the target response *night*—increased the frequency with which 'night' was given as a response to 'dream' (from 0.09 to 0.32 in this example). Mediated priming may also affect performance on direct tests of memory. Words associatively related to target words have been found to produce more false recognitions (Underwood 1965; see also Juola *et al.* 1971; Hermann *et al.* 1975) and are given more often as recall intrusions (Cramer 1965; Deese 1959) than comparable unrelated words (Roediger and McDermott 1994).

Some of the best evidence that semantic cues can automatically elicit previously encountered information comes from work with amnesics (see Moscovitch *et al.* 1993). Shimamura and Squire (1984) presented memory-impaired Korsakoff patients with a list of single words (e.g. *hot*) and later presented semantic associates of these words (e.g. *stove*) with indirect free-association instructions. Despite the amnesics' nearly complete inability to recall list items, their production of target words in the free-association test was equivalent to that of a matched control group. A similar result was found when the groups were presented with highly related cue-target pairs at study (e.g. table–chair) and later asked to produce the first word that came to mind in response to the cue (*table*–?). For both groups of subjects, production of the target words was almost three times above baseline. Schacter (1985; Schacter and McGlynn 1989) has obtained analogous results using idioms such as 'sour grapes' and 'small potatoes'.

In addition to word association, other conceptual indirect tests include category-exemplar generation (Hamann 1990; Rappold and Hashtroudi 1991; Srivinas and Roediger 1990) and answering general knowledge questions (Blaxton 1989; Hamann 1990). As with word association, these tests contain no perceptual information that could directly specify the target response, and thus facilitation as a function of prior presentation is often taken as demonstrative of conceptual priming. However, a potentially important issue is whether these tests are measuring prior meaning-based processing or simply an increased tendency to output the target in response to any cue, conceptual or perceptual. In many of the experiments using conceptual indirect tests, priming is found after simple presentation of the target at study (e.g. Blaxton 1989; Schacter 1985) and even following *non-semantic* encoding tasks (e.g. Hamann 1990). Thus, prior presentation can increase the probability that an item will be output, independent of any specific meaningful processing at study. Analogous to findings with perceptual indirect tests (e.g. Masson and Freedman, 1990; Ratcliff *et al.* 1989), these observations raise the question of whether so-called conceptual priming reflects the tranfer of prior meaning-based processing, or simply a bias to respond with previously encountered items irrespective of prior processing. An important goal for future research is to disentangle the effects of prior meaning-based processing versus those arising from simple item registration (cf. Moscovitch 1992).

As an operational definition of a conceptually driven test, Roediger *et al.* (1989) proposed that words generated at study should produce superior transfer in comparison to those that were read in 'no context' conditions. Presumably, the idea behind this approach is that if you know what kind of *test* you have, you can infer the nature of the *processes* which produce priming on that test. On the basis of this logic, it has been argued that category-exemplar generation and tests of general knowledge measure unconscious influences of prior conceptual processing (Blaxton 1989; Srivinas and Roediger 1990; see also Smith and Branscomb 1988). As with perceptual indirect tests, however, the effects found with conceptual cues generally parallel those found on direct tests, raising the question of conscious contamination. In fact, one of the first studies applying the process-dissociation methodology to a conceptual indirect test (category-exemplar generation) found evidence that apparent conceptual priming actually reflected conscious uses of memory (Jaciw and McAndrews 1993).

From our perspective, the problem with Roediger *et al.*'s operational approach is its underlying assumption that indirect tests are process-pure measures of implicit memory. If, in constrast to this assumption, performance on indirect tests is contaminated by conscious uses of memory, then Roediger *et al.*'s operational criteria will not validly identify unconscious conceptual processing. Toth *et al.* (1994) suggested a more stringent criterion for identifying conceptual transfer: Apply Roediger *et al.*'s (1989) generate/read comparison to estimates of unconscious influences derived from the process dissociation procedure. For this approach, unconscious conceptual influences would be demonstrated if estimates of automatic influences for words generated without perceptual support at study exceeded baseline; or, more impressively, if the generation estimates exceeded those of previously read items. LoP effects on estimates of automatic influences would also suggest unconscious conceptual transfer. Both of these results have been obtained on tests of recognition memory (Jacoby 1991; Toth 1992), but not on tests using physically degraded stimuli such as word stems (Jacoby *et al.* 1993*b*; Toth *et al.* 1994). One potentially important difference between the two tasks is the goal of retrieval: stem completion requires the identification of a perceptual/lexical pattern, whereas recognition requires a subject to localize an item in a particular episodic context. An important goal for future research is the application of process-dissociation procedures to tests employing only semantic retrieval cues.

Unconscious influences from new and pre-existing associations

Another phenomenon that has been related to the issue of conceptual priming is the unconscious use of associative information, either between items having a pre-existing semantic relationship or between unrelated items that have been not been previously associated. The general procedure for this paradigm is to present a cue-target pair at encoding and then to elicit retrieval using a combination of perceptual and conceptual cues. Generally, retrieval cues consist of a part of the target (e.g. a word-stem) presented either in the context of the cue with which it was paired at study (intact condition) or in the context of a different cue, often taken from another studied pair (recombined condition). Unconscious influences of associative information are revealed by the difference between stem-completion performance in the intact and recombined conditions. Because both target words were previously presented, the advantage for intact over recombined pairs can only be explained by memory for associative information.

This paradigm was first used in a series of experiments by Graf and Schacter (1985; Schacter and Graf, 1986*a*,*b*) to explore the possibility of 'implicit memory for new associations'. Initial studies suggested that new associations could produce unconscious influences in both amnesics and controls, but only when the unrelated cue-target pairs had been processed semantically and relationally at encoding. Subsequent research, however, has uncovered an inconsistent pattern of positive and negative results (see Bowers and Schacter 1993, for a review). On the basis of post-test interviews, Bowers and Schacter (1990) classified subjects as either 'test-aware' or 'test-unaware' and found that only the former group showed implicit memory for new associations. Also, studies with amnesics have shown that the acquisition of novel associations is negatively correlated with the severity of amnesia (Schacter and Graf 1986*b*; Shimamura and Squire 1989). Both results suggest that the basic effect may often be due to conscious uses of memory.

In an attempt to determine whether 'implicit memory' for new associations is actually implicit, Reingold and Goshen-Gottstein (in press) used both indirect test instuctions and the process-dissociation procedure. Performance on the indirect test following elaborative encoding revealed the usual advantage for stems presented in intact, as compared with recombined, test pairs (0.46 vs. 0.36). Process-dissociation estimates of conscious control also showed an advantage for intact as compared to recombined conditions (0.30 vs. 0.10), confirming that reinstatement of a recently encountered associative context can enhance recollection of individual items (Tulving and Thompson 1973). However, estimates of unconscious influences showed little difference between performance in intact and recombined conditions (0.29 vs. 0.32, n.s.), suggesting that many results obtained with this 'implicit' paradigm may reflect conscious contamination. Interestingly, using a *non-semantic* task in which subjects simply copied the unrelated word pairs (Micco and Masson 1991), Reingold and Goshen-Gottstein did find evidence that associative information can unconsciously influence performance. This finding suggests that meaningful elaboration, in and of itself, may be less important for acquiring new associations than has been claimed (see Schacter and Graf 1986*a*). Perhaps the critical factor is that the items be strongly related or integrated so as to produce at least some degree of unitization (Hayes-Roth 1977). Important questions for future research include the extent and nature of the relational processing required.

Although unconscious influences from new associations has produced equivocal results, Jacoby (1994) has used the process-dissociation procedure to provide evidence that exposure to pre-existing associations can produce subsequent unconscious influences. At encoding, subjects made relatedness judgements to both related (e.g. knee–bone) and unrelated (e.g. apple–shell; turtle–cider) pairs, under conditions of either full or divided attention. Unrelated pairs were formed by randomly pairing members of related pairs that were rejoined at test. At test, subjects were presented with a cue word followed by the initial letter of the associatively related target word (e.g. knee–b; apple–c). For the inclusion test condition, subjects were told to complete the target with an associatively related word from the study list or, if they could not remember an appropriate study item, to compete the stem with the first related word that came to mind. For the exclusion test condition, subjects were instructed to complete stems with related words that were not presented at study (e.g. acceptable responses to *knee* would be *bend, brace, band,* etc.). As expected, divided, as compared to full, attention to study pairs significantly reduced conscious recollection for the individual words, but had no effect on estimates of unconscious influences (cf. Jacoby *et al.* 1993*b*). Most important, estimated unconscious influences were significantly greater when the original associative context was reinstated (i.e. intact condition) in comparison to when the prior context was not reinstated (i.e. recombined condition). In subsequent research, Jacoby (in press) has shown that this automatic associative effect survives a divided attention manipulation at study, and a change in modality from study to test (cf. Schacter and Graf 1989).

2.3.3 Conceptual unconscious influences in context

In all of the studies reviewed above, the focus has been on the type of cues provided at test. However, as indicated in our historical review, there are reasons to question whether one can infer the cognitive processes involved in a task simply on the basis of the cues provided. This conclusion would appear to be supported by the studies reviewed above in that conceptual encoding manipulations were found to influence 'perceptual' tests and perceptual (non-semantic) encoding tasks enhanced performance on 'conceptual' tests. While an analysis of retrieval cues is certainly important for understanding memory, classification of processes on the basis of test cues alone misses the broader context in which retrieval is taking place. In this section, we review evidence for the influence of context and set in the production of unconscious influences of memory.

List-wide context and the priming of interpretation

One of the first studies to suggest an important role of the retrieval context in the production of unconscious influences was done by Jacoby (1983*a*) who found that facilitation in word identification was enhanced when the test list contained a high, as opposed low, proportion of previously studied words (see also Kasserman *et al.* 1987). Allen and Jacoby (1990) replicated this effect (but see Challis and Roediger 1993) and provided additional data suggesting that the effect was not due to conscious uses of memory. An interesting aspect of these experiments, one that suggests an effect of set on retrieval, is that performance on new items decreased as the number of old items increased. Experiencing a large number of test items originating from a specific prior episode (e.g. the encoding task) may act to establish an anticipatory set for encountering similar items. Such a set may inhibit or otherwise interfere with performance on non-set (i.e. 'new') items. As the number of old items increases, so does the anticipatory set; new items suffer in this context because they do not fit the expected pattern.

A further experiment by Jacoby (1983*a*) also suggested the operation of cognitive set. In an experiment investigating facilitation effects over a five-day period, Jacoby (1983*a*) found that identification performance was larger if the test list contained only items studied in a single session. When items from multiple sessions were tested in a mixed list, much less facilitation was found. Although not designed to investigate conceptual priming, these studies provide evidence that unconscious influences are sensitive to the context in which retrieval occurs. Moreover, they suggest that perceptual processing alone is not sufficient to mediate priming and, in this regard, anticipate more recent work suggesting an integration of perceptual and conceptual processes (e.g. Jacoby *et al.* 1992*a*; Levy and Kirsner 1989; Masson and Freedman 1990).

The experiments by Jacoby (1983*a*) suggests that contextual factors can alter the expression of unconscious influences by affecting which particular episodes, and what aspects of those episodes, are recruited to support current performance. It could be argued, however, that these effects, although context-dependent, are essentially taking place with the perceptual domain. Is there any evidence that prior conceptual operations can be evoked through contextual reinstatement? A suggestive example is provided by Jacoby and Witherspoon (1982) who found evidence for what could be called *interpretive priming*. In the first phase of their experiment, amnesics and controls heard questions that biased the low-frequency meaning a homophone embedded in the questions (e.g. 'Name a musical instrument that employs a *reed*'). In a later indirect spelling task, both groups showed a large increase in the number of words spelled in accordance with their previously biased meaning, an effect on spelling that was independent of recognition memory for the previously presented words.

Is homophone biasing a perceptual or data-driven effect? Given that the test word was presented in isolation, spelling would seem to fit popular descriptions of data-driven tests (e.g. Bainbridge *et al.* 1993; Moscovitch 1994). In contrast, we believe that the critical aspect of any task is not whether the cue is isolated or presented in the context of other items—whether it is 'perceptual' or 'conceptual'—but what the subject must do with that cue given the overall task demands. Spelling of a homophone requires that a particular meaning be instantiated. In line with this goal, results showed that it was the episodic interpretation of the initial event that was used to guide the interpretation of the subsequent event (see Masson and Freedman 1990).

Another study which shows repetition priming for episodic interpretations was done by McAndrews *et al.* (1987) who presented amnesics with sentences that were difficult to interpret without the knowledge of a key word or phrase. For example, the sentence 'The haystack was important because the cloth ripped' makes little sense in isolation, but is readily understood when contextualized with the key word 'parachute'. Amnesics with severe memory deficits were initially shown a set of these puzzle sentences and then given the key word. Facilitation was measured by their ability to produce the key word or phrase when later presented with the sentences alone. Despite showing substantial impairment on tests of free recall and recognition memory, the amnesic's ability to solve the puzzle sentences was nearly three times above baseline solution rates, a level of comprehension that did not show signs of decay after a delay of one week. The puzzle sentences used by McAndrews *et al.* (1987) can be viewed as distinctive context cues that helped to retrieve specific (i.e. episodic) interpretations encountered earlier.

The homophone-bias and puzzle-sentences studies show that when an ambiguous stimulus pattern is presented, prior conceptual processing surrounding its initial interpretation may be recruited to influence its subsequent interpretation. Other experiments, using more traditional data-driven tests, have also suggested the importance of episodic interpretations for subsequent priming effects. For example, Masson and Freedman (1990) found that lexical decisions to repeated homogrpahs may produce no priming when a context word precedes them and biases different meanings on their first and second occurrence. Vriezen *et al.* (in press) have also looked at the effects of repeated interpretations by presenting subjects with isolated words and manipulating the type of judgement made on the first and second presentation. They found that making a semantic judgement to a visually presented word resulted in a small but significant priming effect on a subsequent naming or lexical decision task. However, no facilitation was found when the order of tasks was reversed (i.e. from naming or lexical decision to semantic judgements), even though the same perceptual/lexical unit was presented on both occasions (see also Ratcliff *et al.* 1985). Perhaps more surprising, although performance on a specific word was facilitated when a semantic judgement was repeated (e.g. 'Is it bigger than a breadbox?'), no facilitation was found when the second judgement made reference to a different semantic domain (e.g. 'Is it man-made?'). Overall, these results pose problems for views that treat data-driven processing as independent from the more general context in which that processing is carried out, and instead suggest that repetition priming effects are specific to the match between prior and current task goals.

Text as context

Taken as a whole, the studies reviewed so far suggest an important role for context in the production of unconscious influences. Additional evidence for contextual factors is provided by research using connected discourse. Oliphant (1983) investigated the relationship between context and repetition priming in a single-word lexical decision task. Repeated words had first been encountered either in isolation (as part of a study list or a previous lexical decision task) or in meaningful passages (pre-experimental questionnaires or task instructions). Oliphant found that, unlike words presented in isolation, words presented in text did *not* facilitate performance on the lexical decision task. A similar pattern of results was reported by MacLeod (1989) using fragment completion: target words embedded in meaningful passages produced much less priming than did words presented as part of a to-be-learned list. Both the Oliphant and MacLeod results have been interpreted as showing that context reduces the amount of perceptual analysis given to specific word forms, thereby producing a memory trace unable to support subsequent perceptual priming (Jacoby 1983*b*; Roediger and Blaxton 1987). For example, MacLeod (1989, p. 398; see also Masson and MacLeod 1992) has stated that '. . . context plays a critical role in priming: As a word moves from being contextually bound in meaningful discourse to being isolated in a list, its probability of priming increases'.

That context plays a critical role in mediating the effects of prior experience is in accord with the present framework. However, MacLeod's conclusion focuses on contextual factors at encoding without considering the importance of contextual factors at retrieval. That unrelated words presented in isolation at study show the highest level of priming would be expected on an indirect retention measure which itself contains little meaningful structure. The present analysis suggests that if the context provided by meaningful discourse were available at retrieval, even 'contextually bound' words would show performance facilitation or priming.

Our interpretation receives strong support from a study by Levy and Kirsner (1989) who manipulated the surface characteristics of both meaningful passages and word-lists in order to study word- and text-level transfer on indirect measures of memory. Replicating Oliphant (1983), they found that words embedded in natural text did not facilitate performance on a subsequent measure of word identification. Words presented in isolation, however, did facilitate identification performance, the magnitude of which varied with the similarity of surface characteristics (e.g. modality, type font) from study to test. More importantly, when the earlier-read passages were re-presented at test, performance (reading time) was significantly facilitated *and varied with surface-level similarity*. The latter finding rules out the possibility that the failure to find text-to-word transfer on isolated-word tests (e.g. word identification, lexical decision, or completion) was due to context reducing the role of data-driven processing at encoding (cf. Jacoby 1983*b*; MacLeod 1989; Roediger *et al.* 1989). Contrary to this account, Levy and Kirsner's results show that memory for perceptual characteristics was integrated with other, more conceptual, aspects of the prior reading experience (see also Jacoby *et al.* 1992*a*; Kolers and Roediger 1984). Apparently, whether a particular aspect of prior processing will influence subsequent performance depends on the context in which that performance is assessed. Transfer is most comprehensive when the test reinstates the context surrounding the original encoding episode.

Reading tasks offer one of the most flexible paradigms for investigating the nature of contextual reinstatement because, in addition to the repetition of specific words, other forms of contextual information can be manipulated including syntactic, semantic, and thematic structures. Space limitations restrict us from reviewing that literature here (see Levy 1993), but we believe it confirms a powerful role for contextual (as well as episodic) factors in the production of unconscious influences. As one brief example that provides some symmetry with the studies reviewed above, Levy *et al.* (1991) found that reading particular words can result in little or no transfer to the reading of texts composed of those words, unless higher-order textual characteristics (i.e. syntax, thematics, etc.) were also encoded as part of the original event. This was true even when surface characteristics (i.e. type fonts) were perfectly matched.

Orientation to the past as a context for the present

We have argued that conceptual priming is best revealed when the context surrounding prior processing is reinstated at retrieval. Unfortunately, using indirect tests to investigate context and set effects is difficult, if not impossible, because of the possibility that subjects will become aware of some critical past event. This is a serious limitation for the indirect test approach because there are reasons to believe that unconscious influences may be sensitive to the context set by awareness and intent (Jacoby *et al.* 1993*a*; Wegner 1993). Direct tests of memory focus a subject's awareness on the past, thus encouraging the intentional reinstatement of an earlier episodic context. Jacoby *et al.* (1993*a*) have shown that performance on *direct* tests is often supported by unconscious influences of memory. Thus, if we are correct about the importance of context in producing unconscious conceptual influences, we should find conceptual influences on the unconscious processes that support performance on direct tests such as recognition memory.

Toth (1992) found such evidence using an exclusion test in combination with a response deadline technique. In phase 1 of his second experiment, subjects made semantic and non-semantic judgements to different sets of words presented under incidental study instructions. In the second phase, subjects were presented with an auditory word-list which they were told to remember. In the recognition memory test that followed, subjects were told to accept only the words they had been asked to remember (i.e. those presented aurally); both new words and those from phase 1 were to be rejected. Results showed that the ability to reject words from phase 1 depended on both retrieval time and prior processing. At the long deadline (1500 ms), where subjects had ample time for recollection, incorrect acceptance of phase 1 words did not differ as a function of prior processing (semantic = 0.20; non-semantic = 0.21). In contrast, at the short deadline (500 ms), where recollection was curtailed and responses more familiarity-based, false acceptance was significantly higher following a prior semantic (0.56), as opposed to non-semantic (0.30), orienting task. This result suggests that, contrary to previous claims (e.g. Jacoby and Dallas 1981; Mandler 1980) automatic familiarity is not based only on perceptual factors (i.e. 'perceptual fluency') but can also reflect prior conceptual processing (see also Jacoby 1991). This conclusion was supported in a follow-up experiment that used the process-dissociation procedure to estimate the magnitude of conscious recollection and automatic familiarity. As expected, estimated recollection was significantly affected by both levels of processing (LoP) and response time at retrieval; that is, estimates were higher following semantic processing and at the long response deadline. In contrast, estimates of familiarity did not change across the response deadline, but were significantly higher following semantic, in comparison to non-semantic, study at both points in retrieval.

As a final example of how orientation to the past can set the context for unconscious influences, consider two experiments by Ste-Marie and Jacoby (1993). They were interested in factors which result in spontaneous recollection of a prior event, but wanted to measure such factors indirectly. In order to do this, they used a variant of the flanker paradigm (Eriksen and Eriksen 1974). Subjects studied a list of visually presented words and were then given a speeded, visual test of recognition memory. Words presented for recognition memory judgements (henceforth 'targets') were flanked above and below with another word that could have been either previously presented in the experiment ('old') or not previously presented ('new'), but subjects were told to attend and respond only to the centre (target) word. Results showed that when the flanking and target words were both of one type (i.e. old or new) subjects were facilitated in their reaction times to make correct recognition decisions. This result indicates both that selective attention to the middle word was not perfect and that the nature of the flanking word (i.e. its status as old or new in the experiment) may influence responses to the target.

What factors might be important for mediating this flanker (spontaneous recognition) effect? If one thought that automatic influences were completely data-driven or based on perceptual fluency, then decreasing the perceptual similarity between a word's prior presentation and its use as a flanker—for example, having the word be presented auditorily at study—should reduce its influence. However, in experiments designed to test this hypothesis, Ste-Marie and Jacoby (1993) found something much more interesting and, we believe, important. They found that whether a flanking word had an influence on responses to the target depended, not on the perceptual similarity of the flanker from study to test, but rather on the relationship between the target and the flanker. That is, flanking words previously seen at study only influenced responding when the target itself had previously been experienced visually. When the target had previously been presented auditorily, only words that were earlier heard influenced reaction times to targets; study words that had been presented visually had no influence on previously heard targets. Apparently, attention (intention?) to the target word created a set which allowed events of a similar kind (i.e. previously heard or previously read words) to gain access to the response system and influence responding. Words from a different 'category', although potentially having all the characteristics for perceptual priming, had no influence. Similar results have emerged in studies of attentional orientation (Folk *et al.* 1992). These findings suggest that automatic influences, rather than being absolute or the by-product of cognitively impenetrable perceptual modules, are senstive both to the context of processing and to the goals set by intentions (Jacoby *et al.* 1993*a*).

2.4 SUMMARY OF CONTEMPORARY RESEARCH

One of our main goals in this chapter was to review critically the evidence for unconscious uses of prior conceptual processing in order to provide guidelines for future research and theory on the topic. The results of our review were both positive and negative. On the positive side, we find clear evidence that prior conceptual processing can unconsciously influence subsequent behaviour. Conceptual priming appears to occur whenever there is a high overlap between the processing context at study and test. Such contextual reinstatement can be either in the form of associative or semantic cues (e.g. Jacoby 1994, in press) or, possibly, from a high degree of perceptual overlap (Gardiner 1988*a*; Toth and Hunt 1990). Perhaps more important, unconscious conceptual influences appear very sensitive to the match between the processing goals operating at encoding and retrieval. Congruent task goals were found to recruit prior conceptual operations in both isolated word paradigms (e.g. the spelling of homographs; lexical decision) and in more contextually rich environments (e.g. reading text; solving puzzle sentences). Also, an intentional orientation to the past may allow prior conceptual processing to unconsciously influence performance, possibly through reinstatement of the earlier context, a recreation of the prior set for processing, or perhaps both.

On the negative side of our review, the majority of claims for the existence of conceptual priming are based on research using indirect test paradigms which, although suggestive of unconscious influences, do not rule out the possibility of conscious contamination. Research using the process-dissociation procedure, post-test interviews, and inconsistencies in the indirect test literature, all suggest that many apparent examples of conceptual priming are due to conscious uses of memory. Although some researchers might question the validity of estimates derived from the process-dissociation procedure, we want to emphasize that the results from this procedure are very consistent with those obtained using indirect tests. For example, estimates derived from the procedure show that manipulations of LoP, attention, retrieval time, presentation duration, and ageing can have large influences on consciously controlled uses of memory but leave automatic, unconscious influences unchanged (for reviews see Jacoby *et al.* 1992*a* in press; Jacoby and Begg submitted; Toth *et al.* 1994). Moreover, when uncontaminated by conscious uses of memory, performance on indirect tests closely matches estimates of unconscious influences gained from the procedure (Jacoby *et al.* 1993*b*; Reingold and Goshen-Gottstein, in press; Toth *et al.* 1994).

Of course, findings obtained with the process-dissociation procedure do not rule out the possibility that conceptual priming could occur given the cues provided in many of the indirect test paradigms discussed above. Indeed, to the extent that these tests reinstate the prior encoding context, we believe that many of these tests have the appropriate characteristics for eliciting conceptual transfer. But this is part of the problem with indirect test paradigms: the very conditions that are conducive to unconscious use of prior conceptual processing—the reinstatement of context and set—are the exact conditions that often result in spontaneous recollection of the study episode. Conceptual priming may often occur in a variety of tasks and situations but is overlooked because of conscious contamination. For this reason, we believe that further specification of unconscious uses of prior meaning-based processing will require researchers to adopt methods other that those offered by the indirect test approach (see Reingold and Toth, chapter 4). Obtaining uncontaminated results from indirect tests is not impossible, but it requires that one present items so 'out of context' that little direct contact is made with prior processing episodes; hence, little can be learned about conceptual unconscious influences.

As discussed by Jacoby (in press), there are always two potential effects of reinstating context, one automatic, the other controlled. The process-dissociation procedure allows one to reinstate context and still measure unconscious influences despite the potential increase in conscious recollection. Even if one is reluctant to adopt the process-dissociation procedure, the data reviewed here support our claim that conceptual priming is most likely to be found in environments with high contextual overlap and thus demand methodologies that go beyond indirect tests given 'out of context'. One conservative option, shown in the experiment by Toth (1992), is to use an opposition ('exclusion') condition which is often sensitive enough to demonstrate the automatic effects or prior conceptual processing.

2.5 CONCLUSIONS: GETTING 'SET' FOR FUTURE RESEARCH ON UNCONSCIOUS INFLUENCES

Imagine an experiment in which an entire past event—including the perceptual stimuli, the meaning of the stimuli, the context in which they were encountered, the distribution of attention, and the subject's processing goals or set—was repeated. We imagine that in this situation all measured aspects of performance, including perceptual and conceptual processing, would be facilitated. Of course, entire events cannot be repeated, only aspects of prior events. In this sense, tasks can be viewed as filters that allow some aspects of prior processing to be used in current performance, but not others. Current views of unconscious influences of memory are biased toward perception because perceptual factors are relatively easy to manipulate and measure; that is, we have ready access to available filters. However, other factors—such as set (executive processes) and context—may be equally, if not more, important to understanding the nature of unconscious influences, but they have not been studied by contemporary researchers because of their propensity to evoke awareness of the past.

A central theme in this chapter has been that it is the neglect of context, specifically the context for retrieval, that has limited the scope of conceptual priming observed in the laboratory. This same neglect has limited theoretical approaches to memory because of the tacit assumption that perception and conception can be treated as separate, independent domains of inquiry. Presumably conceptual processes can be ignored because they arise in a separate system (Tulving and Schacter 1990; Squire 1992) or involve a qualitatively different set of processes (Roediger

1990) than those mediating memory for prior perceptual operations. In contrast to these views, we believe that understanding effects of the past requires that one take into account how perception and conception, either separately or together, are integrated with contextually defined goals. As stated by Bargh (1990, p.98): 'Automatic, preconscious influences on behavioral decisions certainly exist . . . but the decisions themselves are made intentionally and in the service of the current goal'

The majority of laboratory demonstrations of unconsious influences of memory has been interpreted as showing almost complete dependence on prior perceptual or data-driven processing; few researchers have worried about whether these demonstrations would be invariant across changes in context or the subjects processing goals. The idea that data-driven processing can be used to account for unconscious influences is similar to the claim that automaticity is stimulus-driven. Indeed, the data-driven/conceptually driven distinction is very similar to the contrast between stimulus-driven and intention-driven processing that has been popular in theorizing about attention (e.g. Posner and Snyder 1975). Is performance ever controlled entirely by external stimuli (i.e. data) or entirely by conscious intent? After extensive learning, automatic processes are said to become as encapsulated and uncontrolled as reflexes. However, even reflexes can be modified by attention (Anthony 1985). Neumann (1984) argued that automatic processes (and, we would add, unconscious influences) are not a characteristic of stimulus-driven processing, but rather are an emergent property of the exercise of specific skills in specific environments. That is, automatic or unconscious uses of the past arise from the integration of stimulus parameters and memory for skills in the context of consciously controlled goals and intentions. Priming effects from a prior encounter with a word, for example, may arise only in the context of task goals, such as completing stems or judging some property of a word or its referent; in other contexts, with other task demands, prior encounters with a word may produce different automatic effects (e.g. Vriezen *et al.* in press)—or no effects at all (e.g. Ste-Marie and Jacoby 1993).

The notion of transfer-appropriate processing provides a very appealing and intuitive framework for thinking about memory. Memory is the repetition of a set of operations that occurred together in the past. A more exact theory of memory, however, will require that this 'set of operations' is better specified. As a first step toward specification, researchers have focused on the broad distinction between perception and conception. However, while this distinction provides some help in describing the overlap in processing from study to test, it neglects the goals of that processing and the context in which it occurs. When these factors are taken into account, the unit of analysis for a theory of memory becomes the stimulus–goal configuration, rather than isolated perceptual or conceptual processes. Entire events cannot be repeated but similar contexts and sets (goal orientations) often recur, and it in these instances that memory for prior conceptualizations can influence current thought and behaviour. Often, such prior conceptualizations are apprehended consciously and thus we can intentionally choose to exploit, or to avoid, the prior influence. More often, we believe, our views of the world are coloured covertly and we simply *perceive* the *meaning* of the event.

ACKNOWLEDGEMENTS

Preparation of this chapter was supported by a fellowship awarded to Jeffrey P. Toth by the Rotman Research Institute of Baycrest Centre and the Clarke Institute of Psychiatry, Toronto, Canada; and by a Natural Science and Engineering Research Council (NSERC) of Canada operating grant to Eyal M. Reingold. We thank R. Hunt, L. Jacoby, B. Levine, M. Masson, N. Meiran, H. Roediger, and M. Wheeler for their comments on an earlier draft of this chapter.

REFERENCES

Alejano, A. R. and Carr, T. H. (1991). *The development of abstract processing operations in reading: Repetition benfits as a diagnostic tool.* Paper presented at the Midwestern Psychological Association, Chicago, IL.

Allen, S. W. and Jacoby, L. L. (1990). Reinstating study context produces unconscious influences of memory. *Memory and Cognition*, **18**, 270–8.

Anthony, B. J. (1985). In the blink of an eye: Implication of reflex modification for information processing. In *Advances in psychophysiology*, Vol. 1, (ed. P. K. Ackles, J. R. Jennings, and M. G. H. Coles), pp. 167–218. JAI Press, Greenwich CT.

Bainbridge, J. V., Lewandowsky, S., and Kirsner, K. (1993). Context effects in repetition priming are sense specific. *Memory and Cognition*, **21**, 619–26.

Bargh, J. A. (1990). Auto-motives: Preconscious determinants of social interaction. In *Handbook of motivation and cognition*, (ed. E. T. Higgins and R. M. Sorrentino), *Vol. 2*, pp. 93–130. Guilford Press, New York.

Bassili, J. N., Smith, M. C., and MacLeod, C. M. (1989). Auditory and visual word-stem completion: Separating data-driven and conceptually driven processes. *The Quarterly Journal of Experimental Psychology*, **41A**, 439–53.

Biederman, I. and Cooper, E. E. (1991). Evidence for complete translational and reflectional invariance in visual object priming. *Perception*, **20**, 585–93.

Biederman, I. and Cooper, E. E. (1992). Size invariance in viual object priming. *Journal of Experimental Psychology: Human Perception and Performance*, **18**, 121–33.

Blaxton, T. A. (1989). Investigating dissociations among memory measures:

Support for a transfer appropriate processing framework. *Journal of Experimental Psychology: Learning, Memory, and Cognition*, **15**, 657–68.

Bowers, J. S. and Schacter, D. L. (1990). Implicit memory and test awareness. *Journal of Experimental Psychology: Learning, Memory, and Cognition*, **16**, 404–16.

Bowers, J. S. and Schacter, D. L. (1993). Priming of new information in amnesic patients: Issues and data. In *Implicit memory: New directions in cognition, development, and neuropsychology*, (ed. P. Graf and M. Masson), pp. 303–26. Erlbaum, Hove, UK.

Bransford, J. D., McCarrell, N. S., Franks, J. J., and Nitsch, K. E. (1977). Toward unexplaining memory. In *Perceiving, acting, and knowing*, (ed. R. Shaw and J. Bransford), pp. 431–66. Erlbaum, Hillsdale, NJ.

Brown, A. S. and Mitchell, D. B. (1994). Levels of processing in implicit memory: A reevaluation. *Memory and Cognition*, **22**, 533–41.

Brown, A. S., Neblett, D. R., Jones, T. C., and Mitchell, D. B. (1991). Transfer of processing in repetition priming: Some inappropriate findings. *Journal of Experimental Psychology: Learning, Memory, and Cognition*, **17**, 514–25.

Bruner, J. S. and Goodman, C. C. (1947). Value and need as organizing factors in perception. *Journal of Abnormal Social Psychology*, **42**, 33–44.

Challis, B. H. and Brodbeck, D. R. (1992). Level of processing affects priming in word-fragment completion. *Journal of Experimental Psychology: Learning, Memory, and Cognition*, **18**, 595–607.

Challis, B. H. and Roediger, H. L. III (1993). The effect of proportion overlap and repeated testing on primed word fragment completion. *Canadian Journal of Psychology*, **47**, 113–23.

Chiarello, C. and Hoyer, W. J. (1988). Adult age differences in implicit and explicit memory: Time course and encoding effects. *Psychology and Aging*, **3**, 358–66.

Clark, R. and Morton, J. (1983). Cross-modality facilitation in tachistoscopic word recognition. *Quarterly Journal of Experimental Psychology*, **35A**, 79–96.

Clifton, C. (1966). Some determinants of the effectiveness of priming word associates. *Journal of Verbal Learning and Verbal Behavior*, **5**, 167–71.

Cofer, C. N. (1967). Conditions for the use of verbal associations. *Psychological Bulletin*, **68**, 1–12.

Cohen, N. J. and Squire. L. R. (1980). Preserved learning and retention of pattern analysing skill in amnesia: Dissociations of knowing how and knowing that. *Science*, **210**, 544–54.

Corteen, R. S. and Dunn, D. (1974). Shock-associated words in a nonattended message: A test for momentary awareness. *Journal of Experimental Psychology*, **102**, 1143–4.

Corteen, R. S. and Wood, B. (1972). Autonomic responses to shock-associated words in an unattended channel. *Journal of Experimental Psychology*, **94**, 308–13.

Craik, F. I. M (1991). On the specificity of procedural memory. In *Memories, thoughts, and emotions*, (ed. W. Kessen, A. Ortony, and F. I. M. Craik), pp. 183–97. Erlbaum, Hillsdale, NJ.

Craik, F. I. M. and Lockhart, R. S. (1972). Levels of processing: A framework for memory research. *Journal of Verbal Learning and Verbal Behavior*, **11**, 671–84.

Cramer, P. (1964). Successful mediated priming via associative bonds. *Psychological Reports*, **15**, 235–8.

Cramer, P. (1965). Recovery of a discrete memory. *Journal of Personality and Social Psychology*, **1**, 326–32.
Cramer, P. (1966). Mediated priming of associative responses: The effect of time lapse and interpolated activity. *Journal of Verbal Learning and Verbal Behavior*, **5**, 163–6.
Deese, J. (1959). On the prediction of occurrence of particular intrusions in immediate recall. *Journal of Experimental Psychology*, **58**, 17–22.
Durso, F. T. and Johnson, M. K. (1979). Facilitation in naming and categorizing repeated words and pictures. *Journal of Experimental Psychology: Human Learning and Memory*, **5**, 449–59.
Dunn, J. C. and Kirsner, K. (1989). Implicit memory: Task or process. In *Implicit memory: Theoretical issues*, (ed. S. Lewandosky, J. C. Dunn, and K. Kirsner), pp. 17–31. Erlbaum, Hillsdale, NJ.
Ellis, A. (1982). Modality-specific repetition priming of auditory word recognition. *Current Psychological Research*, **2**, 123–8.
Erdelyi, M. H. (1985). *Psychoanalysis: Freud's cognitive psychology*. Freeman, New York.
Erdelyi, M. H. (1992). Psychodynamics and the unconscious. *American Psychologist*, **47**, 784–7.
Eriksen B. A. and Eriksen, C. W. (1974). Effects of noise letters upon the identification of a target letter in a nonsearch task. *Perception and Psychophysics*, **16**, 143–9.
Fisher, R. P. and Craik, F. I. M. (1977). Interaction between encoding and retrieval operations in cued recall. *Journal of Experimental Psychology: Human Learning and Memory*, **3**, 701–11.
Folk, C. L., Remington, R. W., and Johnston, J. C. (1992). Involuntary covert orienting is contingent on attentional control settings. *Journal of Experimental Psychology: Human Perception and Performance*, **18**, 1030–44.
Gardiner, H., Boller, F., Moreines, J., and Butters, N. (1973). Retrieving information from Korsakoff patients: Effects of categorical cues and reference to the task. *Cortex*, **9**, 165–75.
Gardiner, J. M. (1988*a*). Generation and priming effects in word-fragment completion. *Journal of Experimental Psychology: Learning, Memory, and Cognition*, **14**, 495–501.
Gardiner, J. M. (1988*b*). Functional aspects of recollective experience. *Memory and Cognition*, **16**, 309–13.
Gardiner, J. M. (1989). A generation effect in memory without awareness. *British Journal of Psychology*, **80**, 163–68.
Gardiner, J. M., Dawson, A. J., and Sutton, E. A. (1989). Specificity and generality of enhanced priming effects for self-generated study items. *American Journal of Psychology*, **102**, 295–305.
Gibson, J. J. (1941). A critical review of the concept of set in contemporary experimental psychology. *Psychological Bulletin*, **38**, 781–817.
Graf, P. and Mandler, G. (1984). Activation makes words more accessible, but not necessarily more retrievable. *Journal of Verbal Learning and Verbal Behavior*, **23**, 553–68.
Graf, P. and Schacter, D. L. (1985). Implicit and explicit memory for new associations in normal and amnesic subjects. *Journal of Experimental Psychology: Learning, Memory, and Cognition*, **11**, 501–18.

Graf, P., Mandler, G., and Hayden, P. E. (1982). Simulating amnesic symptoms in normal subjects. *Science*, **218**, 1243–44.

Graf, P., Squire, L. R., and Mandler, G. (1984). The information that amnesic patients do not forget. *Journal of Experimental Psychology: Learning, Memory, and Cognition*, **10**, 164–78.

Grand, S. and Segal, S. J. (1966). Recovery in the absence of recall: An investigation of color-word interference. *Journal of Experimental Psychology*, **72**, 138–44.

Greenwald, A. G. (1993). New Look 3: Unconscious cognition reclaimed. *American Psychologist*, **47**, 766–79.

Hayes-Roth, B. (1977). Evolution of cognitive structures and processes. *Psychological Review*, **84**, 260–78.

Hamann, S. B. (1990). Level-of-processing effects in conceptually driven implicit tasks. *Journal of Experimental Psychology: Learning, Memory, and Cognition*, **16**, 970–7.

Hermann, D. J., McLaughlin, J. P., and Nelson, B. C. (1975). Visual and semantic factors in recognition from long-term memory. *Memory and Cognition*, **3**, 381–4.

Hirshman, E., Snodgrass, J. G., Mindes, J., and Feenan, K. (1990). Conceptual priming in fragment competion. *Journal of Experimental Psychology: Learning, Memory, and Cognition*, **16**, 634–47.

Hunt, R. R. and Toth, J. P. (1990). Perceptual identification, fragment completion, and free recall: Concepts and data. *Journal of Experimental Psychology: Learning, Memory, and Cognition*, **16**, 282–90.

Isen, A. M. and Diamond, G. A. (1989). Affect and automaticity. In *Unintended thought*, (ed. J. S. Uleman and J. A. Bargh). Guilford Press: New York.

Jaciw, M. and McAndrews, M. P. (1993, November). *Elaborative processing effects on conceptual priming: A process dissociation analysis*. Paper presented at the 34th Annual Meeting of The Psychonomic Society. Washington, DC.

Jackson, A. and Morton, J. (1984). Facilitation of auditory word recognition. *Memory and Cognition*, **12**, 568–74.

Jacoby, L. L. (1983*a*). Perceptual enhancement: Persistent effects of an experience. *Journal of Experimental Psychology: Learning, Memory, and Cognition*, **9**, 21–38.

Jacoby, L. L. (1983*b*). Remembering the data: Analysing interactive processes in reading. *Journal of Verbal Learning and Verbal Behavior*, **22**, 485–508.

Jacoby, L. L. (1991). A process dissociation framework: Separating automatic from intentional uses of memory. *Journal of Memory and Language*, **30**, 513–41.

Jacoby, L. L. (1994). Measuring recollection: Strategic versus automatic influences of associative context. In *Attention and performance XV*, (ed. C. Umilta and M. Moscovitch). Bradford, Cambridge, MA.

Jacoby, L. L. (in press). Dissociating automatic and controlled effects of study/test compatibility. *Journal of Memory and Language*.

Jacoby, L. L. and Begg, I. M. (submitted). In defense of functional independence: Violations of assumptions underlying the process-dissociation procedure? *Journal of Experimental Psychology: Learning, Memory, and Cognition*.

Jacoby, L. L. and Brooks, L. R. (1984). Nonanalytic cognition: Memory, perception and concept learning. In *The psychology of learning and motivation: Advances in research and theory*, Vol. 18, (ed. G. H. Bower), pp. 1–47. Academic Press, New York.

Jacoby, L. L. and Dallas, M. (1981). On the relationship between autobiographical memory and perceptual learning. *Journal of Experimental Psychology: General*, **3**, 306–40.

Jacoby, L. L. and Hayman, G. A. (1987). Specific visual transfer in word identification. *Journal of Experimental Psychology: Learning, Memory, and Cognition*, **13**, 456–63.

Jacoby L. L. and Kelley, C. M. (1987). Unconscious influences of memory for a prior event. *Personality and Social Psychology Bulletin*, **13**, 314–36.

Jacoby L. L. and Kelley, C. M. (1990). An episodic view of motivation: Unconscious influences of memory. In *Handbook of motivation and cognition, Vol. 2*, (ed. E. T. Higgins and R. M. Sorrentino) pp. 93–130. Guilford Press, New York.

Jacoby, L. L. and Witherspoon, D. (1982). Remembering without awareness. *Canadian Journal of Psychology*, **36**, 300–24.

Jacoby, L. L., Baker, J., and Brooks, L. R. (1989). Episodic effects on picture identification: Implications for theories of concept learning and theories of memory. *Journal of Experimental Psychology: Learning, Memory, and Cognition*, **15**, 275–281.

Jacoby, L. L., Levy, B. A., and Steinbach, K. (1992*a*). Episodic transfer and automaticity: The integration of data-driven and conceptually driven processing in rereading. *Journal of Experimental Psychology: Learning, Memory, and Cognition*, **18**, 15–24.

Jacoby, L. L., Toth, J. P., Lindsay, D. S., and Debner, J. A. (1992*b*). Lectures for a layperson: Methods for revealing unconscious processes. In *Perception without awareness*, (ed. R. F. Bornstein and T. S. Pittman), pp. 81–120. Guilford Press, New York.

Jacoby, L. L., Ste-Marie, and Toth, J. P. (1993*a*). Redefining automaticity: Unconscious influences, awareness and control. In *Attention: Selection, awareness and control. A tribute to Donald Broadbent*, (ed. A. D. Baddeley and L. Weiskrantz), pp. 261–282. Oxford University Press.

Jacoby, L. L., Toth, J. P., and Yonelinas, A. P. (1993*b*). Separating conscious and unconscious influences of memory: Measuring recollection. *Journal of Experimental Psychology: General*, **122**, 139–54.

Jacoby, L. L., Yonelinas, A. P., and Jennings, J. M. (in press). The relationship between conscious and unconscious (automatic) influences of memory: Toward showing independence. In *Scientific approaches to the question of consciousness*, (ed. J. Cohen and J. W. Schooler). Erlbaum, Hillsdale, NJ.

James, W. (1890/1950). *Principles of psychology*. Holt: New York.

Jolicoeur, P. (1985). The time to name disoriented natural objects. *Memory and Cognition*, **13**, 289–303.

Juola, J. F., Fischler, I., Wood, C. T., and Atkinson, R. C. (1971). Recognition time for information stored in long-term memory. *Perception and Psychophysics*, **10**, 8–14.

Kasserman, J. E., Yearwood, A. A., and Franks, J. J. (1987). Contextual priming effects in perceptual identification. *Bulletin of the Psychonomic Society*, **25**, 233–35.

Kelley, C. M., Jacoby, L. L., and Holingshead, A. (1989). Direct versus indirect tests of memory for source: Judgments of modality. *Journal of Experimental Psychology: Learning, Memory, and Cognition*, **15**, 1101–8.

Kihlstrom, J. F. (1987). The cognitive unconscious. *Science*, **237**, 1445–52.

Kirsner, K. and Smith, M. C. (1974). Modality effects in word identification. *Memory and Cognition*, **2**, 637–40.

Kirsner, K., Milech, D., and Standen, P. (1983). Common and modality-specific processes in the mental lexicon. *Memory and Cognition*, **11**, 621–30.

Kirsner, K., Milech, D., and Stumpfel, V. (1986). Word and picture identification: Is representational parsimony possible? *Memory and Cognition*, **14**, 398–408.

Kirsner, K., Dunn, J. C., and Standen, P. (1989). Domain specific resources in word recognition. In *Implicit memory: Theoretical issues*, (ed. S. Lewandowsky, J. C. Dunn, and K. Kirsner), pp. 99–122. Erlbaum, Hillsdale, NJ.

Kolers, P. A. and Roediger, H. L. III (1984). Procedures of mind. *Journal of Verbal Learning and Verbal Behavior*, **23**, 425–49.

Levy, B. A. (1993). Fluent rereading: An implicit indicator of reading skill development. In *Implicit memory: New directions in cognition, neuropsychology, and development*, (ed. P. Graf and M. E. J. Masson), pp. 49–73. Academic Press, New York.

Levy, B. A. and Kirsner, K. (1989). Reprocessing text: Indirect measures of word and message level processes. *Journal of Experimental Psychology: Learning, Memory, and Cognition*, **15**, 407–17.

Levy, B. A., Masson, M. E. J., and Zoubek, M. A. (1991). Rereading text: Words and their context. *Canadian Journal of Psychology*, **45**, 492–506.

Lindsay, P. H. and Norman, D. A. (1977). *Human Information processing*. Academic Press, New York.

Logan, G. D. (1988). Toward an instance theory of automatization. *Psychological Review*, **95**, 492–527.

McAndrews, M. P., Glisky, E. L., and Schacter, D. L. (1987). When priming persists: Long-lasting implicit memory for a single episode in amnesic patients. *Neuropsychologia*, **25**, 497–506.

MacLeod, C. M. (1989). Word context during intial exposure influences degree of priming in word fragment completion. *Journal of Experimental Psychology: Learning, Memory, and Cognition*, **15**, 398–406.

Mandler, G. (1980). Recognizing: The judgment of previous occurrence. *Psychological Review*, **87**, 252–71.

Masson, M. E. J. and Freedman, L. (1990). Fluent identification of repeated words. *Journal of Experimental Psychology: Learning, Memory, and Cognition*, **16**, 355–73.

Masson, M. E. J. and MacLeod, C. M. (1992). Reenacting the route to interpretation: Enhanced perceptual identification without prior perception. *Journal of Experimental Psychology: General*, **121**, 145–76.

Micco, A. and Masson, M. E. J. (1991). Implicit memory for new associations: An interactive process approach. *Journal of Experimental Psychology: Learning, Memory, and Cognition*, **17**, 1105–23.

Morris, C. D., Bransford, J. D., and Franks, J. J. (1977). Levels of processing versus transfer appropriate processing. *Journal of Verbal Learning and Verbal Behavior*, **16**, 519–533.

Moscovitch, M. (1992). Memory and working-with-memory: A component process model based on modules and central systems. *Journal of Cognitive Neuroscience*, **4**, 257–67.

Moscovitch, M. (1994). Models of consciousness and memory. In *The cognitive neurosciences*, (ed. M. S. Gazzaniga), pp. 1341–56. MIT, Cambridge, MA.
Moscovitch, M., Vriezen, E. R., and Gottstein, J. (1993). Implicit tests of memory in patients with focal lesions or degenerative brain disorders. In *Handbook of neuropsychology* Vol.8, (ed. H. Spinnler and F. Boller), Elsevier, Amsterdam.
Neumann, O. (1984). Automatic processing: A review of recent findings and a plea for an old theory. In *Cognition and motor processes*, (ed. W. Prinz and A. F. Sanders), pp. 255–93. Springer, Berlin.
Niedenthal, P. M. (1992). Affect and social perception: On the psychological validity of rose-colored glasses. In *Perception without awareness*, (ed. R. F. Bornstein and T. S. Pittman) pp. 211–35. Guilford Press, New York.
Norman, D. A. (1981). Categorization of action slips. *Psychological Review*, **88**, 1–15.
Norman, D. A. and Shallice, T. (1986). Attention to action: Willed and automatic control of behavior. In *Consciousness and self-regulation: Advances in research, Vol.4*, (ed. R. J. Davidson, G. E. Schwartz, and D. Shapiro) Plenum, New York.
Oliphant, G. W. (1983). Repetition and recency effects in word recognition. *Australian Journal of Psychology*, **35**, 393–403.
Posner, M. I. and Snyder, C. R. R. (1975). Attention and cognitive control. In *Information processing in cognition: The Loyola Symposium*, (ed. R. L. Solso) pp. 55–85. Erlbaum, Hillsdale, NJ.
Rajaram, S. and Roediger, H. L. (1993). Direct comparison of four implicit memory tests. *Journal of Experimental Psychology: Learning, Memory, and Cognition*, **19**, 765–76.
Rappold, V. A. and Hashtroudi, S. (1991). Does organization improve priming? *Journal of Experimental Psychology: Learning, Memory, and Cognition*, **17**, 103–14.
Ratcliff, R. Hockley, W. E., and McKoon, G. (1985). Components of activation: Repetition and priming effects in lexical decision and recognition. *Journal of Experimental Psychology: General*, **114**, 435–50.
Ratcliff, R. and McKoon, G. (1993). Bias in implicit memory tasks. Paper presented at the 34th Annual Meeting of The Psychonomic Society. Washington, DC.
Ratcliff, R., McKoon, G., and Verwoerd, M. (1989). A bias interpretation of facilitation in perceptual identification. *Journal of Experimental Psychology: Learning, Memory, and Cognition*, **15**, 378–87.
Reason, J. T. (1984). Lapses of attention in everyday life. In *Varieties of attention*, (ed. R. Parasuraman and D. R. Davies, pp. 515–49. Academic Press, New York.
Reason, J. T. (1990). *Human error*. Cambridge University Press.
Rees, H. J. and Israel, H. E. (1935). An investigation of the establishment and operation of mental sets. *Psychological Monographs*, **46**, No. 210, 1–26.
Reingold, E. M. and Goshen-Gottstein, Y. (in press). Separating consciously controlled and automatic retrieval processes in memory for new associations. *Journal of Experimental Psychology: Learning, Memory, and Cognition*,
Reingold, E. M. and Merikle, P. M. (1990). On the inter-relatedness of theory and measurement in the study of unconscious processes. *Mind and Language*, **5**, 9–28.
Roediger, H. L. III (1990). Implicit memory: retention with remembering. *American Psychologist*, **45**, 1043–56.
Roediger, H. L. III and Blaxton, T. A. (1987). Effects of varying modality, surface

features, and retention interval on priming in word fragment completion. *Memory and Cognition*, **15**, 379–88.

Roediger, H. L. III and McDermott, K. B. (1993). Implicit memory in normal human subjects. In *Handbook of neuropsychology*, Vol. 8, (ed. H. Spinnler and F. Boller), pp. 63–131. Elsevier, Amsterdam.

Roediger, H. L. III and McDermott, K. B. (1994). Creation of false memories: Remembering words not presented in lists. Paper presented at the 35th Annual Meeting of The Psychonomic Society. St Louis, MO.

Roediger, H. L. III, Weldon, M. S., and Challis, B. H. (1989). Explaining dissociations between implicit and explicit measures of retention: A processing account. In (ed. H. L. Roediger and F. I. M. Craik), *Varieties of memory and consciousness: Essays in honour of Endel Tulving*, pp. 3–41. Erlbaum, Hillsdale, NJ.

Roediger, H. L. III, Weldon, M. S., Stadler, M. A., and Riegler, G. H (1992). Direct comparison of word stems and word fragments in implicit and explicit retention tests. *Journal of Experimental Psychology: Learning, Memory, and Cognition*, **18**, 1251–69.

Sanford, R. N. (1936). The effects of abstinence from food upon imaginal processes: A preliminary experiment. *The Journal of Psychology*, **2**, 129–36.

Sanford, R. N. (1937). The effects of abstinence from food upon imaginal processes: A further experiment. *The Journal of Psychology*, **3**, 145–59.

Schacter, D. L. (1985). Priming of old and new knowledge in amnesic patients and normal subjects. *Annals of the New York Academy of Sciences*, **608**, 543–71.

Schacter, D. L. (1992). Priming and multiple memory systems: Perceptual mechanisms of implicit memory. *Journal of Cognitive Neuroscience*, **4**, 244–56.

Schacter, D. L. and Church, B. (1992). Auditory priming: Implicit and explicit memory for words and voices. *Journal of Experimental Psychology: Learning, Memory, and Cognition*, **18**, 915–930.

Schacter, D. L. and Graf, P. (1986*a*). Effects of elaborative processing on implicit and explicit memory for new associations. *Journal of Experimental Psychology: Learning, Memory, and Cognition*, **12**, 432–44.

Schacter, D. L. and Graf, P. (1986*b*). Preserved learning in amnesic patients: Perspectives on research from direct priming. *Journal of Clinical Experimental Neuropsychology*, **8**, 727–743.

Schacter, D. L. and Graf, P. (1989). Modality specificity of implicit memory for new associations. *Journal of Experimental Psychology: Learning, Memory, and Cognition*, **15**, 3–12.

Schacter, D. L. and McGlynn, S. M. (1989). Implicit memory: Effects of elaboration depend on unitization. *Americal Journal of Psychology*, **102**, 151–81.

Segal, S. J. and Cofer, C. N. (1960). The effects of recency and recall on free association. *American Psychologist*, **15**, 451 (Abstract).

Shallice, T. (1982). Specific impairments in planning. *Philosophical Transactions of the Royal Society of London, B*, **298**, 199–209.

Shallice, T. (1988). *From neuropsychology to mental structure*. Cambridge University Press.

Shiffrin, R. M. and Schneider, W. (1977). Controlled and automatic information processing II: Perceptual learning, automatic attending and a general theory. *Psychological Review*, **84**, 127–90.

Shimamura, A. P. and Squire, L. R. (1984). Paired-associate learning and priming in amnesia: A neuropsychological approach. *Journal of Experimental Psychology: General*, **113**, 556–70.

Shimamura, A. P. and Squire, L. R. (1989). Impaired priming of new associations in amnesia. *Journal of Experimental Psychology: Learning, Memory, and Cognition*, **15**, 721–8.

Siipola, E. (1935). A group-study of some effects of preparatory set. *Psychological Monographs*, **46**, No. 210, 27–38.

Slamecka, N. J. and Graf, P. (1978). The generation effect: Delineation of a phenomenon. *Journal of Experimental Psychology: Human Learning and Memory*, **4**, 592–604.

Smith, E. R. and Branscombe, N. R. (1988). Category accessibility as implicit memory. *Journal of Experimental Social Psychology*, **24**, 490–504.

Snodgrass, J. G. and Feenan, K. (1990). Priming effects in picture fragment completion: Support for the perceptual closure hypothesis. *Journal of Experimental Psychology: General*, **119**, 276–96.

Srinivas, K. and Roediger, H. L. (1990). Classifying implicit memory tests: Category association and anagram solution. *Journal of Memory and Language*, **29**, 389–412.

Ste-Marie, D. M. and Jacoby, L. L. (1993). Spontaneous versus directed recognition: The relativity of automaticity. *Journal of Experimental Psychology: Learning, Memory, and Cognition*, **19**, 777–88.

Storms, L. H. (1958). Apparent backward association: A situational effect. *Journal of Experimental Psychology*, **55**, 390–5.

Stuss, D. T. (1991). Self, awareness, and the frontal lobes: A neuropsychological perspective. In *The self: Interdisciplinary perspectives*, (ed. J. Strauss and G. R. Goethals), pp. 255–78. Springer, New York.

Squire, L. R. (1992). Memory and the hippocampus: Synthesis of findings with rats, monkeys, and humans. *Psychological Review*, **99**, 195–231.

Toth, J. P. (1992). *Familiarity is affected by prior conceptual processing: Differential effects of elaborative study and response-time at test on separable processes in recognition memory*. Unpublished data and manuscript.

Toth, J. P. and Hunt, R. R. (1990). Effect of generation on a word-identification task. *Journal of Experimental Psychology: Learning, Memory, and Cognition*, **16**, 993–1003.

Toth, J. P., Reingold, E. M, and Jacoby, L. L. (1994). Toward a redefinition of implicit memory: Process dissociations following elaborative processing and self-generation. *Journal of Experimental Psychology: Learning, Memory, and Cognition*, **20**, 290–303.

Tulving, E. (1983). *Elements of episodic memory*. Oxford University Press.

Tulving, E. (1985). How many memory systems are there? *American Psychologist*, **40**, 385–98.

Tulving E. and Schacter, D. L. (1990). Priming and human memory systems. *Science*, **247**, 301–5.

Tulving, E. and Thompson, D. M. (1973). Encoding specificity and retrieval processes in episodic memory. *Psychological Review*, **80**, 352–73.

Underwood, B. J. (1965). False recognition produced by implicit verbal responses. *Journal of Experimental Psychology*, **70**, 122–9.

Vriezen, E. R., Moscovitch, M., and Bellos, S. (in press). Repetition priming effects for words accompanied by repeated and non-repeated orienting questions. *Journal of Experimental Psychology: Learning, Memory, and Cognition.*

Warrington, E. K. and Weiskrantz, L. (1968). New method of testing long-term retention with special reference to amnesic patients. *Nature*, **217**, 972–4.

Warrington, E. K. and Weiskrantz, L. (1970). Amnesic syndrome: Consolidation or retrieval? *Nature*, **228**, 629–30.

Warrington, E. K. and Weiskrantz, L. (1974). The effect of prior learning on subsequent retention in amnesic patients. *Neuropsychologia*, **12**, 419–28.

Wegner, D. M. (1993). Ironic processes of mental control. *Psychological Review*, **101**, 34–52.

Weldon, M. S. (1991). Mechanisms underlying priming on perceptual tasks. *Journal of Experimental Psychology: Learning, Memory, and Cognition*, **17**, 526–41.

Weldon, M. S. (1993). The time course of perceptual and conceptual contributions to word-fragment completion priming. *Journal of Experimental Psychology: Learning, Memory, and Cognition*, **19**, 1010–23.

Weldon, M. S. and Jackson-Barrett, J. L. (1993). Why do pictures produce priming on the word-fragment completion test? A study of encoding and retrieval factors. *Memory and Cognition*, **21**, 519–28.

Weldon, M. S. and Roediger, H. L. III (1987). Altering retrieval demands reverses the picture superiority effect. *Memory and Cognition*, **15**, 269–80.

Winnick, W. A. and Daniel, S. A. (1970). Two kinds of response priming in tachistoscopic word recognition. *Journal of Experimental Psychology*, **84**, 74–81.

Woodworth, R. S. and Schlosberg, H. E. (1954). *Experimental psychology*. Holt, New York.

3

Memory: task dissociations, process dissociations and dissociations of consciousness

Alan Richardson-Klavehn, John M. Gardiner, and Rosalind I. Java

3.0 TASKS, RETRIEVAL STRATEGIES, AND STATES OF CONSCIOUSNESS: A FRAMEWORK

Striking dissociations between explicit and implicit tests of memory have led to an explosion of research addressing the relationship of conscious awareness of the past to observed memory performance (for reviews see Gardiner and Java 1993*a*,*b*; Richardson-Klavehn and Bjork 1988*a*; Roediger and McDermott 1993; Schacter *et al.* 1993). Despite the vast quantity of data, there is no firm agreement on the theoretical implications of such task dissociations. Two levels of theoretical debate can be identified, the first 'shallower' than the second. The debate at the first level concerns the extent to which task dissociations represent evidence for differences in retrieval strategies and/or memorial states of awareness (e.g. Bowers and Schacter 1990; Dunn and Kirsner 1988, 1989; Challis and Brodbeck 1992; Jacoby 1991; Jacoby *et al.* 1993*b*; Merikle and Reingold 1991; Reingold and Merikle 1990; Richardson-Klavehn and Bjork 1988*a*; Schacter *et al.* 1989). The debate at the second, 'deeper', level concerns the encoding and retrieval mechanisms underlying the hypothesized strategies and states of awareness. Some theorists, for example, have argued that different manifestations of memory are attributable to the operation of distinct memory systems (e.g. Schacter 1989; Squire 1992; Tulving 1993; Tulving and Schacter 1990). Others argue that these different manifestations are consistent with a process viewpoint (e.g. Jacoby *et al.* 1989*a*; Kolers and Roediger 1984; Roediger 1990; Roediger *et al.* 1989*a*,*b*).

We believe that progress on the former issue is likely to be a precondition for progress on the latter one. The present chapter, therefore, reviews and integrates recent data from our laboratory that contribute to understanding of the relationship between task performance, retrieval strategies, and states of awareness. Our data have led us to adopt a framework that makes a threefold distinction between: (a) method of testing memory as defined by task instructions (*intentional* vs. *incidental*); (b) retrieval strategy (*voluntary* vs. *involuntary*); and (c) subjective state of awareness with respect to the past (*conscious* vs. *unconscious*). Conscious memorial states are subdivided into *recollective experiences* and *feelings of familiarity*. Recollective experiences are referred to as *remembering*, and feelings of familiarity in the absence of recollection are referred to as *knowing*. This terminology is used throughout the chapter, so we explain it briefly here.

3.0.1 Intentional and incidental tests of memory

The *explicit/implicit* (Graf and Schacter 1985) and *direct/indirect* (Johnson and Hasher 1987; Segal 1966) distinctions are currently popular ways of classifying tests. We deviate from current practice because we now believe that both classifications have outlived their usefulness. The explicit/implicit terminology is used interchangeably to refer both to tasks and to the hypothetical forms of memory assumed to be tapped by those tasks. The logical problems of making such an identification have been discussed at length (Richardson-Klavehn and Bjork 1988*a*), the principal one being that this interchangeability can lead one to make an *a-priori* assumption that explicit and implicit test performance reflect different underlying retrieval strategies and states of awareness. Richardson-Klavehn and Bjork (1988*a*) adopted and refined the direct/indirect nomenclature in order to draw attention to, and avoid, such *transparency* (Dunn and Kirsner 1989) or *process-purity* (Jacoby 1991) assumptions. As defined by Richardson-Klavehn and Bjork, the two kinds of tests are distinguished solely in terms of observables, the most important difference being one of instructions: in a direct test the instructions refer to a past event, whereas in an indirect test they do not. However, as noted by Roediger and McDermott (1993), the direct/indirect distinction has the disadvantage that it is potentially confusable with the distinction between *direct* (repetition) and *indirect* (associative) priming introduced by Cofer (1967). In addition, these terms have been taken by some to reflect an assumption of process-purity that was not originally intended—a debasement that represents a violation of the principle of *inconvertibility of terms* (Gardiner and Java 1993*a*). This principle prohibits the use of the same labels for tasks, theoretical constructs, and subjective states of awareness.

Here we follow Jacoby (1984) in suggesting that the well-known distinction between *intentional* and *incidental* learning can be fruitfully applied to the classification of memory tests. In an *intentional* memory test the subjects are instructed to try to retrieve information concerning a prior event. In an *incidental* memory test, subjects engage in a cognitive task that makes sense without mental reference to the event whose impact is under study, and subjects are not instructed to try to retrieve information concerning that event. The label *incidental*—in contrast to the more typical *implicit* or *indirect* nomenclature—highlights two important points:

1. The instructions in an incidental test *may* or *may not* make reference to a past event. Recent data (reviewed here) suggest that informing subjects of the relation between the study and test phases of an experiment, but requesting that they nevertheless do not try to retrieve items encountered in the study phase, may be the best way of ensuring that test performance reflects involuntary—and not voluntary—retrieval. Such tests do not qualify as indirect tests (as defined by Richardson-Klavehn and Bjork) because the instructions make reference to a prior event. Furthermore, labelling such tests as implicit is potentially misleading because explicit reference is made to the study–test relationship.

2. The fact that the subject is not instructed to try to recollect past events in an incidental test *does not guarantee* that they will not adopt a voluntary retrieval strategy. In much the same way, incidental learning instructions at encoding do not guarantee that a subject will not adopt a strategy of trying to remember the studied material. Whether or not incidental test performance reflects voluntary or involuntary retrieval must be determined from data. Similarly, involuntary retrieval might contribute to performance in an intentional test (e.g. Jacoby *et al.* 1993*b*; Richardson-Klavehn and Bjork 1988*a*). This test classification, therefore, avoids the pitfalls inherent in equating retrieval strategies with tasks.

3.0.2 Retrieval volition and memorial state of awareness

Dissociations between intentional and incidental memory tests have been assumed to require a distinction between underlying forms of memory, such as that between *memory with* and *memory without awareness* (Jacoby and Witherspoon 1982), *explicit* and *implicit memory* (Graf and Schacter 1985), *intentional consciously controlled memory* and *automatic unconscious memory* (e.g. Jacoby 1991), or simply *conscious* and *unconscious memory* (e.g. Merikle and Reingold 1991). All of these dichotomies fail to distinguish consciousness of memory in the sense of *volition* (i.e. the will to retrieve previously encountered information from memory) from consciousness of memory in the sense of *awareness* in relation to past events (i.e. the knowledge that a current mental state is 'about' the past). In consequence, they fail to accommodate Ebbinghaus' (1885/1964, p. 2) observation that 'mental states once present in consciousness return to it with apparent spontaneity and without any act of the will; that is, they are reproduced *involuntarily*'. Following Ebbinghaus, we classify such phenomena as instances of *involuntary conscious memory*. The framework we put forward here explicitly distinguishes between *retrieval strategy* (*voluntary* vs. *involuntary*) and *memorial state of awareness (conscious* vs. *unconscious*), so that involuntary conscious memory can be accommodated.

Involuntary conscious memory apparently occurs commonly in everyday mental life, such as when the reinstatement of certain environmental cues (e.g. an odour, a melody, or a physical location) triggers spontaneous recollection of events associated with those cues. Involuntary conscious memory has also been implicated in analogical reminding in problem solving tasks (Lockhart and Blackburn 1993), and may be implicated in post-traumatic stress disorders in which patients are unable to avoid vivid and unpleasant recollective experiences corresponding to the stressful event. Involuntary cueing effects that lead to conscious awareness of past events can be masked in studies in which all subjects are instructed to try and retrieve previously encountered information (Bjork and Richardson-Klavehn 1989). In consequence, incidental tests, in which subjects are not instructed to engage in voluntary retrieval, should be more likely than are intentional tests to reveal involuntary conscious memory. We will present evidence that involuntary conscious memory occurs frequently in incidental tests, and will trace the consequences of taking involuntary conscious memory into account when interpreting task dissociations.

It is not often recognized that Ebbinghaus made an explicit distinction between retrieval volition and memorial state of awareness (for an exception, see Roediger and Blaxton 1987). In fact, Ebbinghaus distinguished two classes of memory in addition to involuntary conscious memory, one of which we label *voluntary conscious memory*. This term refers to cases in which '. . . we can call back into consciousness by an exertion of the will directed to this purpose the seemingly lost states; that is, we can reproduce them *voluntarily*' (p. 1). The remaining class of memories consists of cases in which 'vanished mental states give indubitable proof of their continuing existence even if they themselves do not return to consciousness at all . . . Employment of a certain range of thought facilitates under certain conditions the employment of a similar range of thought, even if the former does not come before the mind directly either in its methods or in its results' (p. 2). Here Ebbinghaus uncannily anticipates cases in which effects of prior experiences have been revealed in incidental tests in the absence both of a voluntary retrieval strategy *and* of conscious awareness of the prior events leading to priming (e.g. Eich 1984; Kunst-Wilson and Zajonc 1980). We refer to such cases as instances of *involuntary unconscious memory*.

To emphasize the distinction between awareness and volition in our framework, we refer to voluntary and involuntary *retrieval strategies*. The expression *involuntary strategy* may initially seem to involve a contradiction, because the term *strategy* implies purpose or intention. What we mean, however, is that such a strategy is involuntary *with respect to memory for the events whose impact is under study*. It is a convenient shorthand way of distinguishing, for example, a strategy of responding with the first item coming to mind from a strategy of responding with studied items. Further, this term has the distinct advantage that it makes clear that the subject's behaviour is *always* strategically guided, even when it is not guided by a strategy of retrieving previously encountered information.

In contrast to Ebbinghaus's framework, ours allows the logical possibility that a voluntary retrieval strategy is not accompanied by conscious awareness of a past event. Little systematic evidence is available with respect to this issue, and the existence of such cases is not critical to the arguments presented in the current chapter. One kind of case we have in mind, though, is when constructive retrieval strategies produce information about a prior event for which subjects have no recollective experience or feelings of familiarity. A further difference between our framework and that of Ebbinghaus is that we make a distinction between two forms of conscious awareness of a prior event, *recollection and familiarity*. Following Tulving (1985), *remembering* refers to recollection of a prior event—the ability, for example, to recollect what one was thinking when a particular study-list item was presented. *Knowing* refers to conscious feelings of familiarity in the absence of recollection. A wide variety of evidence supports the validity of this distinction (for reviews see Gardiner and Java 1993*a*,*b*; Rajaram and Roediger in press), and we do not review that literature here. We will, however, describe powerful new data showing that these forms of memorial awareness can be separated empirically, and discuss the extent to which memorial experiences of these two types are involved in incidental tests of memory.

The major thesis of the current chapter is that any adequate theoretical approach to issues of memory and consciousness must make clear distinctions between different levels of theoretical description. Descriptions of subjective states of memorial awareness must not be conflated with descriptions of retrieval strategies, which in turn must not be conflated with descriptions of retrieval processes or the memory representations on which those processes operate. Most critically, failure to distinguish retrieval strategies from memorial states of awareness can lead to serious misinterpretation: (a) of task dissociations in experiments comparing intentional and incidental memory tests; (b) of the results of Jacoby's (1991) *process-dissociation analysis*; and (c) of the implications of experiments in which subjects report directly on their state of consciousness at test by making 'remember' or 'know' responses. We consider each of these issues in turn.

3.1 TASK DISSOCIATIONS: THE ROLES OF RETRIEVAL VOLITION AND SUBJECTIVE AWARENESS OF THE PAST

Recent publications reflect increasing concern that the performance of normal subjects in incidental tests of memory is 'contaminated' by explicit or conscious memory (e.g. Jacoby *et al.* 1993*b*). In terms of our framework, such contamination could either mean that subjects in incidental tests engage in voluntary retrieval of studied items, or that subjects become aware of the global relationship between the encoding and test phases of the experiment, and perhaps also of particular previously encountered items, but that they nevertheless use an involuntary rather than a voluntary retrieval strategy. Confusing these possibilities could lead to serious overestimation of the problem of 'explicit contamination'.

3.1.1 The problem of voluntary retrieval in incidental tests

Although not instructed to do so, subjects may make deliberate attempts to retrieve studied items in an incidental test owing to demand characteristics (e.g. if they suspect the 'true purpose' of the task), or owing to a desire to avoid failure in difficult tasks like fragment completion and perceptual identification. The possibility of such contamination makes it difficult to interpret the growing number of reports of parallel effects of manipulated variables on intentional and incidental tests (e.g Blaxton 1989; Challis and Brodbeck 1992; Eich 1984; Graf and Mandler 1984; Hamann 1990; Jacoby and Dallas 1981; Macleod 1989; Sloman *et al.* 1988; Srinivas and Roediger 1990). Parallel effects of this kind have been interpreted as showing that voluntary and involuntary retrieval were similarly influenced by the experimental manipulation (e.g. Jacoby 1983*a*; Jacoby and Brooks 1984). However, such data are also compatible with the view that voluntary retrieval strategies played a role in both types of test (Richardson-Klavehn and Bjork 1988*a*).

An obvious response to these concerns is to argue that research on memory and awareness should rely primarily on memory-disordered subjects, who are unlikely to engage in voluntary retrieval in an incidental test. Amnesic subjects, for example, often show unimpaired incidental test performance in conjunction with severely impaired or chance performance in an intentional test (Shimamura 1986). Such a response, however, is less than satisfactory. Subject groups in studies of memory-disordered populations are typically small and variable. Under these conditions, it can in practice be difficult to determine whether or not incidental test performance is completely unimpaired (Ostergaard and Jernigan 1993; Shimamura 1993). Moreover, there are now a considerable number of published reports in which amnesics and other memory-disordered subjects have shown significant deficits (compared to normal controls) in both incidental and intentional tests (e.g. Cermak *et al.* 1986; Cohen and Squire 1980; Johnson *et al.* 1985; Martone *et al.* 1984; Squire *et al.* 1987; for reviews see Bowers and Schacter 1993; Ostergaard and Jernigan 1993; Richardson-Klavehn and Bjork 1988*a*). In consequence, it is essential to know whether the deficit in the incidental test reflects the use of a voluntary retrieval strategy by control subjects, or whether the brain structures responsible for involuntary memory have been damaged in the memory-disordered subjects (Ostergaard and Jernigan 1993; Schacter 1985). One cannot escape the conclusion that research on memory and awareness will need to rely on normal as well as amnesic subjects.

In normal subjects, *crossed double dissociations* (Dunn and Kirsner 1988) between intentional and incidental tests have seemed to be the strongest evidence that incidental test performance does not reflect voluntary retrieval (e.g. Allen and Jacoby 1990). Such dissociations occur when the same variable influences intentional and incidental tests in opposite ways (for reviews see Richardson-Klavehn and Bjork 1988*a*; Roediger and McDermott 1993). For example, generating a word at study produces better recall and recognition memory than does reading that word; in contrast, priming in a test of perceptual identification is greater following reading than following generating (e.g. Jacoby 1983*b*; Winnick and Daniel 1970). The argument concerning retrieval volition is simple: how could priming depend on voluntary retrieval when generating (compared to reading) enhances performance in a test requiring voluntary retrieval (recognition memory), but simultaneously impairs priming in a test not requiring voluntary retrieval (perceptual identification)? This argument seems particularly powerful because of the measurement properties of crossed double dissociations. Such patterns of data consist of an ordinal rearrangement of the population means corresponding to the encoding conditions across the two kinds of test. In consequence, the claim that the tests have been dissociated does not depend on the tests having comparable measurement scales.

Unfortunately, the conclusion that such patterns represent evidence for a difference in retrieval volition between tests is not necessarily sound—despite the indisputable measurement properties of crossed double dissociations. Studies showing such patterns have typically used intentional and incidental tests that present different cues to the subject, as well as different instructions. In the Jacoby (1983*b*) study, for example, the cues were either data-limited (perceptual identification) or non-data-limited (recognition memory). That differences in retrieval cues can create similar data patterns in the absence of differences in retrieval volition is clearly indicated by reports of crossed double dissociations between intentional tests such as meaning- and appearance-based recognition memory (Stein 1978), free recall and graphemically cued recall (Blaxton 1989), and free recall and cued recall with word-fragment cues (Weldon *et al.* 1989). These dissociations can be attributed to an interaction between the informational demands of the tests, which have been differentiated in terms of the distinction between *conceptually driven* and *data-driven processing* (e.g. Jacoby 1983*b*; Roediger and Blaxton 1987), and the type of information encoded in the study phase (conceptual vs. perceptual).

Richardson-Klavehn *et al.* (1994*b*) examined whether the kind of dissociation reported by Jacoby (1983*b*) is attributable to a difference in retrieval volition between tests or to a difference in test cues. They used a within-subject manipulation of conceptual versus perceptual processing at encoding that was designed to have the same effect as a generate/read manipulation: In the Auditory-Deep condition, words were presented auditorily and subjects judged how recently they had encountered the referent of each word; in the Visual-Shallow condition, words were visually presented and subjects counted the number of enclosed spaces in the letters of each word (cf. Graf and Mandler 1984). Subjects then received either a visual recognition memory test, or a visual perceptual identification test. The perceptual identification test was conducted under two instructional conditions: one group of subjects was instructed to use their memory for studied items to help them identify the test items (intentional test group). The other group was simply asked to identify the test items, and no mention was made of the presence of previously encountered words (incidental test group). The data from the simplest of Richardson-Klavehn *et al.*'s three experiments are presented in Table 3.1.

Comparing the data for the recognition memory and incidental test groups reveals a crossed double dissociation similar to that reported by Jacoby (1983*b*). The pattern observed in this case is particularly impressive

Table 3.1 Proportions of items recognized and identified in Richardson- Klavehn *et al.* (1994*b*, experiment 3)

Test type (Instructions)	Studied		
	Auditory-deep	Visual-shallow	Unstudied
Recognition memory	0.97	0.52	0.17[a]
Perceptual identification (Incidental)	0.40 (0.07)	0.50 (0.17*)	0.33
Perceptual identification (Intentional)	0.57 (0.20*)	0.52 (0.15*)	0.37

Means in parentheses are priming scores. Significant priming is indicated by an asterisk.
[a] False alarm rate.

because Auditory-Deep encoding led to excellent recognition memory performance ($d' = 3.1$), but did not produce significant priming in perceptual identification. On the other hand, Visual-Shallow encoding led to rather poor recognition memory performance ($d' = 1.1$), but produced significant priming in perceptual identification. The critical new data come from the intentional test group in perceptual identification. In contrast to the incidental test group, this group showed significant priming in both encoding conditions, Auditory-Deep encoding producing somewhat greater (although not significantly greater) priming than Visual-Shallow encoding.

To confirm that the use of a voluntary retrieval strategy in the intentional test of perceptual identification removed the crossed double dissociation between recognition memory and the incidental test of perceptual identification, Richardson-Klavehn *et al.* (1994*b*) performed a non-parametric analysis, pooling the data across their three experiments, which had similar designs and showed similar data patterns. Subjects were classified as to whether they showed a numerical advantage of Auditory-Deep over Visual-Shallow encoding, a numerical advantage of Visual-Shallow over Auditory-Deep encoding, or no difference between encoding conditions. Classification was based on d' scores for recognition memory subjects ($n = 72$), and on priming scores for perceptual identification subjects ($n = 64$ for each instructional group). The resulting frequencies are presented in Table 3.2. Sign tests indicated a highly significant advantage of Auditory-Deep over Visual-Shallow encoding for recognition memory, and a highly significant advantage of Visual-Shallow over Auditory-Deep encoding for the incidental test group in perceptual identification. Most critically, however, there was a significant advantage of Auditory-Deep over Visual-Shallow encoding for the intentional test group in perceptual identification ($P < 0.025$, two-tailed). This difference between encoding conditions was consistent across experiments, and quite consistent across

Table 3.2 Frequency of ordinal arrangements of scores for the two encoding conditions in Richardson-Klavehn *et al.* (1994*b*, experiments 1–3)

Test type (Instructions)	Ordinal arrangement of scores: Auditory-deep> Visual-shallow	Visual-shallow> Auditory-deep	Auditory-deep = Visual-shallow
Recognition memory ($n = 72$)	72	00	00
Perceptual identification (Incidental; $n = 64$)	11	39	14
Perceptual identification (Intentional; $n = 64$)	34	17	13

subjects, but was not numerically large enough to be significant at the level of the individual experiment.

To summarize, these data provide strong evidence that the observed crossed double dissociation between recognition memory and priming was attributable to a difference in retrieval volition between tests, and not just to a difference in test cues, because that dissociation disappeared when voluntary retrieval was encouraged in perceptual identification. Under intentional retrieval instructions, the relationship of priming to recognition memory changed from negative to weakly positive. Formally speaking, therefore, the overall data pattern qualifies as a *reversed association* (Dunn and Kirsner 1988, 1989) between tests. A reversed association occurs when the same pair of tests shows both a negative association (i.e. a crossed double dissociation) and a positive association (i.e. a parallel effect).

The data presented by Richardson-Klavehn *et al.* (1994*b*) encourage the conclusion that incidental test performance predominantly reflects involuntary retrieval when a crossed double dissociation between intentional and incidental tests is observed. Further strong evidence for this conclusion comes from a study by Java (1994), who used a stem-completion task, administered under either intentional or incidental test conditions. In the former test condition, subjects attempted to complete the three-letter stems with words from the study list; in the latter test condition, subjects simply completed the stems with the first word coming to mind. As in the Jacoby (1983*b*) study, items were either generated (e.g. *Not a victory*: D———) or read (e.g *DEFEAT*) in the study phase. The data from Java's experiment 2 are presented in Table 3.3. As would be expected from prior results, intentional test instructions resulted in a strong advantage for generate over read items in terms of proportion correctly recalled. Under incidental test conditions a different pattern was observed: both generating and reading at study enhanced the tendency to complete stems with target items, but this priming effect was greater for read items than for generate items. Java's design conforms strictly to the *retrieval intentionality criterion* proposed by Schacter *et al.* (1989). That is, the physical test cues were identical across the intentional and incidental

Table 3.3 Proportions of stems completed with target items in Java (1994, experiment 2)

	Studied		
Instructions	Generate	Read	Unstudied
Intentional	0.41	0.22	0.04
Incidental	0.34	0.47	0.15

test conditions. Remarkably, a crossed double dissociation between tests was nevertheless observed. As in the Richardson-Klavehn *et al.* (1994*b*) study, therefore, the observed dissociation can be conclusively attributed to a difference in retrieval volition between tests.

The data presented thus far seem to give strong support to the argument that incidental test performance in normal subjects does not reflect voluntary retrieval. However, these data do not justify such a strong conclusion; they only justify the conclusion that intentional test performance relies *predominantly* on voluntary retrieval and that incidental test performance relies *predominantly* on involuntary retrieval. Incidental test performance, therefore, might still reflect voluntary retrieval by some subjects on some test items, but might not be sufficiently contaminated to remove the dissociation between tests. Under other experimental conditions, a degree of contamination that would not remove a crossed double dissociation might be sufficient to produce the kind of parallel effects on intentional and incidental tests referred to above. In consequence, as argued by Richardson-Klavehn and Bjork (1988*a*), parallel effects across intentional and incidental measures must be interpreted with caution, and convergent evidence must be sought to show that such effects do not reflect an influence of voluntary retrieval on the incidental test. We address the problem of contamination by voluntary retrieval strategies further in relation to Jacoby's (1991) process-dissociation procedure, which is claimed to overcome these problems. Next, however, we turn to the question of whether the striking task dissociations we have described constitute evidence for systematic inter-task differences in memorial awareness, as well as evidence for inter-task differences in retrieval strategy.

3.1.2 Awareness of the study–test relationship in incidental tests

Researchers have often attempted to 'disguise' incidental tests by administering them as one of a number of other tasks, by describing the test as a filler or distractor activity prior to a 'real' memory test, or by incorporating only a small proportion of studied items in the test phase. The assumption is that such measures prevent subjects from becoming aware of the relationship between the test and prior encoding events. Recent data render this assumption highly questionable. Richardson-Klavehn *et al.* (1994*b*) explored the relationship between awareness of the encoding episode and incidental test performance in the context of the crossed double dissociation between recognition memory and perceptual identification priming described previously. They used the kind of *test-awareness* measure initially developed by Bowers and Schacter (1990). After completing the perceptual identification test, subjects filled out a questionnaire that asked them whether or not they were aware

Table 3.4 Reported state of awareness and retrieval strategy in perceptual identification in Richardson-Klavehn *et al.* (1994*b*, experiments 1 and 3)

	Test-aware		
Instructions	Voluntary	Involuntary	Test-unaware
Incidental (n = 48)	19 (1)	27 (6)	02
Intentional (n = 48)	43	05	00

Data in parentheses are the numbers of test-aware subjects in the incidental group who suspected prior to the test that studied items would appear. The remainder realized during the test.

that some of the flashed items had been presented to them prior to the test phase. If they classified themselves as test-aware, they answered the remaining questions, which asked them: (a) whether they had suspected prior to the test that previously encountered items would be presented, or whether they had realized at some point during the test; and (b) whether or not they had actively tried to use their memory for previously encountered items to help them identify test items. The questionnaire was administered to subjects in both the intentional and incidental test groups in experiments 1 and 3 (a total of 48 subjects per instructional condition). The results are displayed in Table 3.4.

Responses to the questionnaire for intentional test subjects were consistent with expectation: these subjects were test-aware by virtue of the instructions, and the vast majority reported use of a voluntary retrieval strategy. However, the responses of incidental test subjects were surprising, especially when considered in relation to their perceptual identification performance. Only 2 of 48 subjects in that group classified themselves as unaware that the test contained previously encountered items. Test-awareness was ubiquitous even though the percentage of test items that had been previously studied was quite small in both cases (25 per cent in experiment 1 and 30 per cent in experiment 3). Subjects rarely indicated that they had suspected prior to the test that it would contain old items; instead, the majority indicated that they realized at some point during the test. This realization must have occurred spontaneously because the instructions made no reference to previously encountered items. Most importantly, the performance data show that incidental test performance predominantly reflected involuntary retrieval, *despite* this spontaneous awareness: had awareness of the study–test relation always resulted in the use of a voluntary retrieval strategy, incidental test performance could not have shown a crossed double dissociation from recognition memory performance (by the logic described in the previous section). Responses of incidental test subjects to the questionnaire item concerning voluntary retrieval are consistent with this reasoning: the majority indicated that they did not adopt a voluntary retrieval strategy. In sum, the data suggest that awareness of the study–test relationship during an incidental test is compatible with an involuntary retrieval strategy.

Data from self-report measures of this kind must, of course, be interpreted with caution. Demand characteristics may have induced subjects to report awareness of the study–test relation (e.g. because subjects were unwilling to admit that they did not realize that their memory was being tested). Alternatively, subjects might have become aware of the presence of previously encountered items at the time of the questionnaire itself. These artefacts, however, seem highly unlikely in the current case: first, if demand characteristics caused subjects to report test-awareness, such demand characteristics should also have induced them to indicate suspecting that the test would relate to prior events, and to indicate using a voluntary retrieval strategy. Secondly, Richardson-Klavehn *et al.* (1994*b*), during debriefing in experiment 3, found that subjects were reliably able to indicate on their test protocol at what point in the test they first noticed the presence of a previously encountered item.

The dissociation of strategy and test awareness found by Richardson-Klavehn *et al.* (1994*b*) is also apparent in data obtained by Bowers and Schacter (1990) in a stem-completion paradigm. In their *test-uninformed* condition, these authors went to much greater lengths than did Richardson-Klavehn *et al.* to disguise the nature of their incidental test, and in consequence found a smaller percentage of test-aware subjects (50 per cent). Test-aware subjects showed a significant effect of depth of processing at study on priming, whereas test-unaware subjects did not. Depth-of-processing effects on stem completion are powerful under intentional test conditions, but are typically attenuated or absent under incidental test conditions (e.g. Graf and Mandler 1984), and so are usually assumed to reflect voluntary retrieval strategies (e.g. Schacter *et al.* 1989). This result might, therefore, be taken to mean that awareness of the study–test relationship is perfectly correlated with the use of a voluntary retrieval strategy. This hypothesis, however, is inconsistent with the results of Bowers and Schacter's *test-informed* condition. Subjects in that condition were told that some of the test stems corresponded to studied words, but were asked to employ an involuntary retrieval strategy (i.e. to give the first completion coming to mind) despite this knowledge. Like test-unaware subjects, these subjects showed no effect of depth of processing on priming.

The implication of the Bowers and Schacter (1990) results, taken together with those of Richardson-Klavehn *et al.* (1994*b*), is that awareness of the study–test relationship is not the critical variable determining whether or not dissociations between intentional and incidental tests are observed. What is critical is whether or not incidental test subjects adopt a voluntary retrieval strategy. Spontaneous awareness of the study–test relationship evidently prompts some subjects to adopt such a strategy. It is possible that the extreme measures that Bowers and Schacter took to conceal the purpose of the stem-completion task in their test-uninformed condition resulted in relatively few test-aware subjects, but increased the probability that voluntary retrieval strategies would come into play (e.g. owing to demand characteristics) for those subjects who did become test-aware. In consequence, a strategy of measuring involuntary memory by attempting to 'disguise' memory tests may misfire. In future work, it seems advisable to inform subjects of the study–test relationship, but to request that they nevertheless do not voluntarily retrieve studied items (as in Bowers and Schacter's test-informed condition). It is sobering to note that such instructions were exactly the kind used in some of the early reports of striking dissociations between intentional and incidental tests in normal subjects (e.g. Tulving *et al.* 1982). The value of these incidental test instructions is further illustrated in the work to be described next.

3.1.3 On-line measures of awareness in incidental tests

Questionnaire measures, of course, only allow one to examine subjects' awareness of the global relationship between the study and test phases of an experiment. Subjects will qualify as test-aware even if they only become aware that one test item corresponds to a previously presented item (Bowers and Schacter 1990). Many of their other test responses may nevertheless be unassociated with conscious awareness of the past. In this section we describe experiments in which we have obtained item-by-item measures of awareness in incidental tests. The data provide further strong evidence for the need to distinguish retrieval strategy (voluntary vs. involuntary) from state of awareness with respect to the past (conscious vs. unconscious).

Richardson-Klavehn *et al.* (1994*a*) developed an item-by-item measure of awareness in a word-stem completion paradigm by adapting the *method of opposition* introduced by Jacoby *et al.* (1989*b*). We used three between-subjects test conditions which differed only in terms of instructions, the physical test cues being identical. The first two were an intentional test condition (in which subjects were instructed to use the test stems as cues to retrieve studied words) and an incidental test condition (in which subjects were instructed to complete the stems with the first word coming to mind, and the instructions made no reference to study events). Subjects in the third, and critical, *opposition* test condition were instructed to complete each stem with the first word coming to mind, but to write down another word if the word that initially occurred to them had been previously presented. Depth of processing of study words was manipulated within subjects: the words were presented visually, and subjects either generated a related word (Associate condition) or counted the number of enclosed spaces in the letters of the word (Enclosure condition).

The intentional and incidental test conditions constituted a conceptual replication of a design used on a number of prior occasions (e.g. Graf and Mandler 1984; Roediger *et al.* 1992; Schacter and Graf 1986). Based on the results of those experiments, one would expect to obtain a *single dissociation* (Dunn and Kirsner 1988) between tasks. That is, cued recall (intentional test) should show a strong advantage for Associate over Enclosure encoding. Priming in the incidental test, by contrast, should show no influence of depth of processing—but only if subjects in that condition do not employ a voluntary retrieval strategy. In terms of the framework presented here, this pattern of data would permit the conclusion that the involuntary tendency to produce Associate and Enclosure items in stem completion was approximately the same. One could not conclude, however, that subjects' states of memorial awareness were the same for Associate and Enclosure items. Nor could one conclude that priming was unassociated with awareness of the study event for items in either encoding condition.

We reasoned that the opposition test condition would permit a measure of the extent to which subjects' stem completion responses reflected memory that was not only involuntary, but also unconscious. If involuntary retrieval caused a word to come to mind, but that word was associated with conscious awareness of the study event, subjects should omit that word and write down another word. A facilitatory priming effect, therefore, would be observed only when involuntary influences that were unconscious outweighed involuntary influences that were accompanied by conscious awareness (hence the term *opposition* test). The data are presented in Table 3.5. Performance in the intentional and incidental test conditions was as expected. Depth of processing exerted a strong and significant effect on cued recall ($P < 0.001$), but a weak and non-significant effect on priming when subjects were instructed to

Table 3.5 Proportions of stems completed with target items in Richardson-Klavehn *et al.* (1994*a*)

	Studied		
Test type	Associate	Enclosure	Unstudied
Intentional	0.52	0.06	0.01
Incidental	0.32 (+0.15*)	0.29 (+0.12*)	0.17
Opposition	0.04 (−0.09*)	0.20 (+0.07*)	0.13

Means in parentheses are priming scores. An asterisk indicates a significant difference from the Unstudied baseline.

give the first word coming to mind ($P > 0.20$). In a post-test interview similar to that used by Bowers and Schacter (1990), *all* 24 incidental test subjects qualified as test-aware, but *none* stated that they had used a voluntary retrieval strategy. In conjunction with the performance data, therefore, these self-report data provide further confirmation of the argument made previously—that awareness of the study–test relationship must be distinguished from voluntary retrieval of studied items.

Opposition test performance was strikingly different from incidental test performance. Target items in the Associate encoding condition were less likely to be given as completions than were target items that had not been previously studied—an inhibition effect. On the other hand, items in the Enclosure encoding condition showed a numerically small but statistically reliable facilitatory priming effect ($P < 0.025$), despite the instructions to suppress studied items. We attach particular significance to this combination of inhibition and facilitation within the same group of subjects, because it rules out certain plausible, but uninteresting, explanations of the facilitation effect (e.g. that it occurred because subjects did not understand the test instructions, or because they disobeyed instructions to suppress studied items owing to demand characteristics).

The opposition test was identical to the incidental test in terms of encoding conditions and physical test cues, and the instructions differed only in one critical respect. Both groups of subjects were told to complete stems with the first word coming to mind, but the opposition test instructions additionally required subjects to omit words coming to mind that they had encountered previously. The involuntary tendency to complete stems with studied words should, therefore, have been the same for the two groups. The difference in performance should lie in the fact that opposition test subjects suppressed words associated with awareness of the past, whereas incidental test subjects did not. The Associate encoding condition involved semantic processing, which leads to good recollection of prior events (e.g. Gardiner 1988). The Enclosure condition, on the other hand, involved minimal semantic processing, so subjects should be less likely to be aware that they were producing enclosure words. In consequence, the facilitatory priming effect observed in that condition can be attributed not only to involuntary memory, but also to unconscious memory.

The dissociation in performance between the incidental and opposition tests provides further evidence for a distinction between retrieval strategy (voluntary vs. involuntary) and memorial state of awareness (conscious vs. unconscious). Performance in the incidental test reflected involuntary memory, whether associated or unassociated with conscious awareness of the past, whereas performance in the opposition test reflected only involuntary unconscious memory. By implication, the *difference* in performance (specifically, the difference in priming effects) between

Table 3.6 Stem-completion proportions for unrecognized items in the incidental test condition in Richardson-Klavehn *et al.* (1994*a*)

	Studied		
Test type	Associate	Enclosure	Unstudied
Incidental	0.05	0.25	0.15
Opposition	0.04	0.20	0.13

the two tests represents an estimate of involuntary conscious memory. This difference was much larger in the Associate condition than in the Enclosure condition, leading to the conclusion that Associate encoding resulted in a higher level of conscious memory than did enclosure encoding, even though the two encoding conditions produced an approximately equivalent involuntary tendency to complete stems with studied words.

The interpretation of opposition test performance that we have advanced involves two critical assumptions: (a) that voluntary retrieval played a minimal role in stem completion in both the incidental and opposition tests; and (b) that the facilitation effect in the opposition test caused by Enclosure encoding was associated neither with recollection of a prior event nor with feelings of familiarity. Evidence consistent with both these assumptions comes from a recognition test administered to both test groups after the stem-completion test. Subjects examined their own stem completions and judged whether or not each item they had produced had been previously presented. The first critical finding was that opposition test subjects were completely unable to recognize studied items that they had produced in stem completion. Rates of recognition were very low, and recognition of studied items was somewhat less likely than was 'recognition' of unstudied items. The second critical finding was that incidental test subjects showed good recognition memory for Associate items that they had previously produced, but poor recognition memory for Enclosure items.

Table 3.6 re-presents the stem-completion data for the incidental and opposition test groups, but this time incidental test performance has been conditionalized on later recognition failure. Stem-completion performance in the incidental test was now statistically indistinguishable from stem-completion performance in the opposition test. Incidental test subjects completed the stems with the first word coming to mind, and later attempted to recognize the completions they had produced, so this similarity in performance is consistent with assumption (a) above. Opposition test subjects apparently followed a similar involuntary strategy for bringing completions to mind, but actually completed stems only with items that they failed to recognize. Such a strategy is also consistent with least-effort considerations, because bringing to mind an alternative completion for a stem costs time and effort. For most test items, the first completion coming to mind would not be from the study list, saving the effort of bringing an alternative completion to mind.[1]

Assumption (b) is supported by the finding that opposition test subjects could not recognize the studied items that they had produced. If the tendency to produce Enclosure items in stem completion was attributable to failure to recollect the context of the prior encounter, but was associated with feelings of familiarity as a result that of the prior encounter, then that familiarity should have served as the basis for discriminating studied from unstudied items in the recognition test. Moreover, the argument that the priming effect in the Enclosure condition was associated with feelings of familiarity in the absence of recollection renders the concept of familiarity almost meaningless. Familiarity is universally assumed to increase, not decrease, hit rate in recognition tests (e.g. Jacoby 1991; Jacoby *et al.* 1989*b*; Mandler 1980). Priming in the opposition test was inversely related to recognition hit rate, so feelings of familiarity would have rendered studied items *less*, not more, likely to be produced as responses.

The data presented thus far are consistent with the assumption that subjects in the opposition test follow an involuntary strategy for bringing candidate completions to mind, replacing with an alternative those candidate completions that are associated with awareness of the past. It would still, however, be possible to argue that voluntary retrieval was involved in bringing candidate completions to mind. One could assume that the most effective—if not the least effortful—strategy in such a test would be to try to retrieve a studied word for each stem. If a studied word was accessible, one could then be confident that one completed the stem with a non-studied word. Such an argument would undermine the claim that retrieval volition is dissociable from memorial awareness in stem completion, and the accompanying claim that the difference in performance between incidental and opposition tests represents a measure of involuntary conscious memory.

To distinguish between the competing assumptions, Richardson-Klavehn and Gardiner (1995) performed an empirical analysis of the mental activities that occur in the opposition test. Our method was to make explicit in subjects' behaviour the activities that are assumed to occur covertly in the opposition test: (a) under the hypothesis that candidate completions come to mind via involuntary retrieval, but that words

1. In debriefing, opposition test subjects often reported difficulty in bringing an alternative completion to mind when the first item coming to mind was from the study list. The accessibility of a particular completion may have the effect of 'blocking' alternative completions (see Nickerson 1984 for a discussion of blocking).

associated with awareness of the past are suppressed; and (b) under the hypothesis that candidate completions come to mind via voluntary retrieval (i.e. a cued-recall strategy). The encoding conditions, materials, and test stems were precisely the same as those used by Richardson-Klavehn *et al.* (1994*a*). The three between-subjects test conditions differed only in terms of instructions ($n = 24$ per group). The instructions in the opposition test condition were the same as those used previously (i.e. to complete each stem with the first word coming to mind, but to omit studied words). There were two novel test conditions. In the incidental condition, subjects were told that some of the stems corresponded to words shown to them previously, but that they should nevertheless complete each stem with the first word coming to mind. If the first word coming to mind had been studied, however, they were to provide a second completion for that stem before moving on to the next stem. In the intentional condition, subjects were told to use the stems as cues for the recall of studied words. For each stem, if they had recalled a word from the study list, they were to provide a second completion for that stem before moving on to the next stem. When they were unable to recall a word from the study list, they were simply to complete the stem with the first word coming to mind.[2]

The incidental test condition involved exactly the same critical mental activities that occur in the opposition test, if opposition subjects complete each stem with the first word coming to mind (an involuntary strategy), omitting and replacing with an alternative those words that are recognized. When a second completion had been written for a particular item in the incidental test, one could infer that the subject believed he or she had initially written down a word from the study list, and that only the second completion would have appeared overtly had the subject received opposition test instructions. If incidental test subjects followed the instructions to use an involuntary strategy to bring completions to mind, the likelihood that a studied target word was written as a first completion should be uninfluenced by depth of processing at encoding. On the other hand, second completions should be more likely to be written after production of Associate words than after production of Enclosure words, indicating that Associate words were more frequently recognized as studied, and that those words would have been more frequently replaced with an alternative completion in an opposition test.

In contrast to the incidental test condition, the intentional test condition

2. After failure to recall, intentional test subjects might complete a stem with the first item coming to mind while recognizing that completion as studied. To indicate such occurrences, subjects were instructed to place an asterisk next to the completed item. In practice, however, such instances were extremely rare, and taking them into account has no influence on the pattern of data to be reported here.

involved exactly the same mental activities that occur in the opposition test, if opposition subjects try to retrieve a word from the study list as a completion to each stem, then omit recalled words and replace them with an alternative completion. Under this hypothesis, if opposition subjects were unable to recall a completion for a particular stem, they would then complete that stem with the first word coming to mind, precisely as intentional test subjects were instructed to do. In the intentional test, the likelihood that a word was classified by the subject as 'recalled' (i.e. the likelihood that the subject wrote a second completion for an item) should be strongly influenced by depth of processing. In addition, the likelihood that study list words would appear in stem completion should should be greater in the intentional test condition than in the incidental test condition, because the former condition involved trying to retrieve studied words, whereas the latter did not. This difference between the test conditions should be greatest for Associate items, because voluntary retrieval strategies typically depend on semantic information. The overall proportion of stems completed with targets should, therefore, also show a depth-of-processing effect, in contrast to the pattern predicted for the incidental test.

The data from both the incidental and intentional tests permit an estimate of opposition test performance to be obtained for each subject. For the incidental test, the estimate was obtained by subtracting the proportion of target items that were recognized from the overall proportion of stems completed with targets. For the intentional test, the estimate was obtained by subtracting the proportion of targets that were recalled from the overall proportion of stems completed with targets. It was then possible to compare these estimated opposition scores to observed opposition scores. The logic was that completions that were recognized (incidental test) or recalled (intentional test) would have been replaced by an alternative completion in an opposition test.[3]

The other measure of principal interest was the time taken to perform the stem-completion test. It was for this reason that incidental and intentional test subjects were required to provide second completions for recognized and recalled items, rather than simply indicate recognition or recall. Having them provide alternative completions meant that they had to engage in all the mental activities hypothesized to occur in the opposition test. We assumed that a voluntary retrieval strategy (i.e. using

3. In the incidental test, subjects could falsely recognize a non-target completion, then produce a target item as a second completion. Similarly, in the intentional test, subjects could falsely recall a non-target completion, then produce a target item as a second completion. In both cases, these target items would appear in overt stem-completion responses in an opposition test, because they would replace the non-target items. Such cases, however, were never actually observed in the incidental test, and occurred so rarely in the intentional test as not to influence the estimated pattern of opposition test performance.

Table 3.7 Mean number of seconds required to complete a test item (with standard deviation and range) as a function of test instructions in Richardson-Klavehn and Gardiner (1995)

	Instructions		
Statistic	Opposition	Incidental	Intentional
M	3.9	3.8	9.2
SD	0.8	0.7	2.5
Range	2.6–5.5	2.7–5.7	5.4–13.7

the stems as cues to retrieve studied words) would be more effortful—and therefore more time-consuming—than an involuntary retrieval strategy (i.e. completing stems with the first word coming to mind). A voluntary strategy should take longer than an involuntary one at the level of the individual item, but also because a voluntary strategy should result in production of more studied words, so that intentional test subjects would have to provide more alternative completions than would incidental test subjects. For both these reasons, intentional test subjects should take longer to perform the test than should incidental test subjects. Most important, if opposition subjects were employing an involuntary stem-completion strategy, their mean time should be similar to that of incidental test subjects; by contrast, if they were employing a voluntary stem-completion strategy, their mean time should be similar to that of intentional test subjects.

The instructions in all three test conditions required subjects to work through the test 'quite briskly', ensuring that the different stem-completion instructions did not create differences in time pressure. Subjects were tested individually, and the experimenter turned on a stopwatch when each subject turned the test booklet over, and turned it off when the subject completed the last test item. The subject's total time in seconds was divided by the number of stems in the test, giving the mean number of seconds per test item. These scores were then averaged to obtain the mean number of seconds per item for each test group (see Table 3.7).

The completion-time data are clearly consistent with the hypothesis that opposition test subjects used an involuntary stem-completion strategy, and inconsistent with the hypothesis that they used a voluntary stem-completion strategy. The mean times for the opposition and incidental test groups were almost exactly the same, and the distributions were almost completely overlapping. On the other hand, the mean time for the intentional test group was much longer than the mean times for the opposition and incidental test groups, and the distribution of times

Table 3.8 Proportion stems completed, proportion completions recognized, and opposition estimates in the incidental test condition in Richardson-Klavehn and Gardiner (1995)

	Studied		
Measure	Associate	Enclosure	Unstudied
Completion	0.31	0.27	0.14
Recognition	0.28	0.04	0.004
Opposition (estimated)	0.03	0.23	0.14
Opposition (observed)	0.05	0.26	0.14

in that group showed little overlap with the distributions in the other two groups.[4] The results of a structured post-test interview given to incidental and opposition test subjects provided convergent evidence for an involuntary strategy. None of the 24 incidental test subjects stated that they had tried to retrieve studied items. Similarly, none of the 24 opposition test subjects stated that they had tried to retrieve studied items; in fact, when asked whether they had tried, a number of these subjects spontaneously responded with a version of the least-effort argument that we made previously. That is, they stated that it would be counterproductive to try to retrieve studied words, because doing so would make it more difficult to find a non-studied completion.

The stem-completion data for the incidental and opposition test conditions are presented in Table 3.8. The opposition test data (fourth row of the table) provide an exact replication of the opposition test data of Richardson-Klavehn *et al.* (1994*a*), presented previously in Table 3.5. Significant facilitatory priming was once again observed in the Enclosure encoding condition ($P < 0.001$), despite the instructions not to complete stems with studied words. The incidental test data also conformed to expectation. As in the incidental condition in the prior study, the proportion of stems completed with studied target words (first row) showed little influence of depth of processing ($P>0.30$), despite the fact that subjects in the current experiment were making on-line recognition decisions as they performed the stem-completion task. However, recognition of completions as studied (as indicated by the production of a second completion) was strongly influenced by depth of

4. As expected, intentional test subjects produced more studied words in stem completion than did incidental test subjects, so that they also had to provide additional completions for more of the stems. Richardson-Klavehn and Gardiner (1995) present additional analyses that show very clearly that the difference in stem-completion times between the incidental and intentional tests is not an artefact of the time taken to write down these additional completions.

processing (second row): the majority of Associate words were recognized, whereas the majority of Enclosure words were unrecognized. As a result, subtracting the proportion of targets recognized from the proportion of targets produced in stem completion resulted in quite accurate estimates of the observed proportion of targets produced in the opposition test (third row). Most critically, taking into account only unrecognized words in the incidental test, a significant facilitatory priming effect was observed in the Enclosure condition ($P < 0.001$), as was observed in the opposition test. In sum, the incidental test data show a striking dissociation of strategy and awareness within the same group of subjects. Stem completion predominantly reflected involuntary retrieval (as indicated by the failure to obtain a depth-of-processing effect on stem completion), but associate encoding produced awareness of the study event much more frequently than did enclosure encoding (as indicated by on-line recognition performance).

Table 3.9 shows the data from the intentional test condition. The opposition test data are once again presented for comparison. The first row of the table shows the overall proportion of stems completed with target words. In contrast to the pattern in the incidental test condition, Associate targets were more likely to be produced than were Enclosure targets, a significant depth-of-processing effect. As predicted, therefore, intentional test subjects produced more studied targets than did incidental test subjects, and this difference was largely confined to the Associate condition. The overall stem-completion proportions, of course, disregard whether a target word was defined as recalled (because a second completion was written), or whether it was simply given as the first completion coming to mind (because no second completion was written). The second row of the table shows the stem-completion proportions for words defined as recalled. These data replicate quite closely the cued recall data from Richardson-Klavehn *et al.* (1994*a*), recall of Associate words being much better than recall of Enclosure words, and false recall of unstudied target words being rare. In relation to the overall proportions of targets produced,

Table 3.9 Proportion stems completed, proportion completions recalled, and opposition estimates in the intentional test condition in Richardson-Klavehn and Gardiner (1995)

	Studied		
Measure	Associate	Enclosure	Unstudied
Completion	0.47	0.31	0.16
Recall	0.45	0.11	0.01
Opposition (estimated)	0.02	0.20	0.15
Opposition (observed)	0.05	0.26	0.14

the majority of Associate targets were recalled, whereas the majority of Enclosure and unstudied targets were produced as the first word coming to mind after a recall attempt had failed. Subtracting the proportions of words recalled from the overall stem-completion proportions gives an estimate of opposition test performance (third row). As for the estimates obtained from the incidental test condition, the pattern in these estimates is similar to that in the opposition test data (fourth row). However, the facilitatory priming effect for unrecalled words in the Enclosure condition was only marginally significant ($0.05 < P < 0.10$). The failure to obtain a significant priming effect for unrecalled Enclosure words (which stands in contrast to the significant effect obtained for unrecognized Enclosure words in the incidental test) could be attributable to the fact that intentional test subjects were able to recall a somewhat larger proportion of Enclosure words ($M = 0.11$) than incidental test subjects were able to recognize ($M = 0.04$). It could also reflect decay of priming, because intentional test subjects took longer to complete the test than did incidental and opposition test subjects. On the other hand, it could simply reflect sampling error.

To summarize, our most recent opposition test data replicate the striking pattern reported by Richardson-Klavehn *et al.* (1994*a*). In particular, a facilitatory priming effect occurred in stem completion following a superficial graphemic analysis at study, even though subjects were attempting not to respond with studied words. The predicted opposition test scores yielded by the incidental and intentional tests were broadly similar, although there was limited evidence to suggest that incidental test performance was a better predictor of stem-completion performance in the opposition test than was intentional test performance. We would expect, therefore, that observed stem-completion performance in an opposition test would be similar, whether or not subjects employed a voluntary or an involuntary strategy for bringing completions to mind. This observation, however, does not vitiate the conclusion made by Richardson-Klavehn *et al.* (1994*a*)—that the difference in performance between incidental and opposition tests provides a measure of involuntary conscious memory. We argued previously that priming in an incidental test predominantly reflects involuntary memory, but that priming is sometimes accompanied, and sometimes unaccompanied, by awareness that the target item has been previously encountered. Opposition test instructions were assumed to 'subtract out' those items that came to mind involuntarily, but were associated with conscious awareness of the past, so that the arithmetic difference in priming between the two tests represents an estimate of the level of involuntary conscious memory produced by a particular encoding condition. Our argument depended on the assumption that studied targets in the opposition test come to mind involuntarily, and not voluntarily. The current data confirm that assumption rather conclusively: (a) because stem-completion times for the opposition and incidental tests were similar, and much shorter than for the intentional test; and (b) because priming of stem completion in the incidental test showed no appreciable effect of depth of processing, even though awareness of completions as studied showed a large effect of depth of processing. The latter data confirm that one can obtain an on-line measure of awareness in a stem-completion task without violating the retrieval intentionality criterion of Schacter *et al.* (1989), and illustrate the value (for measuring involuntary memory) of informing subjects of the study–test relationship, but instructing them not to employ a voluntary retrieval strategy.

3.2 TASK DISSOCIATIONS VS. PROCESS DISSOCIATIONS

In this section we compare the empirical approach to repetition priming that we have adopted with the model-based approach taken by Jacoby and colleagues (e.g. Jacoby *et al.* 1993*b*; Toth *et al.* 1994), who also used a stem-completion test in which subjects were instructed to exclude studied completions from their responses. The purpose of their studies was to apply Jacoby's (1991) *process-dissociation procedure* to stem completion. This analysis was originally developed in order to separate the contributions of familiarity and recollection to observed recognition memory performance. However, it is now being put forward as a general framework for separating conscious and unconscious influences in perception and memory (e.g. Jacoby *et al.* 1992*a*,*b*, 1993).

Like our framework, the process-dissociation framework rejects assumptions of identity between tasks and strategies or processes. Unlike our framework, however, the process-dissociation framework makes a single distinction between forms of memory. These forms have been variously described as *recollection* and *familiarity*, *recollection* and *automatic* influences, *controlled* and *automatic* influences, or *conscious* and *unconscious* influences. In terms of our framework, therefore, the process-dissociation approach views retrieval volition and memorial state of awareness as perfectly correlated. Voluntary retrieval is identified with conscious memory, and involuntary (or automatic) retrieval is identified with unconscious memory. For that reason, the process-dissociation framework cannot accommodate cases in which involuntary influences of memory are accompanied by conscious awareness of the past (*involuntary conscious memory*). Further, the process-dissociation framework links familiarity with unconscious memory (e.g. Jacoby 1991). Our framework, by contrast, views familiarity as a form of conscious awareness of the past, but accommodates the possibility that familiarity can have effects that are not under voluntary control.

In order to separate conscious from unconscious memory, the process-dissociation framework prescribes a comparison of inclusion and exclusion test conditions. In the stem-completion paradigm, subjects in the inclusion condition attempt to recall a studied completion for each stem, but if recall fails they complete the stem with the first word coming to mind. Subjects in the exclusion condition are instructed to complete each stem, but not to use studied words. Inferences about the involvement of the two forms of memory are not made directly from a comparison of performance in the two tests. Instead, a simple probabilistic model is used to extract estimates from the data. Conscious (C) and unconscious memory (U) are assumed to be independent. In an inclusion test, both C and U increase the likelihood that a studied target word will be used to complete a stem [C + U (1 − C)]. In an exclusion test, on the other hand, a studied target word will only be used to complete a stem if it is produced as a result of unconscious memory and not associated with conscious memory [U(1 − C)]. Conscious memory for a word will lead that word to be omitted and replaced with an alternative completion. The difference in observed performance between the two tests then serves as an estimate of the probability of conscious memory (C). The probability of unconscious memory (U) can then be estimated simply by dividing the observed proportion of stems completed in the exclusion test by (1 − C).

3.2.1 Independence, redundancy, and exclusivity

The process-dissociation framework and its accompanying empirical procedures have stimulated—and are likely to further stimulate—a great deal of useful debate concerning the relationship between memory and conscious awareness of the past. In particular, the assumption that conscious and unconscious memory are independent is proving a source of controversy. Given independence, the estimate of the U parameter is obtained by dividing exclusion test performance by (1 − C), because exclusion test performance is assumed to underestimate systematically the proportion of items associated with unconscious memory. That is, there is a proportion of items associated with both conscious and unconscious memory. These items are included in an inclusion test [C + U − (CU)], but excluded in an exclusion test [U − (CU)]. Dividing by (1 − C) boosts the exclusion test score in order to take account of these items [i.e. U = E/(1 − C) = E + (CU)].

Joordens and Merikle (1993) have argued for an alternative assumption concerning the relation between conscious and unconscious memory. This *redundancy* view stems from the *prima-facie* plausible notion that the vast majority of mental processes are unconscious, and that only a small proportion of processes reach the 'threshold' of consciousness. Items associated with conscious memory are therefore assumed to form a subset of those associated with unconscious memory, so that unconscious memory can occur without conscious memory, but conscious memory can never occur without unconscious memory. It follows that the intersect between C and U (CU under an independence assumption) is C—because conscious memory is always accompanied by unconscious memory—and that *inclusion* test performance indexes unconscious memory as a whole [I = C + U − C = U]. As is the case under the independence assumption, exclusion performance [E = U − C] underestimates unconscious memory. Another possible relation between conscious and unconscious memory is that of *exclusivity*. Exclusivity means that conscious and unconscious memory can never co-occur, so that the intersect of C and U is defined as zero. Under this assumption, inclusion test performance indexes both conscious and unconscious memory [C + U], and exclusion test performance provides an estimate of unconscious memory alone [U].

Conclusions about the effects of experimental manipulations on U vary radically depending whether one assumes independence, redundancy, or exclusivity (see e.g. Joordens and Merikle 1993). Jacoby *et al.* (in press; see also Jacoby *et al.* 1993*b*; Toth *et al.* 1994) have argued that the independence assumption is supported over the other two assumptions by findings of null effects of experimental manipulations on U, in conjunction with large effects of the same manipulations on C. An example is the effect of dividing attention at study, which reduces estimates of C, while leaving estimates of U unaffected (Jacoby *et al.* 1993*b*). However, as Russo and Andrade (1995) point out, this argument is circular: the invariance of U obtained in the studies summarized by Jacoby *et al.* (in press) is only observed when the data are analysed *using* the independence assumption, and does not occur if the data are analyzed using the redundancy or exclusivity assumptions. For example, the redundancy assumption leads to the conclusion that U is greater when attention is full at encoding than when it is divided, and the exclusivity assumption leads to the opposite conclusion—that U is smaller when attention is full at encoding than when it is divided. The independence assumption, therefore, cannot be justified on the basis of patterns of effects on C and U that occur only when that assumption has already been adopted.

It remains to be seen whether a decision concerning assumptions can be made on the basis of experimental data. What is already clear, though, is that the process-dissociation analysis will have significant limitations as an all-purpose data-analytic tool, if its underlying assumptions turn out to be difficult to verify. Moreover, the debate over the independence assumption reveals underlying difficulties that are even more profound. Casting the relationship between conscious and unconscious memory in terms of simple two-process models results in considerable oversimplification of the very complex phenomena under investigation. Memory tasks cannot be assumed to be awareness-pure, strategy-pure, or process-pure. But by the same token, it is implausible to assume that a particular memorial state of awareness is uniquely associated with a particular retrieval strategy, or that a particular retrieval strategy is uniquely associated with a particular retrieval process or type of memory representation (Gardiner and Java 1993*a*). Such assumptions reflect a doctrine of *concordance* (Tulving 1989) that is increasingly questionable.

The core of the problem lies in the way in which the terms *conscious memory* and *unconscious memory* are interpreted. In the process-dissociation framework, these terms are used interchangeably to distinguish subjective states of awareness, strategies, and underlying processes by which information is retrieved. By contrast, we have reserved the terms *conscious memory* and *unconscious memory* to refer only to memorial states of awareness with respect to a past event. We recognize that subjects can be aware of a voluntary strategy of retrieving information from the past, in the sense that they can report that they are using such a strategy. They can, however, also be aware of using an involuntary strategy (e.g. completing a stem with the first word coming to mind) even though they may have no awareness at all of prior events. The term *awareness* therefore, has quite different connotations when applied to awareness of events and to the ability to report strategies.

Whereas subjects can be consciously aware of a past event, and able to report on the retrieval strategy that they are using, they can *never* be aware of the underlying processes by which information is retrieved, because subjective awareness of the past is the *product* of such processes (Tulving 1976).[5] For that reason, subjects are no more likely to be aware of the retrieval processes underlying conscious awareness of the past than they are to be aware of the retrieval processes underlying effects of memory on their behaviour that are unaccompanied by conscious awareness. The argument that conscious *awareness* of the past is the product of retrieval processes that are not themselves conscious does not imply that conscious *processes* represent the tip of an iceberg, and are therefore redundant with unconscious *processes*. This inference is mistaken because it confuses states of awareness with processes. Subjects are never conscious of a retrieval process, so that the question of whether or not conscious retrieval processes are a subset of unconscious retrieval processes does not even arise. Similarly, it is a fundamental error to assert that conscious and unconscious *processes* are independent, or that they are exclusive. To make such assertions represents what Ryle (1949) called a *category mistake*—a confusion of the logical status of concepts that 'can

5. By *retrieval processes*, we mean hypothetical processes for accessing information from memory representations, such as *correlation* (e.g. Murdock 1982), *ecphory* (e.g. Tulving 1976, 1983), *resonance* (e.g. Ratcliff 1978), or *spreading activation* (e.g. Anderson 1983).

lead to false contrasts, to misleading analogies, and indeed to downright bad theorizing' (Miles 1987).

When the terms 'conscious' and 'unconscious memory' are used to refer to memorial states of awareness, the independence and redundancy models lead to a conclusion that is logically contradictory, namely that a subject can be simultaneously conscious and unconscious of a past event. Logic dictates that conscious and unconscious memory—as states of awareness—stand in an exclusive relation to each other. One can either be conscious or unconscious of a past event, but not both. Adopting an exclusivity position in respect to conscious and unconscious states of awareness does not, however, imply an exclusivity position with regard to the relations between strategies, processes, or memory representations. Subjects' performance, for example, could reflect involuntary retrieval of studied information, even though they are employing a voluntary strategy for retrieving studied information, so that voluntary and involuntary retrieval could be independent or redundant.

The independence and redundancy assumptions, then, may be plausible in respect to retrieval volition (voluntary vs. involuntary) but not in respect to memorial states of awareness (conscious vs. unconscious), for which logic dictates exclusivity. This reasoning leads to an interesting conclusion: if retrieval volition and conscious awareness *were* perfectly correlated, as the process-dissociation framework assumes, it would not be correct to interpret inclusion/exclusion data using the independence or redundancy models. That is, if voluntary retrieval was a necessary and sufficient condition for conscious awareness of the past, and involuntary retrieval was a necessary and sufficient condition for absence of conscious awareness of the past, then voluntary and involuntary retrieval would have to be exclusive, because conscious and unconscious states of awareness are exclusive. The implication, therefore, is that one must either: (a) accept an exclusivity model for the process-dissociation analysis in paradigms like stem completion; or (b) recognize that memorial state of awareness (conscious vs. unconscious) must be distinguished from retrieval volition (voluntary vs. involuntary).

If the foregoing argument is correct, independence or redundancy assumptions for the process-dissociation analysis could be maintained only if the parameters C and U were estimates of voluntary and involuntary memory, without regard to conscious awareness of the past. The C and U parameters, however, are not estimates of voluntary and involuntary memory. Subjects' memorial states of awareness (conscious vs. unconscious) are intimately involved by the inclusion/exclusion procedure in a task like stem completion. For that reason, both independence and redundancy assumptions are questionable for such tasks, even if memorial state of awareness is not identified with retrieval volition.

In an inclusion condition in stem completion, the pool of studied target items that are produced consists of a mix of items retrieved voluntarily (i.e. because they were recalled) and involuntarily (i.e. because they were given as the first item coming to mind after recall failure). It also represents a mix of items associated and unassociated with conscious awareness of the past. To permit separation of voluntary retrieval from involuntary retrieval, subtracting exclusion from inclusion performance would have to result in an estimate of the proportion of items voluntarily retrieved, without regard to conscious awareness. However, memorial awareness—and not retrieval volition—serves as the criterion for suppressing studied items in an exclusion (or opposition) test. For a studied target to be produced owing to an influence of memory (as opposed to chance factors), it must not only be produced as a result of involuntary memory, but must also be unassociated with conscious awareness of the past. Studied targets associated with awareness of the past are suppressed, whether they initially come to mind as a result of voluntary or involuntary retrieval. This argument is supported by the data showing that items produced in an opposition test are associated neither with recollection of the study episode, nor with feelings of familiarity (Richardson-Klavehn *et al.* 1994*a*). It is also supported by the finding that observed opposition test performance was rather accurately predicted by performance in both the incidental and intentional test conditions in the Richardson-Klavehn and Gardiner study (Tables 3.8 and 3.9). The latter data indicate that exclusion test performance would be similar, whether studied targets initially come to mind voluntarily or involuntarily. This equivalence in outcomes suggests that the process-dissociation analysis will fail to reflect the distinction between voluntary and involuntary retrieval that led to the striking differences in stem-completion performance between the intentional and incidental tests.

Exclusion (or opposition) test performance indexes the proportion of studied target items unassociated with conscious awareness of the past, whether one adopts an independence [$E = U(1 - C)$], redundancy [$E = U - C$], or exclusivity [$E = U$] assumption for the process-dissociation analysis. The C parameter gives an estimate of the proportion of items associated with conscious awareness of the past, without regard to retrieval volition. In terms of our framework, therefore, the U parameter is an estimate of the proportion of items associated with *involuntary unconscious* memory, and not an estimate of the overall proportion of items associated with involuntary memory. For this reason, we question the validity of the treatment of exclusion (or opposition) test performance prescribed by the independence model [i.e. dividing exclusion test performance by $(1 - C)$ to estimate U]. This estimation procedure assumes that a item can be associated both with conscious and unconscious memorial states of awareness. We have argued that this assumption involves a logical contradiction. The redundancy model of Joordens and Merikle

(1993) estimates U directly from the data (because it treats inclusion test performance as an estimate of U), but is equally implausible because it involves the same contradiction. If any model is plausible for the inclusion/exclusion procedure in stem completion, therefore, that model seems to be exclusivity.

3.2.2 Involuntary conscious memory and the inclusion/exclusion procedure

The data presented previously support the assertion that incidental test performance reflects a mix of items associated with, and unassociated with, conscious awareness of the past, even when voluntary retrieval processes play a negligible role in performance. Items associated with involuntary conscious memory in an incidental test would be excluded from the subject's overt responses in an exclusion test, but would appear in the subject's overt responses in an inclusion test. These items would, therefore, form a subset of those that contribute to the estimate of the C parameter.

Richardson-Klavehn *et al.* (1994*a*) argued that involuntary conscious memory would increase the size of the difference between inclusion and exclusion tests, and therefore inflate the estimate of the C parameter. The argument was that subjects in an inclusion test would sometimes produce studied targets as a result of voluntary retrieval, but that on other occasions they would produce studied targets as a result of involuntary retrieval (i.e. by giving the first item coming to mind), while also recognizing them as studied items. In an exclusion test, studied targets produced as a result of involuntary retrieval, but recognized as studied, would be omitted, along with items voluntarily retrieved (see Graf and Komatsu 1994 for a similar claim).

In the study described previously, Richardson-Klavehn and Gardiner (1995) made a preliminary examination of this claim. In their intentional test condition, subjects were instructed to complete each stem with a studied word, but if they could not, to complete each stem with the first word coming to mind. These instructions amount to inclusion test instructions, except for one critical difference: subjects had to provide an additional completion for items they believed they had recalled, allowing separation of the data into proportion recalled and proportion completed with the first item coming to mind. The overall proportion of stems completed with targets serves as an estimate of inclusion test performance. Subtracting the proportion of items for which a second completion was written gives an estimate of exclusion (or opposition) test performance (see Table 3.9). As noted previously (footnote 2, p. 103), subjects were asked to indicate when they had failed to recall a studied item, and completed the stem with the first item coming to mind, while also recognizing that item as studied. These items would be included in an inclusion test and excluded in an exclusion test, and would represent instances of involuntary conscious memory. Occurrences of this type were extremely rare, suggesting that Richardson-Klavehn *et al.*'s argument may have been incorrect: involuntary conscious memory may not contribute to the difference between inclusion and exclusion tests, over and above the contribution made by voluntary retrieval.

The suggestion that involuntary conscious memory does not increase the size of the difference between inclusion and exclusion tests must, however, be interpreted with caution. Subjects may simply have had difficulty in following the instructions to distinguish between cases in which they recalled a word and cases in which the first word coming to mind was recognized as studied. The instructions were already complex without this additional requirement, so that involuntary conscious triggering of studied words may simply have been interpreted as recall. Additionally, if subjects employed a recall strategy of bringing several completions to mind in the hope that one of these would be recognized (as a number of subjects indicated), the distinction that we asked them to make would have been particularly difficult. In consequence, whereas numerous reported instances of completion with the first item coming to mind accompanied by recognition would have supported Richardson-Klavehn *et al.*'s claim, the failure to observe many such instances does not invalidate it.

Furthermore, contrary to the assumption made by Richardson-Klavehn *et al.* (1994*a*) and Graf and Komatsu (1994), involuntary conscious memory may occur frequently in an incidental test, but does not have to inflate the difference between inclusion and exclusion tests. Engaging voluntary retrieval processes (as in Richardson-Klavehn and Gardiner's intentional test) may result in access to the vast majority of those items that would have been associated with involuntary conscious memory in an incidental test. Evidence for this claim comes from a comparison of the opposition (or exclusion) estimates derived from the incidental and intentional tests in Richardson-Klavehn and Gardiner's study. Intentional retrieval instructions increased the overall proportion of stems completed with targets (compared to incidental instructions), but left opposition (exclusion) estimates largely unaffected. Exclusion estimates from the incidental test condition can be regarded as reflecting the role of involuntary conscious memory, because the proportion of studied targets coming to mind showed no appreciable depth-of-processing effect. This result suggests that the majority of items associated with involuntary conscious memory are simply a subset of those that are accessible to voluntary retrieval processes under intentional test conditions.

If voluntary retrieval plays an equal and opposite role in inclusion and exclusion test performance, very few items may actually be associated with involuntary conscious memory. However, to the extent that involuntary retrieval brings completions to mind in either the inclusion or the exclusion test conditions, involuntary conscious memory *will* contribute directly to estimates of C in the process-dissociation analysis. Richardson-Klavehn *et al.* (1994*a*) assumed that an involuntary strategy for bringing completions to mind in an exclusion (or opposition) test would be least effortful, because it would throw up fewer studied completions, saving the effort of producing alternative completions. Using the opposition instructions employed by Richardson-Klavehn *et al.* (which emphasized an involuntary strategy), Richardson-Klavehn and Gardiner (1995) found strong support for this assumption. Jacoby *et al.* (1993*b*) used somewhat different instructions in their exclusion test conditions. In two of their experiments (3 and 4), subjects were told to treat the stem-completion test as a creativity test, and therefore not to complete stems with studied words. In the other two experiments (1 and 2), subjects were told to try to retrieve a studied word, and then to exclude it. Whether these differences in instructions actually influence stem-completion performance needs to be conclusively determined. We think it likely that subjects will adopt an involuntary strategy in the exclusion condition in some situations, regardless of what the instructions ask them to do, because such a strategy is demonstrably less effortful and time-consuming than a voluntary one. Finally, Nyberg *et al.* (in prep.) found evidence suggesting that subjects given inclusion instructions in a fragment-completion task adopted an involuntary retrieval strategy, despite instructions to try to complete fragments with studied items.

To summarize, we have argued that the process-dissociation framework oversimplifies the relationship between retrieval volition and conscious awareness of the past, and in particular that it ignores involuntary conscious memory. Failure to accommodate involuntary conscious memory would be a disadvantage of the process-dissociation approach as a general theoretical framework, even if that failure had no consequences in terms of measurement. Measurement consequences, however, are apparent. The inclusion/exclusion procedure, when applied to stem completion and other repetition priming paradigms, does not permit separation of voluntary from involuntary memory. Rather, it separates conscious memory (both voluntary and involuntary) from involuntary unconscious memory. Unless alternative procedures can be developed, the price of being able to separate voluntary memory from involuntary memory is the continued use of comparisons between intentional and incidental memory test, despite their potential disadvantages.

3.2.3 Involuntary conscious memory and generation/recognition models

In response to Richardson-Klavehn *et al.*'s (1994*a*) assertion that retrieval in an opposition test is involuntary, and that items associated with awareness of the past are omitted, Toth *et al.* (1994) have suggested that we are committed to a generate/recognize model of performance in stem completion like the one proposed by Jacoby and Hollingshead (1990). Such a model is taken to imply a redundancy assumption concerning the relationship between C and U, because the pool of items that can be recognized is a subset of those generated. This suggestion, however, oversimplifies our position in two ways. First, generate/recognize models incorporate the assumption that recognition occurs following generation. Our position makes no such sequentiality assumption: when involuntary conscious memory occurs, the involuntary tendency to produce a studied word and the awareness that the word has been previously encountered may occur simultaneously, and may not even be distinguishable from each other. What we have in mind, therefore, is a kind of *spontaneous reminding*, as discussed by Schacter *et al.* (1989, see also Lockhart and Blackburn 1993). Secondly, the argument that we are committed to a two-component model involving unconscious generation followed by conscious recognition only makes sense within the context of a framework (like the one adopted by Jacoby and colleagues) in which conscious memory is *identified* with voluntary memory and unconscious memory is *identified* with involuntary memory. Our framework does not make this identification. As emphasized previously, our framework distinguishes conscious and unconscious states of awareness, which have to be exclusive, from voluntary and involuntary retrieval. In terms of our framework, therefore, it makes no sense to treat conscious memory as redundant with unconscious memory.

3.2.4 Process dissociation and contamination of incidental test performance

Jacoby and colleagues have argued that the process-dissociation technique overcomes the problems of 'contamination by conscious memory' in standard incidental tests that we addressed previously. Our analysis suggested that there are two critically different interpretations of 'contamination'. One is that incidental test performance is contaminated by voluntary retrieval strategies. The other is that incidental test performance reflects an involuntary retrieval strategy, but that involuntary retrieval is sometimes accompanied by conscious awareness of the past. Because the process-dissociation framework does not distinguish these possibilities either conceptually or methodologically, seriously mistaken conclusions can be drawn about contamination in incidental tests.

One major strategy adopted by Jacoby and colleagues involves studying inclusion, exclusion, and incidental test performance as a function of the similarity in perceptual form between study and test items. In Jacoby *et al.* (1993*b*, experiments 3 and 4), for example, subjects either read study words or generated them as solutions to anagrams. In other experiments (Jacoby *et al.* in press), words were either visually or auditorily presented at study. In both sets of experiments the test items were presented visually, so that the degree of perceptual overlap between study and test items was greater in the former than in the latter study condition. In respect to the issue of contamination, the question of principal interest was the extent to which priming across perceptual forms was obtained. The consistent finding was that cross-form priming was obtained in the incidental test, but that the U parameter showed no evidence of transfer across perceptual forms. As the process-dissociation framework only distinguishes between voluntary conscious memory (C) and involuntary unconscious memory (U), any cross-form effects that cannot be attributed to involuntary unconscious memory are attributable by default to contamination by voluntary retrieval of studied items. If this conclusion were correct, the implications would be serious for research using comparisons between within- and cross-form priming effects in incidental tests to draw conclusions about the organization of lexical representations (e.g. Kirsner *et al.* 1989; Monsell 1985).

The conclusion that cross-form priming reflects voluntary retrieval is, however, premature. The term U cannot be used as an estimate of the probability of involuntary memory in an incidental test, because involuntary memory is sometimes associated with awareness of the past (involuntary conscious memory). In consequence, cross-form priming effects in an incidental test that are not attributable to involuntary unconscious memory (U) cannot be conclusively attributed to voluntary retrieval of studied items. The information that supports transfer across perceptual forms is necessarily more abstract (i.e. less perceptually specific) than is the information that only supports transfer within perceptual forms, and it seems likely that it is this more abstract information that supports involuntary conscious memory. In consequence, the pool of items that shows cross-form transfer may consist largely of items that are associated with involuntary conscious memory. The assertion that involuntary cross-form priming is likely to result in spontaneous conscious awareness receives additional support from the finding that cross-form priming is more likely to occur for low-than for high-frequency words (Kirsner *et al.* 1983; Kirsner *et al.* 1986; Kirsner *et al.* 1993). The pool of items that shows involuntary cross-form transfer could, therefore, also be biased to contain the low-frequency items from the total pool under study. Those items, in turn, would have a higher probability of being recognized as studied than would items in the overall set.

If our arguments concerning involuntary conscious memory and cross-form priming are correct, applying the process-dissociation procedure would be expected to have exactly the effect that Jacoby and colleagues have observed: cross-form priming would not be reflected in the parameter estimate U, even if cross-form priming in an incidental test did not reflect the use of a voluntary retrieval strategy. It should be noted, however, that we are not arguing that cross-form priming in an incidental test *never* reflects contamination by voluntary retrieval strategies. On the contrary, it is quite possible that cross-form priming sometimes *does* reflect voluntary retrieval (see e.g. Richardson-Klavehn *et al.* 1994*b*). Our argument is simply that the process-dissociation procedure does not allow one to determine *whether or not* cross-form priming in an incidental test reflects voluntary retrieval, because it cannot distinguish between cross-form priming attributable to voluntary retrieval, and involuntary cross-form priming that is accompanied by conscious awareness of the past (i.e. involuntary conscious memory).

Finally, there are two powerful pieces of evidence that encourage us to believe that cross-form priming in an incidental test can occur in the absence of 'contamination' by voluntary retrieval strategies. The first is that amnesic subjects have shown significant cross-modality priming in an incidental test of stem completion—and at a level not significantly worse than controls—when they were significantly impaired compared to controls in an intentional test (Graf *et al.* 1985). The second is that normal subjects have shown significant cross-modality priming in an incidental stem-completion test, when incidental-test performance conformed completely to the retrieval intentionality criterion, as indicated by the absence of a depth-of-processing effect (Craik *et al.* 1994). These two results strongly support the conclusion that cross-modality priming can be involuntary and, in consequence, they stand in direct conflict with the conclusions concerning cross-form transfer that have been drawn from the process-dissociation procedure. We have recently reproduced the conflict between the results of Craik *et al.* (1994) and those of the process-dissociation procedure within a single experiment, and have obtained evidence (using the empirical techniques described previously) that the conflict can be resolved if involuntary conscious memory is taken into account (Richardson-Klavehn and Gardiner in press).

3.2.5 On the meaning of 'process-purity'

Returning to the contrast between the independence, redundancy, and exclusivity assumptions for the process-dissociation analysis, it is now possible to appreciate the major underlying reason why the framework adopted by Jacoby and colleagues commits them to an independence assumption: the independence assumption is the only one of the three possible assumptions that does not involve treating either the inclusion test or the exclusion test as a process-pure measure. That is, on a redundancy assumption, inclusion test performance is a process-pure measure of U, and on an exclusivity assumption, exclusion test performance is a process-pure measure of U. Following the reasoning used by Jacoby and colleagues, the process-dissociation procedure does not represent much of an advance over the use of traditional 'contaminated' or process-impure incidental tests, unless that procedure avoids the 'process-purity' assumption that is argued to be *intrinsic* to the use of incidental tests (e.g. Jacoby *et al.* 1993*b*). By implication, therefore, if the redundancy or exclusivity assumptions were to hold, the process-dissociation procedure would not represent much of an advance over traditional methods, and so the independence assumption must be adopted.

This line of reasoning, however, once again reflects a failure to distinguish different levels of theoretical description for states of awareness, for retrieval strategies, and for underlying retrieval processes or memory representations. First, the use of traditional incidental tests does not *necessarily* involve process-purity assumptions (notwithstanding the fact that a number of contributors to the literature have made such assumptions). It has in fact been appreciated for some time that incidental tests can potentially be contaminated by voluntary retrieval strategies (e.g. Schacter 1985). Similarly, researchers studying amnesic subjects have long recognized that involuntary retrieval can contribute to performance on intentional tests (for a review, see Richardson-Klavehn and Bjork 1988*a*). It was for precisely these reasons that Richardson-Klavehn and Bjork (1988*a*) criticized the popular use of the terms *implicit* and *explicit* as labels for memory tests and for hypothetical forms of memory underlying performance. Secondly, the problem of 'process-purity' in the context of incidental memory tests is first and foremost a problem of verifying whether subjects follow test instructions. In an incidental stem-completion test, for example, the researcher needs to know whether or not subjects obey the instructions to complete stems with the first word coming to mind. The 'process-purity' or 'contamination' problem, therefore, is a problem relating to subjects' test strategies. To the extent that researchers, as we have done in the work described here, attempt to verify empirically the strategies that their subjects use in an incidental test—rather than simply assuming that subjects follow instructions—the assertion that they are making 'process-purity' assumptions is incorrect.

When the 'process-purity' problem is viewed as a problem relating to test strategies, it becomes clear that the process-dissociation procedure does not overcome the 'process-purity' problem that it was designed to solve. As previously discussed, one cannot simply assume that subjects' strategies in inclusion and exclusion test conditions operate as the process-dissociation model assumes. Subjects may, for example, adopt an involuntary retrieval strategy in either or both test conditions, even though they are instructed to follow a voluntary strategy. Furthermore, in order to conduct tests of the significance of differences between parameter estimates across experimental conditions, inclusion and exclusion scores are typically obtained from each individual subject, the inclusion and exclusion trials often being interspersed in the test list. The instructions for each test condition are reasonably complicated taken individually, so one cannot simply assume that subjects are able to keep track of what they are to do when the different test trials are mixed together—particularly if the subjects are young, old, or memory-disordered (Graf and Komatsu 1994). Instead, empirical verification of subjects' test strategies is required, just as is required when using standard incidental tests. We have previously emphasized, for example, that subjects in an exclusion (or opposition) condition cannot be assumed to be following instructions to suppress studied items unless they show a combined pattern of inhibition and facilitation (compared to baseline) across two different study conditions. When facilitation is observed regardless of study condition, it may be the case that some exclusion trials were mistakenly treated as inclusion trials, or that some subjects disobeyed the instructions to exclude studied items owing to demand characteristics. It should be apparent that the criteria for verifying subjects' strategies in the inclusion/exclusion procedure are at least, if not more, complicated than those used to verify subjects' strategies in standard incidental memory tests.

Looking at the issue from a more abstract viewpoint, the process-dissociation model treats neither the inclusion nor the exclusion tests as 'process-pure' measures, if independence is assumed. However, it does assume that each test provides an accurate (or 'process-pure') measure of *two* hypothesized types of retrieval [i.e. $I = C + U(1 - C)$ and $E = U(1 - C)$]. The problem is that we cannot simply assume that these two types of retrieval operate in each test exactly as the model suggests (e.g. we cannot assume that the parameters of the model are constant across test conditions; for discussion see Graf and Komatsu 1994; Richardson-Klavehn *et al.* 1994*a*; Roediger and McDermott 1994). Neither can we assume that performance in these tests is a function of these two factors, and only these two factors. If a third factor, unacknowledged in the model, is involved in performance, the tests will not be accurate measures, and the validity of the model will be questionable. The issue of the role of involuntary conscious memory in inclusion and exclusion tests, discussed previously, is a case in point. The problem of 'process-purity', therefore, has simply been altered in form—rather than solved—by application of the process-dissociation model.

3.2.6 Depth-of-processing effects and the process-dissociation analysis: the role of scale factors

As mentioned previously, the intentional test used by Richardson-Klavehn and Gardiner (1995) amounts to an inclusion test, with the additional requirement that subjects indicate which items are recalled, and which

Table 3.10 Depth-of-processing effects in the inclusion/exclusion procedure with parameter estimates for the process-dissociation analysis (based on independence)

Measure	Studied: Deep	Studied: Shallow	Unstudied
Toth *et al.* (1994)*			
Inclusion	0.60	0.47	0.29
Exclusion	0.33	0.43	0.26
C	0.27	0.03	
U	0.42 (0.45)	0.45 (0.44)	
Richardson-Klavehn and Gardiner (1995)			
Inclusion	0.47	0.31	0.16
Exclusion	0.02	0.20	0.15
C	0.45	0.11	
U	0.03	0.22	

*Estimates of U in parentheses were obtained from the mean inclusion and exclusion proportions.

are given as the first completion coming to mind. By subtracting the proportion recalled from the overall proportion of stems completed with targets, exclusion test performance can be estimated. The C and U parameters of the process-dissociation analysis can then be estimated from a single test condition. This procedure has the advantage of avoiding possible differences in strategy and response criteria between inclusion and exclusion tests, which could lead to violations of the assumption that the parameters of the model are constant across tests (Richardson-Klavehn *et al.* 1994*a*).

The mean inclusion and exclusion scores as a function of depth of processing at study are presented in Table 3.10, along with the C and U parameter estimates based on the independence assumption. Depth of processing was also manipulated by Toth *et al.* (1994, experiment 1) in a study using inclusion and exclusion conditions in stem completion. The data and parameter estimates from that study are also presented in Table 3.10, because a comparison between the results of the two studies shows interesting similarities and discrepancies. Both studies show an inverse relationship between inclusion and exclusion performance as a function of depth of processing, and in consequence, estimates of C show a depth-of-processing effect in both experiments. By contrast, the effect of depth of processing on U differs strikingly between studies. Toth *et al.* found no significant effect, whereas Richardson-Klavehn and Gardiner found a highly significant effect ($P < 0.001$), with U being smaller in the deep processing condition than in the shallow processing condition.

What is responsible for this difference in conclusions? Three differences in observed inclusion and exclusion performance are apparent:

1. The baseline level of stem-completion performance in Richardson-Klavehn and Gardiner's study, although comparable to many published results from incidental tests, was lower than the baseline level in Toth *et al.*'s study.

2. The depth-of-processing effect in Richardson-Klavehn and Gardiner's study was about twice as large (in terms of mean values) as the one in Toth *et al.*'s study.

3. Richardson-Klavehn and Gardiner's exclusion estimates show a combination of inhibition (compared to baseline) for items that received deep processing at study, in conjunction with facilitation for items that received shallow processing at study, whereas Toth *et al.*'s exclusion data show facilitation in both study conditions.

These outcomes combined to produce a mean exclusion estimate for semantically processed items that was close to zero in the Richardson-Klavehn and Gardiner study. Exclusion values close to zero will inevitably result in small estimates of U, because the U parameter in the independence model is estimated by computing a ratio measure [i.e. $U = E/(1 - C)$]. The level of exclusion test performance, therefore, constrains the effect that the independence correction can have.[6]

Problems for the independence model relating to low exclusion performance are not limited to cases in which mean exclusion performance was at the level reported by Richardson-Klavehn and Gardiner. To reinforce the conclusion that U was uninfluenced by depth of processing, Toth *et al.* (who report higher mean levels of performance) found it necessary to re-compute estimates of U based on the mean

6. A solution to the problem of varying overall performance levels that initially suggests itself is to conduct the analysis on priming scores (see Roediger and McDermott 1994). However, if exclusion test performance for studied items is below baseline, conducting the analysis on priming scores results in a negative value for U, when the parameter estimates for the model should only vary between 0 and 1. For example, conducting the analysis on priming proportions from Richardson-Klavehn and Gardiner's deep processing condition results in a C estimate of 0.44 (i.e. the difference between deep and unstudied proportions for inclusion less the difference between deep and unstudied proportions for exclusion), and a U estimate of −0.23 (i.e. priming in the exclusion condition = −0.13, and U = −0.13/0.56). Another technique designed to correct for baseline performance is to subtract a pooled measure of baseline performance (i.e. the average of the inclusion and exclusion values for unstudied items) from estimates of U that have been computed using data uncorrected for baseline responding (see Jacoby *et al.* 1993*b*; Toth *et al.* 1994). For Richardson-Klavehn and Gardiner's deep encoding condition, however, this technique also results in a negative value for U (i.e. U = 0.03 − 0.155 = −0.125).

inclusion and exclusion values (see Table 3.10). Doing so removed a slight (non-significant) trend towards a reverse depth-of-processing effect on U. It remains to be seen whether the reverse depth-of-processing effect on U found by Richardson-Klavehn and Gardiner will persist when exclusion performance in the deep processing condition is increased, by increasing baseline performance or by some other means. Of particular interest is whether the effect persists when the pattern of inhibition and facilitation across the deep and shallow processing conditions found by Richardson-Klavehn and Gardiner (and also by Richardson-Klavehn *et al.* 1994*a*) is maintained. As argued previously, when that pattern of data is not obtained, it is difficult to be sure about the extent to which subjects follow instructions to exclude items associated with conscious awareness of the past.

Although further data are clearly needed, the discrepancy between the available results leads us to make three observations. First, under the independence model, zero or close-to-zero exclusion scores are taken to indicate a methodological deficiency in the experiment that has to be remedied by increasing exclusion performance, either experimentally, or by re-analysing data to minimize the impact of such scores (e.g. Jacoby *et al.* 1993*b*; Toth *et al.* 1994). It should be remembered, however, that low exclusion scores indicate the subject's *success* in suppressing items that they were instructed to suppress. One can ask, therefore, why such data should not be taken at face value, even under the independence assumption. That is, when suppression is essentially perfect (as in Richardson-Klavehn and Gardiner's deep processing condition), there is simply little or no evidence for unconscious memory. Increasing exclusion performance will inevitably exaggerate the extent to which unconscious memory is involved in performance. There is, in addition, a danger that what are regarded as floor effects in the process-dissociation procedure can be used to explain away failures to obtain predicted outcomes.

Secondly, even if one accepts that low exclusion values *do* reflect a methodological deficiency, one is forced to the minimal conclusion that scaling problems can render the analysis (under the independence assumption) uninterpretable, when observed dissociations among tests are perfectly interpretable under the same experimental conditions and performance levels. Traditional comparisons of intentional and incidental tests have yielded interpretable data with baseline levels comparable to, or even lower than, the levels reported by Richardson-Klavehn and Gardiner (e.g. Graf and Mandler 1984). And, most critically, methodological difficulties related to performance levels do not complicate the inferences that we have drawn within our framework from comparisons of opposition, incidental, and intentional tests. At very least, therefore, one can conclude that the process-dissociation procedure (using the independence assumption) has more limited applicability than do the traditional methods based on observed dissociations among tests, which do not rely on derived ratio measures.

Finally, an exclusivity model for C and U avoids the scaling problems that occur when the independence model is used, because it treats exclusion performance as a measure of U. Such a model also renders the conclusions from the Toth *et al.* and the Richardson-Klavehn and Gardiner studies consistent—and, in our opinion, more sensible. That is, U showed a reverse depth-of-processing effect in both studies. The work reported here (as well as elsewhere, e.g. Craik *et al.* 1994; Roediger *et al.* 1992) has indicated that depth of processing has a minimal influence on priming in incidental tests of stem completion, but large effects on intentional tests. Such results confirm prior assertions (e.g. Graf and Mandler 1984; Schacter and Graf 1986) that involuntary memory in stem completion is largely uninfluenced by depth of processing. Stem-completion times and reports of retrieval strategy obtained in the work reported here provide strong convergent evidence for the conclusion that voluntary retrieval exerts a minimal influence when subjects are properly instructed prior to an incidental test. Although involuntary effects of memory are similar across processing levels, our data show that there is a large difference in the extent to which those effects are accompanied by conscious awareness of encoding events. Our data also show quite conclusively that it is this conscious awareness that determines which items are suppressed in stem completion under exclusion (or opposition) instructions. In terms of our framework, therefore, it is counterintuitive that U should show no effect of depth of processing (as in Toth *et al.*). In stem completion (and other priming paradigms), U is a measure of involuntary unconscious memory, and not a measure of involuntary memory, both conscious and unconscious. U *should*, therefore, be smaller following deep processing at encoding than following shallow processing.

3.2.7 Interim summary

In this section, we have compared our approach to priming paradigms, which distinguishes retrieval volition (voluntary vs. involuntary) from memorial state of awareness (conscious vs. unconscious), to the process-dissociation approach, which equates voluntary retrieval with conscious awareness of the past, overlooking involuntary conscious memory. We have made the following major arguments:

1. While voluntary and involuntary retrieval could be independent, redundant, or exclusive, conscious and unconscious memorial states of awareness should be treated as exclusive.

2. The process-dissociation procedure in priming paradigms like stem completion separates items according to a criterion of memorial state of awareness (conscious vs. unconscious), and not according to a criterion of retrieval volition (voluntary vs. involuntary). Independence and redundancy assumptions for such paradigms are, therefore, highly questionable.

3. Traditional comparisons of intentional and incidental tests address the distinction between voluntary and involuntary retrieval, so that such comparisons cannot be replaced by the use of the process-dissociation procedure.

4. The process-dissociation procedure can lead to misleading conclusions concerning the extent to which incidental tests are contaminated by voluntary retrieval, because it cannot separate voluntary retrieval from involuntary retrieval that is accompanied by conscious awareness of the past (involuntary conscious memory).

5. The 'process-purity' problem for incidental tests is a problem of verifying subjects' retrieval strategies: when the 'process-purity' problem is considered as a strategy-purity problem, the process-dissociation procedure does not avoid this problem.

6. The process-dissociation procedure, using the independence assumption, suffers from scaling problems that do not beset traditional techniques (based on observed dissociations) to the same extent.

In support of the claim that the process-dissociation procedure in priming paradigms separates items according to a criterion of memorial awareness (conscious vs. unconscious), we cited data showing that stem-completion priming under exclusion (or opposition) conditions is associated neither with recollection nor with feelings of familiarity. These data imply: (a) that recollection and familiarity are both types of conscious memory, so that the distinction between recollection and familiarity cannot be equated with the distinction between conscious and unconscious memory; and (b) that procedures designed to separate recollection and familiarity in recognition memory paradigms must be carefully distinguished from procedures designed to separate conscious states of awareness from unconscious states of awareness in priming paradigms. We consider these issues in more detail in the following section.

3.3 PROCESS DISSOCIATIONS VS. DISSOCIATIONS IN REPORTS OF SUBJECTIVE AWARENESS

The process-dissociation analysis and its accompanying empirical procedures were originally developed in connection with the distinction between familiarity and recollection in recognition memory. As applied to recognition memory by Jacoby (1991; see also Verfaellie and Treadwell 1993), the inclusion/exclusion procedure is rather different. Subjects must study two sets of items prior to the test, the sets being distinguished by some critical attribute (e.g. presentation modality). In the inclusion condition, they are to respond 'yes' to any item encountered previously in the experiment. In the exclusion condition, they are to respond 'yes' only to items from one set (e.g. only to auditorily presented items), and 'no' to items from the other set (e.g. visually presented items). The responses of interest are those to items from that the set designated to receive 'yes' responses in the inclusion condition, and 'no' responses in the exclusion condition. The contrast of interest is, therefore, between the proportion of hits in the inclusion condition and the proportion of false alarms in the exclusion condition. Both recollection (R) and familiarity (F) are assumed to lead to a 'yes' response in the inclusion condition, because all studied items are to receive 'yes' responses, that is, $I = R + F\ (1 - R)$. In the exclusion condition, only familiarity in the absence of recollection will lead to a 'yes' response (i.e. a false alarm); recollection should lead an item to be rejected as not being from the set designated to receive 'yes' responses [i.e. $E = F\ (1 - R)$]. Independence of recollection and familiarity is once again assumed. The estimates for R and F are obtained in the same way as are C and U in stem completion [i.e. $R = I - E$, and $F = E/(1 - R)$].

The theoretical framework proposed by Jacoby and colleagues does not make a principled distinction between recollection and conscious memory, and between familiarity and unconscious memory. For example, performance in priming paradigms like stem completion is described in terms of *recollection* (R) and *automatic* (A) influences (e.g. Jacoby *et al.* 1993*b*), as is performance in recognition memory (e.g. Jacoby 1991). Elsewhere, performance in stem-and fragment-completion tests is described in terms of *recollection* and *familiarity* (Jacoby *et al.* in press). These terms are also used interchangeably with the terms *conscious* and *unconscious* influences. And 'know' responses in recognition memory, which index subjective feelings of familiarity in the absence of recollection, are treated as reflecting unconscious influences of memory (Jacoby *et al.* in press). The function of the process-dissociation analysis is, therefore, assumed to be equivalent regardless of experimental paradigm. We, on the other hand, believe that the analysis serves an entirely different function in

Table 3.11 Consequences of recollection, familiarity without recollection, and absence of both familiarity and recollection for the inclusion/exclusion procedure

	Task			
	Stem completion		Recognition memory	
Item status	Inclusion	Exclusion	Inclusion	Exclusion
Recollected	+	−	+	−
Familiar but not recollected	+	−	+	+
Neither familiar nor recollected	+	+	−	−

For stem completion, + indicates that an item will tend to be produced as a result of prior study, and − indicates that an item will tend to be omitted as a result of prior study. For recognition memory, + indicates that prior study will tend to elicit a 'yes' response, and − indicates that prior study will tend to elicit a 'no' response.

recognition memory than it does in repetition priming paradigms like stem completion. In stem completion, as previously argued, the analysis is designed to separate conscious from unconscious memory. In recognition memory, by contrast, the analysis is designed to separate two *conscious* forms of memory. When familiarity causes subjects in an exclusion condition to respond 'yes' erroneously to a previously encountered item, those subjects are showing an influence of *conscious* memory (familiarity) that they cannot avoid. Describing such involuntary influences as *unconscious* (e.g. Jacoby 1991; Jacoby *et al.* 1989*b*) once again reflects a failure to distinguish retrieval volition (voluntary vs. involuntary) from state of awareness with respect to the past (conscious vs. unconscious).[7]

The differences between the stem completion and recognition paradigms are illustrated in Table 3.11. In recognition memory, items that are associated neither with recollection nor familiarity will tend to produce 'no' responses when the subject is under exclusion instructions, just as they will under inclusion instructions. For items to produce 'yes' responses in the exclusion test, they must be familiar, but not recollected as studied. The fate of items associated neither with recollection nor with familiarity is quite different in the stem-completion paradigm. As a result of prior presentation, such items will tend to be produced in both the exclusion and inclusion conditions. Conscious memory—whether it consists of recollection or familiarity—leads studied target items to be omitted under exclusion test instructions, but not under inclusion test instructions.

7. In describing the process-dissociation procedure in stem completion we have used the labels C and U for the parameters, and in describing recognition memory, we have used R and F. We have done so in order to emphasize the differences between the two applications of the procedure in terms of our framework.

When a facilitatory priming effect is observed under opposition (or exclusion) instructions, that effect is associated with recognition failure, and not with familiarity or recollection (Richardson-Klavehn *et al.* 1994*a*; Richardson-Klavehn and Gardiner 1995).

In this section we compare the process-dissociation approach to recognition memory to our own approach, which involves direct, first-person reports of states of awareness in recognition memory. The technique that we use was introduced by Tulving (1985) in connection with his (1983) distinction between episodic and semantic memory systems. It relies on having subjects distinguish whether their recognition of an item is accompanied by recollective experience (e.g. remembering something about the circumstances of an item's presentation), or feelings of familiarity (in the experimental context) in the absence of recollective experience. These states of awareness are indicated by 'remember' and 'know' responses, respectively. Most subjects have little difficulty making the distinction between remembering and knowing, once it has been carefully explained to them. The distinction is generally easy to appreciate because it is relatively common in everyday life for people to experience feelings of familiarity in the absence of recollection. One quite often recognizes voices, faces, objects, or places as being familiar, but cannot recollect the encounter that is responsible for the feeling of familiarity. In such situations, memory is personal but not episodic; there is only the sense that there must have been a previous encounter.

There is now considerable evidence that these states of awareness (as indexed by 'remember' and 'know' responses) can be dissociated. A fairly large group of variables strongly influence remembering, but have little or no effect on knowing. Such variables include depth of processing and reading versus generating at study (e.g. Gardiner 1988), word frequency (Gardiner and Java 1990), divided versus full attention at study (for words: Gardiner and Parkin 1990; for faces: Parkin *et al.* in press), retention interval (Gardiner and Java 1991), and the drug lorazepam versus a placebo (Curran *et al.* 1993). Other variables have opposite effects on remembering and knowing. These include non-words versus words (Gardiner and Java 1990), words versus pictures at study with words at test (Rajaram 1993), and elderly versus young adults (Parkin and Walter 1992). Some variables, but not many, have been found to influence knowing and have little or no effect on remembering. For example, Rajaram (1993) found a higher level of knowing when a test word was preceded by a masked prime that was the same word, compared to when the prime was an unrelated word. And Gregg and Gardiner (1994), using an orienting task that strongly emphasized the perceptual characteristics of study items, found a higher level of knowing when study and test modality matched, compared to when they mismatched.

We do not consider these studies in detail here because recent reviews are available (Gardiner and Java 1993*a*,*b*; Rajaram and Roediger in press). Instead, we present data from a new study that shows a particularly impressive dissociation between remembering and knowing, and provides an important link between our experiential approach to recognition memory and prior approaches that have postulated dual bases for recognition judgements.

3.3.1 A 'double dissociation' of consciousness

In the past, positive effects of maintenance rehearsal on recognition, but not on recall, were influential in promoting the idea that there are two distinct bases for recognition memory judgments (e.g. Craik and Watkins 1973; Geiselman and Bjork 1980; Woodward *et al.* 1973). Mandler (e.g. 1980) argued that recognition depended either on familiarity, which depended on *intra-item organization*, or on recollection, which depended on *extra-item organization*. Maintenance rehearsal was assumed to affect intra-item organization by integrating an item with its perceptual features; elaborative rehearsal, on the other hand, was assumed to influence extra-item organization by connecting an item to other studied items. These connections were assumed to subserve performance in recall tests, as well as in recognition tests.

Gardiner *et al.* (1994) set out to establish a link between the evidence from prior studies of rehearsal and the evidence from the experiential approach to measuring familiarity and recollection. We used an item-by-item directed-forgetting paradigm, in which each study-list word was followed by a cue designating that word as to-be-learned or to-be-forgotten. The total trial time for each study word was held constant at 7 s, but the delay between the word and the cue was either short or long. The cue came either immediately after the item was presented (i.e. word for 1 s; cue for 1 s; blank interval for 5 s; next word) or just prior to the presentation of the next study-list item (i.e. word for 1 s; blank interval for 5 s; cue for 1 s; next word). A critical feature of this procedure was that subjects could not predict whether an item was to be learned or to be forgotten until the within-list cue appeared, because learn and forget trials were unsystematically interspersed in the study list. Subjects could not, therefore, apply different rehearsal strategies to to-be-learned and to-be-forgotten items until the cue appeared.

Previous research using this type of paradigm established that subjects engage in maintenance rehearsal of both to-be-learned and to-be-forgotten items until the within-list cue is presented, because it is not in their interest to interassociate an item with other studied items if they are later instructed to forget that item. When the cue is presented, they cease rehearsing to-be-forgotten items; by contrast, if the item is to be learned, they rehearse that item elaboratively (Bjork 1972; Woodward *et al.* 1973).

In consequence, if subjective familiarity is influenced by maintenance rehearsal, knowing should increase with cue delay, regardless of whether an item is to-be-learned or to-be-forgotten. Knowing should not be influenced by to-be-learned versus to-be-forgotten status, because that variable determines whether or not an item receives elaborative rehearsal. Remembering, on the other hand, should be more likely for to-be-learned than for to-be-forgotten items, consistent with prior evidence that remembering depends on semantic elaboration at study. Remembering should be relatively uninfluenced by cue delay, because maintenance rehearsal involves little semantic elaboration.

The results (Table 3.12) bore out the predictions rather conclusively. The influence of cue delay on overall hit rate was associated with a difference in 'know' responses, while the advantage of 'learn' over 'forget' words in overall hit rate was associated with a difference in 'remember' responses. An interesting additional finding is that the advantage for learn over forget words in terms of 'remember' responses was greater when cue delay was short than when it was long. This result makes sense because the short-cue-delay condition allowed 5 s for elaborative rehearsal of learn words prior to the presentation of the next study-list item. The long-cue-delay condition, by contrast, allowed only 1 s for elaborative rehearsal of learn words before the next item was presented. In sum, the data provide further support for the hypothesis that maintenance rehearsal influences recognition memory via an effect on familiarity. They also forge a connection between recent research based on subjective reports and an older tradition (e.g. Mandler 1980) in which the contributions of familiarity and recollection to recognition were inferred indirectly.

The overall data pattern in this study demonstrates a 'double dissociation' between the two states of awareness in recognition memory. The possibility of demonstrating such a 'double dissociation' was raised by studies showing influences on knowing that were unaccompanied by influences on remembering (Gregg and Gardiner 1994; Rajaram 1993). These findings stand in contrast to the most frequent pattern, in which a variable affects remembering but not knowing. As far as we are aware,

Table 3.12 Proportions of 'remember' and 'know' responses as a function of cue delay and instruction to learn or forget in Gardiner *et al.* (1994)

	Short delay		Long delay		
Response type	'Learn'	'Forget'	'Learn'	'Forget'	Unstudied
'Remember'	0.50	0.23	0.40	0.26	0.03
'Know'	0.18	0.20	0.27	0.29	0.10
Σ	0.68	0.43	0.67	0.55	0.13

however, the current study is the first that actually demonstrates such a dissociation within the same subjects and procedures. Strictly defined, a *double dissociation* consists of a pattern in which one variable influences performance in task A but not in task B, while another variable influences performance in task B but not in task A (for a discussion of such patterns and their theoretical implications, see Dunn and Kirsner 1988). Of course, 'remember' and 'know' responses do not represent different tasks. However, the pattern that we observed, like a double dissociation between tasks, places constraints on interpretation that other patterns of data cannot. For example, the hypothesis that 'remember' and 'know' responses simply represent different levels of subjective confidence is virtually impossible to reconcile with this pattern, as is the hypothesis that the level of 'know' responses is simply insensitive to encoding manipulations. The current data provide strong support for the claim that remembering and knowing are qualitatively different conscious states, in the sense that it is possible to influence the likelihood of one without influencing the likelihood of the other.

3.3.2 Relationship between conscious states in recognition memory

We argued previously that voluntary and involuntary retrieval might be independent, redundant, or exclusive, but that logic dictates an exclusivity relation between conscious and unconscious memorial states of awareness. In terms of our framework, familiarity and recollection both qualify as *conscious* states of awareness, so it is logically possible that familiarity and recollection are independent, redundant, or exclusive. 'Remember' and 'know' *responses*, on the other hand, are necessarily exclusive because subjects place each recognized item into only one of two categories. The subject is instructed to respond 'remember' when an item elicits recollective experience, and to respond 'know' when an item elicits feelings of familiarity *in the absence of* recollective experience. Gardiner and Parkin (1990, see also Gardiner and Java 1993*a*) suggested an exclusivity position for remembering and knowing, arguing that one cannot experience recollection at one and the same time as feelings of familiarity in the absence of recollection. This observation is undoubtedly correct, but as Table 3.13 shows, independence and redundancy models of familiarity and recollection do not assume that one can simultaneously be in a recollective state and a non-recollective state. They differ from exclusivity only in that they postulate that recollection can occur *in conjunction* with familiarity. The proportion of 'know' responses reflects the same state of consciousness, regardless of model: it indexes the proportion of items that are familiar but not recollected. The proportion of 'remember' responses, on the other hand, is interpreted differently depending on the model one adopts: under independence it consists of

Table 3.13 Relation between 'remember' and 'know' responses and the conscious memorial states permitted by the independence, redundancy, and exclusivity models

	'Remember'		'Know'	
Model	Recollected and familiar	Recollected and not familiar	Familiar and not recollected	Neither
Independence	YES	YES	YES	YES
Redundancy	YES	NO	YES	YES
Exclusivity	NO	YES	YES	YES

YES = permitted by the model; NO = not permitted by the model.

a mixture of items that are recollected but not familiar and items that are recollected and familiar; under redundancy it consists only of items that are recollected and familiar; and under exclusivity, it consists only of items that are recollected but not familiar. Independence, redundancy, and exclusivity relations between recollection and familiarity are, therefore, not only logically possible, but also completely compatible with the fact that 'remember' and 'know' responses are exclusive.

Whereas all three possible relations between recollection and familiarity are logically possible, they do not all seem equally plausible from an intuitive point of view. In particular, the independence relation implies that recollection can occur both with familiarity and without familiarity—an assumption that does not seem to square with everyday experiences of recognition. It also implies that it should be possible to adapt the 'remember'/'know' procedure so that subjects separate items that are recollected and familiar from items that are recollected and not familiar. Jacoby *et al.* (in press) have, nevertheless, argued that 'remember' and 'know' responses must be reinterpreted according to an independence model. The logic comes from two-component theories of recognition memory (e.g. Mandler 1980), by way of the process-dissociation framework: A 'know' response will be issued only if an item is familiar and not recollected [$K = F(1 - R) = F - (RF)$], so that the observed proportion of 'know' responses underestimates the overall proportion of items associated with familiarity. The correction applied, therefore, is analogous to the one applied to the exclusion condition in the process-dissociation procedure [i.e. $F = K/(1 - R) = K + (RF)$]. It boosts the observed proportion of 'know' responses to account for the joint probability of recollection and familiarity. Making this correction assumes that the proportion of 'remember' responses is an index of R, as obtained by subtracting exclusion from inclusion performance. Jacoby *et al.* suggest that the results of 'remember'/'know' studies fall into line with the estimates of recollection and familiarity from the inclusion/exclusion procedure when the data are corrected for independence in this fashion.

Jacoby and colleagues are committed to an independence assumption for both recognition memory and repetition priming paradigms: (a) because their framework does not make a principled distinction between the concepts of recollection and familiarity in recognition and the concepts of conscious and unconscious memory in priming; and (b) because the independence assumption is the only one—in terms of their two-process model—that does not involve treating either the inclusion or the exclusion test as a 'process-pure' measure. In terms of our framework, however, recognition memory and repetition priming do not have to be treated in the same way. The process-dissociation procedure in recognition memory is designed to produce estimates of two forms of conscious memory (i.e. familiarity and recollection), whereas the process-dissociation procedure in priming paradigms is designed to separate conscious and unconscious memory (see Table 3.11). For that reason, the assumption concerning the relation between states of awareness that is appropriate for repetition priming paradigms may not be appropriate for recognition memory paradigms, and vice versa. There is, in consequence, no particular reason to favour an independence assumption for recollection and familiarity in the 'remember'/'know' procedure, unless that assumption renders the data from 'remember'/'know' studies more meaningful and interpretable.

Table 3.14 shows data and familiarity estimates (computed based on the independence assumption) for a number of different 'remember'/'know' studies, selected to represent the three kinds of data patterns so far obtained. Familiarity estimates for variables like divided versus undivided

Table 3.14 Effect of correcting for independence of familiarity and recollection on estimates of familiarity from the 'remember'/'know' procedure

Variable	Condition	Response proportion		Familiarity
		'Remember'	'Know'	[K/(1 − R)]
Attention	Divided	0.38	0.20	0.32
at study[a]	Full	0.50	0.21	0.42
Lexicality[b]	Non-word	0.19	0.30	0.37
	Word	0.28	0.16	0.22
Age[c]	Elderly	0.20	0.46	0.58
	Young	0.51	0.25	0.51
Masked	Unrelated	0.42	0.18	0.31
test prime[d]	Repetition	0.43	0.24	0.42
Study, test	Different	0.10	0.26	0.29
modalities[e]	Same	0.11	0.51	0.57

[a] Gardiner and Parkin (1990); [b] Gardiner and Java (1990);
[c] Parkin and Walter (1992); [d] Rajaram (1993); [e] Gregg andGardiner (1994).

attention at study, which influence 'remember' and not 'know' responses (Gardiner and Parkin 1990), will always indicate that familiarity is influenced in a similar way to recollection. Familiarity estimates for variables that have reverse effects on 'remember' and 'know' responses, such as lexicality (Gardiner and Java 1990) and age (Parkin and Walter 1992) can lead to different conclusions for different variables. For non-words versus words the familiarity estimates concur with the 'know' responses. For age the familiarity estimates show little difference as a function of age, despite the substantial difference in 'know' responses. Familiarity estimates for variables that influence 'know' but not 'remember' responses, such as same versus different masked test prime (Rajaram 1993) and match in study and test modality (Gregg and Gardiner 1994), inevitably magnify the difference already apparent in the 'know' responses. In our view the familiarity estimates derived by correcting for independence render what was a rather consistent and interpretable pattern of data considerably less, not more, meaningful.

For reasons not yet understood, the pattern of 'remember' and 'know' responses sometimes converges with, and sometimes diverges from, the results of the inclusion/exclusion procedure. For example, the inclusion/exclusion procedure in recognition memory leads to the conclusion that the effect of dividing attention is to decrease recollection, but that familiarity is relatively uninfluenced. The same outcome is found for 'remember' and 'know' responses (Gardiner and Parkin 1990). However, in this instance Jacoby and colleagues would have to argue that the two approaches are at variance, because the independence correction on the 'know' responses leads to the conclusion that both familiarity and recollection are decreased by dividing attention. One could argue that this discrepancy is attributable to subjects' failure to encode study words in the divided attention condition used by Gardiner and Parkin (1990). However, the discrepancy cannot be explained away in this manner because Parkin *et al.* (1990)—using exactly the same encoding procedures and words as were used by Gardiner and Parkin—found no negative effect of dividing attention on priming in an incidental test of fragment completion. Exactly the same problem for the independence interpretation of 'know' responses is presented by evidence that word frequency selectively influences estimates of recollection obtained from the inclusion/exclusion procedure (Guttentag and Carroll 1994). The 'remember'/'know' procedure leads to exactly the same conclusion when 'know' responses are taken at face value (Gardiner and Java 1990), but not when the independence correction is applied to the 'know' responses.

Further difficulites for the independence interpretation of 'know' responses arise when the effects of ageing are considered. The inclusion/exclusion procedure leads to the conclusion that aging decreases recollection, but that familiarity is relatively uninfluenced (Jennings and

Jacoby 1993). Based on this result, Jacoby *et al.* (in press) argue that the increase in 'know' responses with age observed by Parkin and Walter (1992) does not reflect a true increase in familiarity with age, and that the greater number of 'remember' responses observed in the younger adults (compared with the older adults) resulted in a constraint on the number of 'know' responses that the younger adults were able to make. When the 'know' responses are corrected for independence (Table 3.14), there seems to be some support for this view. However, it must be noted that Parkin and Walter's subjects were given no specific encoding task. In studies in which encoding activities have been controlled, older adults have shown *no* increase in 'know' responses, in conjunction with a large decrease in 'remember' responses (Fell 1992; Mantyla 1993; Perfect *et al.* 1995). The implication is that when encoding activities are uncontrolled, older adults rely more on maintenance rehearsal, and less on elaborative rehearsal, than do younger adults. Based on the results of the Gardiner *et al.* (1994) study described previously, this trade-off between maintenance and elaborative rehearsal would be expected to lead to exactly the pattern of results that Parkin and Walter (1992) observed. In support of this interpretation, Parkin and White (in prep.) found that the increase in 'know' responses with age that occurs when encoding activities are uncontrolled is attenuated when items are presented for study at a slower rate. Presumably the older adults, when given more time, become better able to engage in effortful elaborative rehearsal.

Finally, a strong prediction of the hypothesis that the approaches are reducible, given an assumption of independence for the 'remember'/'know' procedure, is that performance in an exclusion test condition in recognition memory should always be influenced in the same way as are 'know' responses by experimental manipulations. The reason is that exclusion performance is assumed to reflect familiarity in the absence of recollection [i.e. $E = F(1 - R)$], and 'know' responses are assumed to index exactly the same state [i.e. $K = F(1 - R)$]. This prediction is clearly inconsistent with data from generate/read manipulations at study: Jacoby (1991) found that subjects were better able to exclude items that were generated at study than items that were read at study, whereas Gardiner (1988) and Java (1994) found no difference in the level of 'know' responses for generate and read items. The predicted similarity in effects on exclusion performance and on 'know' responses is rarely likely to occur in other situations either. The reason is that the proportion of 'yes' responses to critical items in an exclusion test will generally be *inversely* related to recollection, because recollection leads those items to be rejected as not being from the subset of studied items that are designated to receive 'yes' responses. By contrast, there is no particular reason to expect the level of 'know' responses to be inversely related to recollection (except where there are obvious ceiling effects). In fact, whereas 'know' responses sometimes do show such a pattern, the most frequently observed pattern is that 'know' responses are uninfluenced by a manipulation that influences recollection as indexed by 'remember' responses. Moreover, recent experiments show that under some conditions an increase in 'know' responses is accompanied by a parallel *increase* in 'remember' responses (Gardiner, Kaminska, Dixon, and Java in prep.).

In our view, it is much too premature to expect convergence between the results of the process-dissociation analysis of recognition memory and the results of the 'remember'/'know' procedure. The demands they make of the subject are different, and for that reason it is not only possible, but likely, that they will lead to different conclusions until we have a much better understanding of both procedures. Consider, for example, the role of recollection in the two procedures. Exclusion test performance plays a crucial role in determining estimates of recollection in the process-dissociation procedure, because items that are recollected are assumed to lead to 'no' responses. But to respond 'no' to a studied item in an exclusion test, one must not only have some recollective experience: one must be able to retrieve enough information about the item to be able to determine that it was not part of the subset of studied items designated to receive 'yes' responses. By contrast, to issue a 'remember' response for a particular item, it is only necessary to have some recollective experience. Having recollective experience (e.g. remembering what one was thinking when an item was presented) does not necessarily imply the ability to retrieve information that permits discrimination between different sets of studied items. In consequence, an item that elicits a 'remember' response might not always result in a 'no' response in an exclusion test, so that the way in which items contribute to measures of recollection and familiarity in the two procedures might be fundamentally different.

3.3.3 The problem of response criteria in the inclusion/exclusion procedure

Roediger and McDermott (1994) point out that differing rates of false alarms to unstudied items across subject groups—indicating different response criteria—can create problems in interpreting the results of the process-dissociation procedure in recognition memory. Graf and Komatsu (1994; see also Komatsu *et al.* 1995) point to similar problems within a single group of subjects, if inclusion and exclusion instructions lead to different response criteria. Such changes in criterion could occur when the number of test items that is designated to receive 'yes' responses is greater in the inclusion condition than in the exclusion condition (as in list-discrimination paradigms patterned after the one used by Jacoby 1991). The situation is analogous to the one in tasks designed to measure perceptual sensitivity, in which changing the relative percentages of signal and noise trials leads to changes in both hit and false alarm rates (Green and Swets 1974). Changing the relative percentages of studied and unstudied items in recognition memory might be expected to have a similar effect, but to our knowledge this problem has not been widely studied. For that reason, we offer data obtained by Richardson-Klavehn *et al.* (1994*b*, experiment 1) as food for thought.

They used a between-subjects manipulation of the percentage of studied items on the test (25 per cent vs. 75 per cent), which was accomplished by changing filler items in the study and test lists. This manipulation was crossed with the Auditory-Deep versus Visual-Shallow encoding manipulation described previously. The data (presented in Table 3.15) come from a pool of critical studied and unstudied test items that remained constant in size despite the change in the overall percentage of test items that were previously studied. The critical finding is that increasing the percentage of studied test items increased the proportion of 'yes' responses to both studied items (hits) and to unstudied items (false alarms), suggesting that increasing the percentage of studied items caused subjects to relax their criterion for emitting a 'yes' response. The implication is that the difference in the size of the pool of items designated to receive 'yes' responses across inclusion and exclusion conditions may sometimes influence response criterion.

How the impact of such changes in response criterion should be assessed is a thorny issue, both for traditional recognition tests, and for the inclusion/exclusion procedure (e.g. Jacoby *et al.* in press; Roediger and

Table 3.15 Recognition memory performance as a function of percentage of test items studied in Richardson-Klavehn *et al.* (1994*b*, experiment 1)

Test items studied (%)	Studied: Auditory-Deep	Studied: Visual-Shallow	Unstudied
Mean hit and false alarm proportions			
25	0.91	0.34	0.06
75	0.96	0.52	0.16
Hits minus false alarms			
25	0.85	0.28	
75	0.80	0.36	
Signal-detection model (d')*			
25	3.37	1.27	
75	3.14	1.25	

* The signal-detection model yielded mean criterion scores of 1.81 for the 25 percent-studied condition and 1.18 for the 75 percent-studied condition (a significant difference, $P < 0.001$).

McDermott 1994; Verfaellie 1994). The data presented here suggest that the conclusions one draws can vary substantially depending on the model one adopts. Richardson-Klavehn *et al.* were interested in discovering whether increasing the percentage of studied test items would simply influence response criterion, or whether (as hypothesized by Jacoby 1983*a*) it would have an effect akin to a list-context reinstatement effect—in which case the manipulation should influence accuracy *as well as* response criterion. Interpreting the false alarm rate as indicating the probability of guessing correctly, as assumed by a high-threshold model, leads one to subtract false alarm rates from hit rates (Roediger and McDermott 1994). In the current case (see Table 3.15), this correction suggests that increasing the percentage of studied items led to a higher proportion of 'yes' responses due to guessing, and also improved accuracy for Visual-Shallow items, but did not improve accuracy for Auditory-Deep items (owing to a ceiling effect on those items).

Applying a signal-detection model, on the other hand, leads to the conclusion that increasing the percentage of studied test items caused subjects to use a more lenient criterion for a 'yes' response, and exerted no influence at all on discrimination between studied and unstudied items. The latter outcome is exactly the same as the one obtained in signal-detection experiments in which the relative percentages of signal and noise trials are varied (Green and Swets 1974), and it suggests that there was no list-context reinstatement effect. Differential effects of a criterion shift on responses to different types of item make perfect sense on a signal-detection model, because the underlying distributions of mnemonic information are assumed to be approximately gaussian. According to the model, performance on Visual-Shallow items showed a larger influence of a criterion shift than did performance on Auditory-Deep and unstudied items: (a) because the mean of the distribution for those items (as indicated by d') fell closer to the criterion than did the means of the distributions for Auditory-Deep and unstudied items; and (b) because probability density is greatest at the mean of a gaussian distribution.

The correct choice of model for interpreting changes in response criterion is critical, whether those changes occur as a function of experimental manipulations at test (e.g. inclusion vs. exclusion), or as a function of subject group (as in Verfaellie and Treadwell 1993). Roediger and McDermott (1994) argue that a signal-detection model is not appropriate for overall performance, because of evidence that there are multiple bases for recognition memory, rather than a single dimension of strength. However, they also raise 'grave concerns' (p. 286) about the application of a high-threshold model, which leads one to subtract false alarm scores (for unstudied items) from inclusion and exclusion scores before application of the process-dissociation analysis. Jacoby *et al.* (in press;

see also Verfaellie 1994) concur that a signal-detection model is not appropriate for overall performance, but embrace such a model for familiarity, arguing that familiarity can be described in terms of an underlying dimension of strength, whereas recollection cannot be so described. The latter approach depends on the notion that false alarms to unstudied items reflect familiarity, and not 'false' recollection, so that only familiarity estimates need to be adjusted for changes in criterion. It leads one to take estimates of recollection at face value (i.e. to obtain them from unadjusted inclusion and exclusion scores), but to derive estimates of familiarity from a signal detection model after recollection has been estimated.

The model of criterion effects proposed by Jacoby *et al.* (in press) has not yet been thoroughly evaluated, but it seems to us that this model already raises concerns. The first of these relates to the proposal that recollection be estimated from unadjusted inclusion and exclusion scores. This proposal seems to run foul of the core assumption that overall inclusion and exclusion scores reflect the joint contribution of familiarity and recollection. Given this assumption, overall inclusion and exclusion scores will show the influence of shifts in the criterion placed on familiarity values, and estimates of recollection will reflect this change in criterion (e.g. if there is a change in the familiarity criterion across the inclusion and exclusion conditions). The second concern relates to the proposal that recollection (as defined in the process-dissociation procedure) is not subject to criterion effects. It can be argued, quite plausibly we think, that recollection is all-or-none in many situations, and that 'false' recollection is extremely rare for unstudied items (Verfaellie 1994). However, as noted previously, recollection in the process-dissociation procedure for recognition memory is defined in terms of the ability to *discriminate* between sets of items, and it is not hard to envisage situations in which such discrimination is made difficult (e.g. as in Anderson and Bower 1972). In such situations, shifts in response criterion may apply to recollection as well as to familiarity, and a signal-detection model for recollection may be necessary. Whatever the solution to the problem of response criterion in the inclusion/exclusion procedure for recognition memory, it is apparent that such a solution will be complex.

The setting of a criterion in a recognition memory task is a further example of strategic behaviour, and considering the problem in this way further emphasizes a general point made earlier with respect to strategies in repetition priming paradigms. The point is that the application of the process-dissociation model does not exempt one from determining empirically, and accounting for, the strategies that subjects follow in performing a memory test. In that sense, the process-dissociation procedure is no different from any other procedure for studying memory, and claims that it conclusively overcomes problems of 'process-purity' encountered by other approaches must be treated with caution.

3.3.4 The relationship between familiarity and perceptual priming

A consistent theme in dual-component accounts of recognition memory over the last 15 years has been the assumption that the contribution of familiarity to recognition memory reflects perceptual fluency, and that this perceptual fluency is also reflected in repetition priming effects in perceptual tasks (e.g. Cermak 1993; Graf and Mandler 1984; Jacoby and Dallas 1981; Jacoby *et al.* in press; Parkin 1993). As previously discussed, the process-dissociation framework lends itself to this assumption, not least owing to the similar terminology used to describe the components underlying performance in recognition memory paradigms and in priming paradigms. Here we review a number of results that have led us to question the view that familiarity, as assessed by 'know' responses, corresponds with perceptual priming and, in particular, the view that 'know' responses correspond with perceptual priming effects that are unaccompanied by conscious awareness of the past.

If familiarity is reflected in perceptual priming, and if the effect of maintenance rehearsal on recognition memory reflects an effect on familiarity (as argued by Gardiner *et al.* 1994 and others), one should be able to obtain effects of maintenance rehearsal on priming as well as on recognition memory. Richardson-Klavehn and Bjork (1988*b*; Richardson and Bjork 1982) tested this hypothesis by comparing auditory recognition memory to an incidental test of auditory perceptual identification. They adapted a paradigm developed by Geiselman and Bjork (1980), in which subjects rehearse auditorily presented words imaginally. Geiselman and Bjork had their subjects perform either maintenance rehearsal (i.e. imagining the speaker repeat the words over and over), or elaborative rehearsal (e.g. imagining the speaker saying a sentence containing the words). The critical finding was that increasing the duration of maintenance rehearsal improved recognition memory only if voice (male vs. female) was the same at study and test. Increasing the duration of elaborative rehearsal also increased performance, but match in voice between study and test made no difference to performance. These findings were interpreted by Geiselman and Bjork as providing strong support for the hypothesis that maintenance rehearsal influences the familiarity component of recognition memory.

Richardson-Klavehn and Bjork's encoding conditions were the same as Geiselman and Bjork's, except that voice was always the same at study and test, and two (instead of three) rehearsal durations were used (5 and 15 s). The novel predictions were for auditory perceptual identification, which was expected to act as an index of familiarity (after Jacoby and

Table 3.16 Mean proportions recognized and perceptually identified as a function of maintenance and elaborative rehearsal in Richardson-Klavehn and Bjork (1988*b*)

	Rehearsal type				
	Maintenance		Elaborative		
Test type	5 s	15 s	5 s	15 s	Unstudied
Recognition	0.58	0.66	0.81	0.86	0.30[a]
Identification	0.62*	0.64*	0.64*	0.65*	0.55

Significant priming in auditory perceptual identification is indicated by an asterisk.
[a]False alarm rate.

Dallas 1981). Priming should be greater following maintenance rehearsal than following elaborative rehearsal, based on claim that maintenance rehearsal increases familiarity by integrating an item with its perceptual features. This advantage of maintenance over elaborative rehearsal was expected to increase with rehearsal duration, because the difference in the amount of rote processing between rehearsal conditions should become cumulatively larger as rehearsal duration increases.

The results are presented in Table 3.16. There was a strong and highly significant advantage for elaborative over maintenance rehearsal in recognition memory, and performance increased significantly with rehearsal duration for both types of rehearsal, replicating Geiselman and Bjork (1980). The perceptual identification data, however, did not confirm the predictions. Significant priming was observed in all four study conditions, but there was no indication that priming was greater following maintenance rehearsal than following elaborative rehearsal. Nor was there any indication that priming was influenced by rehearsal duration. This result cannot be attributed to simple insensitivity to experimental manipulations, because priming in auditory perceptual identification is highly sensitive to match in study and test modalities (e.g. Jackson and Morton 1984). Moreover, a similar null effect of duration of maintenance rehearsal was obtained by Greene (1986) using intentional and incidental tests of stem completion. These rehearsal data are also consistent with findings of null effects of massed repetition on priming in incidental tests (for a summary, see Roediger and McDermott 1993).

A different line of evidence questioning the link between familiarity and perceptual priming comes from the study by Java (1994) discussed previously (Table 3.3). Following her incidental test of stem completion, she had subjects inspect their responses and judge whether or not each word that they had written had been studied. New target items and non-target items

Table 3.17 Mean proportions of target items remembered, known, and unrecognized following word-stem completion in Java (1994, experiment 2)

Response type	Studied: Generate	Studied: Read	Unstudied
Intentional test condition			
'Remember'	0.32	0.09	0.01
'Know'	0.09	0.13	0.03
Σ	0.41	0.22	0.04
Incidental test condition			
'Remember'	0.20	0.16	0.00
'Know'	0.10	0.08	0.03
Unrecognized	0.04	0.23	0.12
Σ	0.34	0.47	0.15

There were no unrecognized items in the intentional test condition because subjects were instructed to recall only studied items (i.e. subjects believed they had studied the unstudied target items that they produced).

served as unstudied foils in this recognition test. If a word was recognized, they classified it as remembered or known. Subjects who had completed the intentional test also had to make a 'remember'/'know' judgement for each recalled word. The results are displayed in Table 3.17. The results for the intentional test condition show a pattern similar to previous results in recognition memory (e.g. Gardiner 1988). That is, the overall advantage of generate over read encoding in cued recall was associated with an increase in the proportion of 'remember' responses, but the proportion of 'know' responses was similar across conditions.

The critical results for present purposes come from the incidental test. As noted previously, performance in that condition showed a crossed doubled dissociation from cued recall performance, with greater priming in the read condition than in the generate condition. Using the logic of the retrieval intentionality criterion (Schacter *et al.* 1989), this result implies that priming in the incidental test predominantly reflected involuntary memory. If involuntary memory in an incidental test of stem completion was an index of familiarity, one would expect priming to be positively related to the level of 'know' responses. This result was not observed. As in the intentional test condition, the proportion of 'know' responses did not differ depending on the study condition, replicating prior findings. The advantage of the read over the generate condition in the incidental test lay predominantly in the frequency with which subjects completed stems with items that were *unrecognized* (i.e. *neither* recollected as studied *nor* familiar in the absence of recollection).

These 'remember'/'know' data not only argue against identifying familiarity, as indexed by 'know' responses, with priming in incidental tests. Taken together with other data, they also present strong evidence against Jacoby *et al.*'s (in press) assertion that one can equate familiarity, as measured by 'know' responses, with unconscious memory, as estimated from the process-dissociation procedure in perceptual priming paradigms like stem and fragment completion. If one does not distinguish familiarity from unconscious memory, then one has to assume that exclusion performance in priming tasks indexes familiarity in the absence of recollection, as do 'know' responses. Similarly, 'know' responses index unconscious memory in the absence of conscious memory, as does exclusion performance. One must then predict that 'know' responses will respond to experimental manipulations in the same way as does exclusion performance in priming paradigms. This prediction, however, is clearly falsified: (a) by the finding that the level of 'know' responses is uninfluenced by depth of processing (Gardiner 1988), generating versus reading (Gardiner 1988; Java 1994), and divided versus full attention at encoding (Gardiner and Parkin 1990; Parkin *et al.* in press); and (b) by the finding that the same encoding variables influence stem completion under exclusion conditions (Jacoby *et al.* 1993*b*; Toth *et al.* 1994). This conjunction of outcomes, however, makes perfect sense if it assumed that the items suppressed in an exclusion (or opposition) condition in stem completion are not only those that are recollected (i.e. 'remember' items), but also those that are familiar in the absence of recollection ('know' items), as we have argued previously (see Table 3.11). Such an assumption is supported by data showing that stem-completion priming under opposition conditions is unaccompanied by recognition (Richardson-Klavehn and Gardiner 1995; Richardson-Klavehn *et al.* 1994*a*).

To summarize, the results reviewed here, together with other data showing priming in the absence of recognition (e.g. Eich 1984; Squire *et al.* 1985), seem to us to create considerable difficulties for the view that familiarity, as indexed by 'know' responses, resembles perceptual priming. Priming in incidental tests is sometimes accompanied, and sometimes unaccompanied by conscious awareness of the past. However, we suggest that unconscious memory, as revealed in perceptual priming under certain conditions, is exactly that: *unconscious*. In such situations subjects have no sense of pastness at all; that is, they experience *neither* recollection *nor* familiarity. By contrast, the *déjà vu* kind of familiarity that results from a recent encounter with a stimulus is a conscious memorial experience. Familiarity can, however, have effects on behaviour that are not amenable to voluntary control, such as when a subject mistakenly judges a nonfamous name as famous because it is familiar as a result of prior exposure, but not recollected as studied (e.g. Jacoby *et al.*

1989*b*). Indeed, familiarity in the absence of recollection, as indexed by 'know' responses, exhibits at least one major characteristic associated with automaticity—that it is not reduced by dividing attention at encoding (Gardiner and Parkin 1990; Parkin *et al.* in press).

3.4 SUMMARY OF THE ARGUMENTS

In this chapter we have made a case for greater precision of terminology and of theoretical analysis in attempts to understand the relationship between memory and consciousness. In accordance with the principle of *inconvertibility of terms* (Gardiner and Java 1993*a*), we have presented a framework that is designed to avoid the confusion that results when the same terms are used to label tasks, strategies, memorial states of awareness, and underlying theoretical constructs such as retrieval processes or memory systems. We make a clear distinction between memory tasks, which can be defined in terms of instructions and retrieval cues, and the strategies and states of awareness that can be involved in those tasks, thereby avoiding a-priori assumptions of strategy- and awareness-purity. Furthermore, following Ebbinghaus, we distinguish retrieval volition (voluntary vs. involuntary) from memorial state of awareness with respect to the past (conscious vs. unconscious). We also distinguish two forms of conscious awareness of the past, familiarity and recollection. In contrast, the popular distinction between explicit and implicit memory can be applied to tasks, strategies, and memorial states of awareness. The process-dissociation framework recently introduced by Jacoby and colleagues does not equate tasks with strategies or states of awareness, but it does identify voluntary retrieval with conscious awareness of the past and involuntary retrieval with absence of conscious awareness of the past. That is, it replaces the assumption that tasks are strategy- and awareness-pure with the assumption that states of awareness are strategy-pure. It also equates recollection with conscious memory and familiarity with unconscious memory. The process-dissociation framework, therefore, does not accommodate cases in which subjects become aware of a past event without intending to do so (involuntary conscious memory). It also denies the intuitively plausible assumption that familiarity is a conscious memorial experience, and does not accommodate the possibility that conscious awareness of the past can have effects that are not subject to voluntary control.

In support of our framework we have presented several kinds of data. We examined the striking cross doubled dissociations between intentional and incidental tests that are observed in normal subjects, and concluded that such dissociations can be good evidence for differences in retrieval volition between tests, but that they do not necessarily imply dissociations of consciousness. By comparing intentional, incidental, and opposition tests, we showed that retrieval volition can be experimentally dissociated from conscious awareness of the past. In a stem-completion paradigm, the tendency to complete stems with studied items can be held roughly constant as a function of depth of processing, indicating involuntary retrieval, while the level of conscious awareness of encoding events simultaneously shows large differences as a function of depth of processing. We argued that priming in standard incidental tests can be used to index involuntary memory, whether accompanied or unaccompanied by awareness of the past. Priming in an opposition test (in which subjects are instructed to omit studied items) serves as an index of involuntary memory that is unaccompanied by awareness of the past. The difference in performance between the tests is an index of involuntary conscious memory.

Our opposition test data, together with data from post-test recognition measures, suggest that priming can occur in conjunction with a complete absence of awareness of the individual events that led to priming. In such cases, priming is accompanied by recognition failure, not by recollection or by feelings of familiarity. Moreover, we obtained further evidence that maintenance rehearsal influences recognition memory via an effect on subjective familiarity, but we have found no evidence that maintenance rehearsal influences priming. Along with other evidence, these results suggest that familiarity should be viewed as a form of conscious memory, along with recollection. Recollection and familiarity, however, are qualitatively distinct types of conscious memory and are, in consequence, experimentally dissociable.

In terms of our framework, 'contamination by conscious memory' in incidental tests has two critically different meanings. If it is taken to mean that incidental tests involve subjective awareness of past events, then the data we have reviewed indicate that incidental tests *are* badly contaminated. These data, however, also show that subjective awareness of the past is not to be equated with a voluntary strategy for retrieving studied items. The problem with incidental tests, then, is not to rule out subjective awareness of past events, but to rule out contamination by voluntary retrieval strategies. We suggest, with others (e.g. Bowers and Schacter 1990; Roediger and McDermott 1993), that the surest method for minimizing the role of voluntary retrieval strategies in an incidental test is to inform subjects of the study–test relationship, and to point out that they may recognize particular test items as previously studied, but to emphasize that they should nevertheless adopt an involuntary retrieval strategy. Traditional comparisons of intentional and incidental tests in normal subjects are best regarded as elucidating the distinction between voluntary and involuntary retrieval, and not necessarily the distinction between conscious and unconscious memory. The process-dissociation framework advocated by Jacoby and colleagues was designed to overcome problems of 'contamination' of incidental test performance. Because that framework equates conscious memorial awareness with the use of a voluntary retrieval strategy, however, it fails to distinguish the two critically different meanings of the term 'contamination'. The analysis presented here suggests that the process-dissociation procedure cannot replace the use of incidental tests. When applied to priming paradigms like stem completion, comparisons of inclusion and exclusion tests do not permit separation of voluntary from involuntary memory, as comparisons of intentional and incidental tests do. The reason is that the criterion for excluding studied items in the exclusion test condition is one of conscious awareness that the item has been previously encountered (as in our opposition test condition). In terms of our framework, therefore, the U parameter resulting from this procedure is not an estimate of involuntary memory regardless of state of awareness, which is what priming in an incidental test is designed to measure. In consequence, if an incidental test shows evidence of memory when the U parameter does not, the effect in the incidental test cannot be conclusively attributed to contamination by voluntary retrieval processes. This conclusion can, of course, be undermined by questioning our assertion that conscious awareness of the past can occur in the absence of a voluntary retrieval strategy (involuntary conscious memory). However, one would then have to explain away the dissociations of strategy and awareness that we have obtained in our comparisons of intentional, incidental, and opposition tests. One would also have to explain away both anecdotal and systematic evidence that incidental test subjects frequently become test aware without adopting a voluntary retrieval strategy.

In contrast to the conclusions drawn from the inclusion/exclusion procedure, the conclusions we draw from our use of opposition methods are not dependent on the validity of any specific probabilistic model. Facilitatory priming in an exclusion (or opposition) test, as demonstrated in the current experiments, is attributable to involuntary unconscious memory, regardless of whether one adopts an independence [$E = U(1 - C)$], redundancy [$E = U - C$], or exclusivity [$E = U$] assumption for the relationship between conscious and unconscious memory. If one can produce facilitatory priming in an opposition test, as we have done, one can then examine the factors influencing that priming effect, relying only on data to make theoretical inferences about the representations and processes responsible for involuntary unconscious memory. We prefer this model-independent approach to the model-dependent process-dissociation approach, because the conclusions one draws from the process-dissociation approach vary radically depending on whether one assumes independence, redundancy, or exclusivity. Those conclusions can, therefore, always be questioned by questioning the underlying assumption.

According to the independence and redundancy models, opposition test performance underestimates unconscious memory. We have argued, however, that both the independence and redundancy models are questionable for repetition priming tasks like stem completion. While it is plausible that voluntary and involuntary retrieval could be independent or redundant, it is not plausible to assume that conscious and unconscious memorial states of awareness are independent or redundant. Suppression of studied items in an exclusion (or opposition) test occurs when those items elicit an awareness of the past; whether they are retrieved voluntarily or involuntarily is irrelevant. In consequence, the meaning of the U parameter derived from the independence and redundancy models is not at all clear, because a subject cannot be simultaneously conscious and unconscious of a past event. If any model is plausible, then, it is exclusivity. According to an exclusivity model, exclusion (or opposition) test performance provides an unbiased measure of involuntary unconscious memory ($E = U$). An additional reason to prefer an exclusivity assumption is that the cost of making the wrong assumption is to underestimate, rather than to overestimate, unconscious memory. Given the relatively controversial status of unconscious memory in normal subjects, the most conservative assumption seems preferable.

We have argued that familiarity in recognition memory cannot be identified with unconscious memory, and that recollection cannot be identified with conscious memory. Rather, familiarity and recollection are both manifestations of conscious awareness of the past. Assumptions about the relationship between conscious and unconscious states of awareness do not, therefore, constrain assumptions about the relationship between familiarity and recollection. Conscious and unconscious states of awareness with respect to the past can be exclusive, while familiarity and recollection can be independent, redundant, or exclusive. As in the case of our approach to opposition test data, an advantage of our approach to separating familiarity and recollection in recognition memory (which depends on the use of 'remember' and 'know' judgements) is that it is not dependent on the validity of any specific model. 'Know' judgements index familiarity in the absence of recollection, whether familiarity and recollection are independent, redundant, or exclusive.

If independence or redundancy are assumed, 'know' judgements typically underestimate familiarity. However, it is currently by no means clear that independence or redundancy models are preferable to an exclusivity model for familiarity and recollection. Applying an independence model to 'remember'/'know' data renders the overall pattern of data from those studies much less meaningful and interpretable. This finding leads us to question the independence assumption for the 'remember'/'know' procedure, rather than the face validity of 'remember' and 'know' judgements, which are direct reports of subjective states of awareness. Apparent inconsistencies between results from the 'remember'/'know' procedure and results from the process-dissociation procedure in recognition memory (which assumes independence of familiarity and recollection) are currently difficult to interpret owing to methodological differences between the two procedures. For the moment, the two approaches are better regarded as complementary rather than reducible.

The framework we have put forward in this chapter suggests that the relationships among task performance, memorial states of awareness, retrieval strategies, retrieval processes, and memory representations are much more complex than is acknowledged by any other current theoretical scheme or framework. Such complexities are the inevitable consequence of the reintroduction of the concepts of consciousness and volition into accounts of memory. In our view, the most productive approach to unravelling these complexities is to place a firm emphasis on experimental data, together with careful theoretical analysis and use of terminology. Simple quantitative data-analytic models may appear to overcome current difficulties, but can lead to serious oversimplification, to the introduction of assumptions that may be extremely difficult to verify, and to misleading conclusions. The use of such models does not, in the end, exempt us from ensuring that our measurement tools—that is, our memory tasks—accurately reflect the phenomena that we are attempting to measure.

ACKNOWLEDGEMENTS

We are grateful to Eyal Reingold, Roddy Roediger, Jeffrey Toth, and Endel Tulving for constructive comments on the initial version of this chapter, which was prepared while the first author was a Visiting Research Fellow at City University and the third author was a Postdoctoral Research Fellow at the Open University. We also thank Peter Ayton, James Hampton, and the other members of the Memory and Cognition Research Group at City University for useful discussions of the issues addressed here.

REFERENCES

Allen, S. W. and Jacoby, L. L. (1990). Reinstating study context produces unconscious influences of memory. *Memory and Cognition*, **18**, 270–8.

Anderson, J. R. (1983). *The architecture of cognition*. Harvard University Press, Cambridge, MA.

Anderson, J. R. and Bower, G. H. (1972). Recognition and retrieval processes in free recall. *Psychological Review*, **79**, 97–123.

Bjork, R. A. (1972). Theoretical implications of directed forgetting. In *Coding processes in human memory*, (ed. A. W. Melton and E. Martin), pp. 217–35. Winston, Washington DC.

Bjork, R. A. and Richardson-Klavehn, A. (1989). On the puzzling relationship between environmental context and human memory. In *Current issues in cognitive processes*, (ed. C. Izawa), pp. 313–44. Erlbaum, Hillsdale, NJ.

Blaxton, T. A. (1989). Investigating dissociations among memory measures: Support for a transfer-appropriate processing framework. *Journal of Experimental Psychology: Learning, Memory, and Cognition*, **15**, 657–68.

Bowers, J. S. and Schacter, D. L. (1990). Implicit memory and test awareness. *Journal of Experimental Psychology: Learning, Memory, and Cognition*, **16**, 404–16.

Bowers, J. S. and Schacter, D. L. (1993). Priming of novel information in amnesic patients: Issues and data. In *Implicit memory: New directions in cognition, development, and neuropsychology*, (ed. P. Graf and M. E. J. Masson), pp. 303–26. Erlbaum, Hillsdale, NJ.

Cermak, L. S. (1993). Automatic versus controlled processing and the implicit task performance of amnesic patients. In *Implicit memory: New directions in cognition, development, and neuropsychology*, (ed. P. Graf and M. E. J. Masson), pp. 287–301. Erlbaum, Hillsdale, NJ.

Cermak, L. S., O'Connor, M., and Talbot, N. (1986). Biasing of alcoholic Korsakoff patients' semantic memory. *Journal of Clinical and Experimental Neuropsychology*, **8**, 543–55.

Challis, B. H. and Brodbeck, D. R. (1992). Level of processing affects priming in word fragment completion. *Journal of Experimental Psychology: Learning, Memory, and Cognition*, **18**, 595–607.

Cofer, C. N. (1967). Conditions for the use of verbal associations. *Psychological Bulletin*, **68**, 1–12.

Cohen, N. J. and Squire, L. R. (1980). Preserved learning and retention of pattern analysing skills in amnesics: Dissociation of knowing how and knowing that. *Science*, **210**, 207–10.

Craik, F. I. M., Moscovitch, M., and McDowd, J. (1994). Contributions of surface and conceptual information to performance on implicit and explicit memory tasks. *Journal of Experimental Psychology: Learning, Memory, and Cognition*, **20**, 864–75.

Craik, F. I. M. and Watkins, M. J. (1973). The role of rehearsal in short-term memory. *Journal of Verbal Learning and Verbal Behavior*, **12**, 599–607.

Curran, H. V., Gardiner, J. M., Java, R. I., and Allen, D. (1993). Effects of lorazepam upon recollective experience in recognition memory. *Psychopharmacology*, **110**, 374–8.

Dunn, J. C. and Kirsner, K. (1988). Discovering functionally independent mental processes: The principle of reversed association. *Psychological Review*, **95**, 91–101.

Dunn, J. C. and Kirsner, K. (1989). Implicit memory: Task or process? In *Implicit memory: Theoretical issues*, (ed. S. Lewandowsky, J. C. Dunn, and K. Kirsner), pp. 17–31. Erlbaum, Hillsdale, NJ.

Ebbinghaus, H. (1885/1964). *Memory: A contribution to experimental psychology*, (trans. H. A. Ruger and C. E. Bussenius). Dover, New York.

Eich, E. (1984). Memory for unattended events: Remembering with and without awareness. *Memory and Cognition*, **12**, 105–11.

Fell, M. (1992). Encoding, retrieval and age effects on recollective experience. *Irish Journal of Psychology*, **13**, 62–78.

Gardiner, J. M. (1988). Functional aspects of recollective experience. *Memory and Cognition*, **16**, 309–13.

Gardiner, J. M. and Java, R. I. (1990). Recollective experience in word and nonword recognition. *Memory and Cognition*, **18**, 23–30.

Gardiner, J. M. and Java, R. I. (1991). Forgetting in recognition memory with and without recollective experience. *Memory and Cognition*, **19**, 617–23.

Gardiner, J. M. and Java, R. I. (1993*a*). Recognising and remembering. In *Theories of memory*, (ed. A. F. Collins, S. E. Gathercole, M. A. Conway, and P. E. Morris), pp. 163–88. Erlbaum, Hove, UK.

Gardiner, J. M. and Java, R. I. (1993*b*). Recognition memory and awareness: An experiential approach. *European Journal of Cognitive Psychology*, **5**, 337–46.

Gardiner, J. M. and Parkin, A. J. (1990). Attention and recollective experience in recognition memory. *Memory and Cognition*, **18**, 579–83.

Gardiner, J. M., Gawlik, B., and Richardson-Klavehn, A. (1994). Maintenance rehearsal affects knowing, not remembering; elaborative rehearsal affects remembering, not knowing. *Psychonomic Bulletin and Review*, **1**, 107–10.

Gardiner, J. M., Kaminska, Z., Dixon, M., and Java, R. I. (in prep.). Repetition of previously novel melodies sometimes increases both remember and know responses in recognition memory.

Geiselman, R. E. and Bjork, R. A. (1980). Primary versus secondary rehearsal in imagined voices: Differential effects on recognition. *Cognitive Psychology*, **12**, 188–205.

Graf, P. and Komatsu, S. (1994). Process dissociation procedure: Handle with caution! *European Journal of Cognitive Psychology*, **6**, 113–29.

Graf, P. and Mandler, G. (1984). Activation makes words more accessible, but not necessarily more retrievable. *Journal of Verbal Learning and Verbal Behavior*, **23**, 553–68.

Graf, P. and Schacter, D. L. (1985). Implicit and explicit memory for new associations in normal and amnesic subjects. *Journal of Experimental Psychology: Learning, Memory, and Cognition*, **11**, 501–18.

Graf, P., Shimamura, A. P., and Squire, L. R. (1985). Priming across modalities and priming across category levels: Extending the domain of preserved function in amnesia. *Journal of Experimental Psychology: Learning, Memory, and Cognition*, **11**, 386–96.

Green, D. M. and Swets, J. A. (1974). *Signal detection theory and psychophysics*. Krieger, New York.

Greene, R. L. (1986). Word stems as cues in recall and completion tasks. *Quarterly Journal of Experimental Psychology*, **38A**, 663–73.

Gregg, V. H. and Gardiner, J. M. (1994). Recognition memory and awareness: A large effect of study-test modalities on 'know' responses following a highly perceptual orienting task. *European Journal of Cognitive Psychology*, **6**, 137–47.

Guttentag, R. E. and Carroll, D. (1994). Identifying the basis of the word frequency effect in recognition memory. *Memory*, **2**, 255–73.

Hamann, S. B. (1990). Level-of-processing effects in conceptually driven implicit tasks. *Journal of Experimental Psychology: Learning, Memory, and Cognition*, **16**, 970–7.

Jackson, A. and Morton, J. (1984). Facilitation of auditory word recognition. *Memory and Cognition*, **12**, 568–74.

Jacoby, L. L. (1983*a*). Perceptual enhancement: Persistent effects of an experience. *Journal of Experimental Psychology: Learning, Memory, and Cognition*, **9**, 21–38.

Jacoby, L. L. (1983*b*). Remembering the data: Analyzing interactive processes in reading. *Journal of Verbal Learning and Verbal Behavior*, **22**, 485–508.

Jacoby, L. L. (1984). Incidental versus intentional retrieval: Remembering and awareness as separate issues. In *Neuropsychology of memory*, (ed. L. R. Squire and N. Butters), pp. 145–56. Guilford Press, New York.

Jacoby, L. L. (1991). A process dissociation framework: Separating automatic and intentional uses of memory. *Journal of Memory and Language*, **30**, 513–41.

Jacoby, L. L. and Brooks, L. R. (1984). Nonanalytic cognition: Memory, perception, and concept learning. In *The psychology of learning and motivation*, Vol. 18, (ed. G. H. Bower), pp. 1–47. Academic Press, New York.

Jacoby, L. L. and Dallas, M. (1981). On the relationship between autobiographical memory and perceptual learning. *Journal of Experimental Psychology: General*, **110**, 306–40.

Jacoby, L. L. and Hollingshead, A. (1990). Toward a generate/recognize model of performance on direct and indirect tests of memory. *Journal of Memory and Language*, **29**, 433–54.

Jacoby, L. L. and Witherspoon, D. (1982). Remembering without awareness. *Canadian Journal of Psychology*, **36**, 300–24.

Jacoby, L. L., Kelley, C. M., and Dywan, J. (1989*a*). Memory attributions. In *Varieties of memory and consciousness: Essays in honour of Endel Tulving*, (ed. H. L. Roediger III and F. I. M. Craik), pp. 391–422. Erlbaum, Hillsdale, NJ.

Jacoby, L. L., Woloshyn, V., and Kelley, C. M. (1989*b*). Becoming famous without being recognized: Unconscious influences of memory produced by dividing attention. *Journal of Experimental Psychology: General*, **118**, 115–25.

Jacoby, L. L., Lindsay, S., and Toth, J. P. (1992*a*). Unconscious influences revealed: Attention, awareness, and control. *American Psychologist*, **47**, 802–9.

Jacoby, L. L., Toth, J. P., Lindsay, S., and Debner, J. A. (1992*b*). Lectures for a layperson: Methods for revealing unconscious processes. In *Perception without awareness: Cognitive, clinical, and social perspectives*, (ed. R. F. Bornstein and T. S. Pitman), pp. 81–120. Guilford Press, New York.

Jacoby, L. L., Ste-Marie, D., and Toth, J. P. (1993*a*). Redefining automaticity: Unconscious influences, awareness, and control. In *Attention, selection, awareness, and control: A tribute to Donald Broadbent*, (ed. A. D. Baddeley and L. Weiskrantz), pp. 261–82. Oxford University Press.

Jacoby, L. L., Toth, J. P., and Yonelinas, A. P. (1993*b*). Separating conscious and unconscious influences of memory: Measuring recollection. *Journal of Experimental Psychology: General*, **122**, 139–54.

Jacoby, L. L., Yonelinas, A. P., and Jennings, J. (in press). The relation between conscious and unconscious (automatic) influences: A declaration of independence. In *Scientific approaches to the question of consciousness*, (ed. J. D. Cohen and J. W. Schooler). Erlbaum, Hillsdale, NJ.

Java, R. I. (1994). States of awareness following word stem completion. *European Journal of Cognitive Psychology*, **6**, 77–92.

Jennings, J. M. and Jacoby, L. L. (1993). Automatic versus intentional uses of memory: Aging, attention, and control. *Psychology and Aging*, **8**, 283–93.

Johnson, M. K. and Hasher, L. (1987). Human learning and memory. *Annual Review of Psychology*, **38**, 631–68.

Johnson, M. K., Kim., J. K., and Risse, G. (1985). Do alcoholic Korsakoff's syndrome patients acquire affective reactions? *Journal of Experimental Psychology: Learning, Memory, and Cognition*, **11**, 22–36.

Joordens, S. and Merikle, P. M. (1993). Independence or redundancy? Two models of conscious and unconscious influences. *Journal of Experimental Psychology: General*, **122**, 462–7.

Kirsner, K., Milech., D., and Standen, P. (1983). Common and modality specific processes in the mental lexicon. *Memory and Cognition*, **11**, 621–30.

Kirsner, K., Milech, D., and Stumpfel, V. (1986). Word and picture recognition: Is representational parsimony possible? *Memory and Cognition*, **14**, 398–408.

Kirsner, K., Dunn, J. C., and Standen, P. (1989). Domain-specific resources in word recognition. In *Implicit memory: Theoretical issues*, (ed. S. Lewandowsky, J. C. Dunn, and K. Kirsner), pp. 99–122. Erlbaum, Hillsdale, NJ.

Kirsner, K., Speelman, C., and Schofield, P. (1993). Implicit memory and skill acquisition: Is synthesis possible? In *Implicit memory: New directions in cognition, development, and neuropsychology*, (ed. P. Graf and M. E. J. Masson), pp. 119–39. Erlbaum, Hillsdale, NJ.

Kolers, P. A. and Roediger, H. L. III (1984). Procedures of mind. *Journal of Verbal Learning and Verbal Behavior*, **23**, 425–49.

Komatsu, S., Graf, P., and Uttl, B. (1995). Process dissociation procedure: Core assumptions fail, sometimes. *European Journal of Cognitive Psychology*, **7**, 19–40.

Kunst-Wilson, W. R. and Zajonc, R. B. (1980). Affective discrimination of stimuli that are not recognized. *Science*, **207**, 557–8.

Lockhart, R. S. and Blackburn, A. B. (1993). Implicit processes in problem solving. In *Implicit memory: New directions in cognition, development, and neuropsychology*, (ed. P. Graf and M. E. J. Masson), pp. 95–117. Erlbaum, Hillsdale, NJ.

MacLeod, C. M. (1989). Directed forgetting affects both direct and indirect tests of memory. *Journal of Experimental Psychology: Learning, Memory, and Cognition*, **15**, 13–21.

Mandler, G. (1980). Recognition: The judgment of previous occurrence. *Psychological Review*, **87**, 252–71.

Mantyla, T. (1993). Knowing but not remembering: Adult age differences in recollective experience. *Memory and Cognition*, **21**, 379–88.

Martone, M., Butters, N., Payne, M., Becker, J. T., and Sax, D. S. (1984). Dissociations between skill learning and verbal recognition in amnesia and dementia. *Archives of Neurology*, **41**, 965–70.

Merikle, P. M. and Reingold, E. M. (1991). Comparing direct (explicit) and indirect (implicit) measures to study unconscious memory. *Journal of Experimental Psychology: Learning, Memory, and Cognition*, **17**, 224–33.

Miles, T. R. (1987). Gilbert Ryle. In *The Oxford companion to the mind*, (ed. R. L. Gregory), pp. 691–2. Oxford University Press.

Monsell, S. (1985). Repetition and the lexicon. In *Progress in the psychology of language*, Vol. 2, (ed. A. W. Ellis), pp. 147–95. Erlbaum, London.

Murdock, B. B. Jr. (1982). A theory for the retrieval of item and associative information. *Psychological Review*, **89**, 609–26.

Nickerson, R. S. (1984). Retrieval inhibition from part-set cuing: A persisting enigma in memory research. *Memory and Cognition*, **12**, 531–52.

Nyberg, L., Olofsson, U., Gardiner, J. M., and Nilsson, L.-G. (in prep.). Assessment of retrieval strategy in incidental, intentional, and inclusion tests with word-fragment cues.

Ostergaard, A. L. and Jernigan, T. L. (1993). Are word priming and explicit memory mediated by different brain structures? In *Implicit memory: New directions in cognition, development, and neuropsychology*, (ed. P. Graf and M. E. J. Masson), pp. 327–49. Erlbaum, Hillsdale, NJ.

Parkin, A. J. (1993). Implicit memory across the lifespan. In *Implicit memory: New directions in cognition, development, and neuropsychology*, (ed. P. Graf and M. E. J. Masson), pp. 191–206. Erlbaum, Hillsdale, NJ.

Parkin, A. J. and Walter, B. M. (1992). Recollective experience, normal aging, and frontal dysfunction. *Psychology and Aging*, **7**, 290–8.

Parkin, A. J. and White, C. (in prep.). The influence of exposure duration on recollective experience in older people.

Parkin, A. J., Reid, T., and Russo, R. (1990). On the differential nature of implicit and explicit memory. *Memory and Cognition*, **18**, 507–14.

Parkin, A. J., Gardiner, J. M., and Rosser, R. (in press). Functional aspects of recollective experience in face recognition. *Consciousness and Cognition*.

Perfect, T. J., Williams, R. B., and Anderton-Brown, C. (1995). Age differences in reported recollective experience are due to encoding effects, not response bias. *Memory*, **3**, 169–86.

Rajaram, S. (1993). Remembering and knowing: Two means of access to the personal past. *Memory and Cognition*, **21**, 89–102.

Rajaram, S. and Roediger, H. L. III (in press). Remembering and knowing as states of consciousness during recollection. In *Scientific approaches to the question of consciousness*, (ed. J. D. Cohen and J. W. Schooler). Erlbaum, Hillsdale, NJ.

Ratcliff, R. (1978). A theory of memory retrieval. *Psychological Review*, **85**, 59–108.

Reingold, E. M. and Merikle, P. M. (1990). On the inter-relatedness of theory and measurement in the study of unconscious processes. *Mind and Language*, **5**, 9–28.

Richardson, A. and Bjork, R. A. (1982). *Recognition versus perceptual identification: Effects of rehearsal type and duration*. Paper presented at the annual meeting of the Psychonomic Society, Minneapolis, MN.

Richardson-Klavehn, A. and Bjork, R. A. (1988*a*). Measures of memory. *Annual Review of Psychology*, **39**, 475–543.

Richardson-Klavehn, A. and Bjork, R. A. (1988*b*). Primary versus secondary rehearsal in an imagined voice: Differential effects on recognition memory and perceptual identification. *Bulletin of the Psychonomic Society*, **26**, 187–90.

Richardson-Klavehn, A. and Gardiner, J. M. (1995). Retrieval volition and memorial awareness in stem completion: An empirical analysis. *Psychological Research*, **57**, 166–78.

Richardson-Klavehn, A. and Gardiner, J. M. (in press). Cross-modality priming in stem completion reflects conscious memory, but not voluntary memory. *Psychonomic Bulletin and Review*.

Richardson-Klavehn, A., Gardiner, J. M., and Java, R. I. (1994*a*). Involuntary conscious memory and the method of opposition. *Memory*, **2**, 1–29.

Richardson-Klavehn, A., Lee, M. G., Joubran, R., and Bjork, R. A. (1994*b*). Intention and awareness in perceptual identification priming. *Memory and Cognition*, **22**, 293–312.

Roediger, H. L. III (1990). Implicit memory: Retention without remembering. *American Psychologist*, **45**, 1043–56.

Roediger, H. L. III and Blaxton, T. A. (1987). Retrieval modes produce dissociations in memory for surface information. In *Memory and cognitive processes: The Ebbinghaus Centennial Conference*, (ed. D. Gorfein and R. R. Hoffman), pp. 349–79. Erlbaum, Hillsdale, NJ.

Roediger, H. L. III and McDermott, K. B. (1993). Implicit memory in normal human subjects. In *Handbook of neuropsychology*, Vol. 8, (ed. F. Boller and J. Grafman), pp. 63–131. Elsevier, Amsterdam.

Roediger, H. L. III and McDermott, K. B. (1994). The problem of differing false alarm rates for the process-dissociation procedure: Comment on Verfaellie and Treadwell (1993). *Neuropsychology*, **8**, 284–8.

Roediger, H. L. III, Srinivas, K., and Weldon, M. S. (1989*a*). Dissociations between implicit measures of retention. In *Implicit memory: Theoretical issues*, (ed. S. Lewandowsky, J. C. Dunn, and K. Kirsner), pp. 67–84. Erlbaum, Hillsdale, NJ.

Roediger, H. L. III, Weldon, M. S., and Challis, B. H. (1989*b*). Explaining dissociations between implicit and explicit measures of retention: A processing account. In *Varieties of memory and consciousness: Essays in honour of Endel Tulving*, (ed. H. L. Roediger III and F. I. M. Craik), pp. 3–41. Erlbaum, Hillsdale, NJ.

Roediger, H. L. III, Weldon, M. S., Stadler, M. L., and Riegler, G. L. (1992). Direct comparison of two implicit memory tests: Word fragment and word stem completion. *Journal of Experimental Psychology: Learning, Memory, and Cognition*, **18**, 1251–69.

Russo, R. and Andrade, J. (1995). The directed forgetting effect in word fragment completion: An application of the process dissociation procedure. *Quarterly Journal of Experimental Psychology*, **48A**, 405–23.

Ryle, G. (1949). *The concept of mind.* Hutchinson, London.

Schacter, D. L. (1985). Multiple forms of memory in humans and animals. In *Memory systems of the brain*, (ed. N. M. Weinberger, J. L. McGaugh, and G. Lynch), pp. 351–79. Guilford Press, New York.

Schacter, D. L. (1989). On the relation between memory and consciousness: Dissociable interactions and conscious experience. In *Varieties of memory and consciousness: Essays in honour of Endel Tulving* (ed. H. L. Roediger III and F. I. M. Craik), pp. 355–89. Erlbaum, Hillsdale, NJ.

Schacter, D. L. and Graf, P. (1986). Effects of elaborative processing on implicit and explicit memory for new associations. *Journal of Experimental Psychology: Learning, Memory, and Cognition*, **12**, 432–44.

Schacter, D. L., Bowers, J., and Booker, J. (1989). Intention, awareness, and implicit memory: The retrieval intentionality criterion. In *Implicit memory: Theoretical issues*, (ed. S. Lewandowsky, J. C. Dunn, and K. Kirsner), pp. 47–65. Erlbaum, Hillsdale, NJ.

Schacter, D. L., Chiu, C.-Y. P., and Ochsner, K. N. (1993). Implicit memory: A selective review. *Annual Review of Neuroscience*, **16**, 159–82.

Segal, S. J. (1966). Priming compared to recall: Following multiple exposures and delay. *Psychological Reports*, **18**, 615–20.

Shimamura, A. P. (1986). Priming effects in amnesia: Evidence for a dissociable memory function. *Quarterly Journal of Experimental Psychology*, **38A**, 619–44.

Shimamura, A. P. (1993). Neuropsychological analyses of implicit memory: History, methodology and theoretical interpretations. In *Implicit memory: New directions in cognition, development, and neuropsychology*, (ed. P. Graf and M. E. J. Masson), pp. 265–85. Erlbaum, Hillsdale, NJ.

Sloman, S. A., Hayman, C. A. G., Ohta, N., Law, J., and Tulving, E. (1988). Forgetting in primed fragment completion. *Journal of Experimental Psychology: Learning, Memory, and Cognition*, **14**, 223–39.

Squire, L. R. (1992). Declarative and nondeclarative memory: Multiple brain systems supporting learning and memory. *Journal of Cognitive Neuroscience*, **4**, 232–43.

Squire, L. R., Shimamura, A. P., and Graf, P. (1985). Independence of recognition memory and priming effects: A neuropsychological analysis. *Journal of Experimental Psychology: Learning, Memory and Cognition*, **11**, 37–44.

Squire, L. R., Shimamura, A. P., and Graf, P. (1987). Strength and duration of priming effects in normal subjects and amnesic patients. *Neuropsychologia*, **25**, 195–210.

Srinivas, K. and Roediger, H. L. III (1990). Classifying implicit memory tests: Category association and anagram solution. *Journal of Memory and Language*, **29**, 389–412.

Stein, B. S. (1978). Depth of processing reexamined: The effects of precision of encoding and test appropriateness. *Journal of Verbal Learning and Verbal Behavior*, **17**, 165–74.

Toth, J. P., Reingold, E. M., and Jacoby, L. L. (1994). Towards a redefinition of implicit memory: Process dissociation following elaborative processing and self-generation. *Journal of Experimental Psychology: Learning, Memory, and Cognition*, **20**, 290–303.

Tulving, E. (1976). Ecphoric processes in recall and recognition. In *Recognition and recall*, (ed. J. Brown), pp. 37–73. Wiley, New York.

Tulving, E. (1983). *Elements of episodic memory*. Oxford University Press.

Tulving, E. (1985). Memory and consciousness. *Canadian Psychologist*, **26**, 1–12.

Tulving, E. (1989). Memory: Performance, knowledge, and experience. *European Journal of Cognitive Psychology*, **1**, 3–26.

Tulving, E. (1993). What is episodic memory? *Current Directions in Psychological Science*, **2**, 67–70.

Tulving, E., and Schacter, D. L. (1990). Priming and human memory systems. *Science*, **247**, 301–5.

Tulving, E. Schacter, D. L., and Stark, H. (1982). Priming effects in word-fragment completion are independent of recognition memory. *Journal of Experimental Psychology: Human Learning and Memory*, **8**, 336–42.

Verfaellie, M. (1994). A re-examination of recognition memory in amnesia: Reply to Roediger and McDermott. *Neuropsychology*, **8**, 289–92.

Verfaellie, M. and Treadwell, J. R. (1993). Status of recognition memory in amnesia. *Neuropsychology*, **7**, 5–13.

Weldon, M. S., Roediger, H. L. III, and Challis, B. H. (1989). The properties of retrieval cues constrain the picture superiority effect. *Memory and Cognition*, **17**, 95–105.

Winnick, W. A. and Daniel, S. A. (1970). Two kinds of response priming in tachistoscopic recognition. *Journal of Experimental Psychology*, **84**, 74–81.

Woodward, A. E., Bjork, R. A., and Jongeward, R. H. (1973). Recall and recognition as a function of primary rehearsal. *Journal of Verbal Learning and Verbal Behavior*, **12**, 608–17.

4

Process dissociations versus task dissociations: a controversy in progress

Eyal M. Reingold and Jeffrey P. Toth

4.0 OVERVIEW

Much of the long-standing controversial status of the study of unconscious processing revolves around the lack of a general consensus as to what constitutes an adequate operational definition of conscious awareness (see Dixon 1971, 1981; Erdelyi 1985, 1986; Eriksen 1960; Holender 1986; Reingold and Merikle 1988, 1990). An attempt to review definitional issues relevant to the measurement of awareness is quick to reveal a very curious discrepancy between the prominence of the debate of such issues in the context of the study of perception without awareness, and the absence of such discussions in the study of unconscious, or implicit memory. Referring to debates concerning criteria for establishing perception without awareness, Schacter (1987, p. 511) suggested that 'memory researchers would do well to attempt to incorporate some of the lessons from these investigations into research on implicit memory'. Until recently, discussions of definitional criteria relevant to the measurement of awareness remained scarce despite numerous studies exploring dissociations between implicit/indirect and explicit/direct measures of memory.

Following the introduction of the process-dissociation approach (Jacoby 1991; Jacoby *et al.* 1993*b*), there has been a surge of interest in issues pertaining to the relationship between memory and awareness. Much of this newly found interest centres on criticisms of various aspects of the process-dissociation paradigm. This scrutiny is perhaps to be expected given that the process-dissociation approach represents a novel approach both to the measurement of conscious control, and to the study of conscious and unconscious influences on behaviour. However, whereas some authors attempt to provide a thorough and balanced review of the assumptions made within the framework of the process-dissociation approach (henceforth PDA) and the assumptions made by the task-dissociation approach (henceforth TDA) (e.g. Roediger and McDermott 1993), other critiques of the PDA tend to be rather selective and biased (e.g. Graf and Komatsu 1994). The reader of such critiques may be led to believe that while the PDA involves particularly problematic assumptions, the implicit memory TDA is somehow assumption-free. We believe that this distorted impression is largely attributable to the fact that, while the PDA includes explicitly stated assumptions regarding the relationship between memory and awareness, the assumptions of the TDA are often tacit, unacknowledged, and unexamined.

As a case in point, in a recent critique by Graf and Komatsu (1994) readers are forewarned in the title 'Process dissociation procedure: Handle with caution!'. These authors argue that results obtained by applying the PDA cannot be validly compared to results obtained within the TDA. We dispute this claim and argue that, as with any radically new paradigm, the PDA emerged because of issues which were not adequately handled by the dominant paradigm, in this case the TDA. That is, the PDA has taken on problems that the TDA did not solve. Many of these problems are a function, not of the PDA or TDA, but of assuming a two-process/system, rather than a one-process/system, view of memory. Indeed, some issues (e.g. involuntary conscious memory) which have been raised as problems unique to the PDA, were originally introduced as problems for the TDA (see Schacter 1987). In addition, the PDA included an explicit assumption regarding the relationship between conscious and unconscious memory processes. The particular assumption adopted in the original implementation of the PDA was one of independence between these processes. This assumption has generated considerable controversy (see Curran and Hintzman in press; Gardiner and Java 1993; Jacoby and Begg submitted; Jacoby *et al.* 1994, in press; Joordens and Merikle 1993). However, what is easily forgotten is that the need for exploring what is the appropriate relational assumption is not the unique responsibility of the PDA, but should be addressed by any dual-process/system model of memory, including the TDA. Thus, the fact that there was no explicit treatment of this issue within the TDA does not exempt this framework from dealing with it. Hence, many criticisms of the PDA are not intrinsic to the procedure, but are indicative of the current state of memory research. Discarding the PDA will not eliminate these problems, unless the distinction between conscious and unconscious memory is also discarded. Unlike Graf and Komatsu (1994), we emphasize the need for convergent evidence across paradigms. We conclude that the PDA and TDA can, and should coexist, and that the comparison of results obtained by applying these paradigms may be very informative and productive.

Accordingly, rather than attempting to provide a comprehensive review of research performed within the framework of the PDA (for such reviews see Jacoby and Kelley 1991; Jacoby *et al.* 1992, 1993*a*, in press; Toth *et al.* 1992), the present chapter explores three issues as they relate to the PDA and TDA. These issues are response bias, process-purity, and involuntary conscious memory. Following the suggestions of Schacter

(1987), we begin by providing a brief overview of the response bias and process-purity problems as they have been raised in the context of the perception-without-awareness debate. The relevance of these problems to implicit memory research is then illustrated by considering studies by Graf and Mandler (1984), and Graf *et al.* (1984).[1] These studies are widely cited as providing some of the most powerful demonstrations of functional dissociations between explicit and implicit measures of memory in amnesic patients, as well as in normal subjects. In addition, these studies illustrate what has come to be known as the retrieval intentionality criterion, and consequently, we consider the relevance of the process-purity and response bias issues to this criterion. Next, we describe the PDA and outline the solutions it provides to the response bias and process-purity problems. We then consider and respond to recent critiques that have singled out involuntary conscious memory as particularly problematic for the PDA (Graf and Komatsu 1994; Richardson-Klavehn *et al.* 1994, Chapter 3, this volume; Roediger and McDermott 1993). Finally, we focus on the claim that an empirical comparison across the PDA and TDA is invalid (Graf and Komatsu 1994). We examine the implications of this claim, and reject it on both scientific grounds, and within the larger context of the sociology of science as an exemplar of defining a phenomenon in terms of a particular paradigm.

4.1 THE PERCEPTION-WITHOUT-AWARENESS CONTROVERSY

One of the most curious discrepancies between the literatures on perception-without-awareness and implicit memory concerns the employment of the subjective report, or 'claimed awareness' measure. This measure requires the observer or the rememberer to comment on their subjective phenomenal awareness while performing the experimental task. Although this measure has been used for over a century in studies of unconscious perception (see Adams 1957, for a review of early studies), a subjective report measure of awareness has only recently been introduced in the context of the study of implicit memory (see Bowers and Schacter

1. As the chapter neared completion, it became obvious that our focus on studies by Graf and colleagues (Graf and Mandler 1984; Graf *et al.* 1984) in the first part of the chapter, and on the Graf and Komatsu (1994) critique in the final part of the chapter, may be perceived as unduly personalizing the debate. We apologize for this impression, and would like to explain that the first part of the chapter was written before we became aware of the Graf and Komatsu (1994) critique. Our focus on Graf and Mandler (1984), and Graf *et al.* (1984) was motivated by the significance of these studies within the field of implicit memory. Similarly, our focus on Graf and Komatsu (1994) in the final part of the chapter was dictated by our strong opposition to the extreme position it advanced.

1990; Gardiner 1988; Tulving 1985). It is therefore not surprising that the most formidable alternative explanation raised against subjective report measures of awareness, namely the response bias problem, has been virtually ignored in the study of implicit memory. Eriksen's (1959, 1960) classic critique of the perception-without-awareness literature may represent the first effective articulation of the response bias problem. Consider the following caricature by Eriksen (1959, p. 205), which illustrates how response bias can affect the measurement of awareness:

> A psychophysicist in setting about to determine the absolute threshold for light would not use an experimental situation where the subject was to press a button directly in front of him to indicate that he did not see the light and to get up and walk across the room to press a button on the wall if he did. Few would expect such an arrangement would yield as low an absolute threshold as would be obtained if the subject had the two buttons directly in front of him.

Obviously, there are much more subtle ways in which the demand characteristics of an experimental situation may bias subjects against reporting that they perceived a stimulus. However, Eriksen's caricature poignantly highlights a major weakness in any approach to the measurement of awareness which is solely based on subjective report, or claimed awareness. The basic difficulty with this approach is that it places 'on the individual subject the responsibility for establishing the criterion of awareness' (Eriksen 1959, p. 203). Consequently, factors unrelated to awareness, such as demand characteristics and preconceived biases, may lead subjects to adopt a conservative response criterion and report null perceptual awareness even under conditions in which conscious perceptual information is available. Response bias represents a threat not only to the validity of the subjective report measure of awareness, but also to its reliability. In particular, variability in response criteria makes it difficult to compare reports of null subjective confidence across-subjects, or within-subjects across conditions.

Similar considerations led Eriksen (1959, 1960) to reject subjective report as an adequate measure of awareness, and to suggest instead that awareness be operationally defined in terms of performance on tasks that measure perceptual discriminations. Eriksen advocated employing forced-choice discrimination as a measure of awareness. Examples of such tasks include forced-choice presence/absence decisions, and forced-choice discriminations among several stimulus alternatives. Measures based on discriminative responding have two important advantages over measures based on subjective reports. First, they may allow for obtaining a bias-free measure of perceptual sensitivity (Green and Swets 1966; Swets 1964), and secondly, they represent a much more reliable index of perception relative to subjective report. For these reasons, following Eriksen, most researchers have preferred discriminative responding as an index of awareness (but see Dixon 1971, 1981; Henley 1984).

Yet, whether evidence of perception without awareness is obtained crucially depends on how awareness is operationally defined. While perception in the absence of subjective confidence is a very robust phenomenon (see Adams 1957, for a review), evidence of perception under conditions which establish chance discrimination has not been forthcoming. Consequently, Eriksen (1960) concluded that there was no evidence for perception without awareness. Thus, the change in the operational definition of awareness introduced by Eriksen appeared to have completely eliminated the perception-without-awareness phenomenon.

Eriksen's conclusions were challenged when Marcel (1974, 1983) as well as others (e.g. Balota 1983; Fowler *et al.* 1981) reported findings which appeared to demonstrate perception in the absence of detection in a masked priming paradigm. The results of these studies suggested that a stimulus can influence responding even when subjects cannot discriminate between its presence or absence. Unfortunately, it subsequently became clear that while in principle the present–absent discrimination allows for obtaining a bias-free measure of perceptual sensitivity, the implementations of this task in the above studies were inadequate to establish chance discrimination, and these studies more likely demonstrated perception in the absence of subjective confidence (e.g. Cheesman and Merikle 1985; Holender 1986; Merikle 1982; Nolan and Caramazza 1982).

For researchers who assume that measures of discriminative responding represent valid indicators of awareness (e.g. Holender 1986), the failure to demonstrate perception in the absence of discriminative responding provides evidence against the existence of perception without awareness. However, as pointed out by Reingold and Merikle (1988, 1990), the validity of discriminative responding as a measure of awareness crucially depends on its underlying *exclusiveness assumption*. Specifically, discriminative responding may constitute a valid measure of awareness only if it is influenced exclusively by conscious perceptual experience. If on the other hand, a measure of discriminative responding is sensitive to both conscious and unconscious information, then equating awareness with discriminative responding may result in defining unconscious perception out of existence (see Bowers 1984). The exclusiveness assumption has also been referred to as the process-purity assumption (Jacoby 1991) and the selective influence assumption (Dunn and Kirsner 1988). We shall use the term 'process-purity' to describe any assumption that a task is exclusively influenced by a single process. Thus, while response bias represents a difficult problem for the subjective report approach to the measurement of awareness, process-purity represents an equally devastating problem for the discriminative responding approach to the measurement of awareness.

Given that demonstration of perception without awareness crucially depends on which operational definition of awareness is used (i.e. subjective report vs. discriminative responding), converging on a valid indicator of awareness is of the utmost importance.

4.2 GRAF AND MANDLER (1984): A CASE STUDY OF IMPLICIT MEMORY RESEARCH

With a few notable exceptions (e.g. Bowers and Schacter, 1990; see also the Remember/Know paradigm—Gardiner and Java 1993; Tulving 1985), the subjective report measure of awareness has rarely been used in the study of the relationship between consciousness and memory. That is, asking subjects to provide commentary on their subjective phenomenal awareness during retrieval is seldom considered an adequate method for distinguishing conscious from unconscious retention. Instead, just as perceptual discriminations such as detection and identification have been used to assess perceptual awareness, memory discriminations, such as recognition and recall, have been linked to conscious recollection. Conversely, indirect or implicit memory tasks have often been considered as exclusively tapping unconscious memory. Thus, most memory researchers have tacitly adopted some form of the process-purity assumption, equating tasks and processes. In addition, most studies of implicit memory have completely ignored the problem of response bias. To further clarify these points, we next turn to a closer examination of implicit memory research, and in particular, one of the most influential studies in this area, namely Graf and Mandler (1984).

During the past decade, numerous studies have compared the effects of independent variables on explicit versus implicit measures of memory in both amnesic patients and normal subjects (see Moscovitch *et al.* 1993; Richardson-Klavehn and Bjork 1988; Roediger and McDermott 1993; Schacter 1987; Shimamura 1986, for reviews). The basic aim of these studies was to demonstrate functional dissociations between explicit and implicit measures of memory. Briefly, a functional dissociation is observed if the nature of the effect of an experimental manipulation differs across the explicit and implicit tasks (see Dunn and Kirsner 1988, for a critique of the functional-dissociation paradigm). Although many such dissociations have been reported, there is no general consensus as to their interpretation (see Dunn and Kirsner 1989). One problem in interpreting dissociations stems from the fact that the explicit and implicit tasks employed are often quite dissimilar (see Merikle and Reingold 1991; Reingold and Merikle 1988, 1990). Thus, the observed dissociation may simply be an artefact of such task differences. An example of one task dimension which very often differs across the explicit and implicit tasks is the nature of the test cues available during retrieval. For instance, if a word (e.g. TRAVEL) is presented during study, the same word would be presented as a test cue in a recognition task, in a degraded form (e.g. brief presentation followed by a mask) in a perceptual identification task, with only the first three letters in a stem-completion task (e.g. TRA____), with several letters deleted in a fragment-completion task (e.g. T__A__ __L), and not at all in a free-recall task.

It is precisely in this context that Graf and Mandler (1984) made a truly unique contribution. They demonstrated a dissociation between an explicit cued-recall task and an implicit stem-completion task under conditions in which the test cues were identical across the two tasks. That is, during retrieval subjects were always presented with the first three letters of a word (e.g. DEFEND during study, DEF____during test), and were instructed either to complete each stem with a word they had seen during the study phase (cued-recall instructions), or to respond using the first word that came to mind (stem-completion instructions). In addition to the retrieval instructions, Graf and Mandler (1984) also manipulated the encoding task. They examined the effect of level of processing (i.e. semantic vs. non-semantic; Craik and Lockhart 1972) on both the cued-recall and stem-completion tasks.

Graf and Mandler's (1984) findings are summarized at the top of Table 4.1. Two aspects of the results are particularly important. First, level of processing had an effect on the explicit cued-recall task, but not on the implicit stem-completion task (i.e. a functional dissociation). Secondly, there was a very impressive cross-over interaction. For words encoded semantically, the cued-recall task was a more sensitive measure of memory relative to the stem-completion task, whereas the reverse was true for non-semantically encoded words. This pattern of findings is

Table 4.1 Proportions of stems completed with target items in Graf and Mandler (1984) and Graf *et al.* (1984) by task and encoding instructions

		Encoding instructions	
Study	Task	Semantic	Non-semantic
Graf and Mandler (1984)	Cued recall	0.406	0.078
	Stem completion	0.233	0.200
Graf *et al.* (1984)	Cued recall	0.690	0.399
	Stem completion	0.485	0.378

In Graf and Mandler (1984), retrieval task was a within-subject variable. However, in the table, cued-recall data represent the group of subjects who received the cued-recall task first, and stem-completion data represent the group of subjects who received the stem-completion task first. This was done because task order interacted with other variables. The data shown in the bottom half of this table summarize the performance of Graf *et al.*'s (1984) non-amnesic control group.

all the more impressive given that the test cues were identical across both retrieval tasks; consequently, Graf and Mandler's (1984) findings have often been cited as a very powerful demonstration of functional independence between explicit and implicit memory tasks.

Graf and Mandler's (1984) finding that performance on the implicit stem-completion task did not vary as a function of level of processing, whereas the closely matched cued-recall task demonstrated such an effect, had tremendous impact on the field of implicit memory. Indeed, this finding was instrumental in the emergence of the tacit consensus that implicit measures exclusively reflect unintentional, automatic, unconscious retrieval. So ingrained is this belief in the process-purity of implicit measures that it has endured despite recent reviews which clearly document that in the vast majority of implicit tests small, if not always statistically significant, level of processing effects are found (Brown and Mitchell 1994; Challis and Brodbeck 1992). Rather than re-examine the process-purity assumption, some researchers have preferred to account for level of processing effects on implicit tests by assuming another type of automatic priming which is sensitive to lexical and/or semantic processing (e.g. Challis and Brodbeck 1992; see Toth and Reingold, Chapter 2, for further discussion). The alternative, of course, is that such effects reflect a consciously controlled influence on implicit performance, also referred to as conscious contamination (e.g. Toth *et al.* 1994). The potential danger in explaining incidents of conscious contamination as new types of automatic priming is the unwarranted proliferation of memory systems/processes (see Roediger 1990).

However, subsequent findings of level of processing effects on implicit tests do not invalidate the impressive cross-over interaction reported by Graf and Mandler (1984). Unfortunately, the interpretation of this effect is also unclear because, aside from instructions, there is an important difference between the cued-recall task and the stem-completion task used by Graf and Mandler (1984). That is, the two tasks differed in terms of their susceptibility to the influence of response bias: subjects were required to give a response to every stem in the stem-completion task, but not in the cued-recall task. Thus, the dissociation may simply reflect a difference in response bias across tasks. More specifically, failures to provide a response in the cued-recall task are ambiguous. The absence of a response to a stem may reflect the lack of conscious memory. Alternatively, subjects may have completed the stems only when they were very confident that they had seen the words during the study phase, but not when they had a poorer recollection of the prior occurrence of the word. That is, subjects may have simply adopted a conservative response bias.

One possible solution which may allow for ruling out the alternative explanation of response bias in the interpretation of Graf and Mandler (1984) would be to use a forced cued-recall procedure rather than an unforced cued-recall procedure. In the forced cued-recall task subjects would be required to give a response to every stem even if they subjectively feel that they are only guessing. The forced cued-recall procedure guarantees the same number of responses, and consequently the same response criterion, across subjects and tasks. Therefore, if the same pattern of dissociation obtained by Graf and Mandler (1984) occurs using forced cued recall, then the alternative explanation of response bias would have been successfully eliminated. A series of experiments by Graf *et al.* (1984) is relevant in this context. In these experiments, amnesic and non-amnesic patients were tested using a procedure similar to Graf and Mandler (1984) with one of the differences being that forced cued recall was employed rather than unforced cued recall. The data from the non-amnesic patient control group in Graf *et al.* (1984) are presented in the bottom of Table 4.1. An inspection of the results reveals a very different pattern of findings relative to Graf and Mandler (1984). More specifically, in contrast to Graf and Mandler (1984), and consistent with the general pattern in the literature, level of processing affected both the cued-recall and stem-completion tasks. As an interesting aside, the results from the amnesic group (not shown in Table 4.1) demonstrated a sizeable level of processing effect on the implicit stem-completion task. Furthermore, the magnitude of the effect was not significantly different across the amnesic and patient control groups. Most importantly, the cross-over interaction obtained by Graf and Mandler (1984) was not obtained using the forced cued-recall procedure. In particular, while cued recall was more sensitive than stem completion for semantically encoded words, for non-semantically encoded words stem completion was not more sensitive than cued recall. To verify that forced versus unforced cued recall is responsible for the difference in results between Graf *et al.* (1984) and Graf and Mandler (1984), Reingold and Merikle (1991) manipulated cued-recall instructions by requiring subjects either to complete every stem (forced cued recall) or to complete stems only when they were sure that the completion represented an old word (unforced cued recall). As shown in Table 4.2 forced cued-recall instructions (experiment 1) replicated Graf *et al.* (1984) (i.e. a levels effect on the implicit test and no cross-over interaction), while unforced cued-recall instructions (experiment 2) substantially replicated Graf and Mandler (1984) (i.e. a significant levels effect, but importantly, a cross-over interaction).

What is the meaning of the difference in results across the forced versus unforced cued-recall conditions? The interpretation of these findings is ambiguous. It may mean that the cross-over interaction demonstrated in Graf and Mandler (1984) is an artefact of the response bias difference between the unforced cued-recall task and the stem-completion task. Alternatively, it is possible that the employment of the forced cued-recall procedure, despite having the advantage of equating the influence of

Table 4.2 Proportions of stems completed with target items in experiments 1 and 2 in Reingold and Merikle (1991) by task and encoding instructions

Experiment	Task	Encoding instructions		Unstudied words
		Semantic	Non-semantic	
Experiment 1	Forced cued recall	0.513	0.320	0.164
	Stem completion	0.364	0.305	0.139
Experiment 2	Unforced cued recall	0.447	0.180	0.072
	Stem completion	0.363	0.306	0.141

response bias across tasks, changes the nature of the cued-recall task in another, more fundamental way. That is, when forced to provide a response to a stem in the absence of subjective phenomenal awareness, subjects' memory performance may be unconsciously influenced. This unconscious influence may operate similarly in both stem completion and forced cued recall, increasing the similarity across tasks and eliminating the cross-over interaction.

The advantages and pitfalls of the forced cued-recall procedure relative to the unforced cued-recall procedure are very similar to the advantages and pitfalls of a discriminative responding measure of awareness relative to a subjective report measure of awareness. Recall that when subjects claim that they are purely guessing as to whether a stimulus was presented (i.e. claimed null awareness), this may reflect either a true lack of awareness, or the adoption of a conservative response criterion. Similarly, the absence of a response to a stem in the cued-recall task is ambiguous. It may reflect the lack of a subjective experience of remembering on the part of subjects. Alternatively, subjects may have completed the stems only when they fully recollected, but not when they somewhat recollected, the prior occurrence of the word (i.e. a conservative response bias). Thus, the unforced cued-recall procedure is more similar to the subjective report measure of awareness than is immediately apparent. In response to every stem subjects are required to use their own definition of what constitutes remembering. Given that subjective phenomenal awareness is the essence of the subjective experience of remembering (see Tulving 1989), asking subjects to judge whether or not they remember is very similar to asking them to comment on their subjective phenomenal awareness during retrieval. In contrast, the forced cued-recall procedure is very similar to the discriminative responding measure of awareness. Specifically, by eliminating variability in response criteria across both subjects and tasks, the forced cued-recall procedure provides a more reliable and objective assessment of retention, and has the potential of ruling out the response bias interpretation. However, this increased reliability and objectivity may be achieved by sacrificing validity. In particular, forced cued recall may not be a valid measure of conscious remembering because it may in fact be influenced by both conscious and unconscious uses of memory.

4.3 PROCESS-PURITY, RESPONSE BIAS, AND THE RETRIEVAL INTENTIONALITY CRITERION

The difficulties posed by the process-purity and response bias problems for the interpretation of Graf and Mandler's (1984) findings are especially worthy of close examination because these represent a prototypical example of a successful application of the *retrieval intentionality criterion* (henceforth RIC). As proposed by Schacter *et al.* (1989, p. 53) this 'criterion is comprised of two key components. First, the nominal or external cues provided to subjects on implicit and explicit tests should be the same, . . . Second, an experimental manipulation should be identified that selectively affects performance on one of these tasks and not the other'. Graf and Mandler (1984) demonstrated precisely such a functional dissociation. With identical retrieval cues, level of processing affected the explicit cued-recall test but did not affect the implicit stem-completion test.

The RIC represents a refinement of the TDA to the study of unconscious or implicit memory. In part, it acknowledges the danger of equating between tasks and processes. As clearly expressed by Schacter *et al.* (1989 pp. 52–3):

> . . . just because a test does not require a subject to think back to the study episode does not prevent the subject from doing so anyway. Once we acknowledge this possibility, the basis for drawing an implicit vs. explicit distinction becomes hazy indeed; we have no way of determining a priori whether we are dealing with an implicit or explicit form of memory on an allegedly 'implicit test' unless we can convincingly distinguish between intentional and unintentional retrieval of information acquired during the study episode.

This problem is commonly referred to as conscious contamination of indirect or implicit measures (e.g. Toth *et al.* 1994). A similar problem not mentioned by Schacter *et al.* (1989) is that explicit or direct measures of memory, such as recognition and recall, may also reflect both conscious and unconscious uses of memory. That is, direct or explicit measures may be contaminated by unconscious processes (Jacoby *et al.* 1993*b*; Reingold and Merikle 1988, 1990). This is just another way of stating the process-purity problem (Jacoby 1991). Both direct and indirect measures should not be considered process-pure, or exclusive indicators of conscious and unconscious memory respectively. Given that the RIC approach acknowledges the process-purity problem, what solution does it offer? According to Schacter *et al.* (1989, p. 53):

The logic underlying this retrieval intentionality criterion is straightforward: If the external cues are held constant on two tasks and only the retrieval instructions are varied, then differential effects of an experimental manipulation on performance of the two tasks can be attributed to differences in the intentional vs. unintentional retrieval processes that are used in task performance.

Despite the authors' claim that the logic underlying the RIC is straightforward, we do not believe it provides any clear solution to the response bias and process-purity problems. The RIC acknowledges that a prerequisite for attributing any dissociation between explicit and implicit tests to retrieval intentionality is that the tests be matched on all other dimensions. In so doing it recognizes that the vast majority of reported dissociations in the implicit memory literature are open to criticism in that the tests used are not closely matched on dimensions such as retrieval cues. Unfortunately, by the same logic, the RIC does not go far enough because, as illustrated earlier, direct and indirect tests are rarely matched in terms of their susceptibility to response bias, a task dimension which was left out by the RIC.

A more rigorous approach to matching the direct and indirect tests was proposed by Reingold and Merikle (1988, 1990). This approach requires matching the tasks on all dimensions including retrieval cues and response bias. However, as illustrated by the results of the forced cued-recall procedure discussed earlier, once such careful matching is adhered to, dissociations are very difficult to obtain (but see Merikle and Reingold 1991). Furthermore, a thorough review of the literature suggests that dissociations such as the one reported by Graf and Mandler (1984), and required by the RIC, are rarely cleanly obtained. For example, the vast majority of studies using implicit tasks demonstrate a small, if not significant, level of processing effect (Brown and Mitchell 1994; Challis and Brodbeck 1992). Thus, a meta-analysis would not support the conclusion of a functional dissociation as a result of level of processing. In addition, a functional dissociation which is demonstrated when an independent variable (e.g. levels of processing), affects one of the tests (e.g. explicit), but not the other (e.g. implicit) (i.e. a single functional dissociation), by itself provides little evidence for functional independence between intentional versus unintentional retrieval processes because such dissociations may be easily explained by a single-process model (Dunn and Kirsner 1988).

Finally, and perhaps most importantly, Schacter *et al.* (1989) seem to suggest that attaining an experimental dissociation once under conditions of identical external cues may forever after be taken as evidence that the particular implicit measure is process-pure. Specifically, they argue that if a variable produces parallel effects on previously dissociated implicit and explicit tests, it should not be concluded that this is a result of conscious contamination of the implicit measure.

They justify this conclusion in the following manner (Schacter *et al.* 1989, p. 53):

> ... if we have already established that performance on these two tasks can be dissociated by experimental variable Q, then we can argue strongly against the idea that subjects treated the implicit test like an explicit test; if they had, variable Q could not have produced the dissociation that it did.

Even if one accepts that a specific task dissociation constitutes evidence for unintentional retrieval in the performance on the implicit test, there is no guarantee that the implicit measure will always reflect unintentional retrieval under all experimental conditions. Thus, the RIC seems to make the questionable assumption that once uncontaminated is equal to never contaminated, and consequently an implicit measure should be considered as process-pure with the only requirement being that it be dissociated once from its explicit counterpart.

Another attempt to solve the process-purity problem is based on the performance of amnesics on implicit tests. As pointed out by Roediger and McDermott (1993), some researchers seem to make the assumption that if a particular implicit test shows preserved priming in amnesia, then such a test may be considered a process-pure measure of implicit, unintentional retrieval. However, even if preserved priming in amnesia as demonstrated for a particular measure reflects unintentional retrieval, it does not at all follow that under other conditions (e.g. when performed by normal subjects with a specific encoding manipulation), the same measure may not be contaminated by consciously controlled retrieval. The real problem with using the RIC, or amnesia, as empirical benchmarks is that such a practice still tries to preserve the association between a particular task and a particular process. Consequently, conscious contamination is regarded as a red herring or a nuisance factor that can be examined once and then discarded forever.

This attitude is best illustrated by Endel Tulving's critical comment on Roediger and McDermott's (1993) treatment of the process-purity issue. Tulving writes (Roediger and McDermott 1993, p. 79, footnote 5):

> ... your hand-wringing over how to tell a 'pure' implicit task, or implicit memory performance is a bit overdone... The issue is not that important at this early stage of the game ... Putting it into the sharp focus of researchers' attention may overly cramp their style. Instead of finding out about the real brain/mind, they—and editors and referees—may get fixated on the problem of how 'pure' are implicit and explicit tasks.

Thus, Tulving (1985), who had once lamented that 'nowhere is the benign neglect of consciousness more conspicuous than in the study of human memory' (p. 1), is now advocating the neglect of the relationship between consciousness and implicit/explicit task performance. It is important to note that in addition to playing down the importance of the process-purity problem as it applies to implicit measures, the implicit memory literature virtually ignores the possibility that performance on explicit measures is influenced by unconscious, unintentional retrieval (Jacoby *et al.* 1993*b*; Reingold and Merikle 1988, 1990). As shown by our analysis of Graf and Mandler (1984) and Graf *et al.* (1984), both the response bias and process-purity problems have not been adequately dealt with by the TDA. We next examine the PDA and the solutions it provides to the process-purity and response bias problems.

4.4 PDA: ASSUMPTIONS AND CONTRIBUTIONS

The starting point for the PDA is the rejection of the process-purity assumption. The PDA acknowledges that all tasks, whether explicit or implicit, can potentially be sensitive to both conscious and unconscious influences. This contrast represents a fundamental difference between the PDA and TDA philosophies. The PDA is based on the contention that the joint contributions of conscious and unconscious influences on task performance are the rule rather than the exception. It argues that manifestations of process-purity are the true exceptions because they may only be obtainable under very extreme circumstances such as highly impoverished encoding (e.g. brief exposure, unattended input) in normal subjects, or in the case of a pure amnesic patient. From this perspective, if one is indeed a serious student of 'the real brain/mind', one cannot afford to avoid studying conscious and unconscious processes as they interact in the co-determination of task performance. In the remainder of this section we describe how the PDA can yield evidence of unconscious, automatic influences on memory under conditions which rule out a response bias explanation. We then describe how the PDA can be used to derive quantitative estimates of conscious control and unconscious, automatic influences on memory. Finally, we consider the implications of involuntary conscious memory for the PDA and the TDA.

4.4.1 Unconscious influences: exclusion vs. implicit tests

How then can one unambiguously demonstrate unconscious influence under conditions that rule out the response bias criticism? The solution offered to this question within the framework of the PDA is in the form of the exclusion condition which was originally developed by Jacoby and his colleagues under the term 'opposition paradigm' (see Jacoby *et al.* 1989*a*,*b*; Jacoby and Whitehouse 1989; Kelley and Jacoby 1990), and was subsequently incorporated as one of the two conditions which constitute the Process Dissociation Procedure. To illustrate this condition, consider how it was applied in three different investigations

Table 4.3 Proportions of stems completed with target items by level of processing in an exclusion task in Reingold and Merikle (1991); Richardson-Klavehn *et al.* (1994); and Toth *et al.* (1994)

Study	Encoding instructions		Unstudied words
	Semantic	Non-semantic	
Reingold and Merikle (1991)	0.05	0.21	0.14
Richardson-Klavehn *et al.* (1994)	0.04	0.20	0.13
Toth *et al.* (1994)	0.33	0.43	0.26

(Reingold and Merikle 1991; Richardson-Klavehn *et al.* 1994; Toth *et al.* 1994). Each of these was very similar to Graf and Mandler (1984) in that level of processing was manipulated at study, and words stems served as retrieval cues at test. However, in contrast to both stem-completion and cued-recall instructions, subjects were now asked to avoid completing the stems with old studied words. Instead, in the exclusion condition subjects were required to complete as many stems as possible with new, unstudied words. For example, if DEFEND was the studied word, the stem DEF—— should be completed with other words such as DEFECT, DEFINE, and DEFEAT. In this situation, the pattern of results which will support an interpretation of unconscious influence while ruling out the plausibility of a response bias explanation requires two important components. First, it should be demonstrated that for non-semantically encoded words, even when subjects are instructed to avoid old completions (exclusion instructions), subjects nevertheless complete the stems with old words above baseline. Secondly, it should be established that this inability to avoid old completions is not due to a general difficulty in generating new completions. That is, in the exclusion condition, for semantically encoded words, subjects should be better able to avoid old completions relative to their ability to do so for non-semantically encoded words. As shown in Table 4.3, the results from the three studies that manipulated level of processing in the exclusion condition reveal exactly such a pattern of findings.

Above-chance old completions in the exclusion condition are a compelling counterexample to the response bias interpretation in much the same way as Stroop interference is a compelling demonstration of automaticity (Stroop 1935). In both cases, despite a strong incentive to consciously oppose automatic influences, such automatic influences are nevertheless manifested. Thus, the power of the exclusion condition to reject a response bias explanation is a direct result of it being an interference paradigm. This similarity between the exclusion condition and Stroop interference is perhaps not surprising given that theories of attention and automaticity inspired the development of the PDA (Jacoby 1991; Jacoby *et al.* 1993*a*). Theories of attention and automaticity have long recognized that interference such as that in the Stroop paradigm is a much more compelling demonstration of automaticity relative to facilitation paradigms. Implicit tests constitute facilitation paradigms, and consequently, it is unclear to what degree performance reflects automatic facilitation or priming of old completions because such priming is at least sometimes joined by consciously controlled retrieval of old completions. In contrast, in the exclusion condition, automatic influences of memory are in the form of interference to the instructional set to produce new, unstudied completions. Thus, the exclusion instruction, which is an interference condition, has the potential to produce an unambiguous example of automaticity (i.e. above-chance old completions), while implicit performance inevitably confounds conscious remembering with unconscious influences because both will result in old completions.

It is important to note that although above-chance completions in an exclusion condition exclusively reflect unconscious influences on memory, the rate of completion with old words in an exclusion condition cannot by itself be used to estimate the magnitude of such unconscious, automatic influences. This is the case because performance in the exclusion task represents the combined effect of conscious control and unconscious influences. An estimate of unconscious, automatic influences can be derived but, as elaborated later, the relationship between consciously controlled and automatic influences must first be clearly defined (i.e. one must assume either independence, exclusivity, or redundancy).

The exclusion condition is more than just a clever methodological tool intended to rule out the alternative explanation of response bias. Underlying the exclusion condition is the more general view that a major function of consciousness is to oppose unwanted contextually primed or habitual responses. Perseveration is often given as an example of a failure to exercise conscious control in opposing the tendency for repeating an action which is automatically generated in response to contextual cues. Frontal lobe functioning is considered to be crucially involved in conscious control, and consequently, frontal lobe damage due to brain injury or normal ageing often results in perseveration. Other examples of failures of conscious control to oppose unconscious influences include phenomena such as action slips and slips of the tongue (see Erdelyi 1985). In the exclusion condition, consciously controlled and automatic influences are said to result in opposing or qualitatively different behavioural consequences. More specifically, if subjects consciously retrieve an old completion, they are required to replace it with another word. Thus, any above-baseline completion with old words can only result from unconscious influence coupled with a failure to consciously oppose it. As proposed by many investigators, the exploration of qualitative differences between conscious and unconscious processes is vital for the emergence of a general theory of the mind (e.g. Cheesman and Merikle 1985, 1986; Dixon 1971, 1981; Jacoby *et al.* 1989*a*; Kelley and Jacoby 1990; Merikle and Reingold 1990; Reingold 1992; Reingold and Merikle 1990; Shevrin and Dickman 1980). The exclusion condition is ideally suited for demonstrating strong qualitatively different (i.e. opposing) consequences of conscious control versus unconscious influences.

4.4.2 PDA and the measurement of conscious control and unconscious influence

Within the PDA framework the exclusion condition is contrasted with the inclusion condition. In this condition, as implemented with word-stems as cues, subjects are instructed to complete the stems with previously studied words. However, the instructions are similar to a forced cued-recall procedure rather than an unforced cued-recall procedure. That is, subjects are encouraged to complete as many stems as possible. To verify that there are no differences in response criteria across the inclusion and exclusion conditions, both conditions include baseline items (i.e. stems which do not correspond to any of the studied words). Provided that baseline completion rates are equivalent across conditions, proportion of old completions in the inclusion and exclusion conditions can then be used to derive quantitative estimates of the proportion of consciously controlled trials, and the proportion of unconsciously influenced trials. Proportion of trials completed with old words in the inclusion condition will include consciously controlled and/or unconsciously influenced trials, while in the exclusion condition proportion of old completions reflects unconsciously influenced trials which were unopposed by conscious control. Note that, in the exclusion condition, if a trial is both consciously controlled and unconsciously influenced, conscious control overrides the unconscious influence and consequently the stem is completed with an unstudied word. It is therefore essential to specify the proportion of consciously controlled trials in which an unconscious influence also occurred, that is, 'overlap trials'. Given that there currently exists no empirical method for estimating the proportion of overlap trials, three theoretical models have been used to specify this proportion: exclusivity, independence, and redundancy (see Jones 1987).

To facilitate understanding of the implications of the different models for the estimates of the proportion of consciously controlled trials (C), and the proportion of unconsciously influenced trials (U), they are graphically depicted in Fig. 4.1. In the original implementation of the PDA (Jacoby 1991; Jacoby *et al.* 1993*b*) the independence model was adopted. According to this model, C and U are independent, and thus the proportion of overlap

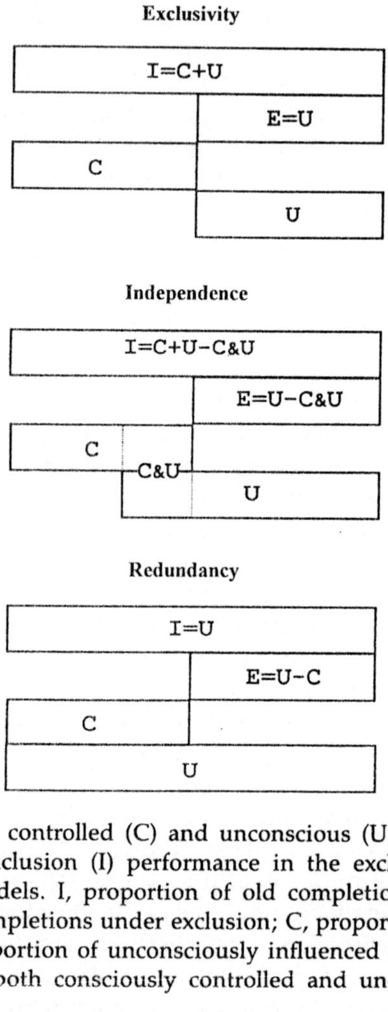

Fig. 4.1 Consciously controlled (C) and unconscious (U) influences underlying exclusion (E) and inclusion (I) performance in the exclusivity, independence, and redundancy models. I, proportion of old completions under inclusion; E, proportion of old completions under exclusion; C, proportion of consciously controlled trials; U, proportion of unconsciously influenced trials; C&U, proportion of trials which are both consciously controlled and unconsciously influenced, equals C times U.

trials equals C times U. Several authors have suggested alternative models. Gardiner and Java (1993) proposed an exclusivity model in which C and U are mutually exclusive, and the proportion of overlap trials equals zero. At the other extreme Joordens and Merikle (1993) argued for a redundancy model in which C is always a subset of U, and, consequently, the proportion of overlap trials equals C.

An inspection of Fig. 4.1 reveals the computation of C does not depend on which model is assumed. Regardless of the model assumed, C equals the proportion of old completions in the inclusion condition (I), minus the proportion of old completions in the exclusion condition (E):

$$C = I - E \quad [1]$$

This is because consciously controlled trials contribute to the proportion of old completions only under inclusion, but not under exclusion, and consequently, they represent the difference between these conditions (but see the later discussion of the differences in the meaning of the estimate of conscious control as a function of the various models). The value of C varies between 0 and 1. Zero represents the value expected in the case of a pure, densely amnesic patient who, regardless of instructional set, produces equal rates of completions with old words in both the inclusion and exclusion conditions. Such patients clearly do not intentionally control the influences of past experiences on their task performance. In contrast, a value of 1 is expected in the case of perfect conscious memory, such as when a single study word is clearly presented to a normal subject just before its corresponding stem with either inclusion or exclusion instructions. In this case one would expect subjects to always complete the stem with the study word when instructed to do so, and to always be able to avoid such a completion when so instructed. Obviously both of these extreme situations can be taken as representing process-pure performance. These examples help to explain the PDA's approach to the measurement of conscious control, but, it should be emphasized that the PDA is especially important under conditions when task performance is co-determined by conscious and unconscious influences.

The basic idea behind the PDA measure of conscious control, is that if memory expression is under intentional conscious control, then subjects can modify and regulate the manner in which they demonstrate their remembering to fit task requirements. To the extent that subjects have conscious control over the act of memory expression, they should be equally capable of completing stems with old words under inclusion, and avoiding such completions under exclusion. Conversely, given that subjects have no control over how unconscious influences of memory are expressed, such influences will affect subjects' responses in an identical manner under both inclusion and exclusion instructions by increasing the probability of old completions.

To illustrate the importance of the concept of conscious control and its relationship to the initiation of an intentional and deliberate action, consider the following compelling example by Marcel (1986, p. 41):

> Cortically blind patients who have no phenomenal experience of an object in the blind field will nonetheless preadjust their hands appropriately to the size, shape, orientation, and 3-D location of that object in the blind field when forced to attempt to grasp it . . . Yet such patients will make no spontaneous attempt to grasp a glass of water in their blind field even when thirsty. Voluntary actions often depend upon conscious perception.

The reason that the blindsight example is compelling is very similar to the reason that preserved learning in amnesia is impressive and compelling.

That is, both cases represent an example of unconscious influences coupled with a complete inability to act intentionally on perceived or remembered information (i.e. a total lack of conscious control). Indeed, one of the most tragic aspects of neurological disorders, such as blindsight and amnesia, is that despite the availability of relevant perceptual and memory information, patients are unable to act on and make conscious use of this information. As illustrated by Marcel's (1986) blindsight example, the idea that conscious awareness is a prerequisite for initiating an intentional action is not new. However, the PDA offers a very elegant operationalization of conscious control as the contrast between trying to respond with target words (Inclusion) versus trying to avoid responding with target words (Exclusion).

Estimating the proportion of unconsciously influenced trials (U), is more complicated, however. This is the case because such an estimate crucially depends on the extent of overlap between consciously controlled and unconsciously influenced trials. As can be seen in Fig. 4.1, the three models vary dramatically with respect to the hypothesized overlap between C and U. If such overlap exists, then the proportion of old completions in the exclusion condition (E) cannot be used as an estimate of U. As mentioned earlier, because conscious control overrides unconscious influence, such trials will not lead to old completions in the exclusion condition, even though an unconscious influence to do so was present. Thus, we need to calculate the proportion of such trials and add them to E to obtain an estimate of U. More precisely, each one of the three models—exclusivity, independence, and redundancy—specifies the conditional probability of U given C [i.e. $P(U|C)$]. The proportion of overlap trials between C and U is equal to the product of $P(U|C)$ and C. Finally, the estimate of U can be obtained using the following equation:

$$U = E + P(U|C)*C \qquad [2]$$

According to the independence model $P(U|C) = U$. When applied to equation 2 we obtain:

$$U = E + U*C \qquad [3]$$

and

$$U = E/(1-C) \qquad [4]$$

The independence model is bracketed by two extreme models of overlap, the exclusivity model, which claims no overlap between C and U [i.e. $P(U|C) = 0$], and the redundancy model, which claims complete overlap between C and U [i.e. $P(U|C) = 1$]. Consequently, for the exclusivity model the estimate for U is:

$$U = E \qquad [5]$$

and for the redundancy model:

$$U = E + C \qquad [6]$$

Elsewhere, Jacoby *et al.* (in press) provided a very compelling case for the independence model. Indeed, the independence model has been tacitly assumed by implicit memory researchers in their quest to demonstrate functional and stochastic dissociations as evidence for independent memory systems or processes. A detailed discussion of the relative merits of the different models is beyond the scope of this chapter (see Curran and Hintzman in press; Gardiner and Java 1993; Jacoby and Begg submitted; Jacoby *et al.* 1994, in press; Joordens and Merikle 1993).

Nevertheless, on the basis of the preceding analysis we would like to argue that, quite separate from the precise relational model adopted (i.e. independence, exclusivity, and redundancy), the PDA constitutes a major contribution to the study of conscious and unconscious influences on behaviour by virtue of its handling of thorny problems such as process-purity and response bias. Furthermore, the explicit relational assumption made in the original exposition of the PDA, namely the independence assumption, served as the impetus for the rapidly growing number of alternative proposals. The mere existence of this debate holds the promise that future theories will no longer be able to avoid specifying the relationship between consciously controlled uses of memory and unconscious influences of memory. Indeed, it is argued here that perhaps one of the most important long-term contributions of the PDA is in highlighting the importance of specifying the relationship between conscious and unconscious influences on task performance as a prerequisite for the study of cognitive processing with and without awareness.

In the next section we examine the implications of the different models as they relate to retrieval processes in general, and to involuntary conscious memory in particular. We argue that it is essential to specify any of the three relational assumptions in terms of a model of retrieval if the goal is to progress beyond a-priori speculation to empirical verification.

4.5 THE PROBLEM OF INVOLUNTARY CONSCIOUS MEMORY

The concept of *involuntary explicit memory* was first introduced by Schacter (1987, p. 510) who defined it as 'cases in which a test cue leads to an unintentional but fully conscious and explicit 'reminding' of the occurrence of a prior episode'. He further stated that 'At present, we know little about the relation between implicit memory and involuntary explicit memory, but future research and theorizing should be directed toward this issue'. It is important to note that contrary to Schacter's (1987) suggestion, this concept has received little theoretical and empirical attention (but see

Richardson-Klavehn *et al.* 1994, and Chapter 3). Ironically, despite its unresolved status within the TDA, this concept has been recently reintroduced as the cornerstone of several critiques of the PDA (Graf and Komatsu 1994; Richardson-Klavehn *et al.* 1994). These critiques have received a tremendous amount of exposure (e.g. Roediger and McDermott 1993), and, in our opinion, have created substantial confusion. Accordingly, we dedicate this section to evaluating the implications of involuntary explicit memory for the PDA framework. We begin by summarizing these critiques. We then argue that in its current form the concept of involuntary explicit memory is too underspecified to serve as a useful theoretical constraint, or as an a-priori objection to either the PDA or the TDA. To clarify this concept, we argue that it is important to differentiate between subjective experience versus retrieval processes. We also highlight the need to specify a model of retrieval, and to operationalize retrieval intentionality. Next, the three relational assumptions (exclusivity, redundancy, and independence) are examined in terms of their implications for modeling retrieval in general, and involuntary conscious memory in particular. Finally, we consider the implications of involuntary conscious memory for the derivation of PDA estimates.

4.5.1 The critiques

A grim assessment of the PDA in the light of the involuntary conscious memory issue was put forward by Graf and Komatsu (1994, p. 116):

> We maintain that the PDP is not suitable for learning about implicit versus explicit memory test performance because it does not distinguish between remembering that is initiated and guided by conscious intention versus remembering that is accompanied by 'consciousness'. . . The failure to distinguish between the different forms of remembering is built into the exclusion condition . . . where subjects are instructed to say NO to two kinds of critical items: those that are remembered as a result of a conscious intention, as well as those whose retrieval is followed by conscious awareness of their occurrence in a previously studied list.

A remarkably similar argument has been independently advanced by Richardson-Klavehn *et al.* (1994, p. 22) who argued 'that it is necessary to make independent distinctions based on retrieval intentionality (intentional vs. involuntary) and awareness (conscious memory vs. unconscious memory), and in particular, that it is necessary to take account of influences of memory that are involuntary, but accompanied by an awareness of the past (involuntary conscious memory)'. They further argued that 'when items associated with conscious memory come to mind involuntarily in an exclusion test, those items will be excluded from subjects' overt responses, reducing observed priming'. As a consequence they argued that, the estimate of unconscious, automatic influence within the PDA 'captures only a subset of involuntary influences—those that are *unaccompanied* by an awareness that an item has been previously encountered'.

As an indication of the impact of these critiques, consider how they are echoed in a thorough and scholarly review by Roediger and McDermott (1993, p. 77):

> [S]ubjects may exclude responses on several distinguishable bases: (a) they may intentionally recollect the item and exclude it, or (b) they may unintentionally retrieve the word and then recognize it and exclude it . . . If subjects covertly produce the response through an automatic process (or through incidental retrieval) and then later exclude it on the basis of recognizing it as being from the list, then the process dissociation procedure will overestimate how contaminated implicit tests are by intentional retrieval processes.

The basic thrust of the critiques is that *in principle* involuntary conscious memory cannot be handled by the PDA. This flaw is said to be related to the exclusion procedure, and to result in an underestimation of unintentional, automatic retrieval. On the basis of this a-priori assessment, a comparison of PDA estimates with implicit/explicit test performance is argued to be invalid and misleading.

4.5.2 The response

To date the concept of involuntary conscious memory is based on an appeal to the introspective experience of subjects in a stem-completion-like task. In such a task it occasionally appears to subjects that the completion popped to mind effortlessly, and only later did they become aware that this completion was a studied word. However, one should be very cautious in formulating theories that are solely based on such introspective experience (see Dennett and Kinsbourne 1992; Nisbett and Wilson 1977). For example, it is widely accepted that subjects are not typically aware of the processes underlying retrieval. Thus, phenomenologically speaking, experiences of involuntary explicit memory may occur in a variety of memory tasks such as explicit cued recall. Given that retrieval intentionality cannot be equated with retrieval instructions, and cannot be directly observed, how is it possible to distinguish empirically involuntary from intentional retrieval? In the absence of an independent measure of retrieval intentionality, such appeals to subjective phenomenal experience can only remain in the speculative realm. Furthermore, if the concept is to be used as a focal point for assessing measures of memory, it is imperative that the concept be considered in the context of specific models of retrieval pertaining to specific experimental tasks. Otherwise introducing this underspecified concept does nothing more than muddy the theoretical waters. In the next section we consider involuntary conscious memory in the context of the direct retrieval and generate/recognize models of retrieval.

Figure 4.2 illustrates the direct retrieval and the generate/recognize accounts of involuntary conscious memory. An inspection of Fig. 4.2 points out some of the key differences between these two interpretations. First, whereas the generate/recognize model assumes sequential dependence between automatic generation and recognition, the direct retrieval model assumes the existence of independent, consciously controlled and automatic retrieval processes. The stem or fragment cues serve as part of the input for both of the retrieval processes assumed by direct retrieval. In contrast, whereas these cues also feed into automatic generation, the input to recognition is a word completion generated automatically. Because part of the input to recognition is the output of generation, recognized items are always a subset of generated items (i.e. a redundancy assumption). Figure 4.2 is not meant to illustrate all test trials, or even a typical test trial as explained by these retrieval models. Rather, this figure illustrates that both models can account for the subjective phenomenal experience which has been termed involuntary conscious memory. This subjective experience is composed of two separate parts, the first being an experience of a completion popping to mind effortlessly without any episodic detail about its prior occurrence. Subsequently, the subject becomes aware of the prior occurrence of the word, and this awareness is accompanied by some amount of episodic detail. Within the generate/recognize model these two aspects of the subjective experience correspond very accurately to the output of generation and the subsequent output of recognition. Note that recognition is not assumed to occur for every generated item, but is a necessary part of involuntary conscious memory. More importantly, in the generate/recognize model the temporal aspect of subjective experience is deemed an accurate reflection of the sequential dependence between processes. This is not the case for direct retrieval. In the latter, the two aspects of the subjective experience are linked to the output of automatic retrieval and consciously controlled retrieval. However, the crucial difference is that these outputs are assumed to be asynchronous. As depicted in Fig. 4.2, in the case of involuntary conscious memory, the output of automatic retrieval is subjectively accessed prior to the output of the consciously controlled retrieval. Such a scenario is quite compatible with notions of the fast acting nature of automatic influences, and the typically slower speed of consciously controlled influences. However, while it is assumed that this is the case for 'involuntary conscious memory' trials, the direct retrieval model does not assume that this is the case in every trial. In fact, the independence of the two processes is likely to result in all kind of patterns of asynchrony between processes, both at input and output. In other words, according to the direct retrieval model, the temporal aspect of the subjective experience of involuntary conscious memory is misleading because it suggests a sequential dependence when independence exists (see also Dennett and Kinsbourne 1992). We thus conclude that the subjective experience of involuntary conscious memory can be accommodated by the PDA and

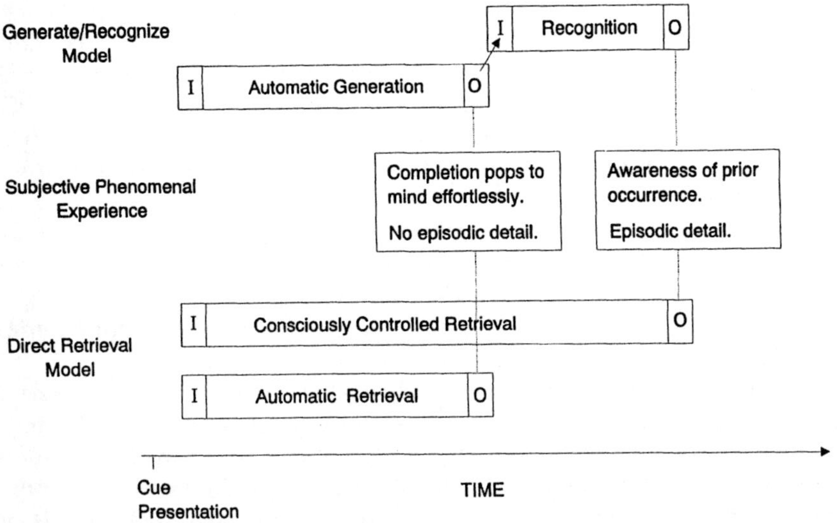

Fig. 4.2 Illustration of the generate/recognize and direct retrieval accounts of involuntary conscious memory. I, input; O, output. (*Note*: the alignment of input stages in the direct retrieval model was done for the purpose of presentation only, and does not imply that the two retrieval processes are synchronous at output.)

the independence assumption within the context of direct retrieval, but is problematic for the independence version of the PDA when cast in the context of a generate/recognize model.

4.5.3 Involuntary conscious memory and exclusivity, independence, and redundancy

By definition, a trial in which involuntary conscious memory occurred represents an automatic, unintentional, unconscious influence coupled with conscious remembering. Such trials have been referred to above as 'overlap trials'. As explained earlier, the three relational assumptions—exclusivity, independence, and redundancy—differ in terms of the hypothesized probability of occurrence of such overlap trials. It is therefore necessary to examine the implications of these assumptions for models of retrieval, and for the issue of involuntary conscious memory.

The exclusivity model assumes that there is no overlap between unconscious and conscious influences (i.e. the probability of overlap trials equals zero). Consequently, we do not see how the concept of involuntary conscious memory can be accommodated to within this framework. Accordingly, Fig. 4.2 only includes the generate/recognize and direct retrieval accounts of involuntary conscious memory that correspond to the redundancy and the independence assumptions respectively. What is ironic is that the same individuals who advocate the exclusivity model (Gardiner and Java 1993; see also Richardson-Klavehn *et al.* Chapter 3), also promote involuntary conscious memory as a difficulty for the PDA (Richardson-Klavehn *et al.* 1994, and Chapter 3). Perhaps the reason for this is that Gardiner and Java (1993) did not really propose a model of retrieval based on the exclusivity assumption. Indeed, any attempt to do so yields the highly counterintuitive notion that on any given trial the occurrence of consciously controlled retrieval somehow precludes unconscious retrieval from occurring, and vice versa. Not surprisingly, as pointed out by Jones (1987), exclusivity models have not been forthcoming in the context of memory theorizing.

Rather than truly arguing for an exclusivity model of retrieval, Gardiner and Java (1993, p. 181) state that the PDA independence model 'merits serious consideration but it does raise the problem of specifying how independent processes can be associated with states of awareness that are exclusive'. In other words, Gardiner and Java (1993) point out that according to the independence model conscious and unconscious influences can and do co-occur. However, conscious and unconscious states of awareness are mutually exclusive; that is, a subject cannot be simultaneously aware and unaware of the prior occurrence of a given word. The key to this confusion is, of course, that the PDA assumes the co-occurrence of conscious and unconscious influences, but does not assume that they co-occur in time (i.e. simultaneity of influence). It appears that Gardiner and Java (1993) tacitly interpret the PDA independence model to mean that consciously controlled and unconscious influences should operate simultaneously. This assumption is clearly not made by the independence model adopted by the PDA. In fact, some asynchrony between conscious and unconscious influences is entirely to be expected. One can further suggest that in line with theories of automaticity, unconscious influences are typically faster than consciously controlled influences. Consequently, it is entirely possible that a fast-acting unconscious influence occurs, and is subjectively experienced as the effortless popping to mind of the target word. Subsequently, when the same target word is independently retrieved in a consciously controlled manner, the result is a full-blown phenomenal awareness of the word's prior occurrence (see Fig. 4.2).

To clarify further how the independence model can accommodate for the subjective experience of involuntary conscious memory, it is important to realize that Jacoby *et al.* (1993*b*) argued for a specific model of retrieval which they referred to as direct retrieval. This model assumes that there are no separate generation and recognition stages involved in the retrieval of target words as a response to stem cues. Rather, the direct retrieval model proposes independent, consciously controlled, and automatic retrieval processes that may or may not access and output studied words as completions (see Fig. 4.2). Thus, there is a certain probability that both processes will retrieve the studied word. On any given trial the probability of such overlap will equal U*C. On some proportion of such overlap trials subjects may subjectively experience the unconscious influence first followed by the consciously controlled influence. However, this temporal aspect of phenomenal experience does not imply sequentiality, or dependence of the underlying processes.

Turning to the redundancy assumption, it is important to note that Joordens and Merikle (1993) focused on reinterpreting the results of Jacoby *et al.* (1993*b*) in the light of the redundancy rather than the independence assumption. These authors did not propose a model of retrieval as a rationale for their preference for redundancy over independence. In fact, a generate/recognize retrieval model which is consistent with the redundancy assumption does exist, and was considered by Jacoby *et al.* (1993*b*). We argue that it is vital to specify relational models at the retrieval level if they are to be meaningfully and empirically contrasted. Accordingly, we take a closer look at current formulations of generate/recognize models of retrieval as they apply to the PDA and TDA.

Jacoby and Hollingshead (1990) proposed a generate/recognize model to explain performance on stem-completion and cued-recall tasks. Jacoby *et al.* (1993*b*) considered the implications of this model in the context of performance in exclusion and inclusion tasks. Recently, Challis and Tulving (1993) proposed a generate/recognize model which is very similar to the one proposed by Jacoby and Hollingshead (1990). Challis and Tulving (1993, p. 1) argued that the 'generation/recognition account of performance on word-fragment cued tests holds that implicit processes of a perceptual and semantic nature underlie generation of items, and depending on the test instructions, recognition is used to select studied items from those generated'. Similarly, Jacoby and Hollingshead (1990, p. 435) suggested that 'a manipulation of cued-recall versus stem-completion instructions has little, if any, effect on generation processes. Rather, the effect of giving cued-recall instructions is to add recognition-memory processes to the generation processes required for stem-completion performance'.

For the present discussion, the important aspects of these generate/recognize models are as follows. First, performance on memory tasks employing stem or fragment retrieval cues is thought to involve two distinct stages—automatic, unintentional generation of completions, sometimes followed by recognition of their prior occurrence. Recognition processes are dependent on generation processes in that unintentional, automatic generation precedes, and is a prerequisite for recognition. In other words, an item can be recognized if and only if it was first automatically generated (i.e. a relationship of redundancy). Recognized items are a subset of generated items because recognition is dependent on prior automatic retrieval.

Most importantly, manipulations of intentional retrieval instructions (e.g. cued recall) versus incidental retrieval instructions (e.g. stem completion) are predicted to have no influence on automatic generation of completions; rather, their impact is thought to be restricted to the recognition process. Thus, cued recall is hypothesized to be equivalent to stem completion in terms of generation. However, cued recall differs from stem completion in that a covert recognition stage is added subsequent to generation.

Jacoby and Hollingshead (1990, experiment 2) tested this prediction by contrasting a generate/recognize test condition with a cued-recall test condition. During study, words were either generated from an anagram, or read. The generate/recognize test condition was designed to simulate the two-stage sequence hypothesized to underlie cued-recall test performance. In the generate/recognize test condition subjects were instructed to complete stems with the first word that came to mind, and then to make an old/new recognition decision. Cued-recall instructions required subjects to complete the stem with studied words. Subjects were asked to avoid completions if the stem did not correspond to a studied word. Both single completion and multiple completion stems were used during test.

An important feature of this experiment was an attempt to equate recognition processes across the cued-recall and generate/recognize conditions. Note that a generate/recognize model assumes that performance in cued recall reflects a two-stage process whereby completions are automatically generated and then subjected to a covert recognition decision. If the decision criterion of this covert recognition stage in cued recall is equated to the decision criterion used in the overt recognition stage in the generate/recognize condition, then, the probability of cued recall should equal the probability of completion plus recognition in the generate/recognize condition. To verify that decision criteria were equated across the overt and covert recognition decisions, baseline stems were included which did not correspond to any of the studied words. If the probability of falsely recognizing a completion of a baseline stem as old did not differ significantly from the probability of false recall (i.e. completion of baseline stems), then decision criteria for overt and covert recognition would be assumed to be equivalent (but see Jacoby and Hollingshead 1990).

As shown in Table 4.4, despite no difference in baseline (i.e. false recognition vs. false recall), the probability of cued recall was higher than the probability of completion plus recognition in the generate/recognize test condition. Importantly, this finding was obtained for both single and multiple completion stems. With multiple completions it can be argued that in the cued-recall test subjects internally performed multiple generate/recognize cycles which increased the probability of studied words being retrieved relative to the single cycle imposed in the generate/recognize condition. However, this explanation cannot account

Table 4.4 Probabilities of cued recall and stem completion plus recognition for single and multiple completion word-stems in Jacoby and Hollingshead (1990, experiment 2)

	Study condition		
Test condition	Anagram	Read	New
Single completion word-stems			
Cued recall	0.79	0.56	0.11
Generate/recognize	0.72	0.45	0.09
Multiple completion word-stems			
Cued Recall	0.34	0.25	0.09
Generate/recognize	0.28	0.18	0.10

for the single completion stem results which are therefore all the more impressive. The generate/recognize condition with single completion stems represents a very close simulation of the hypothesized two-stage process underlying cued-recall performance with these stems. Consequently, the difference in performance across these conditions is very difficult to interpret within the framework of current generate/recognize models. This is the case because the instruction to retrieve studied words in the cued-recall test condition resulted in the retrieval of more words relative to the incidental retrieval instructions in the generate/recognize test condition. Given equivalent baseline performance, this result cannot be easily explained as a difference in response criteria across the generate/recognize and the cued-recall conditions.

We see two potential interpretations for these results, both of which are problematic for current generate/recognize models. The first interpretation would suggest that at least in some trials, the instruction to intentionally retrieve in the cued-recall condition resulted in consciously controlled retrieval of studied words, as would be predicted by a direct retrieval model. The second interpretation would require generate/recognize models to be modified so as to acknowledge the possibility that retrieval instructions can affect both generation and recognition processes, and consequently, an instruction to intentionally retrieve studied words in the cued-recall condition may increase the automatic generation of studied items.

What are the implications of the preceding analysis? Although current implementations of generate/recognize models require modification, it appears that the redundancy relational assumption could be implemented to form a viable, specific model of retrieval. Furthermore, as demonstrated by Jacoby and Hollingshead (1990), the predictions of such models could be empirically tested and contrasted with the predictions of a direct retrieval model. This is obviously a very important direction for future research and theorizing.

The Jacoby and Hollingshead (1990) results may have another important implication. Specifically, several researchers, for example, Richardson-Klavehn *et al.* (1994), modified the instructions in an exclusion task relative to the original instructions used in the PDA. These researchers used generate/recognize-type instructions in the exclusion condition asking subjects to complete stems with the first word that came to mind, and if this word was a studied word, they were to write down another completion instead. In contrast to these generate/recognize retrieval instructions, PDA exclusion instructions provide subjects with an intentional set *vis-à-vis* the retrieval of studied words. In the PDA, subjects are equally oriented toward the study episode in both inclusion and exclusion. However, whereas in the inclusion condition they are required to complete with old words, in the exclusion condition they are to avoid responding with these words. Given the Jacoby and Hollingshead (1990) result, this procedural departure may be more meaningful than immediately apparent. Indeed, in a recent study, Jacoby and Begg (submitted) manipulated retrieval instructions in inclusion and exclusion tasks. They contrasted generate/recognize instructions with the original PDA instructions, and reported that the former yield results consistent with a redundancy model, while the latter yield results consistent with an independence model. This is further support for our conclusion that both redundancy and independence represent viable models of retrieval in specific test conditions. This highlights the need to empirically investigate conditions which produce performance consistent with redundancy versus independence models. Thus, it is futile to look for a single model that applies to all retrieval tasks. However, in contrast to Joordens and Merikle (1993), we argue that current empirical evidence derived from studies implementing the PDA using the original instructions, produced results which are more coherently interpreted by estimates based upon the independence assumption. (For a detailed empirical evaluation see Jacoby and Begg submitted; Jacoby *et al.* in press.)

Finally, it is important to consider how a generate/recognize model can account for the subjective experience of involuntary conscious memory. As seen in Fig. 4.2, in the case of generate/recognize models, the subjective experience of involuntary conscious memory represents a very accurate description of the two-stage sequence of processing underlying performance. Specifically, the unintentional, automatic generation would be subjectively experienced as the completion popping to mind effortlessly unaccompanied by episodic detail. Subsequently, this completion could be recognized, resulting in the subjective experience of remembering the prior occurrence of the completion (i.e. episodic detail). Given this correspondence between phenomenology and retrieval processes, we suspect that the critiques introducing involuntary conscious memory as a problem for the PDA tacitly assume a generate/recognize model. However, if this is the position of Graf and Komatsu (1994), it is not apparent in their critique. In fact, Graf and Komatsu (1994, p. 123) state their commitment to the independence assumption as part of their modified 'general model for inclusion and exclusion test performance'. Similarly, Richardson-Klavehn *et al.* (1994, and Chapter 3), do not acknowledge adopting a generate/recognize retrieval model as part of their critique of the PDA. If the authors of these critiques wish to advance involuntary conscious memory within the context of a generate/recognize model, they should be prepared to state explicitly their commitment to a redundancy assumption. Contrary to the argument advanced in the critiques, it is clear that involuntary conscious memory is not in principle incompatible with the PDA. While it will represent a problem if interpreted within the generate/recognize model, it can be handled in a straightforward manner by the direct retrieval model. Empirical evidence should be obtained to decide between the direct retrieval and the generate/recognize interpretations of the subjective experience of involuntary conscious memory.

4.5.4 Involuntary conscious memory, the exclusion condition, and estimates of the PDA

As mentioned earlier, the critiques of the PDA claimed that a basic flaw in the exclusion procedure makes the PDA ineffective in distinguishing between involuntary conscious memory versus consciously controlled influences on memory, resulting in an underestimation of unconscious automatic influence. In this section we consider the implications of involuntary conscious memory for computing PDA estimates using the independence equations. We do this in turn for the direct retrieval and generate/recognize interpretations of this phenomenon.

Within the context of direct retrieval, a subjective phenomenal experience of involuntary conscious memory may or may not accompany an overlap trial (i.e. a trial in which both conscious and unconscious influences co-occurred). The total proportion of overlap trials is U*C. As pointed out in the critiques, in the exclusion condition overlap trials, and therefore 'involuntary conscious memory' trials, should not result in completions with studied words. Consequently, it is true that the proportion of stems completed with studied words in the exclusion condition, P(Exclusion), may underestimate unconscious, automatic influences (U). The only relational assumption for which this is not true is exclusivity (U = P (Exclusion), see equations 2 and 5). Again this is ironic given that Richardson-Klavehn *et al.* (Chapter 3) and Gardiner and Java (1993) have both raised involuntary conscious memory as a problem unique to the PDA, and at the same time favoured the exclusivity assumption. However, the leap in logic which the critics appear to make is to conclude that because performance in exclusion underestimates unconscious, automatic influence, the PDA underestimates unconscious, automatic influence. This is very puzzling because, as explained earlier, the proportion of overlap trials is added to the proportion of stems completed with studied words under exclusion to provide an estimate of unconscious, automatic influence: U = P(Exclusion) + U*C; see equations 2 and 3, and Fig. 4.1. To summarize, contrary to the criticisms of the PDA, under the direct retrieval interpretation of involuntary conscious memory, the PDA estimates using the independence model are valid. This is not surprising given that within this framework involuntary conscious memory is viewed as an epiphenomenon that is misleading *vis-à-vis* the underlying retrieval processes.

Quite a different picture emerges if a generate/recognize interpretation of involuntary conscious memory is adopted. According to this interpretation 'involuntary conscious memory' trials would inflate the proportion of overlap trials in excess of the U*C value. In the most extreme condition, if all trials in which consciously controlled influences occurred conformed to generate/recognize retrieval, the true proportion of overlap trials would equal C, rather than U*C. This is, of course, the prediction of a redundancy model which holds that consciously controlled influences are a subset of unconscious influences. Under such circumstances computing PDA estimates by applying the independence formulas is obviously inappropriate. If independence formulas are nevertheless applied, the result will be an underestimation of unconscious, automatic influences. Such an inappropriate application of the independence formulas will produce varying degrees of underestimation depending on the difference between the true proportion of overlap trials minus the independence estimate of overlap trials:

$$P(U|C)^*C - U^*C = \text{equation 2} - \text{equation 3} \qquad [7]$$

where P(U/C) is the conditional probability of U given C. The magnitude of the underestimation will vary between **zero** when independence formulas are employed appropriately in the case of true independence, and:

$$C - U^*C = \text{equation 6} - \text{equation 3} \qquad [8]$$

with the latter reflecting the underestimation expected by an inappropriate application of independence formulas in a situation where redundancy holds.

It is also worth contrasting the implications of a generate/recognize implementation of the redundancy assumption versus a direct retrieval implementation of the independence assumption in terms of their impact on the estimate of conscious control. Whereas in both conditions conscious control equals P(Inclusion) − P(Exclusion) (see equation 1 and Fig. 4.1), the meaning of conscious control is different between these two cases in an important way. Specifically, in both models conscious control over the act of memory expression is accurately assessed. However, only in the context of the direct retrieval independence implementation does it also meaningfully reflect conscious control over the act of memory retrieval. For the generate/recognize model, the story is much more complex, and is yet to be specified. Within current implementations of the generate/recognize model, applying the term conscious control to generation is an oxymoron because generation of completions to stems or fragments is assumed to always be unconscious, unintentional, and automatic (but see our discussion of the Jacoby and Hollingshead 1990 result which may conflict with this assumption). In contrast, conscious control of retrieval may be meaningful for the recognition stage in this model. The recognition stage receives the generated completion as part of its input, and it is likely that the generate/recognize model would have to assume that recognition is at least in part under conscious control. It is the responsibility of proponents of generate/recognize retrieval to develop much more explicit models than currently exist. In our discussion of Jacoby and Hollingshead (1990) we have tried to point to potential possibilities. Nevertheless, conscious control of the act of memory expression can still be assessed meaningfully within this model. For generated words which were subsequently recognized, conscious control can be exercised in including or excluding them as completions in a manner consistent with task instructions. In contrast, unrecognized generated studied words result in memory expression over which subjects have no conscious control. This is the case because in both inclusion and exclusion such unrecognized generations will result in an increase in the probability of completing stems with studied words.

Thus, if involuntary conscious memory is equated with a generate/recognize redundancy model, the result will be an underestimation of unconscious, automatic influences. This is the case because the use of independence formulas in this context would be inappropriate. In addition, under these circumstances the meaning of the conscious control estimate is substantially different relative to its meaning within the context of a direct retrieval independence model.

To summarize, involuntary conscious memory cannot be used to invalidate the PDA for the following reasons. First, the critiques introduced involuntary conscious memory in a manner which was vague and underspecified, and which did not distinguish between subjective experience and the underlying retrieval processes. Second, the critiques become meaningful only in the context of a specific generate/recognize implementation of the redundancy model which we provided. In addition, on the basis of evidence obtained by Jacoby and Hollingshead (1990) we argued that current generate/recognize models require modification.

Third, it is not at all clear that a generate/recognize model is assumed in the critiques. In fact, there are indications to the contrary. Fourth, we have demonstrated that the direct retrieval model can accommodate the subjective experience of involuntary conscious memory in a straightforward manner, therefore, soundly rejecting the argument that involuntary conscious memory is inherently incompatible with the PDA. Fifth, our analysis clearly indicated that deciding between various interpretations of involuntary conscious memory requires an empirical evaluation, and cannot be done solely on the basis of a-priori considerations such as the ones advanced in the critiques. Finally, we find it ironic that proponents of the TDA (e.g. Graf and Komatsu 1994) wish to disqualify the PDA on the basis of an issue which was originally introduced as a problem for the TDA (Schacter 1987), and which is yet to be resolved, or even seriously considered, within this framework.

4.6 IS AN EMPIRICAL COMPARISON BETWEEN TDA AND PDA VALID?

We would like to use this final section of the chapter to respond to Graf and Komatsu's (1994) assertion that the PDA is invalid for learning about implicit versus explicit test performance (for a broad response to Graf and Komatsu 1994, see Toth *et al.* in press). We view their statement and its implications as very questionable both on scientific grounds and in terms of the sociology of science. On scientific grounds this assertion ignores the value of convergent evidence across methodologies for studying the relationship between consciousness and memory performance. One strategy employed by PDA researchers has been to compare PDA estimates with implicit performance results using some of the primary experimental variables employed in TDA research (e.g. Jacoby *et al.* 1993*b*; Reingold and Goshen-Gottstein in press; Toth *et al.* 1994). We believe that such a strategy provides vital input without which an evaluation of the validity of either paradigm is impossible. The value of a-priori analyses such as the PDA critiques and the current response notwithstanding, the final test of any theoretical/methodological paradigm is empirical. Such paradigms should be evaluated in terms of their ability to accommodate parsimoniously a large body of empirical evidence, as well as their ability to generate and stimulate empirical research. By discouraging empirical comparisons between paradigms, the possibility of arriving at a unified theoretical explanation is sabotaged, and consequently, fragmentation of the literature prevails, and empirical progress is stifled.

Most importantly, the PDA makes specific predictions about the relationship between PDA estimates and performance on implicit tests, and these predictions should be empirically explored. For example, the PDA predicts that under conditions where conscious control is minimal, the estimate of unconscious, automatic influence should approximate performance on comparable implicit tests. This is the case because under such conditions the indirect measure could be expected to reflect a relatively uncontaminated measure of automatic, unconscious influence. Such a pattern was obtained by Toth *et al.* (1994, experiment 1). In this experiment a level of processing manipulation was used in an indirect stem-completion task, as well as in inclusion and exclusion tasks. In the nonsemantic encoding condition, the estimate of conscious control approximated zero (0.03), and the estimates of automaticity and indirect performance were in close agreement (0.44 vs. 0.45, respectively). In the semantic encoding condition where the estimate of conscious control was substantial (0.27), indirect performance exceeded the estimate of unconscious, automatic influence (0.51 vs. 0.45). The interpretation proposed by Toth *et al.* (1994) was that in the semantic encoding condition, indirect stem-completion performance was not a process-pure measure of unconscious, automatic influence. Rather, it was contaminated by consciously controlled influences. Thus, Toth *et al.*'s (1994) comparison of performance across the TDA and PDA highlights the potential interpretation of level of processing effects in implicit tests as representing the conscious contamination of these tests. The alternative interpretation of these effects based on an assumption of process-purity is one which invokes additional types of priming effects which are sensitive to lexical and/or semantic processing (e.g. Challis and Brodbeck 1992). If for no other reason, parsimony dictates that the conscious contamination explanation should be given serious consideration (for a detailed discussion see Jacoby *et al.* in press; Toth and Reingold, Chapter 2; Toth *et al.* 1994: for additional examples of convergence between implicit performance and PDA estimates see Jacoby *et al.* 1993*b*; Reingold and Goshen-Gottstein in press).

By not acknowledging the process-purity problem within the context of TDA, Graf and Komatsu (1994) fail to appreciate the solution to this problem which is embodied in the PDA. Indeed, once the potential pitfalls of equating processes with tasks are acknowledged, it becomes clear that there are at least two potential strategies that can be pursued in the study of implicit memory. The first involves designing or identifying retrieval tasks which may be less sensitive to the influence of conscious control (e.g. Rajaram and Roediger 1993; Roediger *et al.* 1992). The second strategy is to use a method like the PDA for the purpose of quantifying the separate contributions of consciously controlled and unconscious, automatic processes. Whereas the former strategy focuses on the search for process-pure tasks, the latter strategy searches for an appropriate technique for separating processes within a single task. We have opted for the latter strategy because we believe that in most situations conscious and unconscious influences co-determine task performance. Nonetheless, a PDA-like approach may also prove useful in the search for process-pure tasks. This is the case because the inclusion/exclusion contrast provides a novel approach to the measurement of conscious control. Thus, if inclusion, exclusion, and indirect test conditions are used with the same encoding manipulation (e.g. Toth *et al.* 1994; Reingold and Goshen-Gottstein in press), it may be possible to correlate the magnitude of conscious control with implicit task performance. If the involvement of conscious control in a task is strongly manipulated without an effect on implicit performance this would provide evidence that for the specific manipulations tested, this task was not consciously contaminated. Even in the case of amnesic patients estimating conscious control may prove valuable in determining to what extent a given patient exemplifies 'pure amnesia'. Apart from the potential diagnostic implications of such an application, this possibility may prove important in the context of cognitive neuropsychology research. This is the case because it may be used to evaluate the homogeneity of patient groups for the purpose of between-group comparisons. One of the classic problems facing researchers studying patients with neurological deficits, is that each patient has a unique pattern of deficits making the interpretation of group comparisons difficult. While the possibility of employing the PDA in the search for 'pure tasks' and 'pure amnesics' is intriguing, it is important to remember that both tasks and patients may not be pure across all situations. Thus, the two research strategies should not be viewed as mutually exclusive, rather, as complementary.

As part of their critique of the PDA, Graf and Komatsu (1994, p. 123) proposed 'a more general model for inclusion and exclusion test performance'. The questions then become, is the PDA the appropriate technique for separating consciously controlled versus unconscious influences in a specific task? And which relational assumption should be used? Resolution of these questions must await further empirical evaluation. However, we believe that the PDA takes a meaningful step in the right direction, and that the recent interest in modelling conscious and unconscious influences is a direct result of this change in emphasis brought about by the PDA. One of the motivations underlying the original formulation of the PDA (Jacoby 1991; Jacoby *et al.* 1993*b*) was to start with a minimal number of parameters, as well as with the independence assumption, which as pointed out by Jones (1987), is the most parsimonious of the relational assumptions. The idea was to attempt to model a substantial body of evidence with as simple an approach as possible, and if so indicated, to expand it later on the basis of empirical feedback. In contrast, it is important to point out that the model proposed by Graf and Komatsu (1994) has employed a substantial number of additional parameters without providing a clear operationalization. As such, it is at best a description, not a model (see Toth *et al.* in press). In addition to the emphasis on quantifying the separate contributions of processes, the exclusion condition included in the PDA provides a powerful methodology for conclusive demonstrations of unconscious influences, and for the exploration of qualitative differences between conscious versus unconscious processes.

In order to provide a more complete treatment of the TDA versus PDA controversy, we feel compelled to address the sociological and political context surrounding this controversy. One important reason why we so strongly object to Graf and Komatsu's (1994) statement that the TDA and PDA cannot be validly contrasted empirically, is that we perceive this statement as attempting to establish a territorial claim, and a monopoly on the study of conscious versus unconscious memory. The dominance of the TDA paradigm during the last decade may make it easy to forget that this methodology was initially devised to study phenomena which were previously investigated using a multitude of paradigms, and a variety of different terms such as consciousness, automaticity, attention, intentionality, and awareness. Indeed, the terms 'implicit' and 'explicit' memory were initially defined with respect to conscious recollection at the time of retrieval (e.g. Schacter 1987). As often happens, the initial goal which motivated the development of the TDA methodology has sometimes been replaced with the goal of studying the methodology and tasks for their own sake. That is, redefining the phenomena in terms of the particular methodology which was originally devised with an external research goal distinguishable from this methodology. Thus, some researchers investigate memory tasks such as stem completion, fragment completion, and perceptual identification, while losing sight of the larger goal of studying conscious versus unconscious memory. Similarly, Erdelyi (1985) noted another example of the confusion between theoretical goals and the tasks designed to achieve them. The general consensus in the late 1950s was that 'the failure of experimental methodology to corroborate the existence of unconscious processes was taken, as a matter of course, to reflect a failure of the concept rather than a failure of the extant methodology' (Erdelyi 1985, pp. 58–9), (see Reingold and Merikle 1990 for a detailed discussion). To Graf and Komatsu's (1994) claim that the PDA cannot be used to study performance in implicit and explicit tests we reply that the PDA is not intended to study implicit and explicit performance, rather it is intended to study the phenomena which such tests were originally designed to investigate.

In the present chapter we argued that presenting issues such as the relational assumption problem, and the involuntary conscious memory problem, as unique to the PDA, while ignoring their obvious relevance to the TDA, represents a double standard. As an additional example, consider the argument by Graf and Komatsu (1994, p. 120) that the PDA 'does not take into account false alarm rates'. The irony of this argument should be glaringly apparent in the context of this chapter. As we clearly documented, the TDA completely ignored the issue of response bias, and differences in base rates across contrasted implicit and explicit tests (e.g. Graf and Mandler 1984). In contrast, PDA researchers are extremely careful in comparing base rates across inclusion and exclusion conditions. Indeed, demonstrating no difference in response bias (i.e. base rates) across inclusion versus exclusion has been routinely used as a prerequisite for computing the PDA estimates (see Yonelinas 1994). Thus, a demonstration that base rates differ significantly across inclusion and exclusion, such as the one provided by Komatsu *et al.* (in press), cannot be argued to invalidate the PDA, any more than an example of the violation of the assumptions underlying ANOVA can be used to invalidate that procedure (see Jacoby and Begg submitted). The explicit treatment of the issue of response bias within the PDA, is the best guarantee that when there is a difference across conditions, it will be detected and acknowledged. This cannot be said for the treatment of this issue within the TDA. Similarly, Richardson-Klavehn *et al.* (1994, and Chapter 3), and Gardiner and Java (1993) have criticized the independence assumption of the PDA while at the same time failing to acknowledge that the modified PDA-like procedure they proposed is based on an assumption of independence between involuntary conscious memory and involuntary unconscious memory. This tacit assumption is clearly evident when inspecting the computational formulas they proposed (see pp. 24–6, Richardson-Klavehn *et al.* 1994).

The intensive criticism of the assumptions attributed to the PDA, coupled with the failure to acknowledge their relevance to other paradigms, creates the impression that while the PDA involves especially problematic assumptions, other methodologies, such as the TDA, are much more straightforward and sound on a-priori grounds. The illusion that the TDA is assumptionless is further aided by the fact that its underlying assumptions, (e.g. process-purity, relational assumption) often remain tacit and unacknowledged. The use of the implicit/explicit terms to refer to both tasks and processes/systems contributed in a subtle way to the tacit assumption that implicit and explicit tests exclusively measure implicit and explicit memory respectively (see Reingold and Merikle 1988, 1990; Richardson-Klavehn and Bjork 1988). In contrast, PDA assumptions are stated explicitly, and thus are more open to criticism. In the sociology of science the perception that a particular paradigm is problematic often discourages the use of the paradigm, and impedes publication of research carried out within that paradigm. This may occur regardless of whether or not this perception is justified. When authority figures in a field promote such perceptions, less informed researchers may tend to take such criticisms at face value. This is especially true when the area in question is as complex as the study of consciousness and memory.

The relevance of considering the sociological and political context of the present controversy is vividly illustrated in the previously cited quote in which Tulving cautions that Roediger and McDermott's (1993) treatment of the process-purity issue may result in reviewers becoming overly concerned about this topic, and consequently impede the ability to publish TDA research. We want to emphasize strongly that by discussing issues which may be problematic for the TDA, it is not our intention to impede empirical progress within this framework. Despite our clearly stated theoretical bias, we attempted to provide a serious examination of issues as they apply to both the PDA and TDA. We share Tulving's concern, and we think that it is very unfortunate when empirical data are held hostage awaiting the resolution of theoretical debates. Such an unfortunate, inadvertent effect occurred following Eriksen's (1959, 1960) classic critique of the perception-without-awareness literature, and more recently, following Holender's (1986) critique of the same field. Currently, this area of research has dwindled to a mere trickle. With the recent successful demonstrations of unconscious perception by applying the PDA, and opposition paradigms (i.e. exclusion) (Debner and Jacoby 1994; Jacoby and Whitehouse 1989; Joordens and Merikle 1992; Merikle and Joordens in press) we hope that this trend will be reversed. However, we would add that if this is a concern for an established paradigm such as the TDA, it is definitely a concern for an emerging paradigm such as the PDA. Consequently, we object to the use of a-priori critiques as a basis for rejecting empirical PDA research. At the same time, we do not think the solution to the potential danger that a preoccupation with assumptions will stifle empirical research, is to ignore important theoretical issues. Obviously, paradigms differ in their ability to handle certain theoretical issues, as well as some empirical findings. But it is precisely because all paradigms have some weaknesses that convergence across paradigms is imperative. The solution, therefore, is to promote an atmosphere in which the broader implications of issues are recognized as challenges for the entire field. Otherwise, the TDA versus PDA controversy may become more polarized, and the field may become more fragmented, to the detriment of scientific progress.

ACKNOWLEDGEMENTS

Preparation of this chapter was supported by a Natural Science and Engineering Research Council (NSERC) operating grant to Eyal M. Reingold and by a fellowship awarded to Jeffrey P. Toth by the Rotman Research Institute of Baycrest Centre and the Clarke Institute of Psychiatry. We wish to thank Elizabeth Bosman, Bob Lockhart, Colin MacLeod, Phil Merikle,

Morris Moscovitch, Stephan Kohler, and especially Larry Jacoby, for their helpful comments on earlier versions of this paper.

REFERENCES

Adams, J. K. (1957). Laboratory studies of behavior without awareness. *Psychological Bulletin*, **54**, 383–405.

Balota, D. A. (1983). Automatic semantic activation and episodic memory. *Journal of Verbal Learning and Verbal Behavior*, **22**, 88–104.

Bowers, K. S. (1984). On being unconsciously influenced and informed. In *The unconscious reconsidered*, (ed. K. S. Bowers and D. Meichenbaum), pp. 227–72. Wiley, New York.

Bowers, J. S. and Schacter, D. L. (1990). Implicit memory and test awareness. *Journal of Experimental Psychology: Learning, Memory, and Cognition*, **16**, 404–16.

Brown, A. S. and Mitchell, D. B. (1994). Levels of processing in implicit memory: A reevaluation. *Memory and Cognition*, **22**, 533–41.

Challis, B. H. and Brodbeck, D. R. (1992). Level of processing affects priming in word-fragment completion. *Journal of Experimental Psychology: Learning, Memory, and Cognition*, **18**, 595–607.

Challis, B. H. and Tulving, E. (1993). *Further support for a generation/recognition account of performance on word-fragment cued tests.* Paper presented at the 34th annual meeting of The Psychonomic Society, Washington, DC.

Cheesman, J. and Merikle, P. M. (1985). Word recognition and consciousness. In *Reading Research: Advances in theory and practice*, Vol. 5, (ed. D. Besner, T. G. Waller, and G. E. MacKinnon), pp. 311–52. Academic Press, New York.

Cheesman, J. and Merikle, P. M. (1986). Distinguishing conscious from unconscious perceptual processes. *Canadian Journal of Psychology*, **40**, 343–67.

Craik, F. I. M. and Lockhart, R. S. (1972). Levels of processing: A framework for memory research. *Journal of Verbal Learning and Verbal Behavior*, **11**, 671–84.

Curran, T. and Hintzmann, D. L. (in press). Violations of the independence assumption in process dissociation. *Journal of Experimental Psychology: Learning, Memory, and Cognition.*

Debner, J. A. and Jacoby, L. L. (1994). Unconscious perception: Attention, awareness, and control. *Journal of Experimental Psychology: Learning, Memory, and Cognition*, **20**, 304–17.

Dennett, D. C. and Kinsbourne, M. (1992). Time and the observer: The where and when of consciousness in the brain. *Behavioral and Brain Sciences*, **15**, 183–247.

Dixon, N. F. (1971). *Subliminal perception: The nature of a controversy*. McGraw-Hill, New York.

Dixon, N. F. (1981). *Preconscious processing*. Wiley, Chichester.

Dunn, J. C. and Kirsner, K. (1988). Discovering functionally independent mental processes: The principle of reversed association. *Psychological Review*, **95**, 91–101

Dunn, J. C. and Kirsner, K. (1989). Implicit memory: Task or process? In *Implicit memory: Theoretical issues*, (ed. S. Lewandowsky, J. C. Dunn, and K. Kirsner), pp. 17–31. Erlbaum, Hillsdale, NJ.

Erdelyi, M. H. (1985). *Psychoanalysis: Freud's cognitive psychology*. Freeman, New York.

Erdelyi, M. H. (1986). Experimental indeterminacies in the dissociation paradigm. *Behavioral and Brain Sciences*, **9**, 30–1.

Eriksen, C. W. (1959). Unconscious processes. In *Nebraska symposium on motivation, 1958*, (ed. M. R. Jones), pp. 169–227. University of Nebraska Press; Lincoln.

Eriksen, C. W. (1960). Discrimination and learning without awareness: A methodological survey and evaluation. *Psychological Review*, **67**, 279–300.

Fowler, C. A., Wolford, G., Slade, R., and Tassinary, L. (1981). Lexical access with and without awareness. *Journal of Experimental Psychology: General*, **110**, 341–62.

Gardiner, J. M. (1988). Functional aspects of recollective experience. *Memory and Cognition*, **16**, 309–13.

Gardiner, J. M. and Java, R. I. (1993). Recognizing and remembering. In *Theories of Mind*, (ed. A. Collins, M. A. Conway, S. E. Gathercole, and P. E. Morris), pp. 163–88. Erlbaum, Hillsdale, NJ.

Graf, P. and Komatsu, S. (1994). Process dissociation procedure: Handle with caution! *European Journal of Cognitive Psychology*, **6**, 113–29.

Graf, P. and Mandler, G. (1984). Activation makes words more accessible, but not necessarily more retrievable. *Journal of Verbal Learning and Verbal Behaviour*, **23**, 553–68.

Graf, P., Squire, L. R., and Mandler, G. (1984). The information that amnesic patients do not forget. *Journal of Experimental Psychology: Learning, Memory, and Cognition*, **10**, 164–78.

Green, D. M. and Swets, J. A. (1966). *Signal detection theory and psychophysics*. Wiley, New York.

Henley, S. H. A. (1984). Unconscious perception re-revisited: A comment on Merikle's (1982) paper. *Bulletin of the Psychonomic Society*, **22**, 121–4.

Holender, D. (1986). Semantic activation without conscious identification in dichotic listening, parafoveal vision, and visual masking: A survey and appraisal. *Behavioral and Brain Sciences*, **9**, 1–23.

Jacoby, L. L. (1991). A process dissociation framework: Separating automatic from intentional uses of memory. *Journal of Memory and Language*, **30**, 513–41.

Jacoby, L. L. and Begg, I. M. (submitted). In defense of functional independence: Violations of assumptions underlying the process-dissociation procedure? *Journal of Experimental Psychology: Learning, Memory, and Cognition*.

Jacoby, L. L. and Hollingshead, A. (1990). Toward a generate/recognize model of performance on direct and indirect tests of memory. *Journal of Memory and Language*, **29**, 433–54.

Jacoby, L. L. and Kelley, C. M. (1991). Unconscious influences of memory: Dissociations and automaticity. In *The neuropsychology of consciousness*, (ed. D. Milner and M. Rugg), pp. 201–33. Academic Press, San Diego, CA.

Jacoby, L. L. and Whitehouse, K. (1989). An illusion of memory: False recognition influenced by unconscious perception. *Journal of Experimental Psychology: General*, **118**, 126–35.

Jacoby, L. L., Kelley, C. M., and Dywan, J. (1989*a*). Memory attributions. In *Varieties of memory and consciousness: Essays in honour of Endel Tulving*, (ed. H. L. Roediger III and F. I. M. Craik), pp. 391–422. Erlbaum, Hillsdale, NJ.

Jacoby, L. L., Woloshyn, V., and Kelley, C. (1989*b*). Becoming famous without being recognized: Unconscious influences of memory produced by dividing attention. *Journal of Experimental Psychology: General*, **118**, 115–25.

Jacoby, L. L., Ste-Marie, D., and Toth, J. P. (1993*a*). Redefining automaticity: Unconscious influences, awareness and control. In *Attention, selection, awareness and control. A tribute to Donald Broadbent*, (ed. A. D. Baddeley and L. Weiskrantz), pp. 261–82. Oxford University Press.

Jacoby, L. L., Toth, J. P., and Yonelinas, A. P. (1993*b*). Separating conscious and unconscious influences of memory: Measuring recollection. *Journal of Experimental Psychology: General*, **122**, 139–54.

Jacoby, L. L., Toth, J. P., Lindsay, D. S., and Debner, J. A. (1992). Lectures for a layperson: Methods for revealing unconscious processes. In *Perception without awareness*, (ed. R. F. Bornstein and T. S. Pittman), pp. 81–120. Guilford Press, New York.

Jacoby, L. L., Toth, J. P., Yonelinas, A. P., and Debner, J. A. (1994). The relationship between conscious and unconscious influences: Independence or redundancy? *Journal of Experimental Psychology: General*, **123**, 216–19.

Jacoby, L. L., Yonelinas, A. P., and Jennings, J. (in press). The relation between conscious and unconscious (automatic) influences: A declaration of independence. In *Scientific approaches to the question of consciousness*, (ed. J. D. Cohen and J. W. Schooler). Erlbaum, Hillsdale, NJ.

Joordens, S. and Merikle, P. M. (1992). False recognition and perception without awareness. *Memory and Cognition*, **20**, 151–9.

Joordens, S. and Merikle, P. M. (1993). Independence or redundancy? Two models of conscious and unconscious influences. *Journal of Experimental Psychology: General*, **4**, 462–7.

Jones, G. V. (1987). Independence and exclusivity among psychological processes: Implications for the structure of recall. *Psychological Review*, **94**, 229–35.

Kelley, C. M. and Jacoby, L. L. (1990). The construction of subjective experience: Memory attributions. *Mind and Language*, **5**, 49–68.

Komatsu, S., Graf, P., and Uttl, B. (in press). Process dissociation procedure: Core assumptions fail, sometimes. *European Journal of Cognitive Psychology*.

Marcel, A. J. (1974, July). *Perception with and without awareness*. Paper presented at the meeting of the Experimental Psychology Society, Stirling, Scotland.

Marcel, A. J. (1983). Conscious and unconscious perception: Experiments on visual masking and word recognition. *Cognitive Psychology*, **15**, 197–237.

Marcel, A. J. (1986). Consciousness and processing: Choosing and testing a null hypothesis. *Behavioral and Brain Sciences*, **9**, 40–1.

Merikle, P. M. (1982). Unconscious perception revisited. *Perception and Psychophysics*, **31**, 298–301.

Merikle, P. M. and Joordens, S. (in press). Measuring unconscious influences. In *Scientific approaches to the question of consciousness*, (ed. J. D. Cohen and J. W. Schooler), Erlbaum, Hillsdale, NJ.

Merikle, P. M. and Reingold, E. M. (1990). Recognition and lexical decision without detection: Unconscious perception? *Journal of Experimental Psychology: Human Perception and Performance*, **16**, 574–83.

Merikle, P. M. and Reingold, E. M. (1991). Comparing direct (explicit) and indirect (implicit) measures to study unconscious memory. *Journal of Experimental Psychology: Learning, Memory, and Cognition*, **17**, 224–33.

Moscovitch, M., Vriezen, E., and Goshen-Gottstein, Y. (1993). Implicit tests of memory in patients with focal lesions or degenerative brain disorders. In *Handbook of neuropsychology*, Vol. 8, (ed. H. Spinnler and F. Boller), pp. 133–73, (F. Boller and J. Grafman, volume editors). Elsevier, Amsterdam.

Nisbett, R. E. and Wilson, T. D. (1977). Telling more than we can know: Verbal reports on mental processes. *Psychological Review*, **84**, 231–59.

Nolan, K. A. and Caramazza, A. (1982). Unconscious perception of meaning: A failure to replicate. *Bulletin of the Psychonomic Society*, **20**, 23–6.

Rajaram, S. and Roediger, H. L. III (1993). Direct comparison of four implicit memory tests. *Journal of Experimental Psychology: Learning, Memory, and Cognition*, **19**, 765–76.

Reingold, E. M. (1992). Conscious versus unconscious processes: Are they qualitatively different? *Behavioral and Brain Sciences*, **15**, 218–19.

Reingold, E. M. and Goshen-Gottstein, Y. (in press). Separating consciously controlled and automatic retrieval processes in memory for new associations. *Journal of Experimental Psychology: Learning, Memory, and Cognition.*

Reingold, E. M. and Merikle, P. M. (1988). Using direct and indirect measures to study perception without awareness. *Perception and Psychophysics*, **44**, 563–75.

Reingold, E. M. and Merikle, P. M. (1990). On the inter-relatedness of theory and measurement in the study of unconscious processes. *Mind and Language*, **5**, 9–28.

Reingold E. M. and Merikle, P. M. (1991). *Stem completion and cued recall: The role of response bias.* Paper presented at the 32nd annual meeting of the Psychonomic Society, San Francisco, CA.

Richardson-Klavehn, A. and Bjork, R. A. (1988). Measures of memory. *Annual Review of Psychology*, **39**, 475–543.

Richardson-Klavehn, A., Gardiner, J. M., and Java, R. I. (1994). Involuntary conscious memory and the method of opposition. *Memory*, **2**, 1–29.

Roediger, H. L. III (1990). Implicit memory: A commentary. *Bulletin of the Psychonomic Society*, **28**, 373–80.

Roediger, H. L. III and McDermott, K. B. (1993). Implicit memory in normal human subjects. In *Handbook of neuropsychology*, Vol. 8, (ed. H. Spinnler and F. Boller), pp. 63–131, (F. Boller and J. Grafman, volume editors). Elsevier: Amsterdam.

Roediger, H. L. III, Weldon, M. S., Stadler, M. L., and Riegler, G. L. (1992). Direct comparison of two implicit memory tests: Word fragment and word stem completion. *Journal of Experimental Psychology: Learning, Memory, and Cognition*, **18**, 1251–69.

Schacter, D. L. (1987). Implicit memory: History and current status. *Journal of Experimental Psychology: Learning, Memory, and Cognition*, **13**, 501–18.

Schacter, D. L., Bowers, J., and Booker, J. (1989). Intention, awareness, and implicit memory: The retrieval intentionality criterion. In *Implicit memory: Theoretical issues*, (ed. S. Lewandowsky, J. C. Dunn, and K. Kirsner), pp. 47–65. Erlbaum, Hillsdale, NJ.

Shevrin, H. and Dickman, S. (1980). The psychological unconscious: A necessary assumption for all psychological theory? *American Psychologist*, **35**, 421–34.

Shimamura, A. P. (1986). Priming effects in amnesia: Evidence for a dissociable memory function. *Quarterly Journal of Experimental Psychology*, **38A**, 619–44.

Stroop, J. R. (1935). Studies of interference in serial verbal reactions. *Journal of Experimental Psychology*, **18**, 643–61.

Swets, J. A. (1964). *Signal detection and recognition by human observers.* Wiley, New York.

Toth, J. P., Lindsay, D. S., and Jacoby, L. L. (1992). Awareness, automaticity, and memory dissociations. In *Neuropsychology of memory,* (2nd edn), (ed. L. R. Squire and N. Butters), pp. 46–57. Guildford Press, New York.

Toth, J. P., Reingold, E. M., and Jacoby, L. L. (1994). Toward a redefinition of implicit memory: Process dissociations following elaborative processing and self-generation. *Journal of Experimental Psychology: Learning, Memory, and Cognition,* **20**, 290–303.

Toth, J. P., Reingold, E. M., and Jacoby, L. L. (in press). A response to Graf and Komatsu's (1994) critique of the process-dissociation procedure: When is caution necessary? *European Journal of Cognitive Psychology.*

Tulving, E. (1985). Memory and consciousness. *Canadian Psychology,* **26**, 1–12.

Tulving, E. (1989). Memory: Performance, knowledge, and experience. *European Journal of Cognitive Psychology,* **1**, 3–26.

Yonelinas, A. P. (1994). Receiver-operating characteristics in recognition memory: Evidence for a dual-process model. *Journal of Experimental Psychology: Learning, Memory, and Cognition,* **20**, 1341–54.

5

How implicit is implicit learning?

Dianne C. Berry

In everyday life there are many examples of our learning to respond in some rule-like way without being able to state the rules or regularities that govern our behaviour. For example, most of us learn to recognize and produce grammatical utterances without ever being able to describe the underlying rules of the grammar. The term 'implicit learning' has been used to characterize such situations, and has been the subject of increasing interest and debate in recent years. In fact, understanding the processes involved in implicit learning, and its relationship to explicit learning, have become central goals in current cognitive psychology.

Implicit learning has been investigated in a wide range of experimental paradigms including artificial grammar learning, control of complex systems, and sequence learning. What these situations have in common is that a person typically learns about the structure of a fairly complex stimulus environment, without necessarily intending to do so, and in such a way that the resulting knowledge is difficult to express. In terms of controlling complex systems, for example, people can learn to reach and maintain specified levels of target variables without being aware of the basis on which they are responding (e.g. Berry and Broadbent 1984; Stanley *et al.* 1989). Similarly, people can learn to classify exemplars of an artificial grammar, and can acquire knowledge about the sequential structure of stimuli, without adopting explicit code-breaking strategies and without being able to articulate any rule they might be using or the basis on which they are responding (e.g. Reber 1989; Nissen and Bullemer 1987). In addition, recent studies have provided convincing demonstrations of implicit learning in neuropsychological patients (e.g. Squire and Frambach 1990; Knowlton *et al.* 1992; see Berry and Dienes 1993 for a review).

Despite these wide-ranging empirical demonstrations, however, a number of researchers have argued against the existence of implicit learning. They have suggested that reported discrepancies between measured performance and explicit verbalizable knowledge can be accounted for without resorting to the notion of implicit or unconscious learning (e.g. Shanks and St. John 1994). This chapter reviews much of the evidence that has contributed to the recent debate over the existence of implicit learning. In particular, it assesses the evidence in relation to the two main features of implicit learning proposed by Reber (1989); first, that it gives rise to abstract knowledge; and secondly that it is an unconscious process. Following this, it suggests that given the problem of assessing implicitly acquired knowledge, and of interpreting the results of the different knowledge measures, a more profitable approach might be to see whether such knowledge can be distinguished on other grounds. In line with this, it looks at whether implicitly acquired knowledge is associated with distinct properties of storage and retrieval. Finally, it suggests that the answer to the question 'how implicit is implicit learning' depends on the criteria employed to identify implicit learning; learning may be considered to be implicit in some senses, but not in others.

5.0 EARLY DEMONSTRATIONS OF IMPLICIT LEARNING

5.0.1 Artificial grammar learning

Reber's (1967) study is generally recognized as being the starting point for current work on artificial grammar learning. He showed that people become increasingly sensitive to the constraints of a synthetic grammar simply from exposure to exemplary strings. In the first part of his experiment, subjects were shown a series of letter strings which were generated by a finite state grammar. They were not informed about the existence of the grammar and were simply told to memorize the letter strings. A control group of subjects were given random strings to learn. In the second phase of the experiment, subjects were told about the existence of the grammar and were given an unexpected classification task. They were presented with a new set of strings (half of which were grammatical and half ungrammatical) and had to classify them as being grammatical or not. Reber found that subjects given grammatical strings to memorize in phase one showed superior memory performance to those given random strings. More importantly, subjects who had seen the grammatical strings performed significantly above chance on the unexpected classification task, even though they were not able to explain how they made their decisions, or what the rules of the grammar might be.

This basic finding has been replicated and extended in a number of follow-on studies (e.g. Reber 1976; Reber and Lewis 1977; Reber and Allen 1978). Reber (1976), for example, compared the original neutral memorization procedure (where subjects simply memorized the letter strings and were then given the unexpected classification task), with one where subjects were informed during the memory phase that the strings conformed to certain grammatical rules. They were told that it might help them to memorize the strings better if they tried to work out what the rules might be. Reber found that this explicit search instruction, as he called it, had a negative effect on performance on all aspects of the experiment. Subjects receiving the search instruction took longer to memorize the exemplars, were poorer at determining well-formedness of strings, and showed evidence of having induced rules that were not representative of the grammar. Reber concluded that explicit processing of complex materials had a decided disadvantage in relation to implicit processing. However, not all subsequent studies (e.g. Dulany *et al.* 1984) have replicated the negative effect of the explicit search instruction. Hence, it is probably safest to conclude that implicitly trained subjects do at least as well on subsequent attempts to discriminate between grammatical and ungrammatical strings as subjects who attempt to work out the rules explicitly.

This conclusion is supported by a recent study by Mathews *et al.* (1989) which employed a more extreme manipulation of implicit versus explicit processing. In their 'implicit' match task, subjects held single exemplars in memory only long enough to select the same item from a subsequent set of five items. They did not know that the items were generated by a grammar. They also had no opportunity or incentive for explicit abstraction of similarities among items. Yet their performance on a subsequent classification task was as good as that of subjects who carried out an explicit edit task in the learning phase, which involved the continuous generation and testing of rules for letter order.

5.0.2 Control of complex systems

In these studies, people have interacted with computer-controlled tasks and have been required to reach and maintain specified levels of a target output variable by manipulating one or more input variables. Berry and Broadbent (1984), for example, required subjects to control either a sugar production factory or a computer-simulated person. (The tasks were in fact mathematically identical.) It was found that in both cases practice significantly improved ability to control the tasks but had no significant effect on ability to answer post-task written questions. In contrast, verbal instructions about the best way to control the tasks had no significant effect on control performance, although they did make people significantly better at answering the questions. As well as these differential effects, there was also no evidence for a positive association between task performance and question answering. People who were better at controlling the tasks were significantly worse at answering the questions. Berry and Broadbent concluded that these tasks might, under certain conditions, be performed in some implicit manner.

Broadbent *et al.* (1986) came to a similar conclusion using Broadbent's (1977) city transport system. They found that subjects improved in ability to control the tasks with practice, but there was not a corresponding increase in the number of correct answers to verbal questions about the system. They also found that verbal explanation had no effect on task performance (although in this case the verbal explanation simply consisted of presenting the written questionnaire with the correct answers filled in).

One criticism of the Berry and Broadbent and Broadbent *et al.* studies is that the particular questions used in the post-task questionnaires may not have been appropriate to the particular ideas of the people learning to control the systems. The subjects might have had knowledge that was relevant to controlling the tasks, but which was not tested by the questions. Berry (1984, 1991), however, used a number of question types and still found evidence for a dissociation. Furthermore, Stanley *et al.* (1989) asked people to practise at either the sugar production or person interaction task and then to explain verbally to somebody else how to control it. Although in this case people could choose their own form of words, their own performance improved before they could tell somebody else how to succeed. Individual learning curves associated with the tasks showed sudden improvements in performance which were not accompanied by a similar increase in verbalizable knowledge. Stanley *et al.* suggested that there is a considerable difference between the amount of time it takes to acquire verbalizable knowledge, and knowledge used to perform the control tasks. Subjects tend to become quite skilled in controlling the tasks long before there is much gain in verbalizable knowledge.

5.0.3 Sequence learning

Most studies in this area have focused on two main tasks: the serial reaction time task initiated by Nissen and Bullemer (1987) and the matrix scanning task initiated by Lewicki and colleagues (e.g. Lewicki *et al.* 1988). Nissen and Bullemer (1987) used a reaction time task in which a light appeared at one of four locations (arranged horizontally) on a video monitor. Subjects were required to press the one key, out of four keys, that was directly below the position of the light. The sequence of lights was either determined randomly, or else they appeared in a repeating 10-trial sequence. The results showed a rapid decrease in reaction time with training in the repeating sequence condition, but not in the random condition. Furthermore, when subjects in the repeating condition were switched to a random sequence, reaction times increased substantially. The majority of subjects in the repeating sequence condition reported noticing the sequence, and some were able to describe parts of it spatially.

This contrasts with the performance of a group of amnesic patients, who showed a similar pattern of performance to the normal subjects but were totally unaware of the existence of the repeating pattern.

In a follow-up study, Willingham *et al.* (1989) attempted to determine whether there were normal subjects who demonstrated procedural learning of the sequence in the absence of explicit verbalizable knowledge of it. They identified two subgroups of subjects: the unaware subjects who either claimed they had not noticed that there was a pattern or failed to specify more than three positions of the sequence correctly; and the aware subjects who claimed to have noticed a pattern and could reproduce the sequence. Both groups showed substantial procedural learning of the sequence. In particular, the response times of the unaware group decreased by nearly 100 ms. Furthermore, their performance on a subsequent generate task was at the same level as that of control subjects who had not been exposed to the repeating sequence. The generate task involved displaying the repeating sequence but required subjects to predict the next stimulus position, rather than responding to the present stimulus position. (Hartman *et al.* 1989 reported similar findings with a verbal analogue of the serial reaction time task.)

Lewicki *et al.* (1988) used a matrix scanning task, in which the sequential structure of the material was manipulated to generate sequences of five elements according to a set of simple rules. Each rule defined where the next stimulus could appear as a function of the locations at which the two previous stimuli had appeared. The first two elements of each sequence were unpredictable, whereas the last three were determined by their predecessors. Lewicki *et al.* (1988) reported a progressively widening difference between the number of fast and accurate responses, elicited by predictable and unpredictable trials, emerging with practice. They also found a sharp increase in response latencies when they altered the sequential structure of the stimuli. Again, when asked after the task, subjects failed to report having noticed any pattern in the sequence of exposures, and none of them even suspected that the sequential structure of the material had been manipulated.

5.0.4 Acquisition of invariant characteristics

Finally, Burton and colleagues have recently reported two studies (McGeorge and Burton 1990; Bright and Burton 1994) demonstrating implicit learning of an invariant feature. In the original McGeorge and Burton study, subjects were exposed to a set of 30 four-digit strings during a 'learning phase' in which they concentrated on a cover task involving mental arithmetic on each string. Subjects then carried out a forced-choice 'memory' test on 10 pairs of new strings. They were led to believe that one string of each pair had appeared in the learning phase. Although this was not the case, one string of each pair did contain an invariant digit that had appeared in each learning string. McGeorge and Burton showed that subjects selected significantly more strings that contained the invariant digit, even though they expressed considerable surprise when the hidden rule was subsequently explained.

In a follow-up study, Bright and Burton (1994) suggested that the earlier results could be accounted for in terms of a simple feature frequency counting mechanism rather than implicit learning of an abstract rule. They therefore adapted the McGeorge and Burton task so that the invariant feature did not appear in the same form on every trial in the learning phase. Subjects were presented with a series of clock faces rather than number strings; the invariant feature being that all the clock faces in the learning phase were between 6 and 12 o'clock. In the test phase, subjects were again led to believe that they were taking part in a recognition memory experiment and were presented with pairs of new clock faces, one of each pair showing a time between 6 and 12 o'clock, and one not. In line with the original study, subjects were significantly more likely to select clock faces which conformed to the hidden rule, despite having no explicit awareness of the rule.

5.1 SUBSEQUENT CHALLENGES

Reber (1989) proposed two main features of implicit learning: first, that it gives rise to abstract knowledge; and secondly that it is an unconscious process. Both have become the subject of considerable debate in the literature.

5.1.1 How abstract is implicitly acquired knowledge?

Reber originally claimed that implicit learning is an unconscious abstraction process that gives rise to abstract knowledge. Hence, people categorize novel instances on the basis of some memorial representation of the patterns of invariance inherent in the exemplar set. This type of model presumes that individuals abstract structural or featural information from the training examples and store this information as a high-level generalization. An alternative suggestion is that decisions about category membership of novel items are based solely on retrieval of information about specific exemplars rather than on more abstract information (e.g. Brooks and Vokey 1991). Thus, classification decisions are guided by similarity of test items to stored exemplars (or parts of them).

Most of the debate on this topic has centred on artificial grammar learning. Studies attempting to provide evidence for implicit abstraction rather than for instance- or similarity-based processing in this area have focused on the issue of transfer. An early study by Reber (1969) required subjects to memorize two sets of grammatical letter strings, one after the other. For some subjects the letter strings in the second set were made up of the same letters as those in the first set, but the underlying rules were modified. For other subjects the rules were the same, but the actual letters changed. Reber found that changing the rules had a disruptive effect on subjects' performance, but changing the letter set had no detrimental effect. More recently, Mathews *et al.* (1989) have also shown that subjects are fairly resilient to changes of letter set. Their experiment was run over a four-week period. They found that subjects who received a new letter set each week (which was based on the same underlying grammatical structure) performed as well as subjects who worked with the same letter set throughout the experiment.

At first glance, it is difficult for similarity-based models to account for transfer across different letter sets. According to such accounts, classification performance should decline as a function of distance from training items. However, as Brooks and Vokey (1991) have recently pointed out, similarity-based models can account for transfer across different letter sets if it is assumed that transfer to 'changed letter set' strings is due to abstract similarity between test strings and specific training stimuli. For example, a string such as MXVVVM could be seen as similar to BDCCCB in that they both start and end with the same letter and have a repeated letter triplet next to the end. Hence, transfer to a different letter set could be due to reliance on abstract (relational) analogies to individual items, rather than to reliance on knowledge of the structure of the grammar abstracted across many training items. Vokey and Brooks (1992) showed that abstract similarities to specific study exemplars had a large effect on transfer performance regardless of the grammaticality of the transfer items. Thus, transfer across letter sets is not evidence in itself for abstract knowledge. (Perruchet 1994, put forward a similar account to Vokey and Brooks, but shifted the level of analysis from whole exemplars to small chunks such as bigrams and trigrams.)

Mathews *et al.* (in prep.) have recently attempted to distinguish between similarity and abstractionist theories. They suggest that the critical feature that distinguishes abstraction from similarity-based models is the selective weighting of relevant versus irrelevant features. According to abstractionist theories, it should be possible to find exceptions to the typical distance from training-item effects reported by Brooks and Vokey (1991) and Vokey and Brooks (1992). That is, it should be possible to find transfer tasks in which many features of the stimuli are altered without loss in classification accuracy. Mathews *et al.* presented evidence in favour of abstractionist models from five artificial grammar learning experiments showing that implicit learning induces selective responding to category-relevant cues. Similarity to training-item effects were found when changed features of training items were relevant (valid) cues for classification, but not when irrelevant cues were changed to produce transfer items. Thus, the results could not be completely accounted for by the notion of similarity-based processing.

Bright and Burton (1994) have also recently argued in favour of implicit rule abstraction in relation to performance on their invariant clock face task. As well as finding transfer between analogue and digital representations of time in the learning and testing phases, they found no advantage at test of previously seen old items over new items that conformed to the hidden rule. They argued that any instance or exemplar model would predict that subjects should have performed better on the old items. Conversely, however, Cock *et al.* (1994) have recently shown that performance on McGeorge and Burton's invariant digit task can be better accounted for in terms of similarity-based processing than in terms of implicit rule abstraction.

Taking the various findings together, it seems safe to conclude that neither extreme position is likely to be tenable. As Berry and Dienes (1993) propose, performance in most implicit learning tasks is likely to involve a combination of exemplar-based processing and implicit rule abstraction. Indeed, successful computational models for artificial grammar learning and sequence learning contain elements of both (see also Nosofsky *et al.* 1989; Cleeremans 1993).

5.1.2 How unconscious is implicitly acquired knowledge?

Reber originally claimed that knowledge acquired during artificial grammar learning was completely unconscious (see also Lewicki *et al.* 1992). More recently, Reber (1989, p. 229) has modified his position to suggest that 'knowledge acquired from implicit learning processes is knowledge that, in some raw fashion, is always ahead of the capability of its possessor to explicate it'. However, other researchers (e.g. Perruchet and Pacteau 1990; Shanks and St. John 1994) believe that such modifications are insufficient and argue that there is no evidence that knowledge acquired during artificial grammar learning is implicit in nature. Similar debates have arisen in relation to the computer control and sequence learning tasks. In these fields also, earlier claims have been modified in the light of more recent evidence.

Artificial grammar learning

Reber's original claim that knowledge acquired during artificial grammar learning is completely unconscious was based on subjects' post-task introspections. Subjects were able to classify new strings as being grammatical or not with a greater than chance accuracy, but were not able to describe how they did this or on what basis they were making their decisions. However, it soon became apparent that Reber's original claim was, at the least, an oversimplification. Studies in his own laboratory (e.g. Reber and Lewis 1977; Reber and Allen 1978) showed that subjects could report some of what they knew. For example, Reber and Allen (p. 202) reported that 'specific aspects of letter strings were often cited as important in decision making . . . first and last letters, bigrams, the occasional trigams and recursions were mentioned'. Unfortunately, Reber and Allen did not analyse subjects' verbal reports in such a way as to be able to predict performance levels.

More recent investigators have adopted more systematic approaches to assess whether subjects' verbalizable knowledge can account for their classfication performance. Mathews *et al.* (1989), for example, used a teachback technique, in which during the classification task subjects were asked to provide instructions for an unseen partner on how to classify the strings. The transcribed instructions were subsequently given to yoked control subjects who were then tested on the same classification task. Mathews *et al.* found that although the yoked control subjects performed significantly above chance, and improved across blocks in the same manner as the original experimental subjects, their performance remained behind that of the experimental subjects, at roughly half their level of accuracy. As Dienes *et al.* (1991) have recently pointed out, however, there are some problems with using yoked subjects to assess the validity of rules stated by experimental subjects.

Dienes *et al.* (1991) employed a more direct method of assessing the validity of rules elicited in free recall. In this study, following the learning and classification phases, subjects were asked to describe as fully as possible the rules or strategy they had used to classify the strings. Dienes *et al.* then used the elicited rules to simulate classification performance and found that simulated performance (53 per cent) was considerably less than that of actual classification performance (63 per cent). Hence, as with the Mathews *et al.* (1989) study, not all of subjects' classification knowledge could be elicited with free recall. These findings could be taken as evidence that learning on such tasks gives rise to a relatively specific knowledge base that can not be tapped by free report. However, as other researchers (e.g. Brewer 1974; Brody 1989) have argued, free recall is a relatively insensitive and incomplete measure. Poor performance on free-recall tests may simply reflect the problem of having to retrieve large amounts of low-confidence knowledge, rather than reflecting a deeper incompatibility between the mechanisms employed in free recall and the type of knowledge stored.

This possibility has led some investigators to employ forced-choice tests in order to assess acquired knowledge. Whereas free report gives subjects the option of not responding, forced-choice measures do not. Dulany *et al.* (1984), for example, asked subjects during the classification task to underline that part of a string that 'made it right' if it was grammatical, or that part that violated the rules if it was classified as ungrammatical. Dulany *et al.* then analysed the extent to which the rules implied by subjects' underlinings could be used to classify strings as valid or invalid. They found that the induced rules were sufficient to account for the full set of classification decisions made, and argued that knowledge of the grammar must therefore be held consciously. However, Reber *et al.* (1985) have challenged the interpretation of this study, arguing that subjects' underlinings could be the result of vague guesses that could be made on the basis of implicit knowledge.

Another line of attack has come from Perruchet and Pacteau (1990). They have argued that exposure to grammatical strings results in little more than knowledge of particular pairs of letters or bigrams that occur in the grammar. Their claim is based on two main findings. First, subjects exposed to pairs of letters rather than whole strings in phase one of the experiment performed just as well on the subsequent classification task as did subjects who were presented with the whole strings (provided that strings beginning with an illegal first letter were excluded from the analysis). Secondly, in a separate experiment, subjects were exposed to complete exemplars and were asked to rate isolated bigrams for their legitimacy. It was found that they were able to do so with above-chance accuracy, and that their ratings could predict observed classification performance without error. Although it is clear that subjects undoubtedly did acquire appreciable bigram knowledge in this study, there are other studies which show that subjects do learn more than just bigrams (see, for example, Mathews 1990).

Finally, Dienes *et al.* (1991) employed a new knowledge test (the sequential letter dependency, or SLD, test) in which subjects were asked which letters could occur after different stems varying in length from zero letters upwards. They found a positive correlation between classification performance and ability to answer the SLD test (whereas they found no correlation between classification performance and free report). More importantly, there was a close match between classification performance and predicted performance that was based on answers to the SLD test.

Taking the various findings together, it seems clear that there is no evidence to support Reber's original claim that knowledge acquired during artificial grammar learning is completely unconscious. If accessibility is judged in terms of performance on free-recall tests, then there is evidence to support Reber's more recent view that knowledge acquired from implicit learning processes is knowledge that is always ahead of the capability of its possessor to explicate it. However, if accessibility is judged in terms of performance on forced-choice tests, then even Rober's modified position seems questionnable.

Control tasks

The debate over the accessibility of implicitly acquired knowledge has been less extensive in relation to the computer control tasks, but there have been a number of new findings that require some of the earlier claims to be modified. First, Stanley *et al.* (1989) have shown that dissociations between task performance and associated verbalizable knowledge are not as complete as was at first thought. Stanley *et al.* asked subjects to practise at either the sugar production or personal interaction task and then to describe to somebody else how to control it. They found that although there was a marked dissociation between performance and verbalizable knowledge at moderate levels of practice, highly experienced subjects (570 trials) were able to give verbal statements that helped novices to perform more successfully. (Sanderson 1989, similarly reported positive associations between performance and question answering emerging with extensive practice on Broadbent *et al.*'s city transport task.)

Like Stanley *et al.*, McGeorge and Burton (1989) also used a teachback method (getting subjects to provide instructions for the next subject) to elicit verbalizable knowledge after performance on the sugar production task. Rather than presenting the elicited instructions to subsequent subjects, however, they used them to develop computer simulations of subjects' control performance. Comparisons were then made between simulated performance and observed performance. Using this method, McGeorge and Burton found that about one-third of their subjects reported heuristics that resulted in simulated performances that were either equivalent to, or better than, observed performance. Hence, after 90 trials of practice some subjects were able to produce accurate verbal statements.

Marescaux *et al.* (1989), again using the sugar production task, demonstrated that subjects know more about situations that they have personally experienced. Their experiment was set up so that subjects interacted with the sugar production task for two sets of 30 trials, and then answered a number of post-task questions. The questions were matched closely to the task in that they required subjects to estimate how many workers would be needed to reach target in different situations, and in that they were presented on the computer so that subjects saw just what they might have seen on the full task. The questions varied along two basic dimensions. First, the target sugar output was either the same or different to that experienced while controlling the task. Secondly, the mini-history given to subjects at the start of each question was either taken from their own immediately preceding interaction, or was taken from a hypothetical interaction. The results showed superior questionnaire performance when subjects had to reach the same target as they had experienced while interacting with the task, and when the mini-histories were taken from their own past experience. The key factor seemed to be that subjects were tested on specific situations which they themselves had experienced while interacting with the task. They did not seem to have learned anything that could be used in other novel situations.

Taken together, the studies by Stanley *et al.*, McGeorge and Burton, Marescaux *et al.*, and Sanderson suggest that the dissociation between task performance and associated verbalizable knowledge may not be as complete as was at first thought. People appear to develop some explicit knowledge as a result of task experience. The evidence seems to indicate, however, that increases in explicit knowledge occur after improvements in task performance, and that this knowledge may be largely limited to knowledge of specific personally experienced situations.

Sequence learning

A number of investigators (e.g. Perruchet and Amorim 1992; Perruchet *et al.* 1990; Shanks *et al.* 1994) have recently argued against the evidence for the acquisition of implicit knowledge in sequence learning tasks. They have suggested that improvements in performance on such tasks can be accounted for without resorting to the notion of non-conscious processing.

As far as the studies initiated by Nissen and Bullemer (1987) are concerned, Perruchet and Amorim (1992) have identified a number of problems with the generate task. In this task, subjects are exposed to the repeating sequence, but are required to predict the next stimulus position rather than respond to the present stimulus position. The stimulus is typically displayed until the subject makes the correct prediction for the next trial. Perruchet and Amorim put forward two specific criticisms; first, that the instructions given to subjects before the generate task did not mention that subjects should reproduce prior sequences and, secondly, that there were problems with the correction procedure. Perruchet and Amorim therefore adapted the generate task in two ways. First, they changed the instructions to emphasize the relation between study and test phase. Secondly, they did not provide feedback on response accuracy. Using this modified test, they found that subjects could acquire conscious knowledge of substantial portions of the repeating sequence after only two 100-trial blocks of training. In a second experiment, in addition to the generate task, Perruchet and Amorim assessed knowledge using a recognition procedure of the four-trial chunks composing the repeating sequence. As in their artificial grammar learning studies, they found that subjects could recognize chunks that did follow the constraints of the training stimuli. (Shanks *et al.* (1994) have identified other problems with the Nissen and Bullemer serial reaction time task.)

Perruchet *et al.* (1990) have similarly criticized Lewicki *et al.*'s (1988) study. They argued that Lewicki *et al.*'s findings can be accounted for without suggesting that subjects acquire tacit knowledge of the composition rules and that subjects partition the sequence into logical blocks of five trials. Rather, they suggested that the results could be explained by the relative frequency of a few simple sequences of target locations. Perruchet *et al.* focused on the nature of the 'movement' of the target from one location to the next, rather than on the location of targets *per se* (which Lewicki *et al.* were careful to equalize for each quadrant). They suggested that frequent and infrequent movements were not equally distributed over the predictable and unpredictable trials. In particular, infrequent movements occured mainly in unpredictable trials, hence giving rise to longer reaction times. Perruchet *et al.* carried out an extended replication of the Lewicki *et al.* experiment and found that their alternative explanation accounted for many fine-grained features of subjects' performance.

Taken together, the studies by Perruchet and colleagues and Shanks *et al.*, suggest that evidence for implicit learning of sequential structure may not be as convincing as was at first thought. In some cases, subjects have more explicit knowledge available than had previously been believed. In other cases, the results could be accounted for without resorting to the notion of implicit learning at all. (However, see Reed and Johnson 1994, for a recent demonstration of implicit sequence learning.)

Taking the three areas together, it seems clear that evidence in favour of implicit learning is not as convincing as was originally thought. Indeed, some researchers have argued forcibly against its existence (e.g. Perruchet and Pacteau 1990; Shanks and St. John 1994). In their recent review, Shanks and St. John conclude that 'evidence for unconscious learning of any sort is highly questionnable' and that 'human learning is almost invariably accompanied by conscious awareness'.

Shanks and St. John posit two criteria which they argue need to be applied when considering studies in this area. The first criterion (the Information Criterion) concerns that match between the information that is responsible for performance changes and the information that is revealed by the test of awareness. Shanks and St. John suggest that if learning involves the acquisition of information I, but the experimenter is focusing on information I,* then the subject may appear not to be aware of the relevant knowledge when in fact they are. (This is similar to Dulany's 1961 notion of correlated hypotheses.)

The second criterion (the Sensitivity Criterion) states that in order to show the test of conscious knowledge and task performance relate to dissociable underlying systems, we must be able to show that our test of awareness is sensitive to all of the relevant conscious knowledge.

Clearly, many of the studies that have commonly been cited as evidence in favour of implicit learning would fail these two criteria. However, as Berry (1994*b*) and others have argued, it may be that Shanks and St.

John have gone too far in their rejection of the evidence. Despite some problems with individual experiments, it is still the case that many of the tasks labelled as being implicit are associated with a fairly distinct set of features that do not apply to tasks currently labelled as being explicit (Berry and Dienes 1993). It may also be the case that Shanks and St. John have focused too closely on the issue of conscious awareness when evaluating the evidence for implicit learning. One problem is that different authors have used the term 'conscious' in different ways (see, for example, the debate between Dulany *et al.* 1984 and Reber *et al.* 1985). Related to this is the problem of determining whether particular tests (e.g. Dulany's underlinings task or Nissen and Bullemer's generate task) should be considered as being measures of implicit or explicit knowledge.

Because of problems such as these, some researchers (e.g. Mathews *et al.* 1989, Berry and Dienes 1993, Berry 1994*a*) prefer not to equate the term 'implicit' learning with unconscious learning. Rather, they argue that implicitly and explicitly acquired knowledge might be better distinguished on other grounds; for example, by looking at whether they have different properties of storage and retrieval. We will consider this question next.

5.2 DOES IMPLICITLY ACQUIRED KNOWLEDGE HAVE DISTINCT PROPERTIES OF STORAGE AND RETRIEVAL?

Given the problem of assessing implicitly acquired knowledge, and of interpreting the results of the different knowledge measures, an alternative approach is to see whether such knowledge can be distinguished on other grounds. As Berry and Dienes (1993) argue, if implicit knowledge is qualitatively different from explicit knowledge then it may well be associated with different properties of storage and retrieval. One way of demonstrating this would be to show that experimental manipulations affect performance and measures of awareness differently, or affect different measures of performance differently, suggesting the existence of different databases for different output processes. A number of examples are considered below.

5.2.1 Implicit and explicit learning modes

It has been suggested that implicit learning tends to be associated with incidental learning conditions rather than with deliberate hypothesis testing. A number of studies have shown that people who approach the task in a relatively passive manner perform at least as well (and sometimes better) than people who try to work out the underlying structure of the task explicitly.

In terms of artificial grammar learning, Reber (1976) found that subjects who simply memorized a set of randomly ordered grammatical strings performed significantly better on the subsequent classification test than subjects who were told to search for the underlying rules in order to assist their memorization performance. However, other studies (e.g. Dienes *et al.* 1991; Dulany *et al.* 1984) have not replicated this detrimental effect of explicit search instructions and have found no difference between implicitly and explicitly instructed subjects. Interestingly, Mathews *et al.* (1989) found that a much stronger implicit/explicit manipulaton had no effect on learning a finite state grammar but did have a significant effect on learning a biconditional rule. In the latter case, subjects in the explicit condition performed significantly better.

In terms of the control tasks, Berry and Broadbent (1987, 1988) found that the salience of the relationship between the input and output variables was an important factor in determining whether learning was implicit or explicit. In the case of the sugar production and person interaction tasks used by Berry and Broadbent (1984) and Stanley *et al.* (1989), the underlying relationship was relatively non-obvious. Berry and Broadbent (1988) reasoned that if the underlying relationship was made more obvious or salient, performance and verbalizable knowledge might be positively associated. We therefore devised a pair of person interaction tasks to test out this suggestion. In both cases each control action by the person produced an output from the system that depended only on that input and simply added a constant to it. In the salient case the output appeared immediately, whereas in the non-salient case it appeared only after the next input (that is, there was a lag). The results showed that in the case of the salient task, post-task questionnaire scores were high and positively associated with control performance, whereas in the case of the non-salient version, post-task questionnaire scores were low and uncorrelated with control performance. Like Reber, we also found that salience interacted with the provision of an explicit search instruction. Telling people to search for the underlying rule had a detrimental effect on controlling the non-salient person, but a beneficial effect on controlling the salient person.

Further evidence for the distinction between implicit and explicit learning modes was provided by Hayes and Broadbent (1988) and Berry (1991). In the latter case it was found that experience of watching another person interacting with the salient person control task had a beneficial effect on subsequent control performance with the same task, whereas experience of watching another person interacting with the non-salient person control task had no beneficial effect on subsequent control performance.

Finally, in the area of sequence learning, Howard *et al.* (1992) showed that if subjects initially simply observed a sequence then their later responses were just as fast as subjects who responded to the sequence from the beginning. However, observing rather than responding led to superior generation performance, indicating a dissociation between generation and reaction time. Similarly, Nissen *et al.* (1987) showed that injecting the drug scopolamine had no influence on learning as assessed by reaction time, but did reduce generation performance.

5.2.2 Robustness of implicit and explicit knowledge

Reber (1989) proposed that implicit learning should be more robust than explicit learning. There are various aspects to this.

Secondary tasks

One suggestion has been that the storage and retrieval of implicit knowledge should be less affected by secondary tasks than should explicit knowledge (e.g. Dienes *et al.* 1991). Unfortunately, the findings on this issue have been somewhat mixed.

Dienes *et al.*, using the artificial grammar learning paradigm, investigated the effect of random number generation on both classification performance and free report of the rules of the grammar. Contrary to predictions, they found that the dual-task manipulation interfered equally with classification performance and free report.

In terms of the control tasks, Hayes and Broadbent (1988) found that performance on Berry and Broadbent's (1988) salient person task (but not their non-salient task) was interfered with by a memory-demanding concurrent task. However, Green and Shanks (1993) failed to replicate this effect. (See Berry and Broadbent, in press, for a full discussion of the effects of secondary tasks on control task performance.)

Finally, a number of studies have examined the effect of a secondary tone counting task on sequence learning performance (e.g. Nissen and Bullemer 1987; Cohen *et al.* 1990; Reed and Johnson 1994). Cohen *et al.* found that subjects could learn simple sequences when carrying out either a difficult or easy tone counting task. However, performance on the generate task was affected by difficulty of the tone counting task. More recently, Reed and Johnson have provided evidence of complex sequence structuring learning (involving at least second-order conditionals) while subjects were engaged in a secondary tone counting task. The results for cued-generation and recognition tests indicated that the learning was indeed implicit.

Time

It has also been suggested that implicitly acquired knowledge 'lasts longer' than explicitly acquired knowledge (e.g. Reber 1989). In other words, people show evidence of implicitly acquired knowledge after long retention intervals, when there is little evidence of explicitly acquired information. Allen and Reber (1980), for example, retested subjects two years after their initial exposure to exemplars of an artificial grammar. They found that performance on the string classification test was still significantly above chance even though subjects had not been re-exposed to the grammar in the intervening period. In contrast, subjects' explicit knowledge was found to be less durable (although it may be that adequate measures were not taken).

Impairment

Finally, there have been claims for robustness in the face of psychological and neuropsychological impairment: that is, implicitly acquired knowledge seems to remain more intact than does explicitly acquired knowledge.

In terms of artificial grammar learning, Abrams and Reber (1988) found that psychiatric patients classified grammatical and non-grammatical strings similarly to normals after exposure to grammatical strings, but were inferior to normals on a task that required determining a mapping between letters and numbers (and that was regarded as requiring explicit knowledge). Similarly, Knowlton *et al.* (1992) found that amnesic patients performed as well as normal control subjects on an initial-string classification task. However, they performed more poorly than the controls on an explicit yes/no recognition test, and on a final classification test where they had to base their decisions on explicit comparisons with original exemplars. Finally, Reber *et al.* (1991) found that performance on an artificial grammar learning task was less affected by IQ differences than was performance on an explicit problem solving task.

In terms of the control tasks, Squire and Frambach (1990) examined whether amnesic patients could learn to control, and answer questions about, the sugar production task at the same level as normal subjects. Their experiment was set up so that patients and control subjects interacted with the task for 90 trials and then completed a 16-item questionnaire (containing simple factual questions, general strategy questions, and specific strategy questions). It was found that the amnesics performed just as well as the control subjects in an initial training session. However, in a second session (approximately 27 days later) they performed significantly worse than the controls. Squire and Frambach suggested that this is because by this stage of practice the normal control subjects were starting to build up explicit knowledge which could be used to improve performance still further. The amnesics, in contrast, were not able to do this. Questionnaire results showed that control subjects scored significantly better on the factual questions, and to some extent on the general strategy questions, but at the same level as the amnesic patients on the specific strategy questions.

In a similar vein, Myers and Conner (1992) showed that older subjects (aged 30–59) were able to control the sugar production task as well as younger subjects (aged 16–19), but performed significantly less well on the post-task questionnaires.

Finally, in terms of sequence learning, Nissen and Bullemer (1987) tested amnesic patients on their serial reaction time task. They found that the amnesics performed at the same level as a group of age-matched controls. That is, they showed the same improvement in reaction time with the repeating sequence, and the same slowing on transfer to the random sequence. Importantly, none of the amnesics reported that they had noticed the repeating pattern, whereas many of the normal controls did. These results were replicated by Willingham *et al.* (1989) who also tested performance on the repeating sequence one week later. It was found that neither group demonstrated forgetting across the one-week delay.

5.2.3 Metacognitive awareness

Berry and Dienes (1993) have argued that one of the primary features of implicit learning is that it is associated with a phenomenal sense of intuition. That is, people do not feel that they actively work out the answers. Rather, they make particular responses because they 'feel right', or typically they may simply believe that they are guessing. In fact, a number of recent studies in the area of artificial grammar learning have shown that people's confidence in their answers is often unrelated to their accuracy (Chan 1992; Dienes and Altmann 1993).

Chan (1992) argued that a characteristic of explicit knowledge is good metaknowledge of it; that is, subjects should know when they know something. On the other hand, he argued that an important characteristic of implicit knowledge is the absence of metaknowledge. Chan trained subjects on an artificial grammar using graphics symbols that pilot subjects found to be highly non-verbalizable. He then gave them a classification test and a version of Perruchet and Pacteau's (1990) bigrams test. After each decision, subjects were required to rate their confidence in that decision.

Chan found that confidence for incorrect responses on the classification test was just as great as for correct responses, even though subjects' classification knowledge was almost entirely veridical. However, there was a significant positive correlation between confidence ratings and performance on the bigrams test (which he took to be a measure of explicit knowledge). In a subsequent experiment, Chan found that explicitly but not implicitly instructed subjects produced substantial correlations between classification accuracy and confidence. Similarly, he found that training on bigrams versus whole exemplars led to roughly equivalent levels of classification knowledge, but to different correlations between confidence and accuracy.

Chan's findings are not peculiar to graphics symbols. In another experiment he used standard letters as the elements in the grammar and again found a substantial correlation between bigram knowledge and confidence ratings, but no correlation between classification knowledge and confidence ratings. Dienes and Altmann (1993) replicated the lack of relationship between confidence and accuracy for letter stimuli. Furthermore, they found that subjects classified better than a control group, even when they only included in the analysis classification decisions that subjects believed were literal guesses.

5.4 CONCLUSION

Despite problems with individual experiments, a number of tasks that have been labelled as being implicit do seem to be associated with a fairly distinct set of features (Berry and Dienes 1993). In particular, they show transfer specificity, they can be learnt under incidental conditions, subjects cannot say how they arrived at their answers, their confidence is unrelated to their accuracy, and performance on the tasks is fairly robust in the face of time and impairment. On the other hand, there are other tasks (usually labelled as being explicit) for which these features do not apply (e.g. Mathews *et al.* 1988). Hence, rather than totally accepting or dismissing all of the evidence in favour of or against implicit learning, a more realistic approach might be to focus on the conditions that give rise to the different types of learning and knowledge. As Reed and Johnson (1994, p. 594) have recently pointed out in relation to sequence learning, 'instances in which sequence structures are learned explicitly do no contradict evidence for implicit learning of other sequences. There is no logical reason to believe that all particular instances of the general class of sequence structure will always be learned in the same manner in relation to conscious awareness'. The same argument applies equally well to learning artificial grammars and the control tasks. In a similar vein, Whittlesea and Dorken (1993) have recently proposed an 'episodic-processing' account of implicit learning that emphasizes the variability of processing that subjects can perform under task control in implicit learning, and the consequent variability of implicit knowledge. They suggest (p. 229) that 'people variously acquire knowledge that is abstract or concrete, general or particular, and superficial or deep, depending on the circumstances in which learning occurs'.

An alternative approach is to assume that individual tasks are not process-pure. Thus, researchers need to look at the relative contribution of implicit and explicit processes to performance on a single task, for example by applying Jacoby's (1991) process-dissociation technique. Experiments in progress by Dienes and colleagues and in our own laboratory are currently doing this.

Finally, to return to the question of how implicit is implicit learning, the answer really depends on the criteria used to establish implicit learning. We have seen in this chapter that learning can be implicit in some senses but not in others. Future research should continue to determine the critical ways in which implicit and explicit learning differ.

ACKNOWLEDGEMENT

Some of the ideas in this chapter grew out of discussions with Zoltan Dienes during the process of writing our recent book on implicit learning.

REFERENCES

Abrams, M. and Reber, A. S. (1988). Implicit learning in special populations. *Journal of Psycholinguistic Research*, **17**, 425–39.

Allen, R. and Reber, A. S. (1980). Very long-term memory for tacit knowledge. *Cognition*, **8**, 175–85.

Berry, D. C. (1984). Implicit and explicit processes in the control of complex systems. Unpublished D.Phil. thesis. University of Oxford.

Berry, D. C. (1991). The role of action in implicit learning. *Quarterly Journal of Experimental Psychology*, **43**, 881–906.

Berry, D. C. (1994*a*). Implicit learning: Twenty-five years on. A tutorial. In *Attention and performance XV*, (ed. C. Umilta and M. Moscovitch) pp. 755–82. MIT Press, Cambridge, MA.

Berry, D. C. (1994*b*). A step too far? *Behavioural and Brain Sciences*, **17**, 397–8.

Berry, D. C. and Broadbent, D. E. (1984). On the relationship between task performance and associated verbalisable knowledge. *Quarterly Journal of Experimental Psychology*, **36**, 209–31.

Berry, D. C. and Broadbent, D. E. (1987). The combination of explicit and implicit learning processes. *Psychological Research*, **49**, 7–15.

Berry, D. C. and Broadbent, D. E. (1988). Interactive tasks and the implicit–explicit distinction. *British Journal of Psychology*, **79**, 251–72.

Berry, D. C. and Broadbent, D. E. (in press). Implicit learning in the control of complex systems. In *Complex problem solving: The European perspective*, (ed. P. Frensch and J. Funke). Erlbaum, Hillsdale, NJ.

Berry, D. C. and Dienes, Z. (1993). *Implicit and explicit knowledge in human performance*. Erlbaum, Hove.

Brewer, W. F. (1974). There is no convincing evidence for operant or classical conditioning in adult humans. In *Cognition and symbolic processes*, (ed. W. B. Weimer and D. S. Palermo). Erlbaum, Hillsdale, NJ.

Bright, J. and Burton, A. M. (1994). Past midnight: Semantic processing in an implicit learning task. *Quarterly Journal of Experimental Psychology*, **47A**, 71–90.

Broadbent, D. E. (1977). Levels, hierarchies and the locus of control. *Quarterly Journal of Experimental Psychology*, **29**, 181–201.

Broadbent, D. E., FitzGerald, P., and Broadbent, M. H. P. (1986). Implicit and explicit knowledge in the control of complex systems. *British Journal of Psychology*, **77**, 33–50.

Brody, N. (1989). Unconscious learning of rules: Comment on Reber's analysis of implicit learning. *Journal of Experimental Psychology: General*, **118**, 236–8.

Brooks, L. and Vokey, J. (1991). Abstract analogies and abstracted grammars: Comment on Reber (1989) and Mathews *et al.* (1989). *Journal of Experimental Psychology: General*, **120**, 316–20.

Chan, C. (1992). Implicit cognitive processes: Theoretical issues and applications in computer system design. Unpublished D.Phil. thesis. University of Oxford.

Cleeremans, A. (1993). *Mechanisms of implicit learning*, MIT Press: Cambridge, MA.

Cock, J., Berry, D. C., and Gaffan, E. A. (1994). New strings for old: The role of similarity processing in an incidental learning task. *Quarterly Journal of Experimental Psychology*, **47**, 1015–34.

Cohen, A., Ivry, R., and Keele, S. (1990). Attention and structure in sequence learning. *Journal of Experimental Psychology: Learning, Memory, and Cognition*, **16**, 17–30.

Dienes, Z. and Altmann, G. (1993, July). *The transfer of implicit knowledge across domains*. Paper presented at the Toronto meeting of the EPS and BBCS.

Dienes, Z., Broadbent, D. E., and Berry, D. C. (1991). Implicit and explicit knowledge bases in artificial grammar learning. *Journal of Experimental Psychology: Learning, Memory, and Cognition*, **17**, 875–87.

Dulany, D. E. (1961). Hypotheses and habits in verbal 'operant conditioning'. *Journal of Abnormal and Social Psychology*, **63**, 251–63.

Dulany, D. E., Carlson, R., and Dewey, G. (1984). A case of syntactical learning and judgement: How concrete and how abstract? *Journal of Experimental Psychology: General*, **113**, 541–55.

Green, R. and Shanks, D. (1993). On the existence of independent explicit and implicit learning systems: An examination of some evidence. *Memory and Cognition*, **21**, 304–17.

Hartman, M., Knopman, D., and Nissen, M. J. (1989). Implicit learning of new verbal associations. *Journal of Experimental Psychology: Learning, Memory, and Cognition*, **15**, 1070–82.

Hayes, N. and Broadbent, D. E. (1988). Two modes of learning for interactive tasks. *Cognition*, **28**, 249–76.

Howard, J., Mutter, S., and Howard, D. (1992). Serial pattern learning in event observation. *Journal of Experimental Psychology: Learning, Memory and Cognition*, **18**, 1029–39.

Jacoby, L. L. (1991). A process dissociation framework: Separating automatic from *intentional uses* of memory. *Journal of Memory and Language*, **30**, 513–41.

Knowlton, B. Ramus, S., and Squire, L. (1992). Intact artificial grammar learning in amnesia: Dissociations of classification learning and explicit memory for specific instances. *Psychological Science*, **3**, 172–9.

Lewicki, P., Hill, T., and Bizot, E. (1988). Acquisition of procedural knowledge about a pattern of stimuli that cannot be articulated. *Cognitive Psychology*, **20**, 24–37.

Lewicki, P., Hill, T., and Czyzewska, M. (1992). Nonconscious acquisition of information. *American Psychologist*, **47**, 796–801.

McGeorge, P. and Burton, M. (1989). The effects of concurrent verbalisation on performance in a dynamic systems task. *British Journal of Psychology*, **80**, 455–65.

McGeorge, P. and Burton, M. (1990). Semantic processing in an incidental learning task. *Quarterly Journal of Experimental Psychology*, **42**, 597–610.

Marescaux, P., Luc, F., and Karnas, G. (1989). Modes d'apprentissage sélectif et nonsélectif et connaissances acquises au control d'un processes. *Cahiers de Psychologie Cognitive*, **9**, 239–64.

Mathews, R. (1990). Abstractiveness of implicit grammar knowledgge: Comments on Perruchet and Pacteau's analysis of synthetic grammar learning. *Journal of Experimental Psychology: General*, **119**, 412–16.

Mathews, R., Buss, R., Chinn, R., and Stanley, W. (1988). The role of explicit and implicit learning processes in concept discovery. *Quarterly Journal of Experimental Psychology*, **40**, 135–65.

Mathews, R., Buss, R., Stanley, W., Blanchard-Fields, F., Cho, J., and Druhan, B. (1989). Role of implicit and explicit processes in learning from examples: A synergistic effect. *Journal of Experimental Psychology: Learning, Memory, and Cognition*, **15**, 1083–100.

Mathews, R., Roussel, L., Blanchard-Fields, F., and Norris, L. (in prep). Implicit induction of abstract knowledge: The nonconscious Sherlock Holmes in us all.

Myers, C. and Conner, M. (1992). Age differences in skill acquisition and transfer in an implicit learning paradigm. *Applied Cognitive Psychology*, **6**, 429–42.

Nissen, M. J. and Bullemer, P. (1987). Attentional requirements of learning: Evidence from performance measures. *Cognitive Psychology*, **19**, 1–32.

Nissen, M. J., Knopman, D. S., and Schacter, D. L. (1987). Neurochemical dissociation of memory systems. *Neurology*, **37**, 789–94.

Nosofsky, R., Clark, S., and Shin, H. (1989). Rules and exemplars in categorisation, identification and recognition. *Journal of Experimental Psychology: Learning, Memory, and Cognition*, **15**, 282–04.

Perruchet, P. (1994). Defining the knowledge units of a synthetic language: Comment on Vokey and Brooks (1992). *Journal of Experimental Psychology: Learning, Memory and Cognition*, **20**, 1–16.

Perruchet, P. and Amorim, M. (1992). Conscious knowledge and changes in performance in sequence learning: Evidence against dissociation. *Journal of Experimental Psychology: Learning, Memory and Cognition*, **18**, 785–800.

Perruchet, P. and Pacteau, C. (1990). Synthetic grammar learning: Implicit rule abstraction or explicit fragmentary knowledge? *Journal of Experimental Psychology: General*, **119**, 264–75.

Perruchet, P., Gallego, J., and Savy, I. (1990). A critical reappraisal of the evidence for unconscious abstraction of deterministic rules in complex experimental situations. *Cognitive Psychology*, **22**, 493–516.

Reber, A. S. (1967). Implicit learning of artificial grammars. *Journal of Verbal Learning and Verbal Behaviour*, **5**, 855–63.

Reber, A. S. (1969). Transfer of syntactic structures in synthetic languages. *Journal of Experimental Psychology*, **81**, 115–19.

Reber, A. S. (1976). Implicit learning of synthetic languages: The role of instructional set. *Journal of Experimental Psychology: Human Learning and Memory*, **2**, 88–94.

Reber, A. S. (1989). Implicit learning and tacit knowledge. *Journal of Experimental Psychology: General*, **118**, 219–35.

Reber, A. S. and Allen, R. (1978). Analogy and abstraction strategies in synthetic grammar learning: A functionalist interpretation. *Cognition*, **6**, 189–221.

Reber, A. S. and Lewis, S. (1977). Toward a theory of implicit learning: The analysis of the form and structure of a body of tacit knowledge. *Cognition*, **5**, 331–61.

Reber, A. S., Allen, R., and Regan, S. (1985). Syntactic learning and judgements: Still unconscious and still abstract. *Journal of Experimental Psychology: General*, **117**, 17–24.

Reber, A. S., Walkenfeld, F., and Hernstadt, R. (1991). Implicit and explicit learning: Individual differences and IQ. *Journal of Experimental Psychology: Learning, Memory, and Cognition*, **17**, 888–96.

Reed, J. and Johnson, P. (1994). Assessing implicit learning with indirect tests: Determining what is learned about sequence structure. *Journal of Experimental Psychology: Learning, Memory, and Cognition*, **20**, 585–94.

Sanderson, P. (1989). Verbalisable knowledge and skilled task performance: Associations, dissociations and mental models. *Journal of Experimental Psychology: Learning, Memory, and Cognition*, **15**, 729–47.

Shanks, D. and St. John, M. (1994). Characteristics of dissociable learning systems. *Behavioral and Brain Sciences*, **17**, 367–447.

Shanks, D., Green, R. and Kolodny, J. (1994). A critical examination of the evidence for nonconscious (implicit) learning. In *Attention and Performance XV*, (ed. C. Umilta and M. Moscovitch), pp. 837–60. MIT Press, Cambridge, MA.

Squire, L. and Frambach, M. (1990). Cognitive skill learning in amnesia. *Psychobiology*, **18**, 109–17.

Stanley, W. B., Mathews, R., Buss, R., and Kotler-Cope, S. (1989). Insight without awareness: On the interaction of verbalisation, instruction and practice on a simulated process control task. *Quarterly Journal of Experimental Psychology*, **41**, 553–77.

Vokey, J. and Brooks, L. (1992). The salience of item knowledge in learning artificial grammars. *Journal of Experimental Psychology: Learning, Memory, and Cognition*, **18**, 328–44.

Whittlesea, B. and Dorken, M. (1993). Incidentally, things in general are particularly determined: An episodic processing account of implicit learning. *Journal of Experimental Psychology: General*, **122**, 227–48.

Willingham, D., Nissen, M., and Bullemer, P. (1989). On the development of complex procedural knowledge. *Journal of Experimental Psychology: Learning, Memory, and Cognition*, **15**, 1047–60.

6

Implicit knowledge in people and connectionist networks

Zoltan Dienes and Josef Perner

6.0 INTRODUCTION

There has been considerable debate about whether and in what way complex cognitive knowledge can be unconscious or implicit (e.g. Berry and Dienes 1993; Cheesman and Merikle 1984; Dulany *et al.* 1984; Holender 1986; Jacoby 1991; Reber 1967, 1989; Reingold and Merikle 1988). This chapter will focus on artificial grammar learning as a paradigm example of the acquisition of knowledge that appears to be implicit by some criteria but not others. In a typical artificial grammar learning task, subjects are first asked to memorize strings of letters generated by a finite state grammar (see Fig. 6.1). Subjects are then informed that the strings were actually generated by a complex set of rules, and the subjects are asked to classify new strings as obeying the rules or not. Typically, subjects can classify well above chance, but they find it difficult to say what the rules are (Reber 1967). Initially, four methodological criteria by which subjects knowledge could be assessed as being implicit will be discussed. Then some ways in which representations can be implicit or explicit are described and related to the preceding criteria. Next a possible connectionist model of artificial grammar learning will be briefly presented. Finally, we will consider if connectionist models illuminate the way in which subjects knowledge can be regarded as implicit.

6.1 METHODOLOGICAL CRITERIA OF IMPLICIT KNOWLEDGE

The unconscious or implicit nature of subjects' knowledge can be assessed according to at least four methodological criteria, which are discussed below.

6.1.1 Knowledge we infer the subject must have is not revealed in free recall

Reber (e.g. 1967, 1989) originally argued that the knowledge acquired during artificial grammar learning was implicit because subjects could not state the rules of the grammar or the strategies that they used in free report, either after or during the classification phase. These initial observations were confirmed by Mathews *et al.* (1989) and Dienes *et al.* (1991). Mathews *et al.* found that the instructions given by trained subjects on how they classified strings were insufficient to allow other subjects who were not trained on the strings to classify as well as the trained subjects. Dienes *et al.* found that when the instructions given by trained subjects were used in computer simulations, the instructions underpredicted the actual classification performance of subjects. Both results strongly suggest that subjects do not convey in free recall all the knowledge underlying classification performance.

As Shanks and St. John (1994) have pointed out, such results are interesting, especially for applied psychology, but they do not imply that there are distinct types of conscious and unconscious knowledge. The sceptic of implicit learning can point out that perhaps the subject is only willing to report high-confidence and not low-confidence knowledge, no matter how much browbeating goes on. After all, if subjects state rules that are wrong they may not appear competent, so they may regard it better to state only rules for which they have some confidence. So, according to

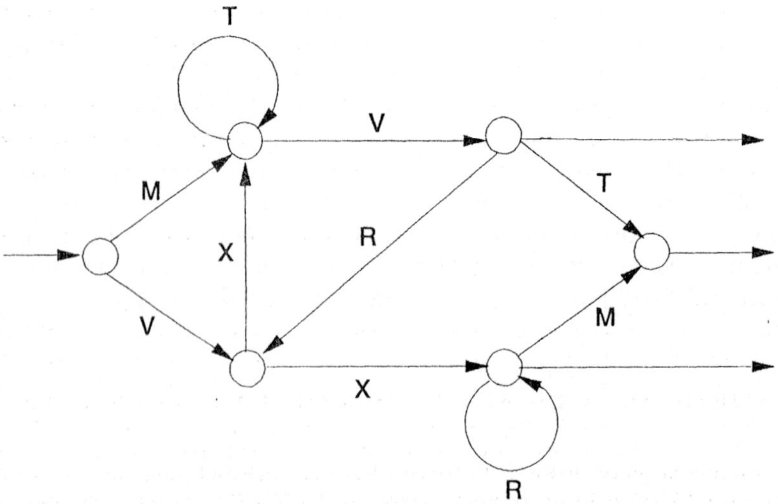

Fig. 6.1 A finite state grammar.

the sceptic, what we need is forced-choice tests to make sure we elicit all of the information available to the subject.

6.1.2 Chance performance on a direct test*

Reingold and Merikle (1993) define a *direct test* as a test in which the subjects are instructed to perform the discrimination of interest, and an *indirect test* as a test that does not make any reference to the discrimination. Following Cheesman and Merikle (1984), we will describe knowledge that shows itself only on indirect tests as knowledge that is below an objective threshold.

However, there is a problem in inferring implicit knowledge from the use of this criterion: the direct test may not be an exhaustive test of relevant knowledge (Dulany 1962; Reingold and Merikle 1993). That is, the direct and indirect tests, of course, have to be literally different—but then there is the logical possibility that the tests might tap slightly different knowledge. In this case, there is no evidence that the knowledge tapped by indirect test is implicit.[1] For example, in artificial grammar learning, we presume that the subjects ability to classify test exemplars indirectly reflects knowledge of some particular rules—for example, knowledge of which bigrams are allowed by the grammar. In order to tell if the putative bigram knowledge is implicit, we need to see if a direct test of what bigrams are allowed by the grammar reveals the knowledge. Chan (1992) found that subjects could classify strings of non-verbal graphic symbols as being grammatical or not (the indirect test), but they could not say which bigrams were legal according to the grammar (the direct test). This could indicate implicit knowledge of bigrams, but perhaps subjects were not using rules, implicitly or explicitly, that referred to bigrams. For example, the rules might be about triplets or symmetry patterns in the string as a whole.

Although, in general, application of this criterion is logically difficult, the criterion may plausibly indicate implicit knowledge in specific cases where the tests plausibly tap the same knowledge. In terms of artificial

* (A forced-choice test) that directly measures some knowledge we infer that the subject must have (because of its indirect effects.

1. Shanks and St. John (1994) argued that an objective threshold criterion in principle could demonstrate unconscious knowledge even if it has not in fact done so to date. They give the example of Lovibond (1992): Lovibond found that if stimulus A elicited a Galvanic Skin Response (GSR) after pairings with shock, then subjects gave a high expectancy of shock in the context of stimulus A. This seems to indicate that the knowledge is conscious. Shanks and St. John point out that the results could have been otherwise; that is, subjects may not have had a high expectancy of shock and so it was logically possible for their criterion to indicate unconscious knowledge. In fact, even if subjects did not expect shock in the context of A we could not conclude that subjects had unconscious knowledge: the GSR may not be indicating an unconscious prediction of shock, but instead it might be indicating, for example, a non-specific anxiety in the context of stimulus A.

grammar learning, no strong cases have yet been made. In fact, the general finding has been that knowledge that may be indirectly revealed by the classification task, is also revealed by direct tests. That is, there is little evidence that the knowledge is implicit by this criterion. For example, Dulany *et al.* (1984) found that subjects could underline that part of a string that made it non-grammatical or grammatical. Presented with MTRTV as a test string, the subject might have said it was non-grammatical and underlined it: M<u>TR</u>TV. When this underlining was treated as a rule of the form 'TR cannot occur in positions 2 to 3,' the subjects' rules predicted classification performance without significant error. Perruchet and Pacteau (1990) hypothesized that subjects' knowledge consisted largely of knowledge of acceptable bigrams. They found that on forced-choice tests subjects could rate the grammaticality of bigrams. Similarly, Dienes *et al.* (1991) found that subjects could predict what letter should come next in a string of letters.

Some people have used the converse of this criterion to indicate explicit knowledge: that is, knowledge is explicit if it can be elicited by a direct test (e.g. Dulany *et al.*, 1984; Perruchet and Pacteau 1990; Shanks and St. John, 1994). Direct tests may usefully indicate the form of subjects' knowledge. For example, if subjects can successfully rate the grammaticality of bigrams we know that the subjects' knowledge is in a form suitable for rating bigrams, and is not, for example, in a form that can only be elicited by complete exemplars. This may allow us to infer something about how holistic or context-dependent the subjects' knowledge is. As we will argue later (6.2), different forms of knowledge map on to our intuitions about how implicit or explicit a representation is: a representation of an examplar in terms of its constituent bigrams makes some of the structure of the examplar more explicit than a representation that simply indicated the complete exemplar. It may be these intuitions, to be elaborated in 6.2, that underlies the idea that successfully rating bigrams indicates explicit knowledge (Perruchet and Pacteau 1990). However, there are problems with inferring explicit knowledge on the basis of good performance on a direct test, when explicit means that the direct test elicits exactly the knowledge that was used for the indirect test. One problem is that direct tests may suggest knowledge that was not originally directly represented. For example, in the prediction task used by Dienes *et al.* (1991), the subject had to say for each letter whether it could occur in a given position. If the subject correctly says that R cannot start a letter string, it may be that this was implied by the subject's existing knowledge (no stored examplars contained an R in the first position) but not directly represented. If forced-choice tests are proper tests of what we already explicitly know, then, following Socrates, we must explicitly know most of mathematics, including theorems yet to appear in mathematical journals.

Another problem is not a problem with applying the methodology but a reason for thinking that even if the methodology were accurately applied, the results would not be particularly useful. The direct and indirect tests have to be very similar in order to make plausible that the direct test was accessing the same knowledge as the indirect test. But then it becomes exceedingly difficult to imagine an information-processing mechanism that would allow performance on the indirect test but not the direct test. For example, take the claim that: (1) subjects' knowledge of an artificial grammar consists of knowledge of fragments of that grammar, say, predominantly bigrams; and (2) this knowledge is conscious. According to Shanks and St. John (1994), these are two orthogonal claims. Let us say we accept claim (1) but not (2), that is, we think that the knowledge is unconscious. How should subjects perform on a bigram-rating task? What sort of mechanism would not apply the knowledge when we give it a task specifically chosen to tap exactly the contents of the knowledge in exactly the situation in which all relevant retrieval cues are present (so that it is a sensitive test)? If the bigram-rating test did not elicit the knowledge we could have no grounds for believing that the knowledge was of *bigrams* and not higher-order fragments. Thus, whenever we have reason to believe that the direct test is actually testing the knowledge we are interested in, it becomes unlikely that an objective threshold would separate qualitatively different types of knowledge.

6.1.3 Knowledge that the subjects do not know that they know

If subjects perform well on various indirect and direct tests, one may still want to regard the knowledge as unconscious if subjects do not know that they know it; that is, if they lack metaknowledge. This criterion rather than the previous one may more closely match everyday intuitions about consciousness; if a person sincerely claims that they do not know something, yet the knowledge is revealed on forced-choice tests, it seems reasonable to call the knowledge unconscious. Following Cheesman and Merikle (1984) we will describe knowledge satisfying this criterion as being below a subjective threshold. A lack of metaknowledge can be revealed in two ways: a lack of correlation between confidence and accuracy (Chan 1992); and accurate performance when subjects believe that they are guessing (Cheesman and Merikle 1984).

Confidence in performance uncorrelated with accuracy.

Chan (1992) investigated whether the incidentally acquired knowledge of an artificial grammar was implicit in the sense that a subject's confidence in his or her decision predicts it's accuracy. Chan initially asked one group of subjects (the incidentally trained subjects) to memorize a set of grammatical exemplars. Then in a subsequent test phase, subjects gave a confidence rating for their accuracy after each classification decision. Chan found that these subjects were just as confident in their incorrect decisions as they were in their correct decisions. He asked another group of subjects (the intentionally trained subjects) to search for rules in the training phase. For these subjects, confidence was strongly related to accuracy in the test phase. That is, incidentally trained subjects lacked metaknowledge, intentionally trained subjects did not. Chan concluded that the correlation between confidence and accuracy could be a useful criterion of consciousness.[2]

To see what is it that subjects lack metaknowledge about in this situation, it will be useful to distinguish between deterministic and stochastic responses. A subject responds deterministically if the same test string always elicits the same response; a subject responds stochastically otherwise. If subjects respond deterministically to all test strings, this may be because subjects are using partially correct rules (e.g. 'say "grammatical" whenever an M starts a string, and "non-grammatical" otherwise'). In this case, subjects may consider all applications of these rules subjectively as cases of knowledge regardless of whether the rules lead to correct or incorrect performance. Hence, subjects' confidence judgements will not correlate with their classification judgements despite insights into the rules they are using (metaknowledge). In other words, a lack of correlation between confidence and classification judgements does not indicate a lack of metaknowledge in this situation. Subject may be perfectly aware of the rules they are applying and when they are applying them (and even why they have formulated those rules and why they are applying them).

In a typical artificial grammar learning experiment, subjects actually respond stochastically to at least some strings. Reber (1989) interpreted these results as indicating that subjects know some exemplars perfectly and guess the rest of the time. If this were the case, the lack of correlation between confidence and accuracy would indicate that subjects do not know *when* they are applying their knowledge (and when they are applying guesses). A more general interpretation is that subjects are using stochastic rules which specify the probability for saying 'grammatical' for each exemplar (Dienes 1992). That is, we need not assume with Reber that the probabilities must be either 0, 0.5, or 1. In this more general scenario, one highly plausible assumption is that the probabilities reflect the degree to which the exemplars satisfy the learned constraints (see Dienes 1992 for an accurate prediction of the subjects' probabilities given this assumption). For example, we assume that if subjects say 'grammatical'

2. Chan (1992), Dienes *et al.* (1995), and Manza and Reber (1994) found that incidentally trained subjects could produce a correlation between confidence and accuracy depending on stimulus materials.

more than 50 per cent of the time to an exemplar, then the exemplar is subjectively more likely to be grammatical than non-grammatical. If subjects had general access to these probabilities, then they should be more confident of 'grammatical' decisions associated with high rather than low probabilities of saying 'grammatical'. The probabilities must correlate with the actual grammaticality of the exemplars if subjects perform above chance. Thus, if subjects could have used the different probabilities to inform their confidence ratings, confidence would have correlated with accuracy. Therefore, under these assumptions a lack of correlation would indicate that subjects lack metaknowledge about the strength of their rules. In summary, a lack of correlation between confidence and accuracy indicates a lack of metaknowledge whenever subjects use stochastic rules that lead to above-chance performance, but not when subjects use deterministic rules.

Subjects show above-chance performance when they believe that they are literally guessing

Cheesman and Merikle (1984, 1986) argued compellingly for the use of this version of the criterion in subliminal perception. That is, if subjects believe that they are at chance in discriminating which stimulus was presented, then the stimulus is below a subjective threshold of consciousness. Cheesman and Merikle found that stimuli below a subjective threshold still influenced subjects' behaviour, and argued that in this sense subliminal perception did exist. Dienes *et al.* (1995) applied the criterion to artificial grammar learning. In the test phase, after each classification decision, subjects gave a confidence rating. There was a substantial proportion of classification responses for which subjects believed that they were literally guessing. That is, any knowledge applying to these responses was unconscious according to Cheesman and Merikle's criterion. Nonetheless, the accuracy of these responses was at a level greater than chance (and at a level greater than that of a control group). This 'unconscious' knowledge seemed to be qualitatively different to knowledge about which the subjects had some confidence. When subjects performed a secondary task (random number generation) during the test phase, the knowledge associated with 'guess' responses was unimpaired, but the knowledge associated with confident responses was impaired (to a level below that of the knowledge associated with 'guess' responses). That is, this criterion is not just another curious way of categorizing knowledge: it may separate knowledge in a way that corresponds to a real divide in nature.

When subjects claim that there is literally no basis to their responding we do not have to infer exactly what the knowledge is to have evidence that the knowledge is unconscious. Whatever the knowledge is, subjects are claiming that there is no knowledge guiding their performance. When subjects claim that there is literally no basis to their responding, we have evidence that subjects are either unaware of the connection between any basis and their responding or that they are unaware of the basis itself. This contrasts with the objective threshold criterion: in that case, we needed to infer exactly what the knowledge was in order to test it with a direct test. As we argued above, making that inference can be problemmatic. So using a subjective threshold may be easier in practice than using an objective threshold.

6.1.4 Knowledge is applied regardless of, or contrary to, the subjects' intentions

If subjects do not want to apply some knowledge but nonetheless it influences the subjects' performance then the subjects do not have conscious control over the knowledge. The usefulness of such a criterion based on intention has been argued for vigorously by Jacoby in a number of different experiments (e.g. 1991). In a typical experiment, subjects were exposed to different words in two different contexts (e.g. reading or hearing). If, in a subsequent test phase, subjects were asked to recognize words from only one of the contexts (e.g. hearing), there was a tendency for words to intrude from the other context. That is, the study of the word from the reading context elicited an 'old' response, despite the fact that the subject was intending not to respond to those words. One of the strengths of Jacoby's work is in the demonstration that the sort of knowledge that applies against intentions is qualitatively different to the knowledge that is responsive to intentions: for example, the latter but not the former was affected by secondary tasks.

Is knowledge of artificial grammars unconscious in this sense of applying contrary to intention? Dienes *et al.* (1995) tested this criterion by training subjects on two grammars and then asking subjects to apply one at a time. Subjects could do this very well. Also, there was no detectable tendency to apply the grammar that subjects were asked not to apply. Subjects seemed to be completely conscious of which grammar was applying. Furthermore, consistent with Jacoby's results, subjects' ability to discriminate the grammars was imparied by a secondary task at test. These results show that subjects have intentional control over which grammar to apply. In contrast, the extent of control over specific aspects of the grammar remains an open question.

In summary, we have considered four criteria by which knowledge could be regarded as implicit. In terms of two of the criteria, subjects' knowledge of artificial grammars appears conscious: the knowledge can largely be elicited by putative direct tests and the subject can control which grammar to apply to a given test. In terms of the other two criteria, the knowledge appears unconscious: the knowledge is difficult to express in free recall and the subject lacks metaknowledge about it. The difficulty of eliciting knowledge in free report may be symptomatic of the lack of metaknowledge: if you do not know that you have knowledge, it is difficult to tell someone about it. Thus, a key discrepancy in the results is that knowledge appears conscious according to an objective threshold but unconscious according to a subjective threshold. Later in this chapter, we will see to what the extent this discrepancy can be resolved in a coherent way by considering what implications a connectionist network model of artificial grammar learning has for the different criteria. For now, we can note that the discrepancy indicates that our intuitions about consciousness are complex and we should not expect that the different aspects of our intuitions cut along the same divide. 'Consciousness', as defined by our intuitions, is probably not a unified thing. (For further discussion on the relation between lack of metaknowledge and intentional control see Dienes *et al.* 1995.)

We will now go on to consider if understanding the way in which knowledge is represented could illuminate the way in which that knowledge is implicit or explicit.

6.2 THE MEANING OF IMPLICIT/EXPLICIT AND THREE TYPES OF EXPLICITNESS

We start from the assumption that a representational system like the mind needs to be able to be in distinct (internal) states that, at least during the acquisition of its representational content, must covary with the states of the world which they represent (e.g. Dretske 1981, 1988; Millikan 1984). Our general linguistic intuition about the meaning of the implicit/explicit distinction is based on this basic observation about representations.

In natural conversation, information is said to be conveyed explicitly if the representational medium in which the information is expressed is in that state whose function it is to covary with the represented fact. Other information that is given is only implicitly conveyed. A paradigm example of this are presuppositions. For instance, the statement 'He did not stop at the stop sign' conveys explicitly the information that *He did not stop at the stop sign,* because the expression used has the function to covary with him stopping or not stopping at the stop sign. However, the sentence also conveys other information, for instance, that there was a stop sign. However, this is not conveyed explicitly because to covary with this fact is the function of a different expression, namely, 'There was a stop sign'. Hence, we say that this was only implicitly conveyed by the original statement.

From this example we observe the following natural language use of the implicit/explicit distinction. Expressions whose function it is to covary with a fact represent this fact explicitly. Other, supportive facts that must hold if the chosen expression is to have the meaning it should have, are said to be implicitly represented by that expression. In the following we use this *linguistic intuition* to justify why different types of explicitness that we are going to distinguish all deserve the label 'explicit' (Perner 1993).

6.2.1 Three types of explicitness

To introduce our three types of explicitness we will peruse simplified examples from artificial grammar learning. For instance, strings that start with an M always have T in second position. Let us say strings with that configuration are more likely to be judged 'grammatical' than 'ungrammatical'.

To illustrate completely implicit knowledge let us focus on how the fact that *M is followed by T* is encoded. Let us assume that a mental representation 'X' is formed which represents the compound property of *M-is-followed-by-T*. This representation does not make the structure of *M is followed by T* explicit, since there is nothing in 'X' whose function it is to covary with *M*, *followed-by*, or *T*. Nevertheless, 'X' stands in some representational relationship to *M*, *followed-by*, and *T* as only strings that have an M followed by a T are to be represented by 'X'. Even though this X detector must have a component that is sensitive to the presence of Ms, the function of that component is not to represent Ms but, at best Ms-that-are-followed-by-Ts. This M-sensitive component would be a representation of Ms only if it were *separable* from the representation of 'followed-by-T', and could be combined with other representations, e.g. 'can-start-a-string' to form: 'M can-start-a-string'. The critical feature of 'M' being separable is, in Davies' (1991) words, that any occurrence of 'M' in different combinations, e.g. in 'M is-followed-by-a-T' as well as in 'M can-start-a-string' has some systematic causal effect (e.g. the system can show some common reaction whenever an M occurs). Only in that case are Ms represented explicitly. Since 'X' does not explicitly represent *M*, *followed-by*, and *T* but still stands in some representational relation to those properties it satisfies our general linguistic intuition that 'X' represents the facts that it is an M that is followed by a T, that it is a following relation that holds between M and T, etc., only *implicitly*.

In contrast, if instead of with 'X' a mental expression like 'M followed by T' is used, in which there are distinct parts whose function it is to covary with properties *having-an-M*, *being-followed-by*, etc. then the facts that the string has an M that is followed by a T, etc. are explicitly represented. We call this type of explicitness '*property-structure explicit*'.

Our next type of explicitness makes use of a possibility introduced by Strawson (1959, p. 206) with the example of a 'naming game': 'Playing the naming-game may be compared with one of the earliest things which children do with language—when they utter the general name for a kind of thing in the presence of a thing of that kind, saying 'duck' when there is a duck, . . . it is logically possible that one should recognize the features without possessing the conceptual resources for identifying reference to the corresponding particulars'. The idea is that one would say 'duck' to the presence of a duck without having the notion of re-identifiable particular ducks. In our case we might think of a person who describes strings as 'M followed by T' and 'grammatical'. These statements represent the fact that the presented (particular, re-identifiable) string, not any string, has the property of *having an M followed by a T*. Yet, the fact that it is *a particular string* which has this property is not explicitly represented since there is nothing in the expression 'M followed by T' whose function it is to covary with that fact. Since this fact is not represented explicitly but, nevertheless, represented in some way our general linguistic intuition about the implicit/explicit distinction applies and we can say that this fact is only implicitly represented.

To make this fact explicit it is necessary to go beyond the mere naming game of exclaiming 'M followed by T' and also express the fact that it is a particular string that is characterized by an M followed by a T. This can be done by forming the mental expression: '*This string* has an M followed by a T'. This extended expression makes the implicit predication of 'M is followed by a T' to a particular string *predication explicit*, because the whole expression does have the function to covary with the fact that the identified particular is characterized by the property in question.[3]

For our third type of explicitness the general linguistic intuition about the implicit/explicit distinction can be applied again from a different angle. The mental representation 'this string has an M followed by a T' informs about the letter sequence of the string. However, it does so only if it is a state of *knowledge*, not if it is part of an erroneous belief or of pretence. So, for the representation to carry this information it is critical that it corresponds to reality, which is implied by the term 'knowledge'. But again, if the representation does correspond to reality (i.e. reflect knowledge), this fact is not explicitly expressed, since the expression does not contain anything whose function it is to indicate

3. To avoid a tempting confusion one should point out that the function (meaning) of the two component terms 'This string' and 'an M followed by a T' depends on their position in the overall expression. The function of the overall expression is to express that something, which is picked out by one of its properties, namely being a string, has the property of having an M followed be a T. Thus the ultimate function of the expression 'string' is not to denote the property of being a string but to identify a particular entity (which happens to be a string). While the function of the expression 'M followed by a T' is to denote that property, in contrast, in the sentence 'The thing with an M followed by a T is a string' the component expression 'string' has the function to denote the property of being a string.

that the representation 'this string has an M followed by a T' corresponds to reality and constitutes knowledge. This can be done with so-called propositional attitude constructions. That is, expressions that embed the represented proposition within a representation of the mental state (attitude) with which that proposition is held (e.g. 'I *know* that this string has an M followed by a T'). Such expressions we call '*mental-state explicit*'. Of course, a belief can be mistaken even if it is represented as knowledge. A belief can be represented as knowledge if it is justified even though it happens to be wrong.

Knowledge that is rather than is not mental-state explicit can be manipulated in more flexible ways. For example, one can decide how to test optimally the piece of knowledge because one can think of it as a possible piece of knowledge. Mental-state explicit representations are closely related to consciousness. In fact, according to Armstrong's (1968) second-order thought theory of consciousness (recently elaborated by Carruthers 1992, 1993; Rosenthal 1986, 1993), consciousness consists of representing (having a second-order thought about) one's first-order mental states with which one holds representations of the world. Our analysis, thus, explains why consciousness is so widely equated with explicitness in learning (Reber 1989) and memory research (Schacter 1987). And since our criterion for mental-state explicitness relates to our general linguistic intuition about the meaning of the implicit/explicit distinction, our analysis also provides some linguistic justification for why knowledge without consciousness is considered implicit.

Before proceeding to the next section which investigates the relationship between our three types of explicitness and the methodological criteria used to decide whether knowledge is implicit or explicit, we need to discuss briefly how the three types of explicitness are to be applied to how a subject knows a grammar. A grammar is a collection of rules (e.g. a string can start with either an M, a V, or an X; an M can be followed by a T, a V by an M or X, etc.). This grammar can be represented in a property-structure implicit way with a set of compound properties that happen to be co-extensive with the combinations of explicitly specified properties. Furthermore, although a grammar is an abstract entity that is defined by this set of rules it is still possible, and often necessary, to conceptualize it as a *particular thing* which has these rules. For instance, it is necessary for being able to ask questions about the grammar: 'Does the grammar allow strings to start with an S?' So we see that the implicit/explicit distinctions for property structure and predication that we elaborated for the properties of particular strings can also be applied to particular grammars.

A representation of a grammar can also be mental-state explicit or not. In fact, there are two types of mental-state explicitness that it will be useful to distinguish: *content explicitness* and *attitude explicitness*, respectively. If the

Table 6.1 The three types of explicitness

Measure of Knowledge	Types of explicitness required		
	Property-structure	Predication	Mental-state
Indirect			
Direct			
Prediction	X	(X)	
Judgement	(X)	(X)	
Voluntary control		(X)	(X)
Free recall	X	X	Content but not attitude
Confidence related to accuracy			Attitude but not content

X, definitely involved; (X), plausibly but not necessarily involved.

subject can represent *I am in possession of propositional content* X (where X could be, for example, *A T can follow an M*) then this shows content explicitness: that is, the representation of X must itself be representable as an object of knowledge (or other, not necessarily specified, propositional attitude). If the representation of X allows the subject to form an attitude towards it that appropriately reflects whether it has been derived from observations or is just a guess, then this shows attitude explicitness. We will elaborate on this distinction further in the next section.

6.2.2 Relating the three types of explicitness to the methodological criteria for deciding whether knowledge is implicit or explicit

We now examine the different tests of knowledge that have been discussed as criteria for detecting the presence of knowledge and whether it is implicit or explicit. We investigate whether and to what degree knowledge revealed by each of these tests requires explicitness of a particular type. The conclusions are summarized in Table 6.1.

Indirect effects

Consider first an indirect measure of knowledge, namely familiarity judgements (and their associated reaction times) of test strings. Judgements of familiarity can be purely implicit. Let us say the subject is sensitive to the fact that strings can have M followed by a T. A representation 'X' (where X stands for the complex, unstructured property of *having-an-M-followed-by-a-T)* which is neither property-structure nor predication explicit can yield familiarity effects and associated reaction time effects. A consequence of having a property-structure implicit M-T representation, is that only M-T sequences will seem familiar, and not T-M or M-S sequences. Only when a separable M representation exists can T-M and M-S be seen as similar to M-T (i.e. in that they share the occurrence of an M). But even with a property-stucture implicit representation, strings that conform to the grammar of the studied instances (e.g. ones that have an M followed by a T, can be processed more easily than other strings). This leads to faster reaction times and to a feeling of familiarity on the basis of which familiarity can be judged. There is no need to encode the precise structure of properties as specified in the grammar that was used to generate the strings. Nor is it necessary to represent that it is a particular grammar which has the familiar properties which elicit that feeling. Nor is it necessary to have any propositional attitude towards the knowledge. So, this result confirms the general intuition that knowledge established with indirect measures of this kind is purely implicit, unless it can also be revealed in one of the following types of test.

Direct tests

A direct measure of knowledge makes reference to the discrimination of interest. One example of a direct test is prediction (e.g. Dienes *et al.* 1991; Willingham *et al.* 1989). The subject is shown the beginning of a string and has to predict its likely continuation. For instance, in case of our simplified example of an M followed by a T, subjects would be shown the M and would have to predict 'T'. This task requires property-structure explicitness but not predication explicitness. If the encountered combinations of Ms being followed by Ts were represented as the unstructured property X then no predictions of T given M would be possible. When being presented the M the system would not respond in any way since it only is sensitive to the complete combination of M followed by a T (i.e. X). Only when the structure of this property is made explicit as 'M followed-by T' can successful predictions be made, because only when the system recognizes M on its own as a familiar input can the prediction mechanism be initiated.

Our analysis also explains why the ability to detect ungrammatical bigrams or trigrams is considered more explicit than classification of whole strings (cf. Perruchet and Pacteau 1990): because it suggests a larger degree of property-structure explicitness. That is, if the subject can say whether bigrams are grammatical, then the knowledge must be finer-grained than knowledge that consists of representations of complete exemplars as compound properties. Successfully rating bigrams indicates some degree of property-structure explicitness, but it might not be complete. For example, the representation used might have been of the form X, where X means *T-can-follow-M*. Thus, predicting single letters requires a greater degree of property-structure explicitness than rating bigrams.

Note, however, that if the knowledge is revealed on the direct test, then a property-structure explicit representation has certainly become formed by the subject. The knowledge may not have been explicitly represented until that point (e.g. when earlier applied on an indirect test). That is, the direct test may create an explicit representation of knowledge that was previously implicitly represented (Reber 1989). However, the direct test might fail to make the knowledge completely explicit. For example, subjects might not know which propositional attitude they have with respect to the content of the knowledge.

At first sight, predication explicitness might be thought to be required for a direct test, since it is on face-validity, crucial to understand that the test string be judged in relation to a *particular grammar* (i.e. the one according to which the training strings were generated). However, predication explicitness might be avoided if the grammaticality judgement—understood as similarity with the training strings—can be made on the basis of familiarity. That is, it is conceivable that subjects reason that if something feels familiar then it must have been similar to something seen before (i.e. 'It must have been generated by the same rules as the things I've seen before'). In this case, the judgement of grammaticality can be made without any predication-explicit representation of the grammatical rules.

In sum, consideration of the proposed types of explicitness explains why direct tests have been considered as measures of explicit knowledge: many direct tests count as 'to-some-degree explicit' because they require property-structure explicitness, and they plausibly (but not necessarily) use predication explicitness. The fact that they require only one type of explicitness, but not both, explains why passing a direct test is only a weak criterion of explicitness of knowledge. The possibility that predication explicitness can be circumvented in some direct tests via judgements based on familiarity illustrates one reason why there is controversy about the validity of direct tests as measures of explicit knowledge (cf. Dienes and Perner 1994).

Voluntary control

In tests of voluntary control subjects have to choose between systems of rules (that is, which of two grammars to apply, e.g. Dienes *et al.* 1995). One way to succeed in such tests is to have direct volitional control over one's knowledge, in the sense that one can decide to use or not to use it because it has been explicitly labelled as the particular body of knowledge one wishes to use or not use. That is, we assume that for direct control it is necessary to have predicate explicitness. But there are alternative ways of controlling which body of knowledge to use that does not require predicate explicitness.

Whittlesea and Dorken (1993) argued that subjects could distinguish different grammars by familiarity judgements. They trained subjects on exemplars from two grammars. The exemplars were distinguished by the task subjects performed on them: for one grammar, subjects pronounced the exemplars; for the other grammar, subject spelled them. Subjects were later asked to pronounce or spell test items, and then classify these strings as either belonging to the 'pronouncing' grammar or to the 'spelling' grammar. Subjects could discriminate the grammars reliably above chance. The important finding for Whittlesea and Dorken's argument is that when test strings were common to both grammars, subjects tended to classify them as belonging to the spelling grammar if they spelt them and as belonging to the pronouncing grammar if they pronounced them. Whittlesea and Dorken argued that because processing is more fluent when a test experience perceptually matches representations of prior experiences (Jacoby *et al.* 1989), fluency or familiarity could be used to discriminate the grammars. A test item belonging only to the 'spelling' grammar if spelt at test would seem familiar and thus the subject could correctly infer that it did belong to the 'spelling' grammar; but if pronounced at test it would seem unfamiliar and the subject could correctly infer that it did not belong to the 'pronouncing' grammar.

One account of these results and those of Dienes *et al.* (1994) is that the choice of grammar can be made by means of a compound property (e.g. *in-context-A,-M-can-follow-T*). Context A could be, for example, the process of spelling a string (Whittlesea and Dorken 1993), or a particular time at which a string was studied (Dienes *et al.* 1995). If context A is reinstated by task demands or imagination, the knowledge of a particular grammar can be isolated without a predication-explicit representation.

Which body of knowledge to use can also be determined by another related strategy. When subjects are told to judge test strings according to the first set of training strings (g1), they may imagine a few of these strings which helps activate that part of their knowledge base used for processing g1 strings. When now a g1-test string is given it seems familiar for the primed knowledge base, whereas a g2-test string will seem unfamiliar. Also, this strategy does not require predication explicitness of the grammatical structures. All it needs is predication-explicit memory of training strings which can be used to prime the network.

Note that reinstating context by externally imposed task demands (Whittlesea and Dorken 1993) is not an illustration of volitional control; however, internally generated context through imagining stimulus material (as is possible in the Dienes *et al.* case) does illustrate volitional control.

Even though the above scenarios are often possible or even plausible, there may be situations in which one can decide plausibly that volitional control was actually mediated (at least partly) by predication-explicitness. For example, if, with a sufficiently sensitive test, measures of familiarity, such as ratings, speed of stimulus identification, do not predict classification response, then these alternative scenarios without predicate explicitness are not supported.

Property-structure explicitness is not required for volitional control. Once the correct *grammar* is chosen, the rules of that grammar can be represented in a different conceptual system (e.g. a property-structure implicit one) than that specified for the generation of strings (typically, a property-structure explicit one). Success on the classification task depends on the extensional overlap between the two conceptual schemes.

It would be natural to assume that voluntary control over one's knowledge also requires mental-state explicitness of that knowledge (i.e. one needs to know that one knows to apply the knowledge strategically). However, on closer inspection this may not be necessary. One could control which body of knowledge (which particular grammar) to use via representation of the material to which it applies (the particular set of training strings) without knowing the structure of that knowledge used to process this material. For instance, in the experiment by Dienes *et al.* (1995) one may have a (predication) explicit knowledge of the two sets of strings that one has studied without a (mental-state) explicit representation of the structures to process them. By mentally focusing on one or the other set of training strings one can influence which processing structures one's mind brings to bear on the test strings. Thus, it is possible that one can apply one's knowledge strategically (explicit by the criterion discussed in Section 6.1.4) and yet fail to have any confidence in what one knows (implicit by the criterion in Section 6.1.3), or even deny that one *knows* anything about the structure of that rule system. In fact, this is what Dienes *et al.* observed: even when subjects believed they were purely guessing, subjects could still choose which of two grammars to apply.

In sum, to exert voluntary control, predication explicitness may be plausible but it is not necessary. However, the directness of the voluntary control depends on whether the representations of the grammar are predication explicit. If the representations are not predication explicit, but control is exerted by mentally reinstating context, then the control is relatively indirect. If, as is possible in the Whittlesea and Dorken (1993) case, responses are determined entirely by externally imposed context, then volitional control is not demonstrated at all.

Property-structure explicitness and mental state explicitness are not necessary for volitional control.

Free recall

To state the rules or strategies that one uses for classification in free recall one needs predication explicitness. For, to know which set of rules one is to describe, one needs to identify the *particular grammar* according to which the training strings have been composed and then describe the rules by which this grammar is characterized. Without this predication explicitness one would not know how to answer the request to describe the rules. ('The rules of what?' one might think.)

Moreover, since the reported rules are to be described linguistically, they must be property-structure explicit at the level of the properties described by words. If the structure of properties one uses to classify strings does not overlap with the actual rules then one's report will not pass as knowledge of the grammar. One could further argue that apart from property-structure and predication explicitness free recall also requires mental-state explicitness. For, when asked to report on the basis of one's classifications, only rules or strategies will be considered which are encoded *as knowledge* (or knowledge in which one has some confidence). Although it is for this reason likely that free recall will only access mental-state explicit (conscious) knowledge, it is conceivable that subjects are able to report the rules without having any confidence in them. Thus, free recall can occur for representations that are content explicit without being attitude explicit. In such a case, the subject does not have insight into whether their recalled rules deserve the status of proper knowledge rather than confabulation. If the subject can confidently recollect, and confidence relates to accuracy, then there must be both content and attitude explicitness.

Knowing that one knows (metaknowledge)

Knowing that one knows requires attitude explicitness. A subject cannot know that he or she knows *V can start a string* unless he or she can represent 'I know that *V can start a string*'. Note that this feeling of knowing must be based on the possession of knowledge of rules for it to count as attitude explicitness, not just, for example, the memory that one has looked at a large number of these strings and therefore one ought to know something about them.

Chan's (1992) criterion can be regarded as a measure of attitude explicitness. As argued in Section 6.1.3, p. 231, the stochastic way subjects respond to test strings plausibly reflects the extent to which the test string satisfies learnt constraints of the grammar, that is, the estimated validity (or rule strength) of the statement 'this string is grammatical'. If the rule strength is 0.50, then that is equivalent to saying 'I guess that this string is grammatical'. If the rule strength is 1.00, then that is equivalent to saying 'I know that this string is grammatical'. Because subjects are correct more often than incorrect, the average rule strength for correct responses is larger than for incorrect responses. Since the rule strengths are the information that should be informing the subjects' propositional attitude (in this case, confidence) towards their grammatical response, if this information were available subjects should be more confident in correct than incorrect responses. If confidence is unrelated to accuracy, confidence is not being informed by rule strength, and the knowledge is attitude implicit.

Full metaknowledge requires confidence ratings that reflect rule strengths combined with the capacity for free recall that is, both attitude and content explicitness. Conversely, subjects can lack metaknowledge in two ways. As described in the previous section, subjects' representations may lack attitude explicitness, even if they have content explicitness, as in the case of verbal reports offered as guesses. But Reber (1993, p. 136) suggested that subjects in his experiments often seemed to know *that* they knew, even though they did not know *what* it was that they knew. That is, subjects' representations may also lack content explicitness, even if they have attitude explicitness. This would arise if rule X were responsible for the representation (feeling) 'I know something about these strings', even if subjects could not say *what* it was that they knew. Both types of lack of metaknowledge are possible and even plausible under different conditions. Chan's (1992) and Cheesman and Merikle's (1984) criteria address lack of metaknowledge due to lack of attitude explicitness but they do not address lack of metaknowledge due to lack of content explicitness.

6.3 A CONNECTIONIST MODEL OF ARTIFICAL GRAMMAR LEARNING

In this section we will describe a specific connectionist model in order to have a concrete example for considering the relation between connectionist models and implicit knowledge in the next section.

Dienes (1992) tested a number of different exemplar and connectionist models of artificial grammar learning. The most successful model could be represented as in Fig. 6.2 (the presentation in Dienes was different but equivalent). The model dealt with strings of up to six letters long, made up of any combination of the five letters M, T, V, R, and X. The first five units coded which letter was in the first position (one unit for each letter), the next five units coded which letter was in the second position, and so on.

In the training phase, a string was applied to the Input units, and activation passed through the weights to the Prediction units. The target value of the **ith** Prediction unit was the same as the activation of the **ith** Input unit. There was no connection between the **ith** Input unit and the **ith** Prediction unit; rather the aim of the **ith** Prediction unit was to predict the **ith** Input unit based on all the other Input units. The weights from the Input units to the Prediction units were adjusted by a small amount (by the delta rule) so that the activation of the Prediction units became closer to the target values given the same input. In effect, the network was learning to predict which letter could occur in the **ith** position given

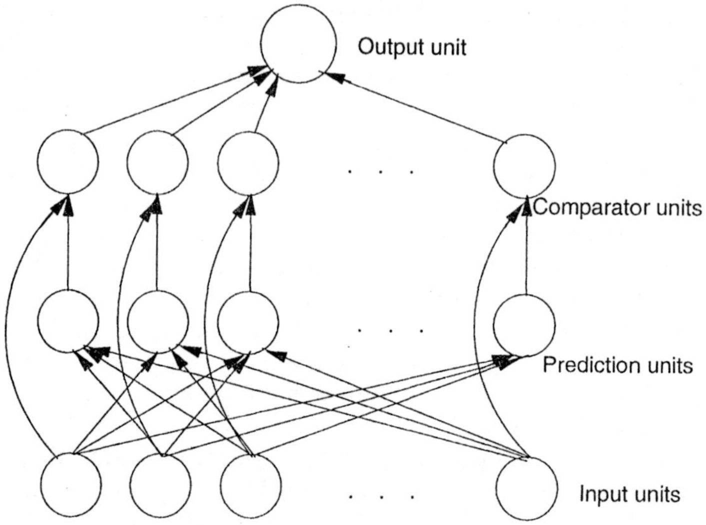

Fig. 6.2 The connectionist network explored by Dienes.

the letters that were in all the other positions. The process was repeated until all the training strings had been applied a number of times. The weights between the Input and the Prediction units then represented the constraints that the network had learnt about the grammar. For example, a positive weight between the *M in first position* unit in the Input layer and the *V in second position unit* in the Prediction layer reflected the rule that 'V can follow M in the first position'.

In the test phase, a novel string was applied to the Input units. If the string was grammatical and the network had captured the regularities in the grammar, then the activation of the Prediction units would closely match that of the Input units. If the string was non-grammatical, there would be some mismatch between the Input and Prediction layers. The network detected matches with a set of Comparator units. The weights of the Comparator units were not learnt but set so that the activation of the **ith** Comparator unit was simply the product of activations of the **ith** Input unit and the **ith** Prediction unit. The more the activation of the Input unit and the Prediction unit matched (e.g. both +1 or both −1) the greater the activation of the Comparator unit. The input to the Output unit was simply the sum of activation of all the Comparator units. This input was monotonically transformed to lie between 0 and 1 and then treated as a probability for saying 'grammatical'. The probabilities so obtained for different test stimuli in fact closely matched the probabilities produced by subjects (Dienes 1992). This is no trivial feat as the exemplar models and other connectionist models considered by Dienes (1992) were not able to match the subjects' probabilities.

6.4 CONNECTIONIST MODELS AND IMPLICIT KNOWLEDGE

6.4.1 Introduction

In this section we will discuss the type of representation used by the network model and see if it illuminates the sense in which subjects' knowledge of an artificial grammar is implicit. Initially, we will describe the related approach of Clark and Karmiloff-Smith (1993), who argued that knowledge in connectionist networks is implicit. Then we will indicate the type of explicitness of the representations in the network in terms of the definitions given in Section 6.2.1. Finally, we will relate the performance of the network to the four criteria of implicit knowledge given in Section 6.1.

Clark and Karmiloff-Smith (1993) argued that the current generation of connectionist models are 'first-order' models which consequently contain only implicit knowledge. First-order models have three characteristics.

First, learning is purely example-driven. Any change in internal representation reflects a change in the statistical properties of the input. In particular, the network does not learn by manipulating its own representations independently of the input to see if it can find a more elegant solution. For example, in the network described above, weights only changed when input was provided. After learning had reached asymptote, weights would only have changed if the regularities in the input strings changed.

Secondly, knowledge of rules in such networks is emergent. They do not depend on symbolic expressions which stand for the elements of a rule. For example, Dienes (1992) demonstrated that the network could follow a certain rule. Specifically, given certain conditions on the training strings, the network classified as perfectly grammatical only strings that were linear combinations of the training strings. However, this rule did not have an explicit representation (property-structure, predication, or mental-state) in the network. The network did not consult this rule, it simply followed it. As we will see below, however, this second characteristic of first-order models is not an entirely accurate description of this network, or of other typical ones.

Thirdly, first-order networks have no self-generated means of analysing their own activity so as to form symbolic representations of their own processing.

Clark and Karmiloff-Smith (1993) argued that these properties of networks mean that they are unable to account for the full flexibility of human beings. Similarly, we argue that connectionist networks may be unable to account for people's use of explicit knowledge but they are good models of implicit learning in such tasks as artificial grammar learning.

6.4.2 Types of explicitness of a representation

In terms of the types of explicitness described in Section 6.2.1, clearly some of the knowledge in the network is not completely property-structure explicit. One example is the rule mentioned above of treating linear combinations of training strings as grammatical. A more detailed rule might be that 'A T can follow another T'. This rule may be true of the grammar and also respected by the network, but because the network does not have a separable representation of T, it cannot have a property-structure explicit representation of the rule. Instead, knowledge of the rule would be distributed over the various T units in different positions. But there are other rules that do have a property-structure explicit representation. For example, the rule 'An M-in-first-position implies (with some likelihood) a T-in-second-position'. There is an Input unit whose function it is to code *An M-in-first-position* and this unit can occur as a property in other propositions (one proposition for each of the weights going from the unit). Also, through learning, the weights to the *T-in-second-position* Prediction unit acquire the function of indicating the predicate *implies (with some likelihood) a T-in-second-position* if learning makes them positive. Thus, the rule 'An M-in-first-position implies (with some likelihood) a T-in-second-position' is represented in a property-structure explicit way. This argument shows that Clark and Karmiloff-Smith's (1993) second characteristic of first-order networks is not a completely accurate characterization of this network, and, by simple extension of the argument, not a completely accurate characterization of many other networks. Note that this conclusion does not just follow from our analysis in terms of property-structure explicitness, but also from the intuition that prediction experiments get at something to-some-degree explicit.

Although some of the network's representations may be property-structure explicit, none of them are predication explicit or mental-state explicit. It would be possible to introduce predication explicitness about the grammar by having a set of units whose function it is to covary with the grammar the network is about (e.g. is it the first or second grammar studied?), and also another set of units to covary with the fact that it is, for example, the first grammar that *has* the structure. A good solution to introducing predication explicitness depends on solving elegantly the binding problem for connectionist networks generally (see Shastri and Ajjanagadde 1993) so that the grammar and the grammatical structure can be bound with the relation of possession.

Mental-state explicitness is profoundly problematic. In this network, and traditionally in connectionist networks, information is transmitted between different parts of the network by the spread of activation. Knowledge in the weights can influence the performance of another part of the network only in so far as the weights determine the activations that can be passed on to that part. Application of the rule 'An M-in-first-position predicts a T-in-second-position', partly encoded in the weights of the network, influences the activation of the Output unit eventually but there is no means by which the system could justify the response given by the Output unit in terms of the rule. The rule is not available to be represented by the network as an object of belief. That is not to say, however, that some of the network's knowledge may not be made mental-state explicit by the use of a second system observing the first (Clark and Karmiloff-Smith 1993), as we discuss later.

The fact that connectionist networks' representations are typically not mental-state explicit underlies the first and third characteristics of first-order systems described by Clark and Karmiloff-Smith (1993). It is difficult to test and reformulate rules that cannot be treated as objects of knowledge.

6.4.3 The four methodological criteria of implicit knowledge

The explicit/implicit status of the representations in the network clearly has implications for which of the methodological criteria of implicit knowledge a system employing this network to learn artificial grammars could be expected to satisfy.

In terms of the first methodological criterion, the network (apparently like subjects) would not be able to freely report its knowledge. The network needs to be cued to give a response. The network's ability to report information freely depends on there being another system that knows how to cue the network appropriately to give informative outputs. To do this, the system needs a theory of how the network works, a theory that cannot be derived directly from the output of the network. The theory cannot be directly derived precisely because the network's knowledge, embodied in its weights, does not consist of mental-state explicit representations.

In terms of the second criterion, the knowledge in the network could be elicited relatively easily by various direct tests; in other words, tests that appropriately cue the network. The network is like subjects in this respect. To perform the direct tests the network just needs to respond on the basis of a partial input, a task that connectionist networks are notoriously good at. No further assumptions need be made about the network in order to conclude that it will be good at forced-choice tasks. Some other more specific suggestions now follow, and some of these suggestions rely on a further assumption that the rest of the system in which the network is embedded can use the activation values of all units in the network. Specifically, the assumption is made that if a unit represents X, then the rest of the system (the part that observes the network) can infer X whenever the unit is active. This can be called the Network Transparency Assumption (NTA). In other words, a forced-choice test makes information in the network content explicit, even if it was not content explicit up to that point.

As described in Section 6.1.2, Dulany *et al.* (1984) asked subjects to underline that part of a test string that made it grammatical or non-grammatical. Subjects' ability to underline parts of strings was found to correspond to their classification performance. Underlining parts of strings is also something the network model could do. One way for the network to do this task would be have the network respond to fragments of each string; another way relies on the NTA. If the Output unit led to the decision that the string was non-grammatical, the positions defined by low activations of the Comparator units could be underlined. If the Output unit led to the decision that the string was grammatical, the positions defined by high activations of the Comparator units could be underlined. Because it is the activations of the Comparator units that determine the value of the Output, the underlining performance of the model should, like subjects, predict its classification performance.

Perruchet and Pacteau (1990) found that subjects could say which bigrams were grammatical and which were not. Again, the model could be easily adapted to do this. For example, bigrams could be given as input to the network. Alternatively (using the NTA), to determine the legal bigrams starting with M, each M unit could be activated in turn, and the letters active in the subsequent Prediction units noted. Dienes *et al.* (1991) found that subjects could say what letter should come next in a sequence. Again, this is not a problem for the network. Sequences with each possible letter as completion could be given as input to the network. An alternative method, using the NTA, was employed by Dienes (1990). He applied sequence stems to the Input units and took the activations of the next position in the Prediction units as the networks prediction for what letters could come next. He showed that the network trained to the same level of classification of subjects could predict the next letter in a sequence to the same degree as subjects.

In summary, when the network is appropriately cued, its knowledge is revealed. This follows, first, from the fact that much of the network's knowledge is property-structure explicit, and secondly, from the ability of connectionist networks to respond on the basis of partial cues and also to complete patterns.

In terms of the third criterion, the network has no metaknowledge about its knowledge because its knowledge does not have a mental-state explicit representation. Could this be changed in an easy way? Although the network, like other connectionist networks, does not derive its results by operating on mental-state explicit representations, it would be possible to observe the network by another system that does construct representations about the first network's representations. For example, using the NTA, after a response has been generated by the Output unit, the value of the associated probability could be made available for confidence ratings. Because the function of the 'confidence' system is to indicate a state of knowledge in the network (i.e. how valid the answer is believed to be), this system forms a mental-state explicit representation, or at least an attitude explicit representation.[4] This allows some metaknowledge. (For current purposes, we will side-step the difficult problem of how *validity* or *truth per se* could come to be represented in a connectionist network.) For example, consider two responses made by the network: in the first case, the response was 'grammatical' and the associated probability was 0.60; in the second case, the response was 'grammatical' and the associated probability was 0.80. If the probabilities were available to a 'confidence' system, they could be used to give a higher confidence rating in the second rather than first case. In this way, confidence could correlate with accuracy and the system would have some metaknowledge according to Chan's (1992) criterion.

In summary, when the activation of the output unit directly reflects the probability, P, of saying 'grammatical', the NTA implies that the knowledge is attitude explicit. Instead of assuming that the Output unit is partially activated to extent P, we could assume that the Output unit is either fully on or fully off on any trial, but it comes on with probability P. In this case, the NTA no longer allows confidence to be based on P. The knowledge would then be attitude implicit (unless the observing system observes the network over time).

Basing confidence on the partial activation of the Output unit could lead to paradoxical behaviour by the model. Sometimes when the probability of saying 'grammatical' is 0.80, the network will say 'non-grammatical'. If the probability is available to a further 'confidence' system, that system would be fairly confident that the string was grammatical, but the response as determined by the lower (observed) network would be 'non-grammatical'. This is possible although not optimal. There are two resolutions to this problem. In both cases, the introduction of the attitude explicit representation allows the system to have 'conscious' or explicit knowledge according to the criterion of metaknowledge (in the sense of knowing *that* one knows).

4. The range of propositional attitudes that can be assumed are very limited, and some may object to the representation being called 'mental-state' explicit. We do not wish to imply that the network has mental states in the same way that we do.

The first alternative is for the 'confidence' system to control the ultimate response, saying 'grammatical' whenever the probability coded by the Output unit is above 0.50, and saying non-grammatical otherwise. Confidence could then be given by how far the probability is from 0.50. This is possible and non-paradoxical. Furthermore, it would lead to a correlation between confidence and accuracy and to chance performance when confidence was 'guessing' (corresponding to a probability of 0.50).

In the second alternative, the network responds stochastically. In this case, the activation of the Output unit is only known to the observing system on some transformed scale (i.e. not directly as a probability). Thus, the system does not know the rational 0.5 cut-off point for saying 'grammatical'. So if the transformed *P* value seems relatively high compared to previous values, the system may say 'grammatical' with high confidence or 'non-grammatical' with low confidence. The result is that the system responds stochastically and confidence is correlated with accuracy.

In terms of the fourth criterion (i.e. whether intentions can control the way knowledge is used) the network is not set up for learning two grammars, and so it sheds no light on subjects' capabilities in this respect. However, keeping two bodies of knowledge separate is a recurring problem for many connectionist networks (McCloskey and Cohen 1989; Kruschke 1993).

6.5 CONCLUSION

In this chapter we have reviewed four methodological ways in which people's knowledge could be assessed as implicit. In respect to artificial grammar learning, people find it hard to express their knowledge in free recall and they lack metaknowledge about their knowledge. That is, their knowledge appears to be below a subjective threshold of consciousness. On the other hand, people's knowledge can be elicited by forced-choice tests (the knowledge is above an objective threshold) and people can decide which of two grammars to use (at this level, the knowledge is applied according to intentions). We argued that the subjective, but not the objective, threshold appears to be the criterion that does the useful work in separating different types of knowledge in people, at least as far as artificial grammars go (see Merikle (1992) for the argument that this is also true of subliminal perception, and Berry and Dienes (1993) for the argument that it could be true of implicit learning paradigms generally).

Considering people's knowledge to be based on a connectionist network illuminates why the subjective rather than the objective threshold does the useful work. The representations employed by the network directly provide accurate responses to input without themselves being represented as objects of knowledge (Clark and Karmiloff-Smith 1993); that is, they are content implicit. Because of this, the knowledge cannot be offered in free recall. The network could also allow either attitude implicitness or explicitness depending on how the output was coded (i.e. as a binary code for grammatical/non-grammatical, or a continuous code for the probability of being grammatical). Thus, this sort of model naturally allows us to see why people's knowledge should be below a subjective threshold.

On the other hand, because networks are excellent pattern-completion devices, and use some property-structure explicit representations, they are very good at successfully responding to forced-choice tests. We argued that it would be natural to assume that relevant knowledge in the network becomes content explicit to an observing system during forced-choice tasks, but only under these conditions (i.e. conditions in which the network is appropriately cued). In summary, the models lead us to expect that people's knowledge would be above an objective threshold.

REFERENCES

Armstrong, D. M. (1968). *A materialist theory of mind.* Routledge: London.

Berry, D. C. and Dienes, Z. (1993). *Implicit learning: theoretical and empirical issues.* Erlbaum, Hove.

Carruthers, P. (1992). Consciousness and concepts. *Proceedings of the Aristotelian Society*, **67**, 41–59.

Carruthers, P. (1993). Language, thought, and consciousness. Unpublished manuscript, Department of Philosophy, University of Sheffield.

Chan, C. (1992). *Implicit cognitive processes: theoretical issues and applications in computer systems design.* Unpublished D. Phil. thesis. University of Oxford.

Cheesman, J. and Merikle, P. (1984). Priming with and without awareness. *Perception and Psychophysics*, **36**, 387–95.

Cheesman, J. and Merikle, P. (1986). Distinguishing conscious from unconscious perceptual processes. *Canadian Journal of Psychology*, **40**, 343–67.

Clark, A. and Karmiloff-Smith, A. (1993). The cognizer's innards: A psychological and philosophical perspective on the development of thought. *Mind and Language*, **8**, 487–519.

Davies, M. (1991). Concepts, connectionism, and the language of thought. In *Philosophy and connectionist theory*, (ed.) W. Ramsey, S. Stitch, and D. Rumelhart), (Eds), pp. 229–57. Erlbaum, Hillsdale, NJ.

Dienes, Z. (1990). Implicit concept formation. Unpublished D.Phil. thesis. University of Oxford.

Dienes, Z. (1992). Connectionist and memory array models of artificial grammar learning. *Cognitive Science*, **16**, 41–79.

Dienes, Z. and Perner, J. (1994). Dissociable definitions of consciousness. *Behavioural and Brain Sciences*, **17**, 403–4.

Dienes, Z., Broadbent, D. E., and Berry, D. C. (1991). Implicit and explicit knowledge bases in artificial grammar learning. *Journal of Experimental Psychology: Learning, Memory, and Cognition*, **17**, 875–87.

Dienes, Z., Altmann, G., Kwan, L., and Goode, A. (1995). Unconscious knowledge of artificial grammars is applied strategically. *Journal of Experimental Psychology: Learning, Memory and Cognition.*

Dretske, F. (1981). *Knowledge and the flow of information.* MIT Press, Cambridge, MA.

Dretske, F. (1988). *Explaining behaviour: Reasons in a world of causes.* MIT Press, Cambridge, MA.

Dulany, D. E. (1962). The place of hypotheses and intentions: An analysis of verbal control in verbal conditioning. In *Behaviour and awareness,* (ed. C. W. Erisken), pp. 102–29. Duke University Press, Durham, NC.

Dulany, D., Carlson, R., and Dewey, G. (1984). A case of syntactical learning and judgement: How conscious and how abstract? *Journal of Experimental Psychology: General,* **113**, 541–55.

Holender, D. (1986). Semantic activation without conscious identification in dichotic listening, parafoveal vision, and visual masking: A survey and reappraisal. *Behavioural and Brain Sciences,* **9**, 1–23.

Jacoby, L. (1991). A process dissociation framework: Separating automatic from intentional uses of memory. *Journal of Memory and Language,* **30**, 513–41.

Jacoby, L. L., Kelley, C. M., and Dywan, J. (1989). Memory attributions. In *Varieties of memory and consciousness: Essays in honor of Endel Tulving,* (ed. H. L. Roediger and F. I. M. Craik), pp. 391–422. Erlbaum, Hillsdale, NJ.

Kruschke, J. K. (1993). Human category learning: Implications for backpropagation models. *Connection Science,* **5**, 3–36.

Lovibond, P. F. (1992). Tonic and phasic electrodermal responses of human aversive conditioning with long duration stimuli. *Psychophysiology,* **29**, 621–32.

McCloskey, M. and Cohen, N. (1989). Catastrophic interference in connectionist networks: The sequential learning problem. In *The psychology of learning and motivation,* Vol 24, (ed. G. Bower), pp. 109–165. Academic Press, New York.

Manza, L. and Reber, A. (1994). Representation of tacit knowledge: Transfer across stimulus forms and modalities. Unpublished manuscript, Pscyhology Department, Brooklyn College of CUNY.

Mathews, R. C., Buss, R. R., Stanley, W. B., Blanchard-Fields, F., Cho, J-R., and Druhan, B. (1989). The role of implicit and explicit processes in learning from examples: A synergistic effect. *Journal of Experimental Psychology: Learning, Memory, and Cognition,* **15**, 1083–100.

Merikle, P. (1992). Perception without awareness: critical issues. *American Psychologist,* **47**, 792–5.

Millikan, R. G. (1984). *Language, thought, and other biological categories: New foundations for realism.* MIT Press, Cambridge, MA.

Perner, J. (1993, April),. *Implicit, explicit, . . . and even consciousness.* Paper presented at the biennial Meeting of the society for Research in Child Development, New Orleans.

Perruchet, P. and Pacteau, C. (1990). Synthetic grammar learning: Implicit rule abstraction or explicit fragmentary knowledge. *Journal of Experimental Psychology: General,* **119**, 264–75.

Reber, A. S. (1967). Implicit learning of artificial grammars. *Journal of Verbal Learning and Verbal Behaviour,* **6**, 855–63.

Reber, A. S. (1989). Implicit learning and tactic knowledge. *Journal of Experimental Psychology: General,* **118**, 219–35.

Reber, A. S. (1993). *Implicit learning and tacit knowledge*. Oxford University Press.

Reingold, E. and Merikle, P. (1988). Using direct and indirect measures to study perception without awareness. *Perception and Psychophysics*, **44**, 563–75.

Reingold, E. and Merikle, P. (1993). Theory and measurement in the study of unconscious processes. In *Consciousness: psychological and philosophical essays. (ed. M. Davies, and G. W. Humphries), Blackwell, Oxford.*

Rosenthal, D. (1986). Two concepts of consciousness. *Philosophical Studies*, **94**, 329–59.

Rosenthal, D. (1993). Thinking that one thinks. In *Consciousness: psychological and philosophical essays*, (ed. M. Davies and G. W. Humphreys). Blackwell, Oxford.

Schacter, D. L. (1987). Implicit memory: History and current status. *Journal of Experimental Psychology: Learning, Memory, and Cognition*, **13**, 501–18.

Shanks, D. R. and St. John, M. F. (1994). Characteristics of dissociable human learning systems. *Behavioural and Brain Sciences*, **17**, 367–448.

Shastri, L. and Ajjanagadde, V. (1993). From simple associations to systematic reasoning: A connectionist representation of rules, variables and dynamic bindings using temporal synchrony. *Behavioural and Brain Sciences*, **16**, 417–94.

Strawson, P. F. (1959). *Individuals: An essay in descriptive metaphysics*. Methuen, London.

Whittlesea, B. W. A. and Dorken, M. D. (1993). Incidentally, things in general are particularly determined: An episodic processing account of implicit learning. *Journal of Experimental Psychology: General*, **122**, 227–48.

Willingham, D. B., Nissen, M. J., and Bullemer, P. (1989). On the development of procedural knowledge. *Journal of Experimental Psychology: Learning, Memory, and Cognition*, **15**, 1047–60.

7

Intuition, incubation, and insight: implicit cognition in problem solving

Jennifer Dorfman, Victor A. Shames, and John F. Kihlstrom

A number of isolated phenomena that usually make up the potpourri of topics grouped under thinking, such as functional fixity, the Einstellung effect, insight, incubation, and so on, must surely be included within the scope of a comprehensive theory. No extensive reanalysis of these phenomena from an information processing viewpoint has been carried out, but they speak to the same basic phenomena, so should yield to such an explanation. (Newell and Simon 1973, pp. 871–2)

Introspective analyses of human problem solving have often focused on the phenomena of intuition, incubation, and insight. The thinker senses that a problem is soluble (and perhaps what direction the solution will take), but fails to solve it on his or her first attempt; later, after a period in which he or she has been occupied with other concerns (or, perhaps, with nothing at all), the solution to the problem emerges full-blown into conscious awareness. These phenomena, which have long intrigued observers of problem solving, have also long eluded scientific analysis—in part because they seem to implicate unconscious processes. The Gestalt psychologists, of course, featured insight in their theories of thinking and problem solving, but interest in intuition, incubation, and insight, among other mentalistic phenomena, declined during the dominance of behaviourism.

With the advent of the cognitive revolution in the 1960s, psychologists returned their attention to thinking, so that a large literature has developed on problems of categorization, reasoning, and judgement, as well as problem solving *per se*. While our understanding of these aspects of thinking has advanced considerably over the past 35 years, most of this research has focused on the subject's *performance* on various problem-solving tasks, rather than the subject's *experience* during problem solving. In this chapter, we wish to revive a concern with problem-solving experience, in particular the experiences of intuition and incubation leading to insight, and to argue that recent work on implicit memory provides a model for examining the role of unconscious processes during problem solving.

7.0 THE STAGES OF THOUGHT

The popular emphasis on intuition, incubation, and insight is exemplified by Wallas' (1926, p. 79) classic analysis of 'a single achievement of thought'. As is well known, Wallas decomposed problem solving into a set of stages. The *preparation* stage consists of the accumulation of knowledge and the mastery of the logical rules which govern the particular domain in which the problem resides. It also involves the adoption of a definite problem attitude, including the awareness that there is a problem to be solved, and the deliberate analysis of the problem itself. Sometimes, of course, the problem is solved at this point. This is often the case with routine problems, in which the systematic application of some algorithm will eventually arrive at the correct solution (e.g. Newell and Simon 1973). Production of the answer must be followed by the *verification* stage, in which the solution is confirmed and refined (or shown to be incorrect).

On other occasions, however, this cognitive effort in the preparation stage proves fruitless and the correct solution eludes the thinker. In these cases, Wallas argued, the thinker enters an *incubation* stage in which he or she no longer consciously thinks about the problem. Wallas (1926) actually distinguished between two forms of incubation: 'the period of abstention may be spent either in conscious mental work on other problems, or in a relaxation from all conscious mental work' (p. 86). Wallas believed that there might be certain economies of thought achieved by leaving certain problems unfinished while working on others, but he also believed that solutions achieved by this approach suffered in depth and richness. In many cases of difficult and complex creative thought, he believed, deeper and richer solutions could be achieved by a suspension of conscious thought altogether, permitting 'the free working of the unconscious or partially conscious processes of the mind' (p. 87).[1] In either case, Wallas noted that the incubation period was often followed by the *illumination* stage, the 'flash' (p. 93) in which the answer appears in the consciousness of the thinker. (This answer, too, is subject to verification.)

Wallas (1926) was quite certain that incubation involved 'subconscious thought' (p. 87), and that the 'instantaneous and unexpected' (p. 93) flash of illumination reflected the emergence of a previously unconscious thought into phenomenal awareness:

1. The idea that unconscious mental processes are more creative than conscious ones is at the heart of many attempts to link creativity with hypnosis and other altered states of consciousness (Bowers and Bowers 1979; Shames and Bowers 1992).

The Incubation stage covers two different things, of which the first is the negative fact that during Incubation we do not voluntarily or consciously think on a particular problem, and the second is the positive fact that a series of unconscious and involuntary (or foreconscious and forevoluntary) mental events may take place during that period (p. 86).

[T]he final 'flash', or 'click,' . . . is the culmination of a successful train of association, which may have lasted for an appreciable time, and which has probably been preceded by a series of tentative and unsuccessful trains (pp. 93–94).

[T]he evidence seems to show that both the unsuccessful trains of association, which might have led to the 'flash' of success, and the final and successful train are normally either unconscious, or take place (with 'risings' and 'fallings' of consciousness as success seems to approach or retire), in that periphery or 'fringe' of consciousness which surrounds the disk of full luminosity (p. 94).

Wallas used the term *intimation* to refer to 'that moment in the Illumination stage when our fringe-consciousness of an association-train is in the state of rising consciousness which indicates that the fully conscious flash of success is coming' (p. 97). In other words, intimations are *intuitions*, in which thinkers know that the solution is forthcoming, even though they do not know what the solution is. This chapter argues that intuition and incubation reflect unconscious processing in problem solving, and that insight reflects the emergence of the solution into phenomenal awareness. Put another way, intuition and incubation are aspects of implicit thought, a facet of implicit cognition.

7.1 THE SCOPE OF IMPLICIT COGNITION

For many years, the notion that unconscious mental processes played a role in thinking and problem solving was widely accepted by non-psychologists (e.g. Koestler 1964), but viewed sceptically by researchers and theorists in the field.[2] In respect to incubation, for example, Woodworth and Schlosberg (1954, p. 840) suggested that 'The obvious theory—unconscious work, whether conceived as mental or as cerebral—should be left as a residual hypothesis for adoption only if other, more testable hypotheses break down'. More recently, however, there has been a shift toward wider acceptance of the idea of the *psychological unconscious*—the idea that mental structures, processes, and states can influence experience, thought, and action outside of phenomenal awareness and voluntary control (Kihlstrom 1984, 1987, 1990, 1995).

To a great extent, the contemporary revival of interest in the psychological unconscious may be attributed to demonstrations of implicit

2. For historical surveys of the psychology of thinking and problem solving, see Dominowski and Bourne (1994) and Ericsson and Hastie (1994).

expressions of memory in neurological patients and normal subjects (e.g. Cermak *et al.* 1985; Graf and Schacter 1985; Graf *et al.* 1984; Shimamura and Squire 1984; Schacter and Graf 1986; Warrington and Weiskrantz 1968). For example, the preservation of priming effects on such tasks as word-stem completion and lexical decision indicates that some memory of words presented during a study episode has been encoded and preserved, despite the subject's inability to remember the words themselves, or even the study task. Based on such results, Schacter (1987; Graf and Schacter 1985) argued for a distinction between explicit and implicit expressions of memory (for complete reviews, see Lewandowsky *et al.* 1989; Schacter 1987, 1992*a*,*b*, 1995; Schacter *et al.* 1993; Roediger 1990*a*,*b*; Roediger and McDermott 1993).[3] Explicit memory refers to conscious recall or recognition of events, while implicit memory refers to any effect on experience, thought, and action that is attributable to past events, in the absence of conscious recollection of those events. Neurological patients suffering from bilateral damage to the medial temporal lobe (including the hippocampus) or the diencephalon (including the mammillary bodies) show a gross impairment of explicit memory (the amnesic syndrome) but preserved implicit memory (for a review, see Shimamura 1994).

Similar dissociations between explicit and implicit memory can be observed in functional amnesias, including those induced by suggestions for post-hypnotic amnesia (Dorfman and Kihlstrom in prep.; Kihlstrom 1980; Kihlstrom *et al.* 1993; Schacter and Kihlstrom 1989; Kihlstrom and Schacter 1995). Moreover, studies of intact, non-amnesic subjects indicate that experimental variables that affect explicit memory do not always affect implicit memory, and vice versa (e.g. Graf and Mandler 1984; Jacoby and Dallas 1981; Tulving *et al.* 1982). For example, elaborative activity at the time of encoding has a major effect on explicit memory, but makes little impact on implicit memory. By the same token, a shift in modality at the time of presentation often affects implicit memory, but usually makes little difference to explicit memory. Thus, dissociations between explicit and implicit memory can be documented in a number of different ways.

A similar distinction can be drawn between explicit and implicit perception (Kihlstrom *et al.* 1992). By analogy to memory, explicit perception refers to conscious perception, as exemplified by the subject's ability to discern the presence, location, movement, and form as well as other palpable attributes of a stimulus. Implicit perception refers to any effect of a current stimulus event on experience, thought, and action, in the absence of conscious perception of that event. As in

3. Similar distinctions have been drawn by others in terms of memory with and without awareness, direct and indirect memory, or declarative and non-declarative memory (e.g. Jacoby and Witherspoon 1982; Johnson and Hasher 1987; Richardson-Klavehn and Bjork 1988; Squire 1992; Squire and Knowlton 1995); the differences among these taxonomic proposals need not concern us here.

the domain of memory, it appears that explicit and implicit perception can be dissociated in a number of different ways. For example, implicit perception is familiar in the literature on so-called 'subliminal' perception, in which a subject's behaviour is shown to be influenced by stimulus events that are too weak or too brief to be consciously perceived (for reviews, see Bornstein and Pittman 1992). It has long been known that priming effects similar to those observed in studies of implicit memory can be produced by stimuli that are presented for very brief durations, or masked by preceding or subsequent events (e.g. Forster and Davis 1984; Fowler *et al.* 1981; Greenwald *et al.* 1989; Marcel 1983). Subliminal perception appears to be analytically limited, in that there are restrictions on the amount of processing subliminal stimuli can receive (Greenwald 1992), and on the amount of information that can be extracted from them. The same sorts of limits obtain in many cases of implicit memory as well. For example, implicit memory produced by degraded stimulus presentations is often limited to knowledge about perceptual structure rather than meaning (Tulving and Schacter 1990). Similarly, subliminal priming is often limited to repetition effects, which can be mediated by perceptual rather than semantic representations of the stimuli. Despite their limitations, subliminal effects provide evidence for a distinction between the subjective threshold, the point at which a stimulus cannot be consciously perceived, and the objective threshold, the point at which all differential response to a stimulus disappears (Cheesman and Merikle 1984, 1985, 1986; Merikle and Reingold 1992). Semantic processing may be possible for stimuli presented near the subjective threshold, while only perceptual processing may be possible for stimuli presented near the objective threshold.

The construct of implicit perception also includes effects attributable to unperceived stimuli that are not themselves subliminal. For example, patients with damage to the striate cortex of the occipital lobe report a lack of visual experience in corresponding portions of their visual fields; yet, they are often able to make above-chance 'guesses' about the properties of stimuli presented to their scotomas (Weiskrantz 1986). This 'blindsight' has a parallel in the behaviour of patients with visual neglect resulting from unilateral lesions in the right temporoparietal regions of the cerebral cortex (Bisiach 1992). These patients appear unresponsive to stimuli in the corresponding portions of the left (contralateral) visual field, but careful observation sometimes reveals that their test performance is in fact influenced by the neglected stimuli (e.g. Marshall and Halligan 1988). Dissociations such as these are also familiar in the functional blindness and deafness associated with the conversion disorders, and in the parallel phenomena induced in normal subjects by hypnotic suggestion (e.g. Bryant and McConkey 1989*a*,*b*; for reviews see Kihlstrom 1992, 1994*b*; Kihlstrom *et al.* 1992, 1993).

Evidence for implicit perception often comes from the same sorts of tasks, such as priming, that provide evidence for implicit memory. Although it could be argued on these grounds that implicit perception and implicit memory are essentially the same phenomena, there are important distinctions between them (Kihlstrom *et al.* 1993). Still, as in any taxonomy, there are borderline cases. For example, demonstrations of implicit memory for items presented during general anaesthesia (for reviews, see Cork *et al.* 1995; Kihlstrom 1993*b*; Kihlstrom and Schacter 1990) probably provide evidence for implicit perception as well, because the patients are (at least ostensibly) unconscious at the time that the target events occurred.

Taken together, implicit memory and implicit perception exemplify the domain of the cognitive unconscious (Kihlstrom 1987). However, there is evidence of implicit processing in other cognitive domains as well. For example, some lines of research provide evidence for *implicit learning*, by which subjects acquire new knowledge in the absence of any conscious intention to learn, and without awareness of what they have learned. For example, in a paradigm refined by Reber (1967, 1993; see also Berry and Dienes 1994; Lewicki 1986), subjects are asked to memorize a list of letter strings that (unknown to them at the time) conform to the rules of an artificial grammar. They are then apprised of this fact, and asked to distinguish between new (unstudied) instances of grammatical strings and ungrammatical ones. Normal subjects can perform such a task with above-chance accuracy, even though they cannot specify the grammatical rules which govern their performance. Questions about the role of consciously accessible knowledge in such paradigms persist, but in principle the findings conform to the general model of the implicit/explicit distinction. Thus, implicit learning may be defined as a change in experience, thought, or action which is attributable to the acquisition of new semantic or procedural knowledge (as opposed to strictly episodic knowledge about past events), in the absence of conscious awareness of that knowledge.

Similarly, at least in principle, *implicit thought* (Kihlstrom 1990) may be observed whenever the subject's experience, thought, and action is affected by a thought (e.g. image, judgement, conclusion, or solution to a problem) in the absence of conscious awareness of that thought. Implicit thought is a difficult concept, because the idea of thinking is part and parcel of our everyday notions of consciousness. For William James (1890), for example, unconscious thought was a contradiction in terms (for a discussion of this view, see Kihlstrom 1984; Kihlstrom and Tobias 1991). In a recent review, Lockhart and Blackburn (1994) presented evidence for the role of implicit memory and implicit learning in problem solving. In this chapter, we consider implicit thought as a category in and of itself, by reviewing experiments which bring into the laboratory the intuition and incubation experiences which Wallas (1926) found in problem solvers who are on the verge of insight.

7.2 THE ROLE OF INTUITIONS IN PROBLEM SOLVING

In philosophy, intuition refers to the immediate apprehension of an idea without any conscious analysis. In ordinary language, however, the term refers to the person's feeling that a decision, judgement, or solution is correct, in the absence of supporting evidence (Bowers 1994). Thus, problem solvers' feelings of warmth reflect their belief that they are getting closer to a solution, even though they do not know what the solution is. Intuition, so defined, is a form of *metacognition* reflecting people's knowledge or beliefs about their cognitive states and processes (Flavell 1979; for reviews, see Metcalfe and Shimamura 1994; Nelson 1992).

In some sense, the problem solver's intuitions and feelings of warmth are analogous to the feeling-of-knowing (FOK; Hart 1965, 1967), the tip-of-the-tongue state (TOT; Brown and McNeil 1966), and other phenomena within the domain of metamemory (Nelson and Narens 1980). In the classic feeling-of-knowing paradigm, the subject is posed a question (e.g. 'What is the capital of Somalia?'); if the answer is not forthcoming, the subject is asked to judge the likelihood that he or she will recognize the correct answer. The accuracy of these self-predictions is then assessed by means of an actual recognition test. In the same way, people can be presented with a difficult problem (i.e. one that is not immediately soluble), and asked to judge the likelihood that they will be able to solve it, or to generate feelings-of-warmth (FOWs) representing how close they think they are to the solution. The accuracy of these FOWs (and other, similar, intuitions) is then determined by whether the subject's attempt to solve the problem is successful.

One difference between metacognition in memory and in problem solving is that while the mechanisms of FOKs are fairly well known, the mechanisms of FOWs are less clear. According to Nelson and his colleagues (Nelson *et al.* 1984), metamemory judgements like the FOK are mediated by two different sorts of processes, trace access and inference. Trace access involves gaining partial access to information stored in a memory trace. Thus, while in the TOT state, subjects can provide accurate information about the orthographic and phonemic features of a word, without being able to produce the word itself. Inference involves the subjects' judgements about whether they might have acquired the critical information at some time in the past. For example, most people give low FOK judgements to Fidel Castro's telephone number, because they know that they have never been in a position to acquire that information. By contrast, people give higher FOK ratings for the White House telephone number, because they can remember many instances (e.g. political advertisements in the newspaper) where they might have encountered that fact.

Just as FOKs are intuitions about knowledge that has not yet been retrieved from memory, so the FOWs experienced in problem solving are intuitions about solutions that have not yet been achieved. A possible metacognitive mechanism for FOWs is suggested by the problem-solving theory known as the general problem solver (GPS; Newell and Simon 1973). According to Newell and Simon, the mental representation of a problem, or *problem space,* includes the initial state, the goal state, intermediate states (or subgoals) to be achieved on the way to the goal state, and operations by which one state is transformed into another. By means of *difference reduction,* for example, the problem solver engages in any activity that reduces the difference between the current state and the goal state. A more complicated strategy is *means–end analysis,* by which the solver analyses the problem space into a set of differences (e.g. between subgoals and the final goal) and identifies and executes operations that will eliminate or reduce the most important differences between the current state and the goal state. The difference between the two techniques is that means–end analysis may sometimes temporarily *increase* the distance between the current state and the goal. Thus, the Hobbits and Orcs problem actually requires that the thinker undo some of the progress made in getting the creatures to the other side of the river (Thomas 1974). Nevertheless, GPS assumes that the thinker has in short-term memory a representation of the distance between the current state and the goal state, and this representation is the basis for feelings of warmth:

> We can now see how cues become available sequentially, and why, consequently, strategies of search that use the cues are possible. Each time a process is applied to an initial state, a new state with a new description is produced. If there are relations (known to or learnable by the problem solver) between characteristics of the state description and distance from the goal (i.e., the final description that represents the solution), these relations can be used to tell when the problem solver is getting 'warmer' or 'colder,' hence, whether or not he should continue along a path defined by some sequence of processes (Newell *et al.* 1962, p. 155).

A clear implication of the GPS analysis of FOWs is that they should be relatively accurate predictors of problem-solving success. However, in contrast to the relative accuracy of FOKs in memory-retrieval situations, intuitions about problem solving are not necessarily accurate. Metcalfe (1986*a*,*b*; Metcalfe and Wiebe 1987) has argued that FOWs are accurate when problems are solved through memory retrieval, but not when they are solved through insight processes. She found that, when subjects are presented with insight problems, their FOW judgements do not predict whether they will actually solve the problems. In fact, Metcalfe has consistently found that incremental warmth ratings over a trial are actually associated with *errors* in problem solving. When insight problems are correctly unravelled, FOWs tend to remain stable at low levels, until virtually the moment that the problem is solved. Thus, either subjects have no intuitions, or their intuitions are in error.

Metcalfe (1986*a,b*; Metcalfe and Wiebe 1987) interpreted this surprising outcome in terms of Gestalt accounts of problem solving (Luchins and Luchins 1970; Scheerer 1963; Wertheimer 1959; for reviews, see Dominowski 1981; Ellen 1982; Ohlsson 1984; Weisberg 1992; Weisberg and Alba 1981*a,b*), which posit a fundamental discontinuity between the deliberate processing of information and the spontaneous restructuring of a problem. Some problems can be solved by memory retrieval, and in these cases FOWs accurately reflect the gradual accumulation of problem-relevant information. Other problems must be solved by restructuring, where metacognitive experiences may be lacking or even invalid. However, many problems seem to admit solution by either retrieval or restructuring. Thus, Metcalfe has classified anagrams as insight problems, on the basis of the finding that metacognitive experiences do not predict success of solution. However, such problems do not require insight for their solution, as the classic insight problems (Maier 1930, 1931) seem to do. That is, anagrams can also be solved by a brute-force process of memory retrieval, in which the thinker rearranges letters systematically and checks each version against the mental lexicon.

In actual practice, it seems difficult to assign problems to insight and non-insight categories on a principled basis, and in the absence of objective criteria, a definition which states that insight problems are those in which intuitions are invalid seems almost tautological. In fact, Lockhart and Blackburn (1994) have defined insight as that component of problem solving which involves conceptual access, as opposed to procedural restructuring. By this criterion, anagrams are not pure insight problems, and may not qualify as insight problems at all. In any event, the requirement that true insight must be unaccompanied by valid metacognitions violates our frequent everyday experience—phenomenological evidence that must also be taken seriously (Shames and Kihlstrom 1994).

In what follows, we wish to use the term *insight problem solving* without entering the debate over what constitutes an 'insight' problem, or 'insight' problem solving. Rather, we wish to use the term *insight* in the same way we use the term *intuition*—in its ordinary-language, folk-psychological sense, which places primary emphasis on the 'aha!' experience (Simon 1986). As described by Simon (1986, p. 483):

> The 'aha' phenomenon differs from other instances of problem solution . . . only in that the sudden solution is here preceded by a shorter or longer period during which the subject was unable to solve the problem, or even to seem to make progress toward its solution. The 'aha' may occur while the subject is working on the problem, or after the problem has been put aside for some period of 'incubation'.

From the point of view of this chapter, insight occurs at the moment when the solution to a problem emerges into consciousness. What concerns us are the precursors to insight: the subject's intuitions, based on the activation of knowledge structures below the threshold for awareness; and the incubation period during which the unconscious becomes conscious.

7.3 EVIDENCE FOR INTUITIONS IN INSIGHT PROBLEM SOLVING

Despite Metcalfe's arguments, some evidence for valid intuitions in insight problem solving comes from a series of studies reported by Bowers *et al.* (1990; see also Bowers *et al.* 1995), and based in turn on the remote associates test (RAT) developed by Mednick (1962; Mednick and Mednick 1967) for the assessment of creativity. Mednick (1962, p. 221) defined creative thinking as the combination of ideas that were not previously associated with each other: 'The more mutually remote the elements of the new combination, the more creative the process or solution'. These associations may occur in a number of ways: serendipitously, by means of similarity between the previously unassociated elements (e.g. words that rhyme but are semantically unrelated), or through mediation by a third idea. In order to distinguish creative associations from the products of mentally retarded or thought-disordered individuals, Mednick further required that these new ideas prove practically useful in some way. It was not enough that they be merely original.

It follows from Mednick's definition that creative individuals are disposed to generate remote associations—literally to connect ideas that other people fail to see as related. Accordingly, Mednick (1962) developed a procedure in which subjects are given a set of three words each unrelated to the others in associative terms, and are asked to generate an associate which all have in common. Barring psychotically loose associations, the only answer is a word which is a remote associate of each of the test items. A favourite example is:

DEMOCRAT
GIRL
FAVOUR. [1]*

Bowers *et al.* (1990, experiment 1) developed a variant on the RAT known as the 'dyads of triads' (DOT) procedure, in which subjects were presented with two RAT-like items. Only one of these was soluble or *coherent*—i.e. the three words did in fact have some distant associate in common. The other was considered insoluble or *incoherent*, because—again barring

* Solutions to problems are to be found on p. 286.

psychotically loose associations—the elements had no associate in common. An example is:

PLAYING	STILL	
CREDIT	PAGES	
REPORT	MUSIC.	[2]

The subjects were asked to inspect the triads and generate the correct solution to the coherent one. After a few seconds, they were asked to indicate which triad was coherent. Of course, in the absence of an actual solution, this judgement represents a guess, hunch, or intuition on the part of subjects. Across five samples of college undergraduates, Bowers *et al.* (1990) found that subjects were able to choose which DOT triads were soluble at rates significantly greater than chance. The subjects were rarely certain of their choices, but greater accuracy was associated with higher confidence ratings. Thus, the subjects' intuitions about the DOT items were accurate more often than not. From Bowers's (1984, 1994) point of view, these choices are not arbitrary—rather, they are informed guessess reflecting the processing of information outside of awareness.

Further analysis of the DOT test by Bowers *et al.* (1990) indicated that there are two types of coherent triads. In *semantically convergent* triads, the remote associate preserves a single meaning across the three elements. Thus, in the triad

GOAT
PASS
GREEN, [3]

the solution preserves a single meaning regardless of the element with which it is associated. On the other hand, some triads are *semantically divergent,* in that the remote associate has a different meaning in the context of each element (or, at least, the meaning of the associate in the context of one element is different from its meaning in the context of the other two). Thus, in the triad

STRIKE
SAME
TENNIS, [4]

the solution has a different meaning in association with each element. Bowers *et al.* (1990) found that the degree of semantic convergence was significantly correlated with the likelihood that subjects would correctly guess which DOT item was coherent.

Bowers *et al.* (1990, experiment 2) performed a conceptual replication of the DOT procedure in the non-verbal domain. For this purpose, they constructed a new test, the Waterloo gestalt closure task (WGCT), consisting of two gestalt closure items similar to those developed by Street (1931), Mooney (1957), and Harshman (1974). Each item of the WGCT contained two components: the coherent portion was a fragmented representation of a familiar object; the incoherent portion was the same stimulus rendered meaningless by rotating and displacing the fragments. As in the DOT procedure, subjects were given a few seconds to generate the name of the coherent gestalt. Then they were asked to guess which figure was coherent. Again, these guesses were significantly greater than chance. Even when subjects rated their confidence levels as zero, their guesses were still correct above chance levels.

Which aspects of the drawings contribute to these successful intuitions is not known at present. In a study reported informally by Bowers *et al.* (1995), subjects were presented with a coherent WGCT item or its incoherent counterpart, followed by a list of four words. When asked to indicate which word was the correct solution to the gestalt, the subjects were correct well above chance on coherent gestalts, compared to chance levels for incoherent ones. Thus, subjects are responding to more or less specific pictorial content in the stimulus.

Returning to the verbal domain, Bowers *et al.* (1990, experiment 3a) obtained further evidence of the role of intuitions in an expansion of the RAT procedure known as the accumulated clues task (ACT). The ACT items consisted of 15 words, all of which had a single associate in common. For the first 12 words, the associate was relatively remote, while for the last three words, the associate was relatively close. An example is:

TIMES
INCH
DEAL
CORNER
PEG
HEAD
FOOT
DANCE
PERSON
TOWN
MATH
FOUR
BLOCK
TABLE
BOX. [5]

In the experiment, the subjects saw the words in sequence, one at a time cumulatively, and were asked to generate the one word which was an associate of all the words in the list. Of course, this was impossible on the first trial, because a word like TIMES has many associates. But relatively few of these are also associates of INCH, and even fewer are also associates of DEAL. Thus, evidence accumulates with each clue as to the correct answer. In the course of solving each item, the subjects were asked to generate at least one free association to each cue, and to indicate whether any of these associations appeared promising as solutions to the problem as a whole. Associates so designated may properly be called *hunches*. Analysis of the responses (experiment 3b) showed that they progressively increased in associative closeness to the actual solution to the problem as the sequence proceeded. Contrary to the findings of Metcalfe (1986*a*, *b*; Metcalfe and Wiebe 1987), subjects rarely attained correct solutions suddenly, without any hunches or premonitions.

A quite different line of research, reported by Durso and his colleagues (Durso *et al.* 1994; see also Dayton *et al.* 1990), also provides evidence that subjects can have correct intuitions in the course of insight problem solving. They presented subjects with the following vignette, which they were asked to explicate:

A man walks into a bar and asks for a glass of water. The bartender points a shotgun at the man. The man says 'Thank you' and walks out. [6]

In order to help them solve the problem, the subjects were allowed to ask the experimenter a series of yes/no questions for up to two hours—at the end of which half of them still had not solved the problem. Then they were asked to rate the relatedness of all possible pairings of 14 words related to the problem. Some of these targets were explicitly stated in the story or otherwise relevant to it (e.g. *man, bartender*), while others were implicit in the correct solution (e.g. *surprise, remedy*). The relatedness judgements were then processed by an algorithm, along the lines of those used in multidimensional scaling, which yields a graphical representation of the links among problem-related concepts in the subjects' minds—literally a map of the problem space. The graphs of subjects who had solved the problem were completely different ($r = 0.00$) from those of subjects who had not done so. That is, concepts implicitly related to the solution were much more closely connected in the minds of those who had achieved insight into the problem than they were in those who had not. For example, the non-solvers' graphs centred on explicit concepts, while the solvers' centred on implicit ones. This suggests that subjects' underlying cognitive structures changed as they achieved insight into the problem.

In a follow-up study, a new group of subjects rated those concepts important to the solution, as well as control concepts, at several points in the course of problem solving. Analysis showed that the insight-related concepts were initially viewed as highly unrelated. Some time before the insight was achieved, the similarity of insight-related concepts increased significantly; another increase was observed when the problem was actually solved. This pattern of ratings indicates that during problem solving subjects gradually increase their focus on those concepts important to the solution. In other words, the subjects' intuitions concerning the insight-relevant concepts, and the relations among them, were affected by the ultimate solution to the problem, even though the subjects were not aware of the solution itself:

> Like dynamite, the insightful solution explodes on the solver's cognitive landscape with breathtaking suddenness, but if one looks closely, a long fuse warns of the impending organization (Durso *et al.* 1994, p. 98).

7.4 THE ROLE OF ACTIVATION IN INTUITION AND INCUBATION

Bowers *et al.* (1990, 1995) concluded from their research that intuitions in problem solving reflect the automatic and unconscious activation and integration of knowledge stored in memory (Anderson 1983; Collins and Loftus 1975; McClelland and Rumelhart 1981; Meyer and Schvaneveldt 1971). This suggestion bears a close resemblance to a spreading activation view of intuition and incubation initially proposed by Yaniv and Meyer (1987) based on a study of retrieval from semantic memory (for a critique of spreading activation theory, see Ratcliff and McKoon 1981, 1988, 1994). In their experiments, Yaniv and Meyer (1987) presented subjects with the definitions of uncommon words, and asked them to generate the word itself. An example is:

LARGE BRIGHT COLORED HANDKERCHIEF; BRIGHTLY COLORED SQUARE OF SILK MATERIAL WITH RED OR YELLOW SPOTS, USUALLY WORN AROUND THE NECK. [7]

After presentation of the definition the subjects were asked to generate the word. If they could do so, they rated their confidence that they were correct; if they could not, they made TOT and FOK judgements. In either case, the trial ended with a lexical decision task in which the subject was presented with six items, including some English words and some legal non-words; among the English words presented on each trial was the answer to the immediately preceding word definition problem and a control item. For example:

SPENDING
DASCRIBE
BANDANNA
TRINSFER
ASTEROID
UMBRELLA.

The general finding was that subjects showed priming on the word targeted by the definition—even when they were unable to generate the word itself. This was especially the case when subjects experienced the TOT state and gave high FOK ratings. Priming was correlated with the magnitude of feeling-of-knowing ratings of the target words, suggesting that the feeling-of-knowing ratings were based on priming-like effects. A second experiment, which extended the period between the definition and the lexical decision task by four minutes (filled by other word generation items), confirmed this finding. This result indicates that the priming detected in the first experiment can last long enough to contribute to incubation effects—despite increased memory load created by the filler task (see also Connor *et al.* 1992; Seifert *et al.* 1995).

Yaniv and Meyer (1987) proposed a model of priming effects in semantic memory which offers a mechanism by which intuition and incubation can occur in problem solving. In their view, presentation of the definition activates relevant nodes in semantic memory. Activation then spreads from these nodes until it reaches a node representing the target and accumulates there to a level sufficient to bring the target into conscious awareness. These levels of activation can persist for a substantial period of time, despite the subject's engagement in other cognitive activities. Incubation effects reflect the accumulated influence of cues contained in the original statement of the problem, inferences generated by the subject's initial work on the problem, and new contextual cues processed during the ostensibly dormant period. But even before the threshold for conscious awareness is crossed, subthreshold levels of activation can sensitize the problem solver to new information pertinent to the solution. According to Yaniv and Meyer, this sensitization, revealed by priming effects in lexical decision, underlies FOKs and other metamemory judgements; we believe, with Bowers *et al.* (1990, 1995), that it underlies intuitions in problem solving as well.

In the present context, the most important point is Yaniv and Meyer's (1987) proposal that subjects are sensitive to, or influenced by, knowledge structures that are activated below the level required for conscious awareness.[4] Similarly, Bowers *et al.* (1990, 1995) argued that subthreshold levels

4. Kihlstrom (1993*a*,*b*, 1994*a*) has argued that superthreshold activation is necessary but not sufficient to support conscious awareness of a percept in memory. According to his view, conscious awareness requires that an activated knowledge structure must also make contact with a representation of the self concurrently active in working memory.

of activation, spreading from nodes representing the clues and converging on the node representing the solution, served as the basis for subjects' intuitions about which DOT and ACT problems were soluble and what the solutions were. A similar process, constructed within the framework of models of object recognition (e.g. Biederman 1987, 1993; Peterson 1994; Tarr 1995), could account for intuitions and insights on non-verbal problems such as those posed by the WGCT.

Unfortunately, the evidence for such a proposal is relatively indirect. In fact, accurate judgements of coherence on the DOT might be based on other kinds of processes. For example, coherent and incoherent test items might differ on a dimension of *interclue relatedness*. Thus, the words PLAYING, CREDIT, and REPORT, which made up a coherent triad in Bowers *et al.*'s experiments, might be more closely associated with each other than are the words STILL, PAGES, AND MUSIC, which comprised an incoherent one. If so, subjects could make accurate judgements of coherence by attending solely to the relations among cues, rather than picking up on the convergence of the activation on some item stored in semantic memory.

To test this hypothesis, Dorfman (1990) constructed RAT-like items consisting of two sets of six words (dyads of sextuples), one coherent and one incoherent. For example:

SCHOOL	KITTEN	
CHAIR	SCOTCH	
JUMP	SALAD	
NOON	BREEZE	
HEELS	MILE	
WIRE	INSURANCE	[8]

Dorfman then asked a group of subjects to rate (on a 0–5 scale) the semantic relatedness of the items in each sextuple. Another group of subjects actually solved the problems (the average subject solved 74 per cent of them) and then made dichotomous judgements of solubility analogous to the coherence judgements of Bowers *et al.* (1990). The judgements of solubility were highly correlated (r = 0.89) with actual ease of solution. More importantly, the items of coherent sextuples were judged to be significantly more semantically related than those of incoherent ones (M = 3.39 vs. 1.90). This indicates that interclue relatedness is a potential clue to coherence. However, correlation analysis indicated that relatedness was only modestly related to either solubility judgements (r = 0.39) or actual solution accuracy (r = 0.29). In a series of subsequent experiments (experiments 1 and 2, described below), relatedness continued to show only modest correlations with solution accuracy (rs = 0.29 and 0.32, respectively). Thus, while interclue relatedness may play some role in metacognitive judgements of coherence, other factors are also important.

In a more direct test of the activation hypothesis, Dorfman (1990, experiments 1 and 2) examined the effects of external cues on metacognitive judgements in problem solving. In experiment 1, subjects saw one clue for each of 40 sextuples (20 coherent and soluble, 20 incoherent and insoluble), and then generated a word that was associatively related to that clue. If this associate was in fact the correct solution to a coherent sextuple, that problem was eliminated from further consideration (the subjects were given no feedback about their performance). In the second phase, the subjects were given two such cues, generated a word that was associatively related to both, and made a judgement of the coherence of the problem. Again, problems that were correctly solved were eliminated from consideration. The problem-solving and coherence tasks were repeated for the sets of three, four, five, and six items.

In this experiment, subjects were more likely to solve coherent problems when they received a greater number of clues. Thus, subjects correctly solved 18 per cent of problems in the initial phase of the experiment, when only one clue was given. This success was, of course, entirely adventitious, reflecting accidents of word association. They solved another 22 per cent of the problems after they received a second clue, and yet another 20 per cent after receiving the third clue. By the time all six clues had been given, the average subject had solved 84 per cent of the problems. Thus, the incremental presentation of cues promoted discovery of insightful solutions. As in the research of Bowers *et al.* (1990), the subjects were able to discriminate coherent from incoherent problems, even though they were unable to provide the correct solutions. Thus, after the second trial, at which point approximately 40 per cent of the items had been solved, the remaining soluble problems received average coherence ratings of 1.34, compared to 1.07 for the insoluble problems. The coherence ratings were especially high for soluble problems which were eventually solved, compared to those to which the subject failed to find the solution (*Ms* = 1.40 vs. 1.13, respectively).

Experiment 2 substituted warmth judgements for coherence ratings, and yielded comparable results. The subjects correctly solved 17 per cent of problems in the initial phase of the experiment, when only one clue was given, another 26 per cent after receiving the second clue, and yet another 20 per cent after receiving the third clue; by the time all six clues had been given, the average subject had solved 91 per cent of the problems. As in the first experiment, the subjects were able to discriminate coherent from incoherent problems, even though they were unable to provide the correct solutions. Thus, after the second trial, with 43 per cent of the items solved, the remaining soluble problems received average warmth ratings of 1.38, compared to 1.09 for the insoluble problems. This time, however, the warmth ratings for soluble problems which were eventually solved were no greater than for those that remained unsolved; in fact, they were somewhat lower (*M*s = 1.36 vs. 1.48, respectively). As in the study by Bowers *et al.* (1990), intuitions were related to solubility; but as in the research of Metcalfe (1986*a,b*; Metcalfe and Wiebe 1987), in this case warmth ratings did not predict the actual emergence of a solution.

In fact, viewed across the six phases of each experiment, the coherence and warmth judgements failed to show consistent signs of an incremental pattern. As a rule, subjects gave relatively low coherence or warmth ratings for unsolved problems, until the trial on which they solved them—at which time, of course, the ratings showed a sharp increase. Thus, items solved in phase 5 of experiment 1, by which time subjects had seen five cues, received average coherence ratings of 3.67 on that trial; prior to this time, however, they had received ratings of 1.18 in phase 2 (two cues), 1.34 in phase 3 (three cues), and 1.02 in phase 4 (four cues). In experiment 2, items that were solved in phase 5 received average warmth ratings of 3.98 in that phase, but ratings of 1.15, 0.99, and 0.44 in phases 2–4, respectively.

Although Dorfman's (1990) experiments 1 and 2 did not reveal the gradual build-up of coherence or warmth envisioned by Bowers *et al.* (1990, 1995), her findings do not necessarily require the sudden, Gestalt-like restructuring process described by Metcalfe (1986*a,b*; Metcalfe and Wiebe 1987). Discontinuous metacognitive experiences need not imply underlying discontinuities in the processing of information. Taken together with the research of Bowers *et al.* (1990), Dorfman's findings suggest that problems of this sort are solved by means of a gradual accrual of information from memory. The thinker's initial unsuccessful attempts to solve a problem activate information in memory, sensitizing him or her to encounters with additional clues (Yaniv and Meyer 1987). Such encounters partially activate other, related memory traces, producing a build-up of underlying coherence which contributes to the intuition that the problem is soluble. Gradually, coherence builds up further to the point at which a novel recombination of information is possible. At this point, the thinker may have an explicit hypothesis or hunch as to the solution to the problem.

When activation of underlying memory traces reaches the threshold needed for discovery of an insightful solution, intuition has led to insight. However, the gradual build-up of coherence may not generate progressively strong intuitions. Metacognitions may be based on activation crossing a threshold, rather than on the absolute magnitude of activation. In this way, coherence could build up preconsciously, but intuitions would emerge only after coherence levels had reached the threshold of conscious awareness. Thus, intuitions could reflect activation processes that occur outside of conscious awareness, and perhaps outside of conscious control as well.

7.5 PRIMING IN INSIGHT PROBLEM SOLVING

Further evidence for the role of unconscious activation in insight problem solving was provided by a doctoral dissertation recently completed by Shames (1994). Shames noted that the intuitions of subjects on the DOT and similar tests, like the intimations described by Wallas (1926), resembled semantic priming effects of the sort familiar in the study of implicit memory—except that it is the thought that is implicit, rather than any representation of current or past experience. Yaniv and Meyer (1987) had made the same argument, but their task involved retrieval from semantic memory. And while retrieval from semantic memory may be a problem in some sense, it does not require establishing (or finding) new associations or connections. Moreover, problem solving on such tasks is usually characterized by a much more mundane phenomenology than problems that are accompanied by insight. Accordingly, Shames imported the RAT into Yaniv and Meyer's priming paradigm.

Shames's first experiment illustrates his basic paradigm. Subjects were presented with RAT-like items and were given five seconds to find a single associate which all three cues had in common. The subjects then indicated, by a simple yes/no response, whether they knew the answer. Under these circumstances of testing, the subjects' responses were negative on a majority of the trials; thus, the bulk of the triads went unsolved. Immediately after their yes/no response, six items were presented for lexical decision. As in Yaniv and Meyer (1987), these items included both words and non-words, and the words included both the item targeted by the RAT problem and a control word. Comparing response latencies to target and control items, both item and subject analyses revealed a significant priming effect for unsolved items. That is, the subjects showed significantly shorter response latencies when making lexical decisions about targets primed by unsolved RAT items, compared to controls. Interestingly, the priming effect observed for solved RAT items was smaller and not significant.

Such a finding deserves replication, especially in the light of the difference obtained between solved and unsolved problems. Accordingly, Shames (1994, experiment 5) developed a larger set of triads and repeated his experiment. Again, he obtained a significant priming effect for unsolved triads, but this time the effect for solved triads was also significant.

One potential problem with Shames' original procedure is that triads are classified as solved or unsolved depending on subjects' self-reports of whether they knew the answer. This reliance on self-reports makes some researchers nervous. For example, subjects might have solved a RAT problem, but withheld this information from the experimenter. In an attempt to overcome this difficulty, Shames (1994, experiment 6) classified RAT items as easy or hard based on the performance of a normative group. Hard items (which are coherent but relatively unlikely to be solved by subjects) produced significant priming on lexical decision, but easy items (which are also coherent, but relatively likely to be solved) did not.

At this point, the matter of whether solved and unsolved triads yield different levels of priming remains uncertain. Two subsequent replications of experiment 1 by Shames (unpublished data) yielded priming for unsolved triads, but not for solved ones. Thus, the general trend of the available evidence is that unsolved problems show priming while solved ones do not. The issue is important, because some theorists (e.g. Merikle and Reingold 1992) have argued that the best evidence for unconscious processes is provided by qualitative differences between explicit and implicit processes. The fact that unsolved items produce priming but solved items do not might be one such difference.

But why might unsolved triads produce more priming than solved ones? One possibility is suggested by Zeigarnik's (1927) classic study of memory and problem solving. Zeigarnik asked her subjects to engage in simple tasks, but interrupted half of these tasks before they could be completed. Later, on a test of incidental memory, the subjects tended to remember uncompleted tasks better than completed ones—a phenomenon enshrined in psychological lore as the *Zeigarnik effect* (for reviews, see Butterfield 1964; Weiner 1966).[5] Zeigarnik's explanation, in the tradition of Lewinian field theory, was that the brain systems involved in task performance remain activated until the task is completed—creating a kind of cognitive tension. When a problem is solved, closure is achieved and the tension dissipates. In much the same way, persisting activation following failure in problem solving might be the basis of the semantic priming effects observed in Shames' experiments. In any event, the fact that semantic priming occurs on trials with unsolved triads is consistent with the hypothesis of implicit problem solving: there is an effect on experience, thought, or action of the solution to a problem, in the absence of conscious awareness of what that solution is.

One thing we know for sure is that the priming effects observed by Shames (1994) reflect actual problem-solving activity. Shames (1994, experiment 2) simply asked subjects to study RAT items in a recognition memory paradigm. On each trial, the subjects were presented with an

5. Zeigarnik also noted that some subjects, who felt that the interrupted problems were beyond their capacity, remembered successful tasks better than unsuccessful ones—a 'reverse' Zeigarnik effect analogous to repression; for a discussion of this effect, see Kihlstrom and Hoyt (1990).

RAT item to memorize, followed by the lexical decision task. They were then presented with a single word and asked whether it had been part of the RAT item just presented. In contrast to the results of experiments 1 and 5, where the RAT items were studied under a problem-solving set, the priming of RAT solutions was not significant. Thus, activation does not spread automatically from nodes representing RAT cues to a node representing their common associate; activation of solutions only occurs when the subject is operating under a particular problem-solving set.

Another line of evidence that automatic spreading activation is not enough to prime RAT solutions came from work on insoluble or incoherent RAT items. Shames (1994, experiment 3) replaced one word in each RAT item with a misleading cue, unrelated to the target remote associate. Thus, two of the words converged on the solution, but the third did not. Under these circumstances, there was no priming effect on lexical decision. If the priming effect were due merely to activation automatically spreading from individual cue nodes, some priming should have been observed, although perhaps the degree of priming would not have been as large as when all three clues were valid. The fact that incoherent RAT items do not prime lexical decisions indicates that the priming reflects progress in problem solving. Taken together, experiments 2 and 3 render it unlikely that the semantic priming observed by Shames is produced merely by the encoding of the individual words in the RAT item, rather than any attempt to find an associate that all three have in common.

In Shames' experiments, subjects proceed to the lexical decision task after only five seconds of problem solving. Therefore, it is possible that the priming reflects the effect of solutions that emerged over the course of the lexical decision task; if this were the case, the observed priming would not reflect implicit problem solving at all, but rather explicit awareness of the solution to the RAT item at hand. Under such circumstances, however, subjects should be able to identify correct solutions to RAT items as such when they appear as targets for lexical decision. Accordingly, Shames (1994, experiment 5) required subjects to make solution judgements rather than lexical decisions after presentation of the RAT items. RAT problems were followed by a series of six words and non-words, as in the lexical decision task. As each of the six probes appeared, subjects were required to determine whether it was an associate of all three RAT cues. On average, it took subjects approximately one second longer to identify RAT targets as such than to identify them as words. Thus, it appears that the subjects do not have enough time during the lexical decision task to consciously identify items as RAT solutions.

The priming effect occurs during the incubation period, after the problem has been posed, but before the solution has arrived in consciousness. The priming effect uncovered by Shames (1994) may underlie the ability of subjects to judge which RAT items are coherent (Bowers *et al.* 1990,

1995). Both phenomena seem to reflect activity in the target node that remains beneath the threshold for conscious accessibility—the 'rising toward consciousness' of which Wallas (1926, p. 94) wrote. Still, further research is required to connect priming with intuitions.

7.6 THE PROBLEM OF INCUBATION

As with intuition, the most convincing evidence for the role of incubation in problem solving is anecdotal. In an early and influential review, Woodworth and Schlosberg (1954, p. 838) cited 'a large mass of testimony from creative thinkers to the effect that laying aside a baffling problem for a while is often the only way to reach a satisfactory solution'. Inventors, scientists, poets, and artists, they noted, routinely testify to the power of incubation (for dramatic and inspiring accounts in a variety of fields, see Koestler 1964); they also tend to characterize incubation as an unconscious process. Campbell (1960) thought that incubation resulted from the random fusion of memory representations, an ongoing process which occurs unconsciously; when the new combination is relevant to the problem at hand, it emerges into consciousness as a creative insight—a mental equivalent of the survival of the fittest.

However, there are other accounts of incubation which afford no role for unconscious processes (for reviews of the possibilities, see Perkins 1981; Posner 1973; Woodworth 1938; Woodworth and Schlosberg 1954). For example, prolonged thought might result in a kind of mental fatigue: after the incubation period, the thinker returns to the problem refreshed and more likely to achieve a solution. According to this view, no work at all, whether conscious or unconscious, is done on the problem during the incubation period. Alternatively, the incubation period merely affords an opportunity for further *conscious* work, activity which is simply forgotten after the problem has been solved—perhaps because it occurred in brief, barely noticed spurts. Thus, what appears to the thinker as unconscious incubation is merely an after-the-fact illusion about what has gone on during the interval.

Perhaps the most popular theoretical account of incubation has been proposed by Simon (1966) (see also Newell *et al.* 1962, pp. 140–1; Simon 1986, pp. 484–5), based on an early version of GPS theory. The theory holds that at each point in problem solving, the current state is held is short-term memory, while the final state, and other subgoals yet to be achieved, is held in long-term memory. If the thinker is interrupted, or for other reasons turns attention away from the problem, the current state will be lost due to decay or displacement. When the thinker returns to the problem, the problem space or subgoal hierarchy likely will have been altered by newly processed information. Thus, thinkers re-enter the problem space at a somewhat different point than they left it. This difference in vantage point, rather than any unconscious work, accounts for the effects of the incubation period. Incubation, then, on this view, is tantamount to a combination of forgetting and prompting. That is, the incubation period provides an opportunity to forget misleading cues, but it also provides an opportunity for the person to encode more appropriate cues newly available in the environment. Woodworth (1938; Woodworth and Schlosberg 1954) offered a similar hypothesis, involving the breaking of inappropriate problem-solving sets. According to this view, the incubation period affords an opportunity to forget (presumably by means of decay or interference) an inappropriate set or direction. Simon's (1966) theory adds to simple forgetting the influence of new information encoded during the incubation period.

Theoretical explanations of incubation may be premature, in view of the fact that attempts to observe incubation under laboratory conditions have not been notably successful (for a review, see Olton 1979). In pioneering research, Patrick (1935, 1937, 1938) observed artists, poets, and scientists as they discussed the content of their ongoing creative projects. She found that ideas recurred in different forms throughout the creative process, separated by periods in which other thoughts were present. Incubation, defined as the early appearance and disappearance of an idea that later appeared in the final product, was observed in the majority of reports. However, Eindhoven and Vinacke (1952) found no evidence of a discrete incubation stage when they asked artists and nonartists to illustrate a poem under what they considered to be more naturalistic conditions. For example (p. 161):

> [T]here was no sharply defined break between preparation and incubation or illumination. Incubation, itself, might be defined as thought about the problem, whether subconscious, or not, and thus would constitute an aspect of creation which persisted throughout the experiment. It probably continues, for instance, even while the subject is finishing his final sketch, at which time it may influence the modification of detail (verification).

From their point of view, Wallas' (1926) stages of thought occur concurrently rather than successively, and are better thought of as component processes of creativity.

More convincing evidence of incubation has been found in a number of more recent experimental studies (e.g. Dreistadt 1969, Fulgosi and Guilford 1968, 1972; Kaplan 1989; Mednick *et al.* 1964; Murray and Denny 1969; Peterson 1974; Silveira 1971), but other studies have either failed to replicate these positive findings or reported negative results (e.g. Gall and Mendelsohn 1967; Olton 1979; Olton and Johnson 1976; Silveira 1971). Moreover, a number of studies have been able to document incubation effects only following certain delays (e.g. Fulgosi and Guilford 1968, 1972), for subjects of certain ability levels (e.g. Dominowski and Jenrick 1972; Murray and Denny 1969; Patrick 1986), with certain kinds of filler tasks (e.g. Patrick 1986), or when certain kinds of environmental cues were available (e.g. Dominowski and Jenrick 1972; Dreistadt 1969). Surveying the literature, Smith and Blankenship (1991, p. 62) concluded that there was 'neither a strong base of empirical support for the putative phenomenon of incubation nor a reliable method for observing the phenomenon in the laboratory'.

Smith and Blankenship (1989, 1991; see also Smith 1994) have recently introduced a method which promises to correct both of these problems. Their method involves presenting a problem along with an ostensible hint about the solution—a hint which is actually misleading. In one variant on their method (Smith and Blankenship 1989, experiment 1), subjects were presented with a series of rebus puzzles (in which pictures, words, or other symbols represent the pronunciation of a word or phrase). For example:

TIMING TIM ING. [9]

The first 15 rebuses were accompanied by helpful clues, in order to establish the subjects' set; however, the last five rebuses were accompanied by misleading clues. A sample misleading item is:

YOU JUST ME
Clue: Beside. [10]

In another variant (Smith and Blankenship 1991, experiment 1), subjects received RAT items to solve, along with misleading associates. An example is:

LICK	(tongue)
SPRINKLE	(rain)
MINES	(gold). [11]

After an initial presentation of the problems, some subjects were retested after a filled or unfilled interval, this time without any clues; others were retested immediately. Across a number of experiments, subjects performed better if they had not been presented with the misleading clues. Where they had received the misinformation, however, the subjects performed better with an incubation interval than if they had been tested immediately. Longer incubation intervals produced superior performance as well as increased forgetting of the misleading cues; both were presumably due to the extended incubation period. Smith and Blankenship (1991) concluded that incubation occurs if subjects suffer from initial fixation in problem solving. Under these circumstances, as hypothesized by Simon (1966), the incubation period facilitates forgetting of the fixation, permitting subjects to restart problem-solving activity at a new, more useful point in the problem space. However, Smith and Blankenship did not claim that forgetting accounts for all incubation effects. Their method shows that the incubation period can be important for overcoming inappropriate sets, but does not shed light on the role of any unconscious processes that might occur during incubation.

In the memory domain, a model for incubation effects may be found in the phenomenon of *hypermnesia*, or the growth of memory over time (for reviews, see Erdelyi 1984; Kihlstrom and Barnhardt 1993; Payne 1987). Following a single-study trial, repeated tests generally reveal that memory for any single item fluctuates over time: some items that are remembered on early trials are forgotten on later ones, and vice versa (Tulving 1964). Usually, inter-trial loss exceeds inter-trial gain, producing the classic forgetting curve of Ebbinghaus (1885). However, under some circumstances the reverse is true, resulting in a net gain in recall (e.g. Erdelyi and Becker 1974). As noted by Mandler (1994), the recovery of previously unremembered items is analogous to the achievement of previously unattained solutions (see also Smith and Vela 1991). The analogy is strengthened by evidence that longer inter-test intervals, analogous to longer incubation periods, produce greater amounts of hypermnesia (Madigan 1976, experiment 2).

How this hypermnesia occurs has been a matter of some debate (Payne 1987). Erdelyi (1988) has speculated that imaginal processing is responsible for the effect, while Roediger (1982; Roediger *et al.* 1982) has proposed that hypermnesia occurs under any conditions that enhance initial recall levels (see also Madigan and O'Hara 1992). Klein and his colleagues (Klein *et al.* 1989) tested the role of encoding factors in hypermnesia, and found that elaborative processing promoted inter-trial recovery, while organizational processing prevented inter-trial forgetting. The finding that elaborative activity underlies the recovery of previously forgotten items is consistent with an activation account: elaboration fosters the spread of activation through the memory network, so that over trials items that were previously activated only to subthreshold levels cross threshold and become available to conscious recollection. This is very similar to the process proposed by Yaniv and Meyer (1987) to account for incubation in problem solving.

7.7 AUTONOMOUS AND INTERACTIVE ACTIVATION IN INCUBATION

But what kind of activation might be involved in incubation? In fact, there are two kinds of activation effects implicated in Yaniv and Meyer's (1987) account of incubation. *Autonomous activation* occurs in the absence of contact with environmental events, while *interactive activation* requires the presentation of environmental cues which make contact with primed knowledge structures. Autonomous activation occurs merely with the passage of time. Interactive activation requires that new information must be available in the environment as well.

The classic view of unconscious incubation seems to implicate autonomous activation processes, inasmuch as they focus on cognitive activity below the threshold of awareness. Thus, Poincaré (cited in Posner 1973, p. 170) reported that after failing to solve some problems having to do with indeterminant ternary quadratic equations, he gave up in disgust, and spent a few days at the seaside thinking of other things. One day, while walking on a bluff, it suddenly occurred to him that the equations which had earlier stumped him were identical with those of non-Euclidean geometry. However, interactive activation may also be important in incubation, if problem solving is particularly facilitated when new environmental cues are processed by a cognitive system that has been prepared for them by means of its own subthreshold activities. Thus, Gutenberg (cited in Koestler 1964, pp. 122–3), while attending a wine harvest, realized that the steady pressure used to crush grapes might also be useful for imprinting letters. Associations of this kind happen frequently in problem solving, even without conscious awareness (Maier 1930, 1931). It seems possible, then, that introspective accounts of insight might underestimate the importance of external stimuli in incubation.

The existing literature offers support for the role of both autonomous and interactive activation in incubation. As noted earlier, Smith and Blankenship (1989) found that a period of inactivity (e.g. sitting quietly or performing a music-perception task) facilitated the solution of verbal rebus problems. The effect of a period of inactivity alone, without the provision of additional external cues, sets the occasion for forgetting to occur; but it also provides an opportunity for autonomous activation to accumulate. Inactivity effects have also been found on the consequences test (Fulgosi and Guilford 1968, 1972; Kaplan 1989, experiments 1–5), anagrams (Goldman *et al.* 1992; Peterson 1974), classic insight problems (Murray and Denny 1969; Silviera 1971), and social-relations problems (Kirkwood 1984). On the other hand, Dominowski and Jenrick (1972) found that inactivity alone was insufficient to produce incubation on a classic-style insight problem; however, the provision of external cues did facilitate performance, providing evidence for interactive activation. Similar results were obtained by Dreistadt (1969), again on an insight problem of the classic type, and Kaplan (1989, experiment 6), with a diverse set of puzzles and riddles.

At least one study has provided evidence for both autonomous and interactive activation in the same experiment. Mednick *et al.* (1964, experiment 2) asked subjects to solve RAT problems; they were retested on unsolved items either immediately, or after a 24-hour delay. One group of delay subjects received no additional cues. However, two additional groups of delay subjects completed an analogy task in which some of the solutions were also solutions to an unsolved RAT item; one of these groups completed the analogies before the incubation period, the other afterwards. Subjects in the delay conditions performed better than those who were retested immediately, providing evidence for autonomous activation; but the effects of the incubation period were greater for those who also completed the RAT-relevant analogies, providing evidence for interactive activation. The subjects who completed the analogies were generally unaware of the connection between the analogies and the RAT problems.

A pair of studies by Dorfman (1990, experiments 3 and 4) directly examined the role of autonomous and interactive activation in incubation effects. In experiment 3, subjects were initially presented with sets of three items from the coherent sextuples described earlier. As before, they were asked to solve each problem and to make a coherence judgement. In the next phase, unsolved problems were repeated, either immediately or following delays of 5 or 15 minutes. In this phase, no additional cues were given. Then subjects received one, two, or three additional cues in successive phases. The short and long intervals were filled with problems from other conditions.

As in Dorfman's (1990) other experiments, coherence ratings were low until just before the solution was achieved, at which point they increased markedly. Moreover, rated coherence was higher for problems which were ultimately solved than for those which remained unsolved (the absence of incoherent problems in this experiment makes it impossible to determine whether subjects could discriminate soluble from insoluble problems). There was no effect of the short or long incubation periods, taken alone, compared to the no-delay condition. That is, the subjects solved approximately the same number of new problems in each of the three delay conditions (no delay, $M = 1.47$; short delay, $M = 1.20$; long delay, $M = 1.33$). However, the incubation period did interact with the cue conditions: provision of one or two additional cues resulted in more new solutions ($M = 3.36$) following the short delay than when there was no delay at all ($M = 2.43$). There was no additional advantage with three cues. Moreover, there was no advantage for extra cues in the long-delay group. Although the results are somewhat puzzling in detail, the interaction indicates that any incubation observed in this experiment was due to interactive rather than to autonomous activation. That is, incubation was only effective when the experimenter provided additional problem-relevant cues after the incubation period.

One potential problem with experiment 3 was that the incubation period was filled with effortful activity, namely, the subjects worked on some problems while others incubated. This methodological feature is common in incubation research, because experimenters want to make sure that subjects do not continue to work consciously on the incubating problem. The finding that subjects are more likely to solve problems after, say, 10 minutes of thought compared to 5 minutes of thought is relatively uninteresting. The question, as far as incubation is concerned, is whether 5 minutes' worth of *not thinking* adds anything to problem solving. Nevertheless, the filled-interval procedure may be less than optimal for studying incubation, because it may create interference which obscures or dampens the effect. Accordingly, Dorfman's (1990) experiment 4 repeated the basic conditions of experiment 3, except that the incubation period was filled with unrelated arithmetic problems; she also added an intermediate-delay condition. Thus, the subjects' minds were still occupied, but with a task that was less likely to interfere with solving the sextuple problems.

Again, coherence ratings remained low until just before the problem was solved, and coherence ratings were higher for solved compared to unsolved problems. This time, however, more problems were solved after the long delay ($M = 5.30$) than after no delay ($M = 3.40$), or after delays of short ($M = 4.50$) or moderate ($M = 3.20$) intervals—even before additional cues were given. There was no additional advantage provided by extra cues. Thus, these findings yielded evidence of autonomous rather than interactive activation.

The main difference between Dorfman's (1990) experiments 3 and 4 concerned the task imposed during the incubation interval. In experiment 3, it consisted of problems of the same sort as those being incubated. In experiment 4, it consisted of qualitatively different sorts of problems. Thus, it seems that incubation can be demonstrated when the filler task does not compete for cognitive resources with the problems being incubated. Apparently, the incubation period allows activation to spread to nodes related to the problem elements, including the target solution. This, in turn, increases the likelihood that the solution will occur to the subject the next time the problem comes up. When autonomous activation alone fails to yield a solution, interactive activation can make an additional contribution. Thus, activation during incubation sensitizes the subject to new information provided by the environment, as suggested by Yaniv and Meyer (1987); activation contributed by this new information then combines with that built-up over the incubation interval to increase further the likelihood of discovering the correct solution.

Although external cues play an important role in problem solving, the importance of the incubation interval itself should not be ignored. In the past, theorists have preferred to shy away from the popular construal of incubation as an unconscious process (e.g. Posner 1973; Smith and Blankenship 1991; Woodworth and Schlosberg 1954). However, many of the mechanisms proposed as an alternative to unconscious processing do not seem to account for Dorfman's (1990) results. For example, the mere recovery from fatigue can be ruled out on the grounds that the subjects were engaged in taxing mental tasks during the incubation interval. For the same reason, we can rule out the possibility of conscious processing during incubation. Campbell's (1960) notion of the random fusion of memory representations also seems unlikely. The activation process is not random, but rather is directed along specific associative pathways. Forgetting may play a role in incubation, as Simon (1966) and Smith (1994; Smith and Blankenship 1989, 1991) have suggested, but the notion of activation building up from subthreshold levels, and eventually (perhaps with additional stimulation from external cues) crossing the threshold of consciousness, remains viable—at least from our point of view.

7.8 IMPLICIT THOUGHT

Thought comes in many forms. Neisser (1967, p. 297) suggested that 'Some thinking is deliberate, efficient, and obviously goal-directed; it is usually experienced as self-controlled as well. Other mental activity is rich, chaotic, and inefficient; it tends to be experienced as involuntary, it just "happens"'. Neisser further suggested that the two forms of thought—rational, constrained, logical, realistic, and secondary process on the one hand, and intuitive, creative, prelogical, autistic, and primary process on the other—reflected serial and parallel processing, respectively. In serial processing, each mental operation is performed in sequence, while in parallel processing a number of operations are performed simultaneously. In current versions of the serial/parallel distinction, such as the parallel distributed processing framework of Rumelhart and McClelland (1986; McClelland and Rumelhart 1986), parallel processes operate too quickly to be accessible to phenomenal awareness.

Another categorization of thought distinguishes between automatic and controlled processes (e.g. Anderson 1982; Hasher and Zacks 1979, 1984; LaBerge and Samuels 1974; Logan 1980; Posner and Snyder 1975; Schneider and Shiffrin 1977; Shiffrin and Schneider 1977, 1984). In theory, automatic processes are inevitably engaged by particular inputs, regardless of the subject's intention—although lately some attention has been given to *conditional* automaticity (Bargh 1989, 1994). Moreover, the execution of automatic processes consumes few or no attentional resources. Thus, automatic processes operate outside of phenomenal awareness and voluntary control. They are unconscious in the strict sense of the word.

Until recently, the notion of unconscious thought was closely tied to the concepts of parallel processing, automaticity, and procedural knowledge more generally. It is almost an article of faith among cognitive psychologists that people lack introspective access to the procedures by which we perceive and remember objects and events, store and retrieve knowledge, think, reason, and solve problems (e.g. Nisbett and Wilson 1977; Wilson and Stone 1985). In large part, the goal of cognitive psychology is to explicate these unconscious procedures and processes (Barsalou 1992). However, there has also been a parallel assumption, mostly unstated, that the declarative knowledge on which these processes operate is accessible to awareness. Put another way, we do not know *how* we think, but we do know *what* we think. Now, however, research on implicit perception, and especially on implicit memory, has made it clear that we do not always know *what* we think and know, either: activated mental representations of current and past experience can influence experience, thought, and action even though they are inaccessible to conscious awareness. By extension, it now seems possible to think of thoughts, images, and judgements which operate in the same way. The unconscious mental representations which underlie our intuitions, and which emerge into consciousness only after a period of incubation, are neither implicit percepts (because they are not representations of the present environment) nor implicit memories (because they are not representations of past experience). Call them implicit thoughts. While implicit perception and memory are well established, the study of implicit thought has only just begun.

ACKNOWLEDGEMENTS

Preparation of this chapter was supported by a post-doctoral fellowship (MH-10042) from the National Institute of Mental Health to Jennifer Dorfman, a Minority Graduate Research Fellowship from the National Science Foundation to Victor A. Shames, and a research grant (MH-35856) from the National Institute of Mental Health to John F. Kihlstrom.

SOLUTIONS TO PROBLEMS

1. The remote associate is PARTY.
2. The solution to the left-hand problem is CARD.
3. MOUNTAIN.
4. MATCH.
5. SQUARE.
6. The man was suffering from hiccups.
7. BANDANNA.
8. The solution to the left-hand problem is HIGH.

9. SPLIT-SECOND TIMING.
10. JUST BETWEEN YOU AND ME.
11. SALT.

REFERENCES

Anderson, J. R. (1982). Acquisition of cognitive skill. *Psychological Review*, **89**, 369–406.

Anderson, J. R. (1983). A spreading activation theory of memory. *Journal of Verbal Learning and Verbal Behavior*, **22**, 261–95.

Bargh, J. A. (1989). Conditional automaticity: Varieties of automatic influence in social perception and cognition. In *Unintended thought* (ed. J. S. Uleman and J. A. Bargh), pp. 3–51. Guilford Press, New York.

Bargh, J. A. (1994). The four horsemen of automaticity: Awareness, intention, efficiency, and control in social cognition. In *Handbook of social cognition*, Vol. 1, (ed. R. S. Wyer and T. K. Srull), (2nd edn), pp. 1–40. Erlbaum, Hillsdale, NJ.

Barsalou, L. W. (1992). *Cognitive psychology: An overview for cognitive scientists.* Erlbaum: Hillsdale, NJ.

Berry, D. C. and Dienes, Z. (ed). (1994). *Implicit learning: Theoretical and empirical issues.* Erlbaum, Hillsdale, NJ.

Biederman, I. (1987). Recognition-by-components: A theory of human image understanding. *Psychological Review*, **94**, 115–47.

Bisiach, E. (1992). Understanding consciousness: Clues from unilateral neglect and related disorders. In *The neuropsychology of consciousness*, (ed. A. D. Milner and M. D. Rugg), pp. 113–37. Academic Press, London.

Bornstein, R. F. and Pittman, T. S. (1992). *Perception without awareness: Cognitive, clinical, and social perspectives.* Guilford Press, New York.

Bowers, K. S. (1984). On being unconsciously influenced and informed. In *The unconscious reconsidered*, (ed. K. S. Bowers and D. Meichenbaum), pp. 227–72. Wiley-Interscience. New York.

Bowers, K. S. (1994). Intuition. In *Encyclopedia of intelligence*, (ed. R. J. Sternberg), pp. 613–17. Macmillan, New York.

Bowers, K. S., Regehr, G., Balthazard, C. G., and Parker, K. (1990). Intuition in the context of discovery. *Cognitive Psychology*, **22**, 72–110.

Bowers, K. S., Farvolden, P., and Mermigis, L. (1995). Intuitive antecedents of insight. In *The creative cognition approach*, (ed. S. M. Smith, T. M. Ward, and R. A. Finke), pp. 27–52. MIT Press, Cambridge, MA.

Bowers, P. G. and Bowers, K. S. (1979). Hypnosis and creativity: A theoretical and empirical rapprochement. In *Hypnosis: Developments in research and new perspectives*, (ed. E. Fromm and R. E. Shor), (2nd edn.) pp. 351–79. Aldine, New York.

Brown, R. and McNeil, D. (1966). The 'tip of the tongue' phenomenon. *Journal of Verbal Learning and Verbal Behavior*, **5**, 325–37.

Bryant, R. A. and McConkey, K. M. (1989*a*). Hypnotic blindness: A behavioral and experiential analysis. *Journal of Abnormal Psychology*, **98**, 71–7.

Bryant, R. A. and McConkey, K. M. (1989*b*). Visual conversion disorder: A case analysis of the influence of visual information. *Journal of Abnormal Psychology*, **98**, 326–9.

Butterfield, E. C. (1964). The interruption of tasks: Methodological, factual, and theoretical issues. *Psychological Bulletin*, **62**, 309–22.

Campbell, D. T. (1960). Blind variation and selective retention in creative thought as in other knowledge processes. *Psychological Review*, **67**, 380–400.

Cermak, L. S., Talbot, N., Chandler, K., and Wolbarst, L. R. (1985). The perceptual priming phenomenon in amnesia. *Neuropsychologia*, **23**, 615–22.

Cheesman, J. and Merikle, P. M. (1984). Priming with and without awareness. *Perception and Psychophysics*, **36**, 387–95.

Cheesman, J. and Merikle, P. M. (1985). Word recognition and consciousness. In *Reading research: Advances in theory and practice*, Vol. 5, (ed. D. Besner, T. G. Waller, and G. E. MacKinnon), pp. 311–52. Academic Press, New York.

Cheesman, J. and Merikle, P. M. (1986). Distinguishing conscious from unconscious perceptual processes. *Canadian Journal of Psychology*, **40**, 343–67.

Collins, A. M. and Loftus, E. F. (1975). A spreading-activation theory of semantic processing. *Psychological Review*, **82**, 407–28.

Connor, L. T., Balota, D. A., and Neely, J. H. (1992). On the relation between feeling of knowing and lexical decision: Persistent subthreshold activation or topic familiarity? *Journal of Experimental Psychology: Human learning and Memory*, **18**, 544–54.

Cork, R. L., Couture, L. J., and Kihlstrom, J. F. (1995). Memory and recall. In *Anesthesia: Biologic foundations* (ed. J. F. Biebuyck, C. Lynch, M. Maze, L. J. Saidman, T. L. Yaksh, and Zapol, W. M.). Raven, New York.

Dayton, T., Durso, F. T., and Shepard, J. D. (1990). A measure of the knowledge reorganization underlying insight. In (Ed.), *Pathfinder associative networks: Studies in knowledge organization*, (ed. R. W. Schvanaveldt), pp. 267–77. Ablex, Norwood, NJ.

Dominowski, R. L. (1981). Comment on 'An examination of the alleged role of "fixation" in the solution of several "insight" problems' by Weisberg and Alba. *Journal of Experimental Psychology: General*, **110**, 199–203.

Dominowski, R. L. and Bourne, L. E. (1994). History of research on thinking and problem solving. In *Thinking and problem solving*, (ed. R. J. Sternbers), pp. 1–35. Academic Press, San Diego, CA.

Dominowski, R. L. and Jenrick, R. (1972). Effects of hints and interpolated activity on solution of an insight problem. *Psychonomic Science*, **26**, 335–37.

Dorfman, J. (1990). Metacognitions and incubation effects in insight problem solving. Unpublished doctoral dissertation, University of California, San Diego.

Dorfman, J. and Kihlstrom, J. F. (in prep.). Implicit memory in posthypnotic amnesia.

Dreistadt, R. (1969). The use of analogies and incubation in obtaining insights in creative problem solving. *Journal of Psychology*, **71**, 159–75.

Durso, F. T., Rea, C. B., and Dayton, T. (1994). Graph-theoretic confirmation of restructuring during insight. *Psychological Science*, **5**, 94–8.

Ebbinghaus, H. (1885/1964). *Memory: A contribution to experimental psychology*, (trans. H. A. Ruger and C. E. Bussenivs). Dover, New York.

Eindhoven, J. E. and Vinacke, W. E. (1952). Creative processes in painting. *Journal of General Psychology*, **47**, 139–64.

Ellen, P. (1982). Direction, past experience, and hints in creative problem solving: Reply to Weisberg and Alba. *Journal of Experimental Psychology: General*, **111**, 316–25.

Erdelyi, M. H. (1984). The recovery of unconscious (inaccessible) memories Laboratory studies of hypermnesia. In G. H. Bower (Ed.), *The Psychology of learning and motivation*, Vol. 18, (ed. G. H. Bower), pp. 95–127. Academic Press, New York.

Erdelyi, M. H. and Becker, J. (1974). Hypermnesia for pictures: Incremental memory for pictures but not words in multiple recall trials. *Cognitive Psychology*, **6**, 159–71.

Ericsson, K. A. and Hastie, R. (1994). Contemporary approaches to the study of thinking and problem solving. In *Thinking and problem solving*, (ed. R. J. Steinberg), pp. 1–79. Academic Press, San Diego, CA.

Flavell, J. (1979). Metacognition and cognitive monitoring: A new area of cognitive-developmental inquiry. *American Psychologist*, **34**, 906–11.

Forster, K. I. and Davis, C. (1984). Repetition priming and frequency attenuation in lexical access. *Journal of Experimental Psychology: Learning, Memory, and Cognition*, **10**, 680–98.

Fowler, C. A., Wolford, G., Slade, R., and Tassinary, L. (1981). Lexical access with and without awareness. *Journal of Experimental Psychology: General*, **110**, 341–62.

Fulgosi, A. and Guilford, J. P. (1968). Short-term incubation in divergent production. *American Journal of Psychology*, **81**, 241–6.

Fulgosi, A. and Guilford, J. P. (1972). A further investigation of short-term incubation. *Acti Instituti Psychologici*, 64–73, 67–70.

Gall, M. and Mendelsohn, G. A. (1967). Effects of facilitating techniques and subject/experimenter interactions on creative problem solving. *Journal of Personality and Social Psychology*, **5**, 211–16.

Goldman, W. P., Wolters, N. C., and Winograd, E. (1992). A demonstration of incubation in anagram problem solving. *Bulletin of the Psychonomic Society*, **30**, 36–8.

Graf, P. and Mandler, G. (1984). Activation makes words more accessible, but not necessarily more retrievable. *Journal of Verbal Learning and Verbal Behaviour*, **23**, 553–68.

Graf, P. and Schacter, D. L. (1985). Implicit and explicit memory for new associations in normal subjects and amnesic patients. *Journal of Experimental Psychology: Learning, Memory, and Cognition*, **11**, 501–18.

Graf, P., Squire, L. R., and Mandler, G. (1984). The information that amnesic patients do not forget. *Journal of Experimental Psychology: Learning, Memory, and Cognition*, **10**, 164–78.

Greenwald, A. M. (1992). New Look 3: Unconscious cognition reclaimed. *American Psychologist*, **47**, 766–779.

Greenwald, A. G., Klinger, M. R., and Liu, T. J. (1989). Unconscious processing of dichoptically masked words. *Memory and Cognition*, **17**, 35–47.

Harshman, R. A. (1974). Harshman figures. Unpublished manuscript, University of Western Ontario.

Hart, J. T. (1965). Memory and the feeling-of-knowing experience. *Journal of Educational Psychology*, **56**, 208–16.

Hart, J. T. (1967). Memory and the memory-monitoring process. *Journal of Verbal Learning and Verbal Behavior*, **6**, 685–91.

Hasher, L. and Zacks, R. T. (1979). Automatic and effortful processes in memory. *Journal of Experimental Psychology: General*, **108**, 356–88.

Hasher, L. and Zacks, R. T. (1984). Automatic processing of fundamental information: The case of frequency of occurrence. *American Psychologist*, **39**, 1372–88.

Jacoby, L. L. and Dallas, M. (1981). On the relationship between autobiographical memory and perceptual learning. *Journal of Experimental Psychology: Learning, Memory, and Cognition*, **110**, 306–40.

Jacoby, L. L. and Witherspoon, D. (1982). Remembering without awareness. *Canadian Journal of Psychology*, **36**, 300–24.

James, W. (1890). *Principles of psychology*, 2 vols. Holt, New York.

Johnson, M. K., and Hasher, L. (1987). Human learning and memory. *Annual Review of Psychology*, **38**, 631–68.

Kaplan, C. A. (1989). Hatching a theory of incubation: Does putting a problem aside really help? If so, why? Unpublished doctoral dissertation, Carnegie Mellon University.

Kihlstrom, J. F. (1980). Posthypnotic amnesia for recently learned material: Interactions with 'episodic' and 'semantic' memory. *Cognitive Psychology*, **12**, 227–51.

Kihlstrom, J. F. (1984). Conscious, subconscious, unconscious: A cognitive perspective. In *The unconscious reconsidered*, (ed. K. S. Bowers and D. Meichenbaum), pp. 149–211. Wiley, New York.

Kihlstrom, J. F. (1987). The cognitive unconscious. *Science*, **237**, 1445–52.

Kihlstrom, J. F. (1990). The psychological unconscious. In *Handbook of personality: Theory and research*, (ed. L. A. Pervin), pp. 445–64. Guilford Press, New York.

Kihlstrom, J. F. (1992). Dissociative and conversion disorders. In *Cognitive science and clinical disorders*, (ed. D. J. Stein and J. Young), pp. 247–70. Academic Press, Sen Diego, CA.

Kihlstrom, J. F. (1993*a*). The continuum of consciousness. *Consciousness and Cognition*, **2**, 334–54.

Kihlstrom, J. F. (1993*b*). Implicit memory function during anesthesia. In *Memory and awareness in anesthesia*, (ed. P. S. Sebel, B. Bonke, and E. Winograd), pp. 10–30. Prentice-Hall, New York.

Kihlstrom, J. F. (1994*a*). Consciousness and me-ness. In *Scientific approaches to the question of consciousness*, (ed. J. Cohen and J. Schooler). Erlbaum, Hillsdale, NJ.

Kihlstrom, J. F. (1994*b*). One hundred years of hysteria. In *Dissociation: Theoretical, clinical, and research perspectives*, (ed. S. J. Lynn and J. W. Rhue), pp. 365–94. Guilford Press, New York.

Kihlstrom, J. F. (1995). The rediscovery of the unconscious. In *The mind, the brain, and complex adaptive systems*, (ed. J. Singer and H. Morowitz), pp. 123–43. Santa Fe Institute Studies in the Sciences of Complexity, Vol. 22. Addison-Wesley, Reading, MA.

Kihlstrom, J. F. and Barnhardt, T. M. (1993). The self-regulation of memory: For better and for worse, with and without hypnosis. In *Handbook of mental control*, (ed. D. M. Wegner and J. W. Pennebaker), pp. 88–125. Prentice Hall, Englewood Cliffs, NJ.

Kihlstrom, J. F. and Hoyt, I. P. (1990). Repression, dissociation, and hypnosis. In *Repression and dissociation: Implications for personality theory, psychopathology, and health*, (ed. J. L. Singer), pp. 181–208. University of Chicago Press.

Kihlstrom, J. F. and Schacter, D. L. (1990). Anaesthesia, amnesia, and the cognitive unconscious. In *Memory and awareness during anaesthesia*, (ed. B. Bonke, W. Fitch, and K. Millar), pp. 22–44. Swets & Zeitlinger, Amsterdam.

Kihlstrom, J. F. and Schacter, D. L. (1995). Functional disorders of autobiographical memory. In *Handbook of memory disorders*, (ed. A. Baddeley, B. A. Wilson, and F. Watts), pp. 337–64. Wiley, London.

Kihlstrom, J. F. and Tobias, B. A. (1991). Anosognosia, consciousness, and the self. In *Awareness of deficit following brain injury: Theoretical and clinical aspects*, (ed. G. P. Prigatano and D. L. Schacter), pp. 198–222. Oxford University Press, New York.

Kihlstrom, J. F., Barnhardt, T. M., and Tataryn, D. J. (1992). Implicit perception. In *Perception without awareness*, (ed. R. F. Bornstein and T. S. Pittman), (pp. 17–54). Guilford Press, New York.

Kihlstrom, J. F., Tataryn, D. J., and Hoyt, I. P. (1993). Dissociative disorders. In *Comprehensive handbook of psychopathology*, (ed. P. J. Sutker and H. E. Adams), (2nd edn), pp. 203–234. Plenum, New York.

Kirkwood, W. G. (1984). Effects of incubation sequences on communication and problem solving in small groups. *Journal of Creative Behavior*, **18**, 45–61.

Klein, S. B., Loftus, J., Kihlstrom, J. F., and Aseron, R. (1989). The effects of item-specific and relational information on hypermnesic recall. *Journal of Experimental Psychology: Learning, Memory, and Cognition*, **15**, 1192–97.

Koestler, A. (1964). *The act of creation*. Macmillan, New York.

LaBerge, D. and Samuels, S. J. (1974). Toward a theory of autoamtic information processing in reading. *Cognitive Psychology*, **6**, 101–24.

Lewandowsky, S., Dunn, J. C., and Kirsner, K. (ed.). (1989). *Implicit memory: Theoretical issues*. Erlbaum, Hillsdale, NJ.

Lewicki, P. (1986). *Nonconscious social information processing*. Academic Press, Orlando, FL.

Lockhart, R. S. and Blackburn, A. B. (1994). Implicit processes in problem solving. In *Implicit memory: New directions in cognition, development and neuropsychology*, (ed. P. Graf and M. E. J. Masson), pp. 95–115. Erlbaum, Hillsdale, NJ.

Logan, G. D. (1980). Attention and automaticity in Stroop and priming tasks: Theory and data. *Cognitive Psychology*, **12**, 523–53.

Luchins, A. S. and Luchins, E. H. (1970). *Wertheimer's seminars revisited: Problem solving and thinking*, Vol. 3. State University of New York at Albany Faculty–Student Association, Albany, NY.

McClelland, J. C. and Rumelhart, D. E. (1981). An interactive activation model of context effects in letter perception: I. An account of basic findings. *Psychological Review*, **88**, 375–407.

McClelland, J. C., Rumelhart, D. E., and the PDP Research Group (1986). *Parallel distributed processing: Explorations in the microstructure of cognition. Vol. 2: Psychological and biological models*. MIT Press, Cambridge, MA.

Madigan, S. (1976). Recovery and reminiscence in item recall. *Memory and Cognition*, **4**, 233–6.

Madigan, S. and O'Hara, R. (1992). Initial recall, reminiscence, and hypermnesia. *Journal of Experimental Psychology: Learning, Memory, and Cognition*, **18**, 421–5.

Maier, N. R. F. (1930). Reasoning in humans: I. On direction. *Journal of Comparative Psychology*, **10**, 115–43.

Maier, N. R. F. (1931). Reasoning in humans: II. The solution of a problem and its appearance in consciousness. *Journal of Comparative Psychology*, **12**, 181–94.
Mandler, G. (1994). Hypermnesia, incubation, and mind popping: On remembering without really trying. In *Attention and performance XV: Conscious and nonconscious information processing*, (ed. C. Umittà and M. Moscovitch), pp. 3–33. MIT Press, Cambridge, MA.
Marcel, A. J. (1983). Conscious and unconscious perception: Experiments on visual masking and word recognition. *Cognitive Psychology*, **15**, 543–51.
Marshall, J. C. and Halligan, P. W. (1988). Blindsight and insight in visuo-spatial neglect. *Nature*, **336**, 766–67.
Mednick, M. T., Mednick, S. A., and Mednick, E. V. (1964). Incubation of creative performance and specific associative priming. *Journal of Abnormal and Social Psychology*, **69**, 84–8.
Mednick, S. A. (1962). The associative basis of the creative process. *Psychological Review*, **69**, 220–32.
Mednick, S. A. and Mednick, M. T. (1967). *Examiner's manual: Remote Associates Test*. Houghton Mifflin, Boston.
Merikle, P. M. and Reingold, E. M. (1992). Measuring unconscious perceptual processes. In *Perception without awareness*, (ed. R. F. Bornstein and T. S. Pittman), pp. 55–80. Guilford Press, New York.
Metcalfe, J. (1986*a*). Feeling of knowing in memory and problem solving. *Journal of Experimental Psychology: Learning, Memory, and Cognition*, **12**, 288–94.
Metcalfe, J. (1986*b*). Premonitions of insight predict impending error. *Journal of Experimental Psychology: Learning, Memory, and Cognition*, **12**, 623–34.
Metcalfe, J. and Shimamura, A. P. (ed.). (1994). *Metacognition: Knowing about knowing*. MIT Press, Cambridge, MA.
Metcalfe, J. and Wiebe, D. (1987). Intuition in insight and noninsight problem solving. *Memory and Cognition*, **15**, 238–46.
Meyer, D. E. and Schvaneveldt, R. W. (1971). Facilitation in recognizing pairs of words: Evidence of a dependence between retrieval operations. *Journal of Experimental Psychology*, **90**, 227–34.
Mooney, C. M. (1957). Closure as affected by viewing time and multiple visual fixations. *Canadian Journal of Psychology*, **11**, 21–8.
Murray, H. G. and Denny, J. P. (1969). Interaction of ability level and interpolated activity (opportunity for incubation) in human problem solving. *Psychological Reports*, **24**, 271–6.
Neisser, U. (1967). *Cognitive psychology*. Appleton-Century-Crofts, New York.
Nelson, T. O. (ed.). (1992). *Metacognition: Core readings*. Allyn and Bacon, Needham Heights, MA.
Nelson, T. O. and Narens, L. (1980). Norms of 300 general-information questions: Accuracy of recall, and feeling-of-knowing ratings. *Journal of Verbal Learning and Verbal Behavior*, **19**, 338–68.
Nelson, T. O., Gerler, D., and Narens, L. (1984). Accuracy of feeling-of-knowing judgments for predicting perceptual identification and relearning. *Journal of Experimental Psychology: General*, **113**, 282–300.
Newell, A. and Simon, H. A. (1973). *Human problem solving*. Prentice-Hall, Englewood Cliffs, NJ.
Newell, A., Simon, H. A., and Shaw, J. C. (1962–1979). The process of creative

thinking. In *Models of thought*, (ed. H. A. Simon), pp. 144–74. Yale University Press, New Haven; CT.

Nisbett, R. and Wilson, T. D. (1977). Telling more than we can know: Verbal reports on mental processes. *Psychological Review*, **84**, 231–59.

Ohlsson, S. (1984). Restructuring revisited: An information-processing theory of restructuring and insight. *Scandinavian Journal of Psychology*, **25**, 117–29.

Olton, R. M. (1979). Experimental studies of incubation: Searching for the elusive. *Journal of Creative Behavior*, **13**, 9–22.

Olton, R. M. and Johnson, D. M. (1976). Mechanisms of incubation in creative problem solving. *American Journal of Psychology*, **89**, 617–30.

Patrick, A. S. (1986). The role of ability in creative 'incubation'. *Personality and Individual Differences*, **7**, 169–74.

Patrick, C. (1935). Creative thought in poets. *Archives of Psychology*, No. 178.

Patrick, C. (1937). Creative thought in artists. *Journal of Psychology*, **4**, 35–7.

Patrick, C. (1938). Scientific thought. *Journal of Psychology*, **5**, 55–83.

Payne, D. G. (1987). Hypermnesia and reminiscence in recall: A historical and empirical review. *Psychological Bulletin*, **101**, 5–27.

Perkins, D. N. (1981). *The mind's best work*. Harvard University Press, Cambridge, MA.

Peterson, C. (1974). Incubation effects in anagram solution. *Bulletin of the Psychonomic Society*, **3**, 29–30.

Peterson, M. A. (1994). Object-recognition processes can and do operate before figure-ground organization. *Current Directions in Psychological Science*, **3**, 105–111.

Posner, M. I. (1973). *Cognition: An introduction*. Scott, Foresman, Glenview, IL.

Posner, M. I. and Snyder, C. R. R. (1975). Attention and cognitive control. In *Information processing and cognition*, (ed. R. L. Solso). Erlbaum, Hillsdale, NJ.

Ratcliff, R. and McKoon, G. (1981). Does activation really spread? *Psychological Review*, **88**, 454–62.

Ratcliff, R. and McKoon, G. (1988). A retrieval theory of priming in memory. *Psychological Review*, **95**, 385–408.

Ratcliff, R. and McKoon, G. (1994). Retrieving information from memory: Spreading-activation theories versus compound-cue theories. *Psychological Review*, **101**, 177–87.

Reber, A. S. (1967). Implicit learning of artificial grammars. *Journal of Verbal Learning and Verbal Behavior*, **6**, 317–27.

Reber, A. S. (1993). *Implicit learning and tacit knowledge: An essay on the cognitive unconscious*. Oxford University Press, New York.

Richardson-Klavehn, A. and Bjork, R. A. (1988). Measures of memory. *Annual Review of Psychology*, **36**, 475–543.

Roediger, H. L. III (1982). Hypermnesia: The importance of recall time and asymptotic level of recall. *Journal of Verbal Learning and Verbal Behavior*, **21**, 662–5.

Roediger, H. L. III (1990*a*). Implicit memory: A commentary. *Bulletin of the Psychonomic Society*, **28**, 373–80.

Roediger, H. L. III (1990*b*). Implicit memory: Retention without remembering. *American Psychologist*, **45**, 1043–56.

Roediger, H. L. III and McDermott, K. B. (1993). Implicit memory in normal human subjects. In *Handbook of neuropsychology*, Vol. 8, (ed. F. Boller and J. Grafman), pp. 63–131. Elsevier, Amsterdam.

Roediger, H. L. III, Payne, D. G., Gillespie, G. L., and Lean, D. S. (1982). Hypermnesia as determined by level of recall. *Journal of Verbal Learning and Verbal Behavior*, **21**, 635–55.

Rumelhart, D. E., McClelland, J. L., and the PDP Research Group. (1986). *Parallel distributed processing: Explorations in the microstructure of cognition. Vol. 1: Foundations.* MIT Press, Cambridge, MA.

Schacter, D. L. (1987). Implicit memory: History and current status. *Journal of Experimental Psychology: Learning, Memory, and Cognition*, **13**, 501–18.

Schacter, D. L. (1992*a*). Consciousness and awareness in memory and amnesia: Critical issues. In *The neuropsychology of consciousness*, (ed. A. D. Milner and M. D. Rugg), pp. 179–200. Academic Press, San Diego, CA.

Schacter, D. L. (1992*b*). Understanding implicit memory: A cognitive neuroscience approach. *American Psychologist*, **47**, 559–69.

Schacter, D. L. (1995). Implicit memory: A new frontier for cognitive neuroscience. In *The cognitive neurosciences*, (ed. M. Gazzaniga), pp. 815–824. MIT Press, Cambridge, MA.

Schacter, D. L. and Graf, P. (1986). Preserved learning in amnesic patients: Perspectives on research from direct priming. *Journal of Clinical and Experimental Neuropsychology*, **15**, 3–12.

Schacter, D. L. and Kihlstrom, J. F. (1989). Functional amnesia. In *Handbook of neuropsychology*, Vol. 3, (ed A. Baddeley, B. A. Wilson, and F. Watts), pp. 337–64. Wiley, London.

Schacter, D. L., Chiu, C.-Y. P., and Ochsner, K. N. (1993). Implicit memory: A selective review. *Annual Review of Psychology*, **16**, 159–82.

Scheerer, M. (1963). Problem-solving. *Scientific American*, **208**, 118–28.

Schneider, W. and Shiffrin, R. M. (1977). Controlled and automatic human information processing: I. Detection, search, and attention. *Psychological Review*, **84**, 1–66.

Siefert, C. M., Meyer, D. E., Davidson, N., Patalano, A. L., and Yaniv, I. (1995). Demystification of cognitive insight: Opportunistic assimilation and the prepared-mind perspective. In *The nature of insight*, (ed. R. J. Sternberg and J. E. Davison), pp. 65–124. MIT Press, Cambridge, MA.

Shames, V. A. (1994). Is there such a thing as implicit problem-solving? Unpublished doctoral dissertation, University of Arizona.

Shames, V. A. and Bowers, P. G. (1992). Hypnosis and creativity. In *Contemporary hypnosis research*, (ed. E. Fromm and M. R. Nash), pp. 334–63. Guilford Press, New York.

Shames, V. A. and Kihlstrom, J. F. (1994). Respecting the phenomenology of human creativity. *Behavioral and Brain Sciences*, **17**, 551–2.

Shiffrin, R. W. and Schneider, W. (1977). Controlled and automatic human information processing: II. Perceptual learning, automatic attending, and a general theory. *Psychological Review*, **84**, 127–90.

Shiffrin, R. W. and Schneider, W. (1984). Automatic and controlled processing revisited. *Psychological Review*, **91**, 269–76.

Shimamura, A. P. (1994). Neuropsychological analyses of implicit memory: History, methodology, and theoretical implications. In *Implicit memory: New directions in cognition, development and neuropsychology,* (ed. P. Graf and M. E. J. Masson), pp. 265–85. Erlbaum, Hillsdale, NJ.

Shimamura, A. P. and Squire, L. R. (1984). Paired associate learning and priming effects in amnesia: A neuropsychological study. *Journal of Experimental Psychology: General,* **113**, 556–70.

Silveira, J. M. (1971). Incubation: The effects of interruption timing and length on problem solution and quality of problem processing. Doctoral dissertation. University of Oregon. (*Dissertation Abstracts International,* 1972, **32**, 5506b.)

Simon, H. A. (1966). Scientific discovery and the psychology of problem solving. In *Mind and cosmos,* (ed. R. Colodny), pp. 22–40. University of Pittsburgh Press.

Simon, H. A. (1986/1989). The information-processing explanation of Gestalt phenomena. In *Models of thought,* Vol. 2, (ed. H. A. Simon), pp. 481–93. Yale University Press, New Haven, CT.

Smith, S. M. (1994). Getting into and out of mental ruts: A theory of fixation, incubation, and insght. In *The nature of insight,* (ed. R. Sternberg and J. Davidson), pp. 229–51. Cambridge, MA. MIT Press,

Smith, S. M. and Blankenship, S. E. (1989). Incubation effects. *Bulletin of the Psychonomic Society,* **27**, 3111–314.

Smith, S. M. and Blankenship, S. E. (1991). Incubation and the persistence of fixation in problem solving. *American Journal of Psychology,* **104**, 61–87.

Smith, S. M. and Vela, E. (1991). Incubated reminiscence effects. *Memory and Cognition,* **19**, 168–76.

Squire, L. R. (1992). Declarative and nondeclarative memory: Multiple brain systems supporting learning and memory. *Journal of Cognitive Neuroscience,* **4**, 232–43.

Squire, L. R. and Knowlton, B. J. (1995). Memory, hippocampus, and brain systems. In *The cognitive neurosciences,* (ed. M. Gazzaniga), pp. 825–37. MIT Press, Cambridge, MA.

Street, R. F. (1931). A Gestalt completion test. *Contributions to Education,* Whole No. 481. Columbia University Teachers College, New York.

Tarr, M. J. (1995). Rotating objects to recognize them: A case study of the role of viewpoint dependency in the recognition of three-dimensional objects. *Psychonomic Bulletin and Review,* **2**, 55–82.

Thomas, J. C. (1974). An analysis of behavior in the hobbits-orcs problem. *Cognitive Psychology,* **6**, 257–69.

Tulving, E. (1964). Intratrial and intertrial retention: Notes toward a theory of free recall verbal learning. *Psychological Review,* **71**, 219–37.

Tulving, E. and Schacter, D. L. (1990). Priming and human memory systems. *Science,* **247**, 301–6.

Tulving, E., Schacter, D. L., and Stark, H. (1982). Priming effects in word-fragment completion are independent of recognition memory. *Journal of Experimental Psychology: Learning, Memory, and Cognition,* **8**, 336–42.

Wallas, G. (1926). *The art of thought.* Franklin Watts, New York.

Warrington, E. K. and Weiskrantz, L. (1968). New method for testing long-term retention with special reference to amnesic patients. *Nature,* **228**, 628–30).

Weiner, B. (1966). Effects of motivation on the availability of memory traces. *Psychological Bulletin,* **65**, 24–37.

Weisberg, R. W. (1992). Metacognition and insight during problem solving: Comment on Metcalfe. *Journal of Experimental Psychology: Learning, Memory, and Cognition*, **18**, 426–31.

Weisberg, R. W., and Alba, J. W. (1981*a*). An examination of the alleged role of 'fixation' in the solution of several 'insight' problems. *Journal of Experimental Psychology: General*, **110**, 169–72.

Weisberg, R. W. and Alba, J. W. (1981*b*). Gestalt theory, insight, and past experience: Reply to Dominowski. *Journal of Experimental Psychology: General*, **110**, 193–8.

Weiskrantz, L. (1986). *Blindsight: A case study and implications*. Oxford University Press.

Wertheimer, M. (1959). *Productive thinking*. Harper & Row, New York.

Wilson, T. D. and Stone, J. I. (1985). Limitations of self-knowledge: More on telling more than we can know. *Review of Personality and Social Psychology*, **6**, 167–83.

Woodworth, R. S. (1938). *Experimental psychology*. Holt, Rinehart, & Winston, New York.

Woodworth, R. S. and Schlosberg, H. (1954). Experimental psychology, (rev. edn). Holt, Rinehart, & Winston, New York.

Yaniv, I. and Meyer, D. E. (1987). Activation and metacognition of inaccessible stored information: Potential bases for incubation effects in problem solving. *Journal of Experimental Psychology: Learning, Memory, and Cognition*, **13**, 187–205.

Zeigarnik, B. (1927). Das Behalten von erledigten und unerledigten Handlungen. *Psychologie Forschung*, **9**, 1–85.

Author index

Subject index

Printed in the United Kingdom
by Lightning Source UK Ltd.
1557

9 780198 52310